Four Years Before the Mast

A HISTORY OF NEW YORK'S MARITIME COLLEGE

Four Years Before the Mast

A HISTORY OF NEW YORK'S MARITIME COLLEGE

Joseph A. Williams

Fort Schuyler Press
State University of New York
Maritime College
Bronx, New York

Copyright © 2013 by Joseph A. Williams
Second printing, with revisions

All rights reserved. This book may not be reproduced, in whole or part, in any form, except by reviewers, without the written permission of the publisher.

Four Years Before the Mast: A History of New York's Maritime College
by Joseph A. Williams

Casebound ISBN: 978-0-9899394-0-9
Paperback ISBN: 978-0-9899394-1-6
Library of Congress Control Number: 2013944849

Edited by Christopher McMillan

Production manager: Jack Estes
Design by Susan Ramundo
Cover by Laura Tolkow

The Fort Schuyler Press is the academic press of the State University of New York
   Maritime College
Fort Schuyler Press
State University of New York Maritime College
6 Pennyfield Avenue
Bronx, New York 10465
Karen E. Markoe: Editor-in-Chief
Ph: 718-409-7247 Fx: 718-409-2873 FSP@sunymaritime.edu

Contents

Introduction xi
Acknowledgments xiii

Chapter 1	American Sailors for American Ships	1
Chapter 2	A Square-Rigged School . . .	17
Chapter 3	"A Barnacle in the School System".	25
Chapter 4	A New Era	35
Chapter 5	The Way of the Schoolship	43
Chapter 6	"The Only Pebble on the Beach"	71
Chapter 7	"We are All Dirty in Consequence"	83
Chapter 8	The Age of Riesenberg	97
Chapter 9	Coming Ashore	121
Chapter 10	The Federal Program	143
Chapter 11	Eighteen Months Before the Mast	153
Chapter 12	The Annapolis of the Merchant Marine	167
Chapter 13	"But Men and Officers Must Obey"	183
Chapter 14	The Dome	201
Chapter 15	"The Way It Is"	217
Chapter 16	"A Very Elegant Man"	229
Chapter 17	"As Military as Mickey Mouse"	241
Chapter 18	First and Foremost	251
Chapter 19	In Step with the Future	269
Chapter 20	The Ship Sails On	279

Appendix A: Names and Places 297
Appendix B: People 305
Appendix C: Vessels 319
Selected Bibliography 331
Notes 339
Illustration Credits 373
Index 377
About the Author 385

For my daughter, Jamie Faye

"The Bells of St. Mary's"

The bells of St. Mary's at sweet even'tide
Shall call her beloved to come o'er her side;
And dear Alma Mater in sound of the sea,
I know you've been waiting, yes, waiting for me.

The bells of St. Mary's Ah! Hear! They are calling
The old lads and the new lads who have gone to sea;
Our dear Alma Mater, we hear your voices calling,
The ship's bells shall ring out—ring out for you and me.

The bells of St. Mary's Ah! Hear! They are calling
The old lads, the new lads who go down to the sea;
And so, my Beloved, when blue seas are calling,
The ship's bells shall ring out—ring for you and me.

Introduction

In the popular imagination nautical history is located in places like the Spanish Main, or Trafalgar, or exotic locales filled with parrots and pirate-hunters—not the Bronx. But in the Bronx, there is a small college based in a defunct 19th century U.S. Army fort which has figured in American maritime history since the 1870s. This is the State University of New York's Maritime College, the oldest active maritime educational institution in the United States.

Thousands of young men and women have graduated from the school during its long history and I was shocked, when I first joined the college in 2008, that there were no published histories of it. This surprise was double-downed, when after a time I found that the college's archives had preserved a remarkable record of the school and how it related to American maritime history.

Yet my decision to write this book came at a freshman orientation seminar that I conducted shortly after I arrived. I was telling the students about the history of Fort Schuyler. I thought it was a good presentation—only two students fell asleep. Then, as the students filed out, their squad leader came to me with a serious look on her face.

"It is Fort Schuyler," she said.

"Oh?" I replied. I had been pronouncing Schuyler as Shoo-ler.

"Yes," she said with such certitude that I knew I was wrong.

I wouldn't let it be, and I mumbled some excuse that both pronunciations were correct. That was, after all, how they said it in graduate school. I even threw out the "I have more and higher degrees than you so I know more" card.

Red-faced, I was determined to learn all I could about this little college under the Throgs Neck Bridge.

Within the first weeks of what became over four years' worth of researching, writing and editing I was pleasantly surprised to find that the school's history was much more dramatic and unique than many other college histories.

Maybe this is because its story is entwined with the sea and its stories. Slowly, my interest in the institution's history grew into an obsession. I am afraid I became a bit of a pedant. To illustrate, there is *no* secret tunnel under Long Island Sound, Riesenberg is pronounced "REE-senberg" not "Rye-senberg," the ship *St. Mary's* is almost certainly spelled *with* an apostrophe, and the school was *never* a reform school. I hope that this history will dispel some of the myths about the school.

Closely tied with the institution are acts of bravery, moments of terror and incredulous episodes that speak volumes about the character of the alumni. In truth, the school's history could only be told because of the graduates who have maintained their connection to the institution and over the years donated their papers and effects to the college archives. I have never encountered a group of alumni who have had such strong ties to their *alma mater*.

Maritime College is special. It is more than a technical college or an old fort with a pretty view. It is a culture and a tradition that keep reverberating through the years. That is why I wrote this book, and that is why I hope you enjoy reading it.

PREFACE TO THE SECOND PRINTING

Since our first printing, the reception to *Four Years Before the Mast* has been enthusiastic. Our readers, in fact, have pointed out some typos and errors that have been corrected in this printing. The greatest change has been to Chapter 19, "In Step with the Future," which was revised to provide a more well-rounded overview of the 1999–2000 crisis. I am specifically grateful to the following astute readers: Gerald Albin, Donald Brennan, David Brown, Jose Femenia, Thomas Fox, John Ingram, and Thomas Keenan.

Acknowledgments

Foremost, I must give thanks to my wife, Michelle. Without her support, initial edits and honest criticism this project would never have come to fruition. Her invaluable assistance can be found in every page of this book.

Special thanks to my editor, Professor Christopher McMillan, who was more blunt and honest than my wife—something I thought impossible. Thank you for showing me my narrative voice.

Thank you to Karen Markoe, editor-in-chief at the Fort Schuyler Press, a great historian, and a fine individual without whom this work could not have been brought to completion.

Thanks to my colleagues at the Stephen B. Luce Library: Constantia Constantinou and Shafeek Fazal. Also a word of thanks to my former colleague and archivist, Elizabeth Berilla, who was wonderful in hunting down esoteric scraps of information.

Special acknowledgement must be given to Richard Corson and Philomena Magavero, Librarians *emeritus* from SUNY Maritime College. It was their work that created the rich institutional archives that allowed this tale to be written.

Finally, thank you to all the alumni and long-time faculty I have spoken with over the several years it took to bring this book to publication. I apologize in advance if I couldn't find space for all your stories or all the personalities that makes the college so special. Maybe a sequel is in order?

CHAPTER 1

American Sailors for American Ships

"Sailors ought never to go to church. They ought to go to hell, where it is much more comfortable."

—H.G. Wells

Richard Henry Dana was a junior at Harvard when he came down with the measles. The disease affected his eyesight and he could no longer keep up with his studies. Doctors could not help him, so he decided to take matters into his own hands and cure himself through a complete change in lifestyle. In August, 1834, he took a break from Harvard and traded in his collegiate frock-coat, kid gloves and silk hat for the "loose duck trousers, checked shirt and tarpaulin hat of a sailor." Like Melville's Ishmael, Dana decided to visit the "watery part of the world."

At Boston, Dana boarded a merchant brig named the *Pilgrim* which was to sail to California via Cape Horn. On his first night, he was ordered by the captain to call all hands due to a shift in wind. He did this sheepishly and suddenly:

> ... everyone was in motion, the sails loosed, the yards braced, and we began to heave up the anchor, which was our last hold on Yankee land. I could take but small part in these preparations. My little knowledge of the vessel was all at fault. Unintelligible orders were so rapidly given, and so immediately executed; there was such a hurrying about, and such an intermingling of strange cries and stranger actions, that I was completely bewildered. There is not so helpless and pitiable an object in the world as a landsman beginning a sailor's life.

Soon after, Dana encountered rough weather. Seasick, he was ordered aloft for the first time to reef topsails. But he was too inexperienced to do anything other than to cling onto the yards for life. "I could not have been of much service," he recalled, ". . . I remember having been sick several times before I left the topsail yard, making wild vomits into the black night. . . ."

Between the rolling sea and the smell of fetid seawater, Dana despaired. He had signed up for two years at the pay rate of $12 per month. This was only the beginning. He reflected, "I had often read of the nautical experiences of others, but I felt as though there could be none worse than mine."

Dana's seasickness lasted for three days. Then, upon the advice of the *Pilgrim's* cook, he ate cold salt beef and biscuit. The illness vanished, and Dana felt like a new man. He then learned the customs and laws of seafaring.

The cigar-chomping captain was "Lord Paramount." He summarized his expectations to the crew at the outset of the voyage:

> If we get along well together, we shall have a comfortable time; if we don't, we shall have hell afloat.—All you've got to do is to obey your orders and do your duty like men,—then you'll fare well enough;—if you don't, you'll fare hard enough,—I can tell you. If we pull together, you'll find me a clever fellow; if we don't, you'll find me a *bloody* rascal.

Beneath the captain was a hierarchy of officers and men that started with the chief mate and descended to the common sailors. These were the lowest of the low and kept constantly at work. Dana commented, "In no state prison are the convicts more regularly set to work, and more closely watched. No conversation is allowed among the crew at their duty. . . ." The work—scrubbing, painting and swabbing—was monotonous. The only time off was at night and on Sundays.

This went on until November 5th. Then, just before 8 p.m., Dana heard the cry of "All hands ahoy!" He hurried onto the deck and saw an immense black cloud which filled the horizon. The chief mate cried, "Here comes the Horn!"

Within a few minutes the sea rose higher than Dana had ever seen. The *Pilgrim* was raised upon a crest of water, then suddenly dropped downward, the sea pouring through open ports. For days they fought heavy seas through rain, hail and snow. On the winds, albatrosses followed the ship. With no other power than wind and current, the little vessel slowly pressed on until the Cape was behind and calmer water ahead. All was well.

Then on November 19th, Dana was woken from his sleep by the call of "man overboard!" Dana raced onto the deck and heard the news. An experienced sailor had fallen from the shrouds into the sea. He wore heavy clothes and could not swim. There was no hope.

Dana reflected:

> Death is at all times solemn, but never so much so as at sea. A man dies on shore; his body remains with his friends . . . but when a man falls overboard at sea and is lost, there is a suddenness in the event, and a difficulty in realizing it, which give to it an air of awful mystery. A man dies on shore,—you follow his body to the grave, and a stone marks the spot . . . but at sea, the man is near you,—at your side,—you hear his voice, and in an instant he is gone, and nothing but a vacancy shows his loss.

One 1850 study of British master mariners showed a 90% higher mortality rate than other occupations. If this was the case for master mariners, inexperienced rank-and-file men, like Dana, were even more likely to perish. Fortunately for him, he survived and recorded his experiences in the classic book, *Two Years Before the Mast*, which educated people on the hard realities of seafaring.

EARLY EFFORTS AT NAUTICAL EDUCATION

In Dana's time, mariners, and especially sailors, were reviled by respectable society. Their tattoos, scars and constant wandering, set them apart from the middle and upper classes. With little government regulation and limited help, the rough lives these men experienced often led to alcoholism and early death. Sailors who retired were often destitute, and society was unwilling to tend to them.

But mariners took care of their own, and the great American port cities developed charitable marine societies starting in the 18th century. New York shipping men founded the Marine Society of the City of New York in 1770 to help "indigent and distressed shipmasters" and their families. In 1801, the wealthy shipping captain, Robert Richard Randall, bequeathed his fortune to found New York's Sailors' Snug Harbor. This organization, which was based on Staten Island until the late 20th century, provided care for "retired, decrepit, and worn-out sailors."

These organizations also recognized that sailors, such as Richard Henry Dana, needed better training. If mariners were properly trained before their first voyage it would lessen accidents, save lives and raise profits. In 1808, the New York Marine Society became the first organization in America to propose establishing a "Marine School" to teach boys navigation. Yet the Society finally resolved that it was impractical without the assistance of the State government. In 1808, there was not even general public education. The idea, well ahead of its time, was soon abandoned.

Advocacy of nautical schools was then taken up by individuals who wanted to create "schoolships" to train American mariners. The first was established by Admiral Sir Isaac Coffin. Coffin was the descendant of the Englishman, Tristram Coffin. With a group of investors, Tristram bought the island of Nantucket and migrated there in 1642. He had nine children who also were prolific. Eventually, Tristram had thousands of descendants, many of whom remained on Nantucket. These offspring were highly influential and involved in the famous whaling and shipping industries out of that island. One of these was Isaac, who became a prominent British Naval officer and British loyalist during the American Revolution.

Although he left New England due to the war, Isaac Coffin never forgot his extensive relations on Nantucket. Since he married later in life and never had an heir he became a philanthropist to his relatives in New England. In 1829, he established a marine school in Nantucket aboard the brig *Clio*. The school was open to any boy of Coffin blood (which was pretty much everybody on Nantucket) and the *Clio* was captained by Alexander Pinkham, another relative. The ship's first cruise, in 1829, took 21 boys to Quebec, Nova Scotia, and the Magdalen Islands. After this, the schoolship operated for several years before finally closing. Not only was it expensive to operate a ship as a school, but the people of Nantucket were not interested in it, preferring to learn how to sail in apprenticeships through their families. Instead, Coffin's funding was used for land-based education.

A few years after, Thomas Goin, a New York shipbroker, called for the establishment of federally financed schoolships. His plan proposed three schoolships to continually cruise the American coast with 500 boys on each vessel. The idea was to "clear the city of wild and idle boys" and provide trained Americans who could fight in the Navy during times of war. Goin went so far as to present a model of a schoolship to the Secretary of the Navy in 1837.

Goin was distressed by the rising percentage of foreign-born crew on merchant and Navy ships. This was a general concern that he shared with others in the American middle and upper classes. It was true that white Anglo-Saxon Protestants predominated among the officers, but throughout the enlisted ranks there were a growing number of "foreigners."

The idea of American sailors for American ships was not new or surprising in a century that embraced xenophobic nationalism. In 1845, an anonymous pamphlet declared that one-third of the Navy was populated by foreigners and argued that American Naval commanders would "feel much more proud and sanguine if they were to go into battle with all American born tars on board their vessels, instead of having a crew mixed up of all nations of the earth. . . ."

"ARE YOU AFRAID OF DEATH?"

Instead of a schoolship like Goin wanted, Congress authorized a Naval apprenticeship system that started in 1838. Under the program, boys between the ages of 13 to 18 were recruited to serve until the age of 21. The program aimed at enlisting native-born Americans to the Navy. Initially, it was successful and at one point there were about 2,000 boys enlisted as apprentices.

One of these early apprentices was a 14 year old boy named Stephen Bleecker Luce who received his appointment as a midshipman-apprentice in 1841 from President Martin Van Buren. Luce was exactly the type of boy that the Navy wanted. An Albany native, he had parents with illustrious pedigrees. His father, Vinal, was descended from William White, the eleventh signer of the *Mayflower Compact*, and his mother, Charlotte Bleecker, came from the old New York Dutch aristocracy. Stephen himself would marry Elisa Henley, a grandniece of Martha Washington, in 1854.

Luce, like Richard Henry Dana, was immersed in maritime training as an apprentice. The boys were funneled onto receiving ships and then dealt out to active vessels. There was no formal instruction, no standardized curriculum and apprentices mixed with the regular crew. Despite these shortcomings, Luce quickly adapted to his surroundings and embraced the Navy wholeheartedly. But his education was lacking. Many years later he commented that apprentices were "thoroughly taught to clean priming wires, scrub side ladders, chew tobacco and to swear with the best of them." Luce's opinion of the apprentice system was also shaped by what happened to Philip Spencer on the brig *Somers* in 1842.

Spencer, whose father was the U.S. Secretary of War, had an obsession with pirates. While Spencer attended Geneva College, he told "murderous stories and tales of blood" from *The Pirates Own Book* by Charles Ellms. The young man proved uncontrollable and his father tried sending him to Union College from which he dropped out. He ran away, hid his identity and signed up to ship out on a Nantucket whaler. Yet his friends located him, told his father, who then used his influence to stop the vessel. His father then got an apprentice commission for his son since that was more suitable to his social class.

Spencer was first assigned to the *North Carolina*, an apprentice receiving ship where he was messmates with Stephen Luce. Aboard, Spencer got into trouble for "mischief and liquor." Luce said, "Spencer was extremely peculiar. He was not all there; he would go aloft and sit in the mizzen-top with his eyes fixed and glaring for hours. When his messmates guyed [made fun of] each other, they never interfered with Spencer." Yet Spencer's father protected the boy, who instead of being dismissed for his antics, was transferred in February, 1842 to the frigate *John Adams*. Again, Spencer got into trouble and avoided a court martial only because of his father. He was reassigned to the brig *Somers* under the command of Captain Alexander Slidell Mackenzie.

On September 13, 1842, the *Somers* sailed out of New York to Madeira. During the outward voyage Spencer did not mix much with the officers, but fraternized with the crew, handing out money and cigars. After Madeira, he ignored his duties but Mackenzie did not punish Spencer thinking he was too incorrigible. More to the point, the captain was afraid of the boy's powerful father.

As the voyage turned toward the West Indies, Spencer approached the purser's steward. He asked:

"Are you afraid of death?"

Then he asked, "Are you afraid to see a dead man?"

And finally . . .

"Are you afraid to kill a man?"

Spencer then babbled about plans to turn the *Somers* into a pirate ship and kill all the officers. He claimed that 20 members of the crew were with him. The steward passed word to the officers, including the executive officer, Guert Gansevoort. Mackenzie ordered Gansevoort to observe Spencer. The executive officer, through the crew, learned that Spencer had been meeting every night in secret with two others. Gansevoort alerted the captain who ordered Spencer and co-conspirators in irons. A search of the 19 year old's belongings revealed a list of men aboard the ship marked "certain," "doubtful," and "to be destroyed."

A trial was held aboard the *Somers* with the captain and the officers investigating the mutiny. Spencer declared the whole thing a prank but none believed him. On December 1, 1842 at 2:15 p.m. Mackenzie hanged him and two suspected co-conspirators from a yardarm. The body swung in the noose for over an hour before the captain ordered it down. That evening, the three bodies of the would-be mutineers were committed to the sea.

After the vessel returned to the United States, a court of inquiry was held and found that the captain had acted within his rights. But Mackenzie believed that a full court martial was needed so that he could be fully cleared and to ensure that he was protected against any reprisals from Spencer's father. The resulting court martial was tied; there was a split decision which resulted in an acquittal. The incident was a major sensation at the time, with strong opinions supporting either Spencer or Mackenzie. In fact, the executive officer, Gansevoort, happened to be the first cousin of Herman Melville. Many years later, in 1888, Melville read an article about the mutiny in the *American Magazine* and was reminded of his cousin's experience. The result was *Billy Budd*.

The *Somers* mutiny hung like a cloud over the entire apprenticeship program. There were other problems as well. Parents were unhappy that being an apprentice did not mean an automatic appointment as an officer. With the program's popularity dropping, the Navy department became clogged with requests for discharges. The Navy ended the program in 1844 and, instead the next year, established an academy at Annapolis to train officers.

"THE NAVY SHOULD BE RE-ORGANIZED"

In 1848 the Navy sent Stephen B. Luce to Annapolis. In the seven years since he had become a midshipman, he had accumulated a great deal of experience with the most significant being a three-year voyage around the globe on the *Columbus* with Commodore James Biddle. Luce must have been excited at the prospect of going to the new academy and becoming an officer.

Yet in those days the Naval Academy did not have the prestige it later held. Originally, it was a five year program with only one year actually spent at Annapolis where the future officers crammed for exams. The cadets did not even wear consistent uniforms. Luce did well, but before he graduated in 1849 was caught in a prank where he and his friends, angry at the commanding officer for not letting them go to the inauguration of Zachary Taylor, ran amuck on the ship by sounding alarms, firing guns and blowing horns. Because of this, Luce's class rank was dropped to tenth from the bottom.

Luce's experiences at the Academy and as an apprentice shaped his views on maritime education. In 1858 he wrote, ". . . the Navy should be reorganized . . . there are *now* in our service, men who wear the navy uniform, but who are totally deficient in education, both as officers and gentlemen, men who are not fit to be entrusted with the command of the meanest scow. . . ."

Luce believed that the Navy should professionalize and standardize ships and training. "Every ship in the service should have the same internal rules and regulations, the same routine of duty, the same form for station bills, the same gun exercises and in fact the same everything. They should differ as little as possible."

REFORMATORY SCHOOLSHIPS

During the 1850s, Luce would have been aware of a renewed effort to develop schoolships for the merchant marine. One advocate was Captain Robert B. Forbes, who lent his ship, the *Jamestown*, to help relieve the Irish during the potato famine. Forbes also obtained most of his considerable fortune by smuggling drugs into China during the Opium Wars. Forbes thought the drugs were not that harmful: ". . . twelve to fifteen million pounds of opium, distributed among three hundred and fifty millions of people, had a much less deleterious effect on the whole country than the vile liquor made of rice, called 'samshue.'"

In an 1851 address to the Boston Marine Society, Forbes declared that a sailor was considered a "mere machine" who worked for the "smallest pittance." He said that sailors were alienated from society and not even able to vote since they were often at sea. "He has no day, no night which he can call his own," said Forbes, "and when he begins to feel the effect of age . . . he often has no *home*."

Forbes went on to establish the Boston Sailors' Snug Harbor in 1855, a charitable organization for retired seamen. He also called for Boston to invest in nautical education. He asked, "If Boston can afford to spend for the education of merchants, lawyers, divines, doctors and mechanics, why cannot she spend something for the special education of seamen . . . ?" Forbes, like Thomas Goin, thought that schoolships would be a social boon to the cities. Forbes declared that a schoolship would "purify the morals of the lower classes. . . ."

While Boston did not immediately respond to Forbes, Baltimore did, and on September 14, 1857 that city opened the sloop-of-war *Ontario* as a schoolship. It was the first attempt in the United States by any governmental body to establish a schoolship for merchant marine training. Aboard, students were taught the basics of life at sea but it was only a simulation since the ship never left the dock. Over the next decade, enrollment declined as the American maritime industry collapsed. Expenses mounted, and on June 5, 1867, the city shut down the *Ontario*.

By 1860, the American merchant marine was in a dramatic tailspin. Since the 1830s, when the Yankee fleet carried up to 90% of the nation's trade, the merchant fleet declined due to subsidy cuts and competition from British iron-screw steamers. The Civil War made matters worse as Confederate raiders and blockades forced shipping insurance rates to skyrocket. Northern ship owners panicked and resorted to "flag flight" registering their vessels in a different country to protect themselves. By the end of the war, American-flagged vessels carried only one third of the nation's trade.

Furthermore, in the mid-1860s there were shipping disasters that drew national attention to the need to have better qualified personnel aboard ships. On April 27, 1865, the SS *Sultana* was overloaded transporting injured and formerly imprisoned Union soldiers. While on the Mississippi River near Memphis, the ship's three boilers exploded leading to over 1,500 deaths. Then, on September 26, 1866, the *Evening Star* sailing out of New York for New Orleans encountered a hurricane. Several large waves flooded the engine room so fast that the ship had to be abandoned. The passengers were told by the captain that the vessel was to be evacuated, but the crew did not deploy the lifeboats. The passengers rushed for the lifeboats and in the confusion another wave swamped the ship causing it to capsize immediately. Of 252 people aboard, only 22 survived.

The decline of the maritime industry and the rise of ship disasters provided fodder for schoolship advocates. They declared that nautical schools could help restore the dying industry to the place of prominence it held earlier in the century. This was misguided since creating schoolships did not create a demand for shipping. Yet it was the only solution that could be agreed upon.

Subsidies for ship owners, common in other countries, were stopped politically by Western congressional members who viewed them as biased toward certain regions of the country. Also, no agreement between ship owners, who wanted to buy foreign-built ships and register them as American, and shipbuilders, who wanted ship owners to buy their product, could be reached. Schoolships by default became an acceptable compromise of governmental action since training ships did not offend either of these interests, and by establishing them the government could look like it was doing something about the depressed state of the maritime trade.

Aside from economic pressures, schoolship advocates, like Goin and Forbes, believed schoolships were an excellent means to uplift and reform the lower classes. In 1860, Boston established a floating reformatory aboard the *Massachusetts* (formerly *Rockall*). New York followed suit in 1869 with its own reformatory aboard a former Le Havre packet vessel named the *Mercury*.

The establishment of the reformatories were part of the 19th century prison reform movement. In the early part of the century convicted juveniles were mixed with the adult population. These boys were usually marginal offenders—poor immigrants or minorities who were found guilty of petty crimes often associated with gangs. When these teenagers were mixed with the adult prison population they often became hardened criminals. To solve the problem, the cities, beginning in 1825, established reformatories to keep youths out of adult prisons and to provide them with a skill by having them work a minimum of six hours a day.

The reformatory ships took on boys guilty of "slight misdemeanors and vagrancy." The commissioners of the *Mercury* pointed out that the ship gave the convicted a "sure and honest means of livelihood suited to their adventurous spirit." At its height, the *Mercury* had about 300 boys and embarked on training cruises where students studied seamanship, ocean temperature, currents, fauna and flora. One administrator crowed that the *Mercury* was "a correctional institution robbed of all objectionable features."

Luce himself thought that reformatory schoolships were not a bad thing. He wrote, "Many smart boys, now preparing to graduate in our penitentiaries, would become valuable members of society, and the benefits would be felt on the land as well as the sea."

The problem was that the boys of the *Mercury* and *Massachusetts* were being forced to learn a trade they were not interested in. As a result, when their sentences were over, few boys went to sea. As potential employees, they were never popular with the shipping industry since reformatories carried a social stigma. Also, it was too expensive to maintain the ships. In 1872, the *Massachusetts* closed followed by the *Mercury* in 1876.

DEVELOPING NAUTICAL EDUCATION

While the reformatory schoolships were at sea, Luce became a specialist in nautical education. In March, 1860 he was assigned to Annapolis as an Assistant Instructor and the next year promoted to head the Department of Navigation. During this time, he reflected on the inefficiency of traditional maritime training. One glaring omission was that the Navy did not have its own textbook. Luce wrote, "Compared to the Army with their wealth of professional literature, we may be likened to the nomadic tribes of the East who are content with the vague tradition of the past."

But Luce's attention to developing a nautical curriculum became distracted at the outbreak of the American Civil War. During the hostilities he was attached to frigate *Wabash* to take part in blockading activities against the Confederacy. On November 7, 1861, the Union Navy sent the *Wabash* as part of a squadron to secure Port Royal Sound off South Carolina. Luce joined in the four-hour battle, where he was given command of one of the frigate's howitzer launches. During a lull in the fighting, a sailor named William Emmet had his cap blown off by the wind. In it was a treasured picture of his sweetheart. The sailor charged down the starboard gangplank and leapt into the water to retrieve the image. Shouts of "man overboard" peeled through the ship. Luce tore off his coat, threw down his sword and dove into the water to save the sailor. But it was no use. Emmet was lost with one witness stating that he was "without a doubt seized and carried down by sharks." Still, Luce's valor was recognized and the next year his class standing at Annapolis, which had been demoted years earlier due to the bell-ringing prank, was restored to fifth from the top.

After Port Royal, the Navy divided Luce's activity between blockade duty and the Naval Academy. At the Naval Academy, he headed the Department of Seamanship and finally filled the gap in maritime educational literature with his 1862 textbook, *Seamanship*. It was a great improvement over the *Kedge*

Anchor, which was the closest thing mariners had to a text until that time. Entries of the *Kedge Anchor* ran like this:

> Turk's heads are made on man-ropes, and sometimes on the foot-ropes of jib-booms in place of an overhanded knot, as the Turk's head is much neater than the knot, and considered by some an ornament. It is generally made of small white line. Take a round turn round the rope you intend to make the Turk's head on—cross the bights on each side of the round turn, and stick one end under one cross, and the other under the other cross. . . .

If the *Kedge Anchor* were given to a man who knew nothing about seamanship it would be easier for him to translate hieroglyphics. Luce's *Seamanship*, while not exactly engaging, (few 19th century textbooks were), provided a curricular framework for a novice mariner.

Luce also trained his cadets practically. He commanded the *Macedonian*, a practice ship used by the midshipmen of the Academy. One cadet at the time recalled, "There was no nonsense about Luce's teaching. It was all practical and to the point." Luce took the vessel in the summer of 1863 to Europe where he observed British and French training methods.

Luce ranked mariners according to ethnicity and race. To him, the British made the ideal sailor. Luce commented that the British petty officers' "physique, intelligence and seaman-like bearing surpassed any men we have seen on this side of the Atlantic for many years." He was highly impressed by Britain's training ships, *Conway* and *Worcester*: "The English Navy is manned, exclusively by young Seamen who have passed through the Training Ships. This is one cause which has brought England to the zenith of her naval power." He later asserted, "We need to look to the example of foreign navies then, to learn how to legislate for our seamen; the very spirit of the age cries out to educate them." Only a schoolship could create the environment necessary to train mariners while at the same time avoiding, as Luce put it, the "spasmodic" results of an apprentice system.*

When Luce became Commandant of Midshipmen at Annapolis at the end of the Civil War, he was in a much better position to push forward his vision of nautical education, not only of the Navy, but also of the merchant

---

*Luce's dislike of the apprentice system was based on his own experiences and observations. When the Navy reestablished the program in 1863, Luce supported it as long as it reformed and standardized its training methods on schoolships.

marine. In 1866, he wrote to prominent Boston men promoting a "Nautical College" to protect "the enormous losses . . . of life and property" such as the *Evening Star*.

Yet the key to Luce's vision was to have the merchant and Naval services manned entirely by Americans. Did this make Luce a nativist? Certainly he expressed contempt for foreigners in the U.S. Navy although paradoxically it did not affect his positive opinion of British mariners. In an 1872 letter to the Secretary of the Navy he wrote, "Our ships go to sea manned by heterogeneous crews representing nearly every country on the face of the globe; men, many of them utterly destitute of any feeling of attachment for or interest in the Navy; whose only care it is to earn a present subsistence till something better can be found . . . The majority are ignorant of the Navy and its traditions, indifferent to honor and reputation; impatient under discipline and who go through with their military duties under protest as it were."

It is not clear if Luce was against naturalized citizens upon American ships. Historian Jennifer Speelman, in her dissertation on the development of nautical education, wrote, "In an era of growing immigration, sailors could easily have been foreign-born and yet served as American citizens. Luce did not perceive the situation as such. He believed only those most in need of employment, such as immigrants, would voluntarily sign up for sea duty when other opportunities presented themselves." Meanwhile, in the merchant service, ships such as the transatlantic packets were filling their crew complements with "Liverpool rats," and whalers obtained sailors from Hawaii, Portugal and islands in the Atlantic Ocean.

Luce became obsessive about the potential of a foreign takeover of the Navy. In 1872, he created data tables showing that only 46.6% of the ships of the Mediterranean Squadron were manned by what he defined as real Americans. In these tables, he went so far as to break the crews down by their nationality. Alongside the "American" entry, he added a footnote which stated "probably a large proportion of the Americans were of Irish parentage."

Whether or not Luce's views on race and ethnicity would be acceptable in later centuries, his ideas on nautical education transformed the Navy. Luce became the intellectual head of the "New Navy." This retooled, professional force would be the spearhead for American global strategy as pronounced by Luce's colleague, Alfred Thayer Mahan, whose seminal work, *The Influence of Sea Power Upon History*, shaped American diplomacy and imperialism in the late 19th and early 20th centuries.

THE ESTABLISHMENT OF THE NEW YORK NAUTICAL SCHOOL

Luce is best known for establishing the U.S. Naval Observatory and the Naval War College, but by extension, Luce also established the training system of the modern merchant marine. To him, the merchant service existed in a symbiotic relationship with the U.S. Navy. The Navy protected American ships, and merchant mariners provided an auxiliary and reserve force for the Navy. Luce believed that individual states should create nautical schools to train mariners with the assistance and oversight of the federal government. To justify federal involvement, Luce cited the 1862 Morrill Act which gave federal land to the states in order for them to create vocational colleges. Luce argued that instead of land, the federal government should give money and Naval personnel to the states to set up and run nautical schoolships.

Meanwhile, one of the dominant industries in New York City was shipping, and it was well represented in the city's Chamber of Commerce. This group, along with the Marine Society, was unhappy with the results of the reformatory *Mercury* and wanted a new school for seamen. They pressed Albany to establish a nautical school that would train a better class of boys than those of the *Mercury*. The legislature responded on April 24, 1873 with a law that authorized the city's Board of Education to found such a school. It is hard to say how much influence Luce had in the creation of this law, but after the school's governing committee was established they consulted with Luce at the recommendation of Admiral John Worden, the Superintendent of the U.S. Naval Academy.

The big problem was that the school was only theoretical since they did not have a training ship. Luce and the Chamber of Commerce approached the Navy to borrow one. The Navy, however, would not lend a ship unless Congress authorized it by law. Luce took up the cause and lobbied Congress through a series of letters to pass a bill that would transform maritime education. He suggested amending the Morrill Act to allow for nautical instruction. The Navy would lend ships to state nautical schools, introduce competency exams to ship masters and officers and create a reserve of graduates for the U.S. Navy.

Most of Luce's proposals were reflected in a bill from the House of Representatives. However, the Senate counter-proposed a version that only allowed the Navy to lend vessels to specific ports for nautical schools—there was nothing about competency exams, amending the Morrill Act, or creating a Navy reserve. This was the bill that became law. While Luce did not fully achieve what he set out to do, it was some progress and he helped the New York Nautical School acquire the old sloop-of-war *St. Mary's*.

The *St. Mary's* had a long history in the Navy before it was assigned as a training ship. Built to help suppress the slave trade, the vessel was designed for speed and long cruises.* Active in the Mexican and Civil wars, the vessel spent most of its career on the Pacific station where it engaged in gunboat diplomacy in Latin America under a series of gutsy commanders. It was a square-rigged vessel with no engines. This was to the liking of Luce who believed that true sailors could only be created under sail.

The Navy could no longer use the vessel and they gave it to Luce. She was taken to Boston where the Navy removed most of the guns, gave her repairs and finally towed her into New York Harbor. The vessel arrived on December 10, 1874 with a new lease on life. Luce transferred her to David Wetmore, the New York Nautical School's chairman. The next month, 26 boys lined up at the Manhattan waterfront to become the first class of the schoolship *St. Mary's*.

---

*Many later sources state that the *St. Mary's* took part in the suppression of the slave trade, but there is no evidence that this was true. The most erroneous accounts of the ship's history come from newspaper articles much later than the time the ship was active in the U.S. Navy. The newspapers also claimed that the *St. Mary's* was the fastest sailing ship the Navy ever built, which is doubtful.

CHAPTER 2

A Square-Rigged School

". . . for thirty-three years this fine old sailing vessel has crossed the ocean nearly every year, sailing altogether between nine and ten thousand miles annually, and that all the work has been done by boys."

—G.C. Hanus, Superintendent of the
Schoolship St. Mary's—1907

On January 11, 1875, twenty-six boys made their way to the foot of East 23rd Street where, tied to a wharf, sat the New York Nautical Schoolship *St. Mary's*. They were going to become sailors in a school that required boots, thread, needles and dark blue overcoats, instead of notebooks and pencils.

That January, the *St. Mary's* was a noisy place. The ship was being refitted into a floating grammar school. Half of her guns were taken out, a temporary schoolroom built on the main deck and hammocks slung on the gun deck. The ship wasn't quite ready by January 11th, but the superintendent and captain of the ship thought that the time was ripe to bring aboard a class of boys.

The students were mixed in age. The youngest, A. Emelius Irving, was just 14 years and 11 months old and needed the minimum age rule of 15 years waived by the Board of Education's Nautical School Executive Committee. The oldest, Richard Moseley, was 21. These boys came from all over Manhattan and the Bronx. In those days, New York City consisted only of those boroughs; by law, only those with a parent or guardian residing in the city could enroll in the school. However, the rules were bent and the very first student enrolled at the school, Alexander Wadsworth, had a guardian from Quincy, Massachusetts. From its beginning, the New York Nautical School was a national enterprise.

The school was governed by an Executive Committee that was composed of members of the Board of Education. It established policies that were suggested by the superintendent, who acted as the captain of the *St. Mary's*. The Executive Committee provided oversight, administered tests, established policies and served as a job placement service for graduates. For the first years of the school's life, this body was headed by David Wetmore.

In addition to the Executive Committee, business interests were represented through advisory committees from the city's Chamber of Commerce and the Maritime Association. These groups represented shipping interests and aside from providing advice, also gave periodic examinations to the boys. The U.S. Navy was also involved. Not only did they furnish the ship, but they often did repairs and provided personnel to be the instructors.

The schoolship's first superintendent was Captain Robert Lees Phythian. He graduated from the U.S. Naval Academy in 1856 and was a Civil War veteran, serving in the Union naval blockade of the Confederacy. After the war, he taught at the Naval Academy and headed its Navigation Department under the direction of Stephen B. Luce. The teaching and practical experience made him such an easy fit for the job that Luce recommended him for the position. One 1876 graduate, Charles Williamson, recalled that Phythian combined the "knowledge of a school teacher" with "the firmness of the disciplinarian and . . . the kindness of a parent." For his trouble, Phythian received in addition to his Navy pay, $2,000 from the city and the right to have his family live aboard the *St. Mary's*—something unheard of in the service. These additional perks made the job a "soft berth" and "the most desirable position in the Navy." Phythian had good cause to be kind.

Phythian and all the officers in the early years of the New York Nautical School were active Navy officers who were assigned to the ship to train the boys to be a reserve for the U.S. Navy. If a boy got out of line, George W. De Long, Phythian's executive officer, would enforce the rules in a military fashion. Naval discipline was the watchword, and Luce's *Young Seaman's Manual* was their text.

Aside from learning rigging, mastwork and vessel identification, the boys, to their great delight, learned how to fire the *St. Mary's* great guns (the half not removed during her reconditioning), use small arms and wield cutlasses. The boys were taught how to make "all knots, splices, hitches, bends, clinches, . . . worming, parceling and serving ropes; turning in deadeyes, securing lanyards and rattling down rigging." They learned the colors and arrangement of running lights, how to sew and how to swim. It was an education that was fun for a boy who learned by doing rather than sitting over a book reading and thinking.

But the boys of the St. Mary's were still required to learn the normal grammar school curriculum which was taught over the winter months. History, math, grammar and the art of penmanship were all given time in repetitive drills.

Yet in the late spring, and every year thereafter, the schoolroom was broken down. The boys put away their *Robinson's Progressive Practical Arithmetic* and *Brown's English Grammar* to turn to the practical work of getting a full-rigged sloop-of-war ready for a sea-voyage. These cruises were the heart and soul of the school.

Phythian did not sail the St. Mary's far that first year and kept within Long Island Sound. After all, he had a completely new set of boys aboard. To take them into the Atlantic would be too hazardous for what was admittedly dangerous training.

On most of the St. Mary's cruises the ship first went to Glen Cove, Long Island. There, stores were loaded and the boys were mercilessly drilled. Then, when the captain thought the boys ready, they sailed into the Atlantic. While Phythian and all his successors strove to make cruises safe—and often gloated in their annual reports when there were no injuries—bad things could happen.

"WILL YOU SAVE HIM?"

On May 2, 1907, while the ship was in Glen Cove, a first year student named Albert Ruffin went to the sickbay with pains in his back and a high fever. Ruffin, at 17 years old, was five foot five and an athletic 127 pounds. He had even won five medals for sports in high school before enrolling in the Nautical School in October, 1906. He was generally well-behaved, and the superintendent at that time, Gustavus Hanus, wrote that Ruffin had "exemplary personal habits" despite being written up several times for leaving his clothes about the ship.

Despite the boy's athleticism, in the sick bay Ruffin fell unconscious. Keran O'Brien, the ship's doctor, examined him and diagnosed him with cerebrospinal meningitis, a bacterial infection of the membranes surrounding the brain and spinal cord. Fever, confusion, headaches and sensitivity to light are all symptoms. If left untreated, it could result in brain damage or death.

This disease was known to the schoolship. In 1881, four cases broke out on the *St. Mary's* resulting in one fatality; and this was in New York City with good medical facilities, not while at sea.

O'Brien told Hanus of the situation. Hanus immediately sent a telegram to the boy's father, a manager of a typewriter company: "Your son Albert is very dangerously ill. Have sent on shore for physician to consult with Dr. O'Brien, come at once."

The shore side doctor was from Glen Cove, and he concurred with O'Brien. Ruffin had to get to a hospital as quickly as possible, and in 1907, Glen Cove did not have a place where he could be treated. Hanus knew that the boy had to be sent to the city, and the quickest way to get there was by boat.

Hanus debarked from the *St. Mary's* and at 9:00 a.m. called Frederick Dalzell, the owner of a large New York City towing company. Hanus said, "We have a sick cadet, who can only be saved by being taken immediately to Bellevue. Will you save him?"

Dalzell called Captain Benson, the master of his fastest tugboat, the *Union*, and ordered him to sail for Glen Cove. The captain rushed to Pier 10, where his boat was tied up, and ordered his engineer to build steam. As the *Union* warmed, Benson saw that he did not have enough crew to work the vessel so he recruited two men from the dock. In fact, he was so rushed that he took only enough coal to fuel a one way voyage to Glen Cove. He would need to depend on the *St. Mary's* supply for the race back. Meanwhile, Hanus sent a telegram to Ruffin's father: "Have sent for a tug to remove Albert to Bellevue Hospital in care of Doctor and assistants; dangerous to delay."

Benson and the *Union* got underway at 10:00 a.m. and shot up the East River whizzing by Man o' War Reef* at a dangerous clip of twelve miles per hour. She then hurried past Blackwell's Island and through the Hell Gate. By the afternoon, the tugboat reached the *St. Mary's*.

Hanus waited for the *Union* by the side ladder, while behind him, O'Brien tended Ruffin in a stretcher. In 20 minutes the transfer was done. The boy, O'Brien, an oxygen tank and coal were loaded aboard the tugboat. Benson then steamed back to New York as quickly as he could. At 3:15 p.m., the *Union* reached the 26th Street pier where an ambulance met them. They whisked the boy to Bellevue Hospital where his father waited.

---

*Now the enlarged Belmont Island.

The newspapers made a splash of the rescue. The press praised Hanus, Benson and Dalzell under the headlines, "Raced with Death to Save Sick Cadet" and "*St. Mary's* Cadet in Race with Death." On May 3rd, Ruffin's father called Hanus and told him that the boy's fever was normal. He had "a fair chance for recovery."

But on May 16th, Ruffin's father sent another telegram to Hanus. While we do not know what the telegram said, Hanus's reply speaks volumes: "Please accept my sincere sympathy and that of everybody on board. I had kept in touch with the hospital and hoped against hope." Hanus sent some of Ruffin's classmates to help lay the boy to rest.

The Nautical School had a built-in set of risks. If the hull was split open by an iceberg, or if a storm foundered the ship, there was no radio to call for help—there was no "Plan B" other than the skills the boys learned from their instructors. It was no accident that in the annual reports of the school, the surgeon's report was highlighted. In it, he talks about how the boys have grown, their health and how the sea life was good for them. Despite tragedies such as the Ruffin incident, the record shows that the *St. Mary's* was a safe school. Between 1875 and 1891 there were only three fatalities; in 1881 a meningitis case, an 1883 accidental drowning when a cadet fell from aloft and an 1888 death from peritonitis, an inflammation of the tissues surrounding the abdominal organs.

"THE SCUM OF NEW YORK"

The New York Nautical School trained sailors, a maligned profession even in ancient times. In Homer's *Odyssey*, Odysseus is challenged by younger men to join sporting competition. Odysseus, worn out by his travels, declines. Then the young athlete Euryalus tries to bait him into competing. "I should never have taken you for an athlete, good at any of the games men play," Euryalus says. "You are more like a skipper of a merchant crew, who spends his life on a hulking tramp, worrying about his outward freight, or keeping a sharp eye on the cargo when he comes home with his extortionate profits." It works. Odysseus is so offended by being called a merchant sailor that he enters the competition and wins. In the 18th century, author Samuel Johnson said, "No man will be a sailor who has contrivance enough to get himself into a jail; for being in a ship is being in a jail, with the chance of being drowned . . . a man in a jail has more room, better food and commonly better company." Sailors were considered low-class derelicts.

What made things difficult for the boys of the New York Nautical School was that they were required to wear traditional sailor uniforms, even when not aboard the *St. Mary's*. For a boy who aspired to be an officer it was a mortifying experience, especially in an era which emphasized class distinction. In 1894, student Frederick McMurray, complained to his mother:

> We have hard times ashore. Men, women, girls and boys stare at us . . . merchants grab us and haul us into their stores . . . Saloon keepers open their side doors and push us in . . . peddlers and beggars annoy us, drunken men clap us on the shoulder and talk to us, and decent people cross the street or clear the sidewalks near us, just because we wear a blue suit with three white stripes and stars and because we have on a round hat and wear a white lanyard.

The end result was that the school was not seen as respectable, even in its beginning. In an 1878 letter to the *New York Times*, a reader wrote:

> The Nautical School is doing grand work in ridding this City of many boys who, in a few years, would be a scourge to it, and in giving to them a chance to become useful citizens. That any body of men could be found in this City who are opposed to a scheme which strengthens our merchant marine and at the same time removes some of the scum of New-York is indeed wonderful.

The *St. Mary's* was confused with the reformatory ship the *Mercury*, which operated simultaneously until 1876. Even after the *Mercury* closed, the bad reputation lingered throughout the *St. Mary's* entire career as a schoolship. While some students, like McMurray, hated this reputation, many other students embraced it as a sign of toughness.

Phythian, all of his successors and the Board of Education fought the reputation problem by constantly stressing that the students were "not offenders to be reclaimed" but came from "respectable birth and parentage, coming, many of them, from country homes, where they have had correct influences and associations." To demonstrate the excellent caliber of the school, Phythian introduced advanced courses in celestial navigation, steamship handling and naval architecture for graduates waiting ashore for jobs. The school from its beginning aspired to train sea officers rather than sailors.

To make sea officers, the boys needed role models and this fell to their instructors. One of them was George W. De Long, who left his position as Phythian's executive officer in 1878 to head a mission to find the North Pole on the *Jeannette*. The men aboard the ship travelled north and were ensnared in the ice. De Long was forced to abandon the *Jeannette* and travelled over the frozen sea for land. Their situation was so dire that they ate their sled dogs before the men were frozen solid, stranded on the coast of Siberia. Such suicidal heroics served as an example to the students on what it meant to be honorable, brave, (and dead) sea officers. In fact, from De Long's mission we can trace a thread of exploration among alumni such as 1902 graduate, Ross Gilmore Marvin.

CHAPTER 3

"A Barnacle in the School System"

". . . the kind of boys who enter on board the St. Mary's are boys who do not like to go to school; they want to go to sea."
—Arent Crowninshield, 1888

THE MADNESS OF ROSS MARVIN

Ross Gilmore Marvin had been going to Cornell when he ran out of money in 1900. Unable to afford his tuition, he enrolled in the New York Nautical School, since it was free. In his early twenties, he was older than the other students and became a leader among them. When he graduated in 1902, he was hired as the schoolship's quartermaster. This money helped him return to Cornell and graduate in 1905.

Marvin was a polymath who was said to be "six men in one. He was a botanist, a geologist, a meteorologist, a mathematician and a navigator." His only flaw was a lip deformity that made his speech "troublesome and awkward." His skills drew the attention of Robert Peary, who recruited him for his 1905–06 expedition to reach the North Pole. On this mission, Marvin acted as Peary's secretary as well as a scientist. Because of the skills he learned on the *St. Mary's*, he was primarily responsible for taking soundings of unexplored ocean bed.

During the expedition, Marvin developed a surprisingly strong relationship with the irascible Peary. Peary noted that Marvin, "grasped more fully than any other man the underlying, fundamental principles of the work."

Marvin also developed a lust for exploration. The mission was unsuccessful and after he returned to America, Marvin commented that the most interesting part about coming home was to find out how the Cornell football team had done. He settled into academia becoming a professor first at Mercersburg Academy, then later, Cornell.

But Peary wanted another try at the Pole. He approached Marvin who jumped at the chance. On this second journey, he brought a banner from the New York Nautical School. The expedition departed in the summer of 1908 on the ship *Roosevelt*.

On this second attempt, Marvin took tidal and meteorological observations and helped Peary plan the trek over the ice. Peary asserted that Marvin, next to the *Roosevelt's* captain, was "the most valuable man in the party. Whenever the captain was not in the field, Marvin took command of the work, and on him devolved the sometimes onerous, sometimes amusing labor of breaking in the new members...."

In the summer of 1908, the expedition set out for Canada. The ship penetrated the polar ice between Etah and Cape Sheridan. When autumn came, the men made a base camp and added to their supplies of tea, biscuit and pemmican, wild game such as polar bear, deer and musk oxen; the bones of the latter used to decorate the *Roosevelt's* rigging. They settled down for the "black and melancholy five months' [of] Arctic night."

Peary decided to push for the North Pole while it was still winter, but just as light returned to the Arctic. They set out on February 15, 1909. Each party was composed of about four men including Inuit assistants. Each sledge was designed to "support the driver and the dog team for about fifty days." Peary noted "by sacrificing a few dogs and using them as food for the other dogs and the men, this time could have been extended to sixty days." The party in total numbered 24 men, 19 sledges and 133 dogs.

Peary's plan to reach the North Pole was to have a pioneer party lead the way, followed by supporting parties to provide logistical assistance. The teams acted as relays, where different groups would take turns inching north. Peary asserted that Marvin helped him develop this strategy.

The dangers of the journey were many: biting cold (up to negative 59 degrees), ever damp clothing and the insidious threat of carbon monoxide poisoning when enclosed shelters were not properly ventilated. Since the polar caps are constantly in motion, collisions between immense frozen ice sheets resulted in mountainous pressure ridges. These icy walls were formidable barriers the explorers had to climb over, go around or find some other way to overcome. It was exhausting work. Peary himself lost 25 pounds during the expedition. Yet the most dangerous threats were leads, channels of open water that suddenly formed from wind and tide. The risk of sudden death by falling into frigid water was a real concern.

Marvin headed his own team, taking soundings when they came to open leads and determining latitude. On March 25th, at 86° 38' north, Peary sent Marvin south, to act as part of the supply chain for his return.

They departed, and Peary claimed to have reached the pole, although some contemporary critics and many modern scholars believe the assertion false. Regardless of Peary's success, when he returned to the *Roosevelt* he was greeted by Marvin's Inuit assistants, Kudlooktoo and Inukitsoq (nicknamed Harrigan). They described how after they broke camp near a large lead, Marvin went ahead of them. The ice broke and he fell into the water and drowned—the body unrecoverable. Peary wrote that the story "staggered" him, "killing all the joy" he had felt. He sent dispatches to the United States and built a memorial cairn to Marvin on Ellesmere Island.

Then in 1926, Kudlooktoo, who had converted to Christianity, told a Danish missionary that Marvin at the time of his death "was like a sane man who for the moment was without the use of his faculties." Kudlooktoo claimed that Marvin attempted to abandon them on the ice. To save themselves, the Inuit shot Marvin with his rifle.

There are problems with this confession, as contemporaries of the expedition asserted that Marvin was "wonderful at getting along" with the Inuits. The New *York Times* condemned Kudlooktoo, writing that he "knows that he need not look out for old age, anyway, because he will probably not live to be old. Before that time he will die by being swept away on a pan of ice in the darkness of the polar night; or by falling into a deep crevasse on the ice cap; or by being caught along the barren coast by a sudden smother of snow and slowly [starve] to death."

Some have suggested that there was a communication problem. The Inuits believed Marvin was abandoning them and they panicked. Jerry Kobalenko, in his book, *Horizontal Everest*, speculated that Marvin may have doubted Peary was going to make it to the North Pole. When Marvin expressed these doubts, Peary may have tried to force Marvin to sign a false affidavit and, as an afterthought, had the Inuits murder him. Was Peary so obsessed with getting to the Pole that he would commit murder? Maybe, but such a conspiracy is a stretch of the imagination, and the former theory seems more likely. Perhaps Marvin did go mad and Kudlooktoo was sincere; otherwise, why else would Kudlooktoo confess to murder and not indict Peary? Kudlooktoo's story is most likely the true version of events.

Even though Marvin never returned, the banner of the New York Nautical School did and found its way to his family. They donated it to the school, which encased it in glass until 1999, when 1989 graduate and astronaut, Scott Kelly, saw the pennant on display. Kelly asked for and received permission to take the pennant as one of two personal items he was allowed to bring on his upcoming spaceflight—the other was a beanie baby. On that mission, Kelly traveled over 3 million miles, much farther than all the voyages of the schoolship *St. Mary's* combined.

The determination and bravery of Ross Marvin was infectious. Many of the boys who graduated from the decks of the *St. Mary's* felt the need to prove themselves as gallant sea officers. They were not common sailors from a reformatory. They were *St. Mary's* boys; that meant quality.

"WHERE BAD BOYS ARE MADE GOOD"

The sacrifices and all the efforts to show how the *St. Mary's* was an institution of high caliber was undermined by stories of savagery. In 1889, Executive Officer Lieutenant William M. Wood brought two ladies aboard and into the wardroom. To impress the women, the officer ordered some of the boys to come into the cabin to "sing and play the banjo for them."

After this, Wood took one of the ship's cutters and escorted the ladies to shore. He returned drunk and summoned the boys out of their hammocks to haul the boat aboard. The boys, fed up with their executive officer, mocked him by singing a parody of the earlier songs as they hoisted up the boat.

Wood cursed the students, and selected one, Charles Harold, for punishment. The officer ordered the boy lashed to the rigging and suspended in the air. Wood then commanded the Master-at-Arms to whip Harold with a rope's end. However, the Master-at-Arms did it too lightly. Wood then seized the rope and completed the punishment himself. Afterwards, Wood was still angry, so he summoned a boy he disliked named Charles Weaver who had just finished a stint in solitary confinement for fighting. Wood ordered another boy to beat up Weaver even though he had already been punished.

Word of the affair reached parents who forced the Board of Education to hold a hearing. Wood denied what happened and even provided a petition from other boys on the ship that supported him. No more mention of the case was made, and Wood quietly left the ship on a leave of absence never to return.

It is fair to say that the Wood case may be exaggerated since accounts are mostly from sensationalizing tabloids. Even so, horrible publicity had done real damage. Parents threatened their truant sons that if they did not behave they would be sent to the schoolship. Almost 20 years after the Wood incident, Superintendent Hanus remarked that a "mistake that the public labors under is the belief that the *St. Mary's* is a kind of reformatory where bad boys are made good." Even as late as 1911, the school's admission application read that the *St.Mary's* was "in no sense a reformatory, or a sanitarium, and only boys of good character, who will appreciate and avail themselves of the instruction are admitted."

The poor reputation of the schoolship grew, especially after Phythian and his competent successor, Henry Erben, were reassigned by the Navy. Maintaining an able staff of officers was a constant problem aboard the ship in its early years. The officers were all active Navy men who were constantly reassigned. As a result, the leadership of the school was in constant flux. The real fixtures of the school were the members of the crew.

The professional crew consisted of cooks, boatswains and other members of the ship who worked on the *St. Mary's*. More often than not they were foreigners, which led Phythian to comment that the number of immigrants aboard the *St. Mary's* justified the school's creation. Some of the crew stayed on for years and imparted to the boys the collective wisdom of hundreds of years of seafaring. The most well-known of them was the colorful Boatswain William Dreilick whose acerbic tongue and quick temper became the stuff of school legend.

Dreilick was an Americanized Finn who served on the schoolship from 1885 to 1922. He was a brilliant and powerful sailor who "had Lot's wife lashed to the mast when it came to saltiness." Graduate Felix Riesenberg wrote how Dreilick "would make the reefing of a topsail in a gale of wind seem like a sea battle, not that he made so much noise, but he conveyed a sense of urgency beyond belief." Frederick McMurray wrote that in emergencies, "he seemed a demigod; with the old ship at an acute angle, her canvas thrashing about and wind force screaming in dirge in the shrouds; pelting rain and the roar of the sea adding to a pandemonium that unnerved the majority of unseasoned sailors during such memorable occasions."

Dreilick was full of choice quotations. When ordered to tack ship, he said to the carpenter in his distinct, Finnish accent, "Dis is too god damn scientific for either you or me to understand." One boy who blundered was asked by the Boatswain, "In vat year ver you born?" After the reply, Dreilick said, "Vell dere were a great many people born dat year, but vy in the hell you were put on dis earth, is a matter entirely beyond my comprehension." Dreilick was so respected that after he died, graduates built a monument over his grave in East Haddam, Connecticut.

THE LATE 19TH CENTURY CRISIS

As the reputation of the school suffered, so too did its enrollment. Attendance at the Nautical School peaked at 117 boys in 1879 under Superintendent Erben. The schoolship was almost at full capacity. After Erben was reassigned, enrollment dropped so that by 1893, there were only 38 students aboard.

Enrollment crashed for four reasons. First, there was the bad reputation. Parents did not wish to send their children to what they were convinced was a reformatory, or those that *did* wish it, often did not have their sons accepted. Second, the school's enrollment was limited to those boys who could claim a parent or guardian in New York City. While boys from outside the city enrolled by having the residency requirement waived by the Board of Education, this was more of the exception than the rule. Third, American oceanic trade was in decline. Statistics show that in 1860 the tonnage of foreign trade carried by the American merchant fleet was 2,379,396 tons. By 1898, this was reduced to 726,213 tons. In 1893, the year that enrollment was at its lowest point, was the also the first year in which the gross tonnage of steam merchant vessels outstripped that of sailing ships like the *St. Mary's*. The fourth reason was that by the 1880s, the *St. Mary's* was in bad condition and the city refused to repair her.

The Nautical School was a free institution supported by city taxpayers. The only fee that students paid was a deposit of $35 to be spent in equipping themselves with appropriate outfits and gear which was refunded after graduation. Unlike shore-based schools, the schoolship had unique expenses. Supplies, food and board for the students, crew and officers were all significant costs.

To pay for the schoolship, the city annually budgeted between $20,000 to $30,000. This covered most expenses since, in good years, the Navy paid for basic maintenance, repairs and needed equipment. All the same, the school was expensive. An 1886–95 analysis tracked the cost per pupil at various schools throughout the city and found that the average annual expense per student in a New York City grammar school was $30.16. For the Nautical School it was $405.93.

The school was held up as an example of government waste. In January, 1878 a report on the Committee of Salaries and Economy stated that the city should not support vocational training, the *St. Mary's* should be gotten rid of, and that nautical education be conducted entirely ashore. That February, the Council of Political Reform stated that the school was unfair since it only trained "a handful of boys in seamanship." They wrote that if the amount of money was justified, then New York should "furnish a trade . . . to all the youth of this City." Yet the only way to reduce costs per pupil was to enroll more students, which was impossible. The ship was designed to handle no more than 120 students.

Politically, the schoolship was seen as a pet project of the Chamber of Commerce. In 1886, while debating New York City's annual budget, Mayor William R. Grace commented that the schoolship was a "mere pet of some few people" and that he did not believe in spending money on it. Yet despite the misgivings, he signed off on the budget anyway, "It is one of those things that we can't wipe out."

This did not stop others in the city government from trying to sink the schoolship. One tactic was to try to move the control of the school to the state. In 1889 and 1891 the States of Pennsylvania and Massachusetts respectively established their own nautical schoolships. These schools were the first since New York, to take advantage of the 1874 federal law. The difference was that these were state, not city, supported institutions. The *New York Times* caught on to the idea and in 1890 wrote that in order for the school to succeed, it needed the financial support of New York State. The newspaper argued that because attendance on the *St. Mary's* was so low, the school was graduating mediocre students just to keep numbers up to justify its budget. As a result, the reputation of the school suffered even more. The *Times* opined that a state takeover would increase the number of applicants which would allow the schoolship to be more selective. The *Times* wrote, "Many a farmer's boy would like to turn his reaping hook and plowshare into a boat hook and marlinspike."

By the 1890s, the situation had grown critical as student desertion increased. Jumping ship was common throughout the history of the New York Nautical School, as students would occasionally disappear in foreign ports. Even John Riis, the son of the famous muckraker, Jacob Riis, deserted the ship in 1899 with three companions while in Gibraltar. He said that the superintendent at that time, William Reeder, was a "hard master." Riis accused him of sending him up on the masthead for up to six hours at a time in the rain, for not studying his navigation lessons. Riis also hated the food. "We had no fresh bread, only hardtack and 'salt horse.' The molasses barrel sprung a leak and we didn't even have that delicacy to soften the hardtack. Stewed prunes were our chief dessert. Condensed milk was doled out in driblets for our coffee which was awful." Unrepentant, the boy claimed that he "left at the first chance" he had.

Several years before Riis deserted, the Chamber of Commerce, which had its own Nautical School Committee, advised the Board of Education in 1891, to take over the management of the *St. Mary's*. They were fed up with the way the city was treating the schoolship, believed it was misunderstood, and needed to be run by people in the maritime industry. Even though the Board of Education refused to transfer the school, the effort was not meaningless. From this date, there was a growing undercurrent that the school needed to be run by the merchant marine.

"FOR BOYS OF MODERATE MEANS"

At that time, Superintendent Arent Crowninshield said that the *St. Mary's* was "for boys of moderate means" since it was free. He said that students who came to the school would "not only earn a livelihood" but "rise to the highest steps in the nautical profession." He denounced those who argued against the school due to its cost:

> Why, several of our wealthy citizens spend more money every year on their yachts than it costs to maintain this school . . . it would indeed be strange if this great, wealthy city, the very existence of which is dependent upon commerce, could not afford to maintain a school so closely connected with commerce as is this institution.

To address the budget issue and to make the school more appealing, Crowninshield said that the *St. Mary's* needed to sail more. He proposed that during the winter the ship should sail to the Caribbean and during the summer to Europe. Crowninshield pointed out:

> You cannot make seamen out of boys simply by their living on board a ship, especially if that ship is tied up to a wharf for six or seven months in a year, her sails unbent and her rigging unrove! . . . the kind of boys who enter on board the *St. Mary's* are boys who do not like to go to school; they want to go to sea; they join the ship with that idea and for that purpose, and look forward most anxiously for the day to arrive when the ship is to sail on her annual cruise.

The Board of Education adopted Crowninshield's suggestions in a 1891 resolution requested an additional $10,000 from the city to finance repairs and a second cruise. But when the Board of Estimate and Apportionment reviewed the allocations, they cut the funding. A tax department bureaucrat quipped that the *St. Mary's* was a "barnacle in the school system." The board gave the schoolship only $20,000, which made a second cruise impossible. Morale ebbed. This was worsened in 1892, when two students died at sea, one being knocked overboard and the other for unspecified reasons. By this time Crowninshield was gone, and his successor, John McGowan, warned that if the *St. Mary's* was not repaired the school would sink.

And the city did nothing. On January 23, 1893, scarlet fever broke out among the boys and crew. The school closed and reopened on February 8th. The bad happenings aboard eroded the remaining political clout of the Nautical School. By the time the school reopened, the ship had become so derelict that she could not sail. McGowan begged the Navy for help, but it refused, so he was forced to spend almost his entire annual budget on repairs. The Nautical School Executive Committee asked the Board of Education for additional monies to fund a summer cruise. The request was refused. That April, out of cash and hope, the schoolship shut down—possibly for good.

Matters were made worse as the Panic of 1893 started that May. The Panic, the worst economic depression the country faced until that point, depleted government coffers and weakened any resolve for the city to finance the school. The school's chief antagonist at that time was Mayor Thomas Gilroy who said ". . . sixteen children could be educated in the grammar schools for the amount now spent for the education of one child in the nautical school." He did not "consider the support or maintenance of a school ship for the education of seamen a proper part of the educational system of the city. . . ." Rather, he wanted the schoolship controlled by the federal or state government since it was already admitting students from all over the country. That July, when Gilroy was notified that additional funds were needed to repair the

St. Mary's, he slammed his fist on a table and said, "Not another cent for that school as long as I am Mayor of this city."

Then Benjamin Megie, an 1888 graduate and naval officer, wrote a letter to Gilroy which said that the Nautical School was a ". . . failure. Of its graduates less than 10 per cent ever follow the sea, and of those at least 50 per cent enter the Navy where their previous 'nautical' training is of no use whatever to them. . . ."

But according to archival records, the majority of schoolship graduates *did* go to sea or worked in the maritime sector. The average percentage of graduates between 1876 and 1906 who did so was a respectable, but not outstanding, 60%. In 1888, the year Megie graduated, 66% of graduates went into the merchant marine, maritime industry, or the Navy.

There is no clear reason why Megie sent the letter. Records indicate that he was generally a good student with the exception of some moderate offenses such as throwing potatoes on deck and insulting the ship's cook. Megie was later court martialed by the Navy and found guilty of "scandalous conduct, tending to the destruction of good morals." He was sentenced to one year in prison before being dishonorably discharged. The details of Megie's court martial have been lost to history, but his letter got into the New York newspapers. It was another broadside at the *St. Mary's*.

Meanwhile, friends of the Nautical School declared that the city was legally obliged to maintain the schoolship and threatened to bring lawsuits. Businessmen circulated a petition demanding that the state take control of the school and have shipping men to run it. Gilroy, however, would not budge and withheld additional funding. The ship remained tied to the pier and school was closed until the beginning of 1894.

Outraged at the situation, the Chamber of Commerce enlisted State Senator Jacob Cantor to introduce a bill to transfer the schoolship to state control. The problem was that the bill called for the same $20,000 budget and that to be admitted, boys needed to be recommended by a State Senator or Assemblyman. When the bill reached the desk of New York Governor, Roswell Flower, he vetoed it, writing that a state nautical school would be a "continuous drain on the State treasury for a doubtful public purpose" and that admission based on political recommendation would introduce a corrupting element to the school. The ship remained in the city's hands—much to everybody's annoyance.

CHAPTER 4

A New Era

"There is no school to-day in the City of Greater New York, public or private, where the discipline, morale, etc., are higher than in the Nautical School."

—W.H. Reeder, 1898

THE RECOVERY

After the disaster of 1893, many students did not return to the *St. Mary's*. In fact, in 1894, there were only seven graduates, and the Chamber of Commerce skipped its annual examination. But new students were recruited, and the school scraped together enough money to hold its annual cruise. By then, Superintendent John McGowan was replaced by Wells Field, who had been Crowninshield's executive officer. He immediately dove into the substantial project of restoring the fortunes of the New York Nautical School.

He wanted the boys of the *St. Mary's* to be the best possible, so he began to deliberately weed out "unworthy graduates." By the time he was done, there were fewer students than he wanted, but their quality was excellent. Field wrote, "I doubt if a better class of boys ever sailed in the *St. Mary's*."

In the meantime, to deal with the endless funding problem, Field eked through 1894 by making no repairs and rationing supplies, which was only possible because there were so few boys. He expected to need more money the next year, since he anticipated higher enrollment and the ship required more repairs. The *St. Mary's* needed to be dry-docked and recoppered for a minimum cost of $2,500.

Between Field's pleading, support from the Chamber of Commerce (which after Flower's veto had given up the plan to transfer the school to the State), and especially after Thomas Gilroy's exit as mayor, new funding was made available to the Nautical School. In 1895, the Board of Education transferred money from the Evening Schools' budget to renew the *St. Mary's*.

The next year brought further progress as more money was given to the schoolship to replace her water tanks and the ceiling of the lower hold. Field declared that even though the *St. Mary's* was 53 years old, it was "the commencement of a new era."

Field continued his bad-boy weeding policy noting that during the cruise of 1896, many upper classmen left. He was not put off by this writing that they were the "the least desirable members of the class." Even better, most of them deserted during the cruise while the *St. Mary's* was docked in Southampton and Havre.

More positive change occurred in 1897, when the city allowed the school to use the newly finished 28th Street recreation pier. This permitted for some land-based training and leisure. Then in 1898, Greater New York City was created. By incorporating five boroughs, the pool of potential candidates widened. After this time, enrollment stabilized at an average of 100 students.

In 1898, Field was replaced by William Reeder, who was immediately reassigned with all the other active Navy officers to fight in the Spanish-American War. The school was placed in the charge of retired Lieutenant Edwin Jacob who made Howard Patterson, an officer of the New York Naval Militia, the acting superintendent for the annual cruise. Patterson, being without an executive officer (the one he had fell ill), and only two junior officers, took direct command of the students, notably referring to them as *cadets* and not *boys* in the official reports.

Patterson thoroughly detailed the cruise of 1898. His report listed 130 examination questions and 19 test problems. His testing was not up to modern standards. Some questions were exceptionally broad and vague, "What do you understand by the mariner's compass?" Others were a bit self-serving, "How would you locate the ship's position on the chart by 'Patterson's Method' of two bearings of the same object?"*

Due to the war and lack of personnel, Patterson kept the cruise close to shore that year. He proved to be so efficient, that an inspector wrote, "A

---

*While Patterson himself did not invent this method, he probably enjoyed teaching it.

complete revolution has been wrought in the organization and administration of the school by the efforts of Captain Patterson." During that cruise, Stephen B. Luce, then a rear-admiral at the twilight of his career, visited the ship several times to witness instruction.

At the end of the Spanish-American War, Reeder returned to the schoolship. He and his successor, Albion Wadhams, focused on increasing the school's prestige by having the boys mingle with bluebloods. Reeder delighted in reporting how, on the cruise of 1900, the King of Portugal visited the ship and that elite military schools were accepting *St. Mary's* graduates. On the cruise of 1901, Wadhams wrote how a British noble gave a lunch for the students in London. Of that same cruise he reported, ". . . the Southampton Ladies' Guild, British and Foreign Sailors' Society, of which the Princess of Wales and Duchess of Fife are patronesses, gave an entertainment for the boys, at which there were many distinguished people."

G.C. HANUS

The superintendent with the greatest impact during this period was the Americanized German, Gustavus Charles Hanus who became superintendent in 1902. He was an 1871 graduate of the Naval Academy who, after a respectable career, retired in 1899. He was the first retired officer to head the school. This allowed him to stay on for six years, far longer than any of his predecessors.* He was an older man. To young officers like Frederick McMurray, who returned to the school as an instructor, Hanus seemed timid. After a storm in 1903, McMurray wrote, "We dragged our anchor so we had to let go the other one. Had a lively time here. The captain was scared to death as usual. He is awfully nervous. Too old. I feel very sorry for him. Hope I won't be like him when I get older or I will have to live life ashore."

Others painted a picture of Hanus as a grandfatherly figure who was ". . . courteous, genial and kind to everyone. His candid smile and frank blue eye as it looked into yours with its characteristic calmness won every one to him at first sight. He took a deep interest in the personal welfare of each boy that entered the school."

Hanus called for the school to be rated as a high school instead of a grammar school. Since the time of the Nautical School's opening, public

---

*Even though Hanus was retired, upon assignment to the *St. Mary's* he was reactivated and given full pay.

education had become more widespread, and to provide a general course of study on the St. Mary's became obsolete. Hanus declared, ". . . all boys in New York City, not mentally defective, have finished their grammar school course. . . . It seems a waste of time to instruct boys who are studying navigation and nautical astronomy, in spelling, reading, history. . . . The limited time can be much more usefully employed in teaching professional branches."

Hanus often hired graduates like McMurray, along with other merchant mariners, to return as officers. In this way, the relationship between the school and its alumni was strengthened. This bond was bolstered in 1903 when Hanus, with McMurray, ran advertisements in newspapers calling for graduates to meet aboard the St. Mary's. Fifty-nine alumni gathered and formed a lasting alumni association* that maintained close ties with the school throughout its history. Hanus was named an honorary alumnus.

Finally, Hanus fought for cadet uniforms instead of sailor uniforms for the students. This issue had been rankling for years and made worse by the fact that the other nautical schools used cadet uniforms. When the city refused to give him money for new outfits, in 1906 he received a $3,000 donation from alumnus John C. Hatzel. The new uniforms were implemented in that February and for the first time, the boys of the St. Mary's could look and feel respectable.

A LONELY BLACK CAT

Yet the St. Mary's herself held the school back. By 1906, the ship had been out-of-date for many years and was no longer able to train modern merchant mariners. Hanus wrote that the ship was "so old that she may become unseaworthy at any time. . . ." He said that Richard Aldcroftt, Jr., the chairman of the Nautical School Executive Committee, wanted to add steam and electrical engineering to its curriculum, which was impossible on a ship like the St. Mary's. Then, in what Hanus called "a miserable ruling," the Board of Inspecting Supervisors ruled that candidates for a second mates license had to be at least 21 years old. Hanus insisted that graduates of the school, who were usually younger, would ". . . desert the sea and stay on land. . . ."

In response one inspector declared, "The graduates of the St. Mary's are well trained. . . . They have, nevertheless, been trained in a sailing vessel which

---

*Other alumni associations had been attempted, but these efforts failed. The 1903 association is, as of this writing, still active as the Fort Schuyler Alumni Association.

has no steam. . . . These graduates should have one or two years experience on a steamer before the responsible position of second mate is given them."

He noted that when the *St. Mary's* was replaced, the ruling could change.

Hanus suggested that they needed to get a new "sailing ship with auxiliary steam. . . ." Hanus wanted Admiral David Farragut's famous sail-steam hybrid, the *Hartford*, a large sloop-of-war that would allow the school to double in size. Hanus, in fact, served on the ship in the 1870s. This particular ship was Farragut's flagship during the Civil War and though old, was almost completely rebuilt in the late 1890s. The Board of Education and the Alumni Association made personal appeals for the ship to President Theodore Roosevelt. Hanus approached Loyall Farragut, David Farragut's son, to garner support.

But Admiral George Dewey and others in the Naval establishment wanted the *Hartford* to go to the U.S. Naval Academy rather than a school that trained the merchant marine. Instead, the Navy offered either the *Yorktown* or the *Vicksburg*, both smaller gunboats. Hanus was not interested since their size "would simply mean maximum expenditures with minimum results." Hanus continued to heatedly insist on the *Hartford* to the point of being threatened with insubordination charges by the Navy Department.

In the end, the school accepted the gunboat *Newport*, which was in the same class as the *Yorktown* and *Vicksburg*. Although small, the *Newport* was a modern vessel being built in 1896 and used during the Spanish-American War. Hanus even sailed on the ship in command of hydrographic parties. She was a sail-steam hybrid which included a full engine room where the students could practice shoveling coal.

Disappointed, Hanus swallowed his pride and advised Aldroftt that the *Newport* was ". . . the best of all the small vessels sought after by others and while she is unsuitable as a home for the Nautical School, you must either take her or in the event of this vessel [the *St. Mary's*] becoming unseaworthy, you would have no ship at all."

It was true that the *St. Mary's* had, once again, fallen into bad condition. The Navy inspected the *St. Mary's* and estimated $40,891 in repairs. Hanus found some repairs that could be delayed making the total $38,691, but it was unclear if the Navy would even pay for that. The *Newport*, however, was up-to-date and free. Also, the press had learned of the *St. Mary's* condition and magnified it the newspapers. There was no choice. The Nautical School had to take the *Newport* and seek a larger ship as soon as possible. Hanus even suggested building a custom-built ship for the school—which, at best, was a fantasy since the city would never pay for it.

Hanus recommended retaining the St. Mary's as a station or classroom ship since he "learned that the Government does not want her." He wrote, "With the crew living on the Newport in the winter, the berth deck of the St. Mary's would become available for a machine shop and lathe instructions, and the cadets could sleep, recite, and live on her. She could also be used as an auditorium and for lecture purposes and the Newport could then be used for cruising purposes and practical instruction in steam engineering."

But the disposition of the St. Mary's rested with the unsentimental Navy. The old ship had an admirable career and still holds the record for the longest serving schoolship in the United States. Hanus wrote, ". . . it is interesting to note that for thirty-three years this fine old sailing vessel has crossed the ocean nearly every year, sailing altogether between nine and ten thousand miles annually, and that all the work has been done by boys." The Alumni Association explored ways to purchase the ship and convert her into a nautical museum. The Secretary of the Navy agreed to this plan with the stipulation that the New York City fund the museum's upkeep. However, the city said no. Then the Alumni Association scrambled to obtain funds to buy the ship and convert her into a clubhouse. But with graduates scattered across the globe, it was impossible to get enough money. When the St. Mary's was struck off the Navy list on June 18, 1908, alumni attempted to set up a stock company to purchase her. This last ditch effort failed.

In August of 1908, the Navy sold the St. Mary's to the Thomas Butler Company, a Boston ship breaking firm, for $5,052. With one last salute by George T. Douglas, the St. Mary's old sail maker, the vessel was emptied of all souls except Thomas, the ship's cat. Thomas took the demise of the St. Mary's personally and hid himself deep within the vessel. He unwittingly became part of the sale. A representative from the Thomas Butler Company said he didn't mind the cat but hoped "he'll have sense enough to leave when we start the fires. . . ."

The old ship was brought to Boston and set down by the Charlestown Bridge where she was dismantled. Thomas held out and hissed at the workmen who sought to remove him.

There is no mention if the cat was removed or not, but afterward the shipbreaker towed the St. Mary's hulk to Point of Pines, and burned her for her metal and fittings. The New York Evening Post eulogized, "So she will go, like the dead old Vikings. At least the *St. Mary's* will escape the axe of the wrecker." As flames licked her wooden frame and smoke rose over the Point of Pines, the ship entered the school's mythology. The following year, at an Alumni Association banquet, Chairman Aldcroftt read a poem in the ship's honor:

Our Boat was beached on a Boston shoal
Where the junkman slings his sledge.
Where her ribs were rent, and only her soul
Was left for her boys to pledge.

But yearly this phantom ship shall sail
On the mystic mere of mem'ries;
And whate'er betide, no man can fail
In his love for old St. Mary's.

The Mary's to-night is a love-feast craft–
Come aboard,
One and all!

Some climb for'ard and a bunch go aft;
Hear the call?
Have a ball!

We won't lower topsails till a good two bells–
Come aboard,
Shake that gig!

Let the air reverberate with lusty sailor yells!
Make 'em big!
Pipe the rig!

Everybody help now with the anchor chain;
We all know how the wild wind varies.
We'll soon be under way on imagination's main,
Raising "Ned" again on the old ST. MARY'S.*

---

*This poem, in effect, served as the unofficial *alma mater* of the school until the adoption of *The Bells of St. Mary's* in 1920.

CHAPTER 5

The Way of the Schoolship

"Harsh treatment thinned them out. . . . Those who remained on board for two years were a seasoned lot."

—Felix Riesenberg

Nobody knows the exact details of daily life aboard the schoolship, but from the stories handed down and from the published material, we can draw an accurate, composite picture of what the experience was like. The story you are about to read is fictional but drawn directly from the memoirs of real Maritime graduates, among them Felix Riesenberg, Frederick McMurray, Nick Carter and Louis Weickum.

TO BE A *ST. MARY'S* BOY

A split-second of warm compressed air rocked against Van Horn's face. He was about to be punched. The blow of a leather-gloved fist struck and weaved down his body like electricity. He staggered for a moment and backed into the ropes where just behind him a crowd of teenage boys *oohed*.

"Watch for that right hook, Van!"

"Don't let him hit you in a clinch!"

"Watch your chin!"

The advice swam in Van Horn's fifteen-year old brain and found its way to his feet, which staggered as the deck of the *St. Mary's* undulated softly at its berth on the East River.

Van Horn gathered his wits. He eyed his 16 year old opponent. Dahl was short and squat with hard arms and broad shoulders. He shifted easily on his feet, a smile egging Van Horn on.

The officer on watch, hearing the commotion, stood back and looked on. It was the benign neglect that the administration unofficially supported. It was the job of the upperclassmen, the "Old Mugs" to trim the underclassmen, the "New Mugs," into submission. Some Old Mugs, like Max Dahl, enjoyed every moment of it.

Halladay Van Horn was 13-years-old when, attracted to the tall ships docked along the Chicago River, he decided to go to sea. But his father forbade it saying, "A sailor? Why don't you just be a tavern owner, or better yet a drunkard?" But Van Horn was obstinate. After one bad argument only a couple of months after falling in love with the ships, he packed his things and ran away.

When he got to the Chicago wharves and tried to sign onto a ship, the captain stopped him and sent him home to his parents. His last words to Van Horn were, "It is a dog's life my lad."

When he got home, his parents brought him into the study. They told him he was unruly and that if he really wanted to go to sea, then he was going to go to a proper school, but he would have to wait two years until he was old enough.

This appeased the boy who waited and finished his grammar school course all the while voraciously reading nautical tales by Richard Henry Dana, Robert Louis Stephenson and Herman Melville. By the time he reached 15, Van Horn's passion for the sea had grown, much to his parents' dismay.

They sent him to New York City to live with his aunt and uncle on the Upper West Side. They became his guardians so that he could attend the Nautical School run by the city. They also took Van Horn out to parties and other social events—to show him the better side of New York.

Van Horn, at first, would look forward to these gatherings. Even though he did not yet have a splendid uniform, he was going to be Cadet Van Horn, 2nd Class, New York Nautical School. Who would not want to entertain such a soon-to-be gallant sea officer?

Men in silk hats and finely dressed ladies would smile kindly at Van Horn as his aunt introduced him.

"And why is he in New York?"

"He's enrolling in the schoolship *St. Mary's*," his aunt would say.

"Oh, a *St. Mary's* boy," they would reply, the inflection of their voices rising as their eyes narrowed.

"It's not what you think. There are good boys aboard that ship."

"Of course, of course. I keep hearing those ridiculous rumors that the schoolship is a reform school. Rubbish! Obviously, if *your* nephew is attending it must be an excellent school."

For the first time in his life, Van Horn had doubts. His stomach boiled as he questioned himself. But his uncle reassured him. "Listen Halladay, when you become the captain of your own ship all these people will be waving to you from the dock." This helped.

NEW MUGS AND OLD MUGS

Van Horn had arrived in New York a few weeks before he was to report aboard the *St. Mary's*. Aside from social events, he spent the time gathering all the required items on a list that was sent to him by the school: thread and needles, three pairs of heavy drawers, pocket handkerchiefs and two pairs of boots were just some of the items he needed. This made a heavy but manageable load that was easily transportable by hansom cab to the East 24th Street pier where the black-hulled and angular schoolship sat that October in the shadows of the late afternoon.

Van Horn paid the cab driver who helped the boy take out his sea bag. The man looked over at the *St. Mary's*, tipped his hat to the boy and sped off as fast as possible.

The boy marched down the pier and up the long gangplank. As he reached the top he stared at the high masts of the *St. Mary's*. He smiled at the thought of climbing the rigging. He then glanced behind him toward the city. The ship was just on the edge of a bad neighborhood that was denoted by the Bellevue morgue, which sat in the gloom staring back at the ship.

The sea is so close to death.

A loud rattling sound shook Van Horn out of his meditation. A boy on the main deck was swinging in his hands a great rattle, a wooden instrument with a large flat head attached to a handle. The clacking noise it made pierced the air and was followed by a rush of feet as boys in sailor uniforms hurried onto the main deck.

"It's an old-fashioned ship," said a voice behind him. "We use a rattle, not a bugle."

Van Horn turned and saw a dark-haired boy, maybe a year or two older than he. He smiled at Van Horn.

"Fred McMurray," said the older boy extending his hand. Van Horn took it and introduced himself.

"Don't be expecting a warmer welcome than what you just got from us Old Mugs," said McMurray. In his hand he had a list of names and put a check mark next to Van Horn's.

"Mugs?" asked Van Horn.

"Mariners Under Guidance—or Midshipman Under Guidance, depends on who you talk to," said McMurray. "You're a landlubber. Now get over there with the other new lads—they won't be hard to find, they ain't in uniform. And hurry up before Ivan the Terrible throws you in the brig on your first day."

Clutching his sea bag, Van Horn hustled onto the main deck. There were dozens of new boys wearing a motley assortment of gear, carrying sea bags and looking as nervous as sheep. Fencing them in was a circle of grinning older boys. They sat easily about the deck, some bare-footed, but all in white sailor uniforms.

"New Mugs! New meat!"

Van Horn felt claustrophobic. The crowding of the new boys and the demonic grins of the older boys made a panic well in his chest.

Then there was a call. "Silence fore and aft!" Two Navy officers parted the ring of white-clad teens. They were a Lieutenant Commander and a Lieutenant.

The Lieutenant Commander was a broad man of early-middle age with narrow-eyes and a dignified handlebar mustache. He had the air of a commanding officer, but what drew Van Horn's attention was a fox terrier that bounded behind him, staring up at the officer with adoration.

The Lieutenant Commander looked at the dog severely and said, "*Avast* Hennessey." The dog sat on its haunches.

Next to the commanding officer was the full-bearded Lieutenant. Each controlled step he took spoke of dignity. His uniform was impeccable with shining brass buttons. His white gloves did not show a speck of dirt.

By this time, the older students had put themselves at attention in somewhat orderly rows. The new recruits were either gawking at the officers (as Van Horn was), or trying to emulate the older students.

The Lieutenant Commander coughed and said, "Welcome cadets. For those of you who do not know me, I am Lieutenant-Commander Field, the captain and superintendent of the schoolship *St. Mary's*. For those of you who study hard and are diligent you will find the next two years profitable. This is an intensive course that requires your complete effort and attention. Anything less will not be countenanced. For those of you who make it through this course, you will receive a certificate from the Board of Education of the

City of New York stating that you are more than qualified to be hired as a third officer aboard one of our merchant ships. Remember, at all times that you are officers-to-be and that you are to represent the best face of our great country to all the corners of the world."

"My executive officer, Lieutenant Hodges," continued the captain motioning to the bearded Lieutenant, "will familiarize you with the discipline aboard and what is expected of you."

The Lieutenant stepped forward. His placid voice spoke, "Cadets, this ship is run as a true man-o-war with naval discipline. For many of you, this may be your first time aboard a ship. Do not worry. If you attend to your studies and your instructors you will do well. The first and most important rule is *obedience*. No argument against orders will be allowed. We expect prompt and cheerful *obedience*."

It went on like that for several minutes. Rules and regulations *ad nauseum*. Some made sense, such as no gambling, even though that would make life dull. Others, such as not being allowed to exchange, sell, or give away property did not make much sense to Van Horn.

Hodges, clearly the "Ivan" that Fred McMurray had referred to, was also much concerned with cleanliness, posture and presentation. He spent about five minutes droning on about it.

Then he turned to the schedule. It was a full day of activity starting at 6:00 a.m. and lasted until 9:15 p.m. when "Pipe Down. Silence fore and aft" ended a typical day.

"As any one of the older First Class students can tell you," said Hodges, "this *light* schedule will become more demanding when it comes time for the cruise. Its purpose is to give you boys a clear idea of what life at sea is like."

Once Hodges finished speaking he looked at the captain. Field nodded, "Very good Lieutenant Hodges. Cadets, you will now be assigned to one of two watches, Port or Starboard. Each watch will have four crews. The maintop, mizzentop, forecastletop and foretop."

The boys were separated into two large groups and then one by one hustled into crews of about 11 boys.

"Halladay Van Horn," called Hodges.

Van Horn went up and stood at attention. Hodges assigned him to Starboard Watch, Mizzentop crew. An Old Mug came forward and said, "I got him, sir."

Van Horn looked at the older boy. It was Fred McMurray.

McMurray hurried the boys of the Mizzentop crew down to the gun deck. The wide deck was once where the *St. Mary's*, in her Navy days, carried the great guns. Now it was a wide chamber filled with folding tables, hammocks and boys.

"They used to have half the battery of guns," said McMurray, disappointment etched on his face. "The old cadets used to practice firing them. But they told me they were removed a while ago."

Also there was a goat, the ship's mascot, as well as a tabby cat. The cat ran over to McMurray who petted her. "Easy Trilly." He then said to Van Horn, "She gave birth to a litter last year. We named two of the kittens Foresail and Mainsail, but we weren't allowed to keep 'em. Ivan said, 'Mr. McMurray, this is a training ship, not a menagerie.' Though I don't see much use for the goat." He glared at it. It glared back at McMurray.

"Watch out for him," McMurray said to Van Horn. "He did his business under my hammock every night last year. I finally got him to stop with a baseball bat."

McMurray guided Van Horn to a corner and said, "This is where you'll berth. Sling your hammock and then muster on deck at five."

After Van Horn set up his hammock and stowed his gear in a locker, the time was getting on. It was already 4:55. The ship's rattle started to clack. He turned to head up to the main deck, and as he did so bumped shoulders with a large boy.

"Watch it Mug," said the boy, his eyes glinting, his fingers curling into fists. "Who are you?"

"Cadet Van Horn, Second Class," he looked the older boy squarely in the eyes.

The older boy drew close and said, "Cadet Dahl, First Class—and I don't like the way you're looking at me.

"Easy Dahl," said another boy coming up. "Muster . . ."

"I know, Sheridan, I know," said Dahl. He then pointed his finger at Van Horn and landed it hard on his chest, "We'll talk later."

Sheridan smiled. Van Horn headed up to the main deck.

When he arrived, all the Tops were already mustered. He made his way through the group when a clear voice said, "You there! Take his name."

Van Horn looked. It was Hodges, who was shouting through a speaking trumpet. An older Mug came up with a little pad. He sniggered as he scribbled down Van Horn's name.

Hodges ambled up, his eyes bright with outrage. He looked at the name on the paper that the Old Mug held and said, "Cadet Van Horn. Being late to muster is unacceptable. When at sea if you are late to your station it might mean death to the ship. Two seams. Late for muster."

Van Horn looked at Hodges and without a sound retreated back to where the mizzentop crew waited. A blond-haired boy said, "You are off to a good start, Van. Two on your first day!"

"And a sore Old Mug," said Van Horn.

"Oh? Who is that?"

"I think his name is Dahl."

"Ooooh," said the blond, his blue eyes twinkling. "He's tough I heard. A real Mug-beater."

"Who are you?" asked Van Horn, his face heated.

"Felix Riesenberg," said the blond boy with a smile.

WHY THE BOYS OF THE *ST. MARY'S* DO NOT FEAR DEATH

Van Horn worked off his two seams of demerits the next day through extra duty. He was sent to paint the side of the ship. The work wasn't as daunting as the boatswain, named Dreilick, to whom he reported. Old and lanky, the man had wide muscular hands and clear eyes that spoke of thousands of leagues on the sea.

"The problem vid you boys," said the boatswain in a clear Finnish accent, "Is that you don't dink. You dink you come aboard a ship, put on a cap and a uniform and den you are a sailor." He leaned down and looked at Van Horn in the eye, his silver mustache vibrating. His face was cracked and tan like leather. "You know vat makes a sailor?"

Van Horn was too afraid of the old man to reply. He didn't have to.

"Vat you vant to do when you get off of dis schoolship is to go 'round the Horn. Then you can shit to the vindvard."

He passed a bucket of black paint to Van Horn and a bundle of tarred fiber oakum. He led the boy to a wooden seat that was set to lower over the side of the ship.

Van Horn looked at the mass of messy cordage and asked, "I'm supposed to paint with that? What about a brush?"

"Dis is how it's done—it is tradition," said Dreilick, his blue eyes glaring at Van Horn from under his cap. "Da best sailors are da ones who do it da old vay. And one of dose traditions is dat you idiot boys need to learn to shut up and follow orders. Over da side vid you."

After painting, Van Horn was next set to practice reefing sails. He and his crew, assigned to the mizzenmast, raced up and down the ratlines at the command of Lieutenant Hodges, whose voice trilled through his speaking trumpet.

"Faster!"

"Don't drop that line or you'll be over the deck!"

"As one! All together now!"

The orders were carried out sloppily. McMurray, who was in charge of the crew, was red-faced from giving commands to no effect. There was much to learn.

Van Horn expected the boys to sing sea shanties while they did this work, but silence pervaded as orders were given and followed. At one point, he and his crew were pulling a rope to haul up the sails. But they yanked so hard that two sails carried away. Boatswain Dreilick, who was nearby, remarked, "Vat is the matter vid you boys? You are too damn lazy to pull and ven you do pull you are too damn lazy to stop."

By eight bells noon, Van Horn was exhausted. He smelled of paint and tar. He made his way down to the gun deck. The hammocks were stowed, and folding tables had been taken out. Dinner was being served.

Van Horn collapsed in his chair. Felix, who was assigned as the table waiter, was bringing over the main meal of the day to the mizzentop crew.

A plate was deposited in front of Van Horn. There was something stiff and meat-like on it as well as something that might have passed for pickles. There was also a side of watery rice. Van Horn poked the meat with his fork.

"Salt beef," said Fred McMurray not looking overly pleased. "They usually reserve this stuff for when we're at sea."

"Don't matter too much then," said another Old Mug. "Food is just as bad here in port. Officers got good food though."

"That's the way it is Paul," said McMurray. "Remember when they made us that special dessert for the Fourth of July last year?"

Paul laughed, "You mean the maggot pudding?"

Van Horn grunted and took a nibble at the salt beef. He almost choked and managed to swallow only because of his severe hunger.

"There really weren't maggots in it?" asked a wide-eyed New Mug, Charlie Williamson.

"Probably would have tasted better with them," said McMurray.

"Well, since Maggot Pudding is off the menu, what's for dessert?" asked Paul. He munched at a pickle.

"Plum duff," said Felix, who had just taken a seat.

"Oh no," several Old Mugs groaned collectively.

"You can drop them right into the drink," said Paul. "Go down like stones."

"Is there any milk?" asked Van Horn.

There was a chortle, "You mean pigeon's milk? I saw Old Pete breaking out a canister today."

A glass was pushed before Van Horn. In it was a white, glue-like substance that might have passed for milk in a cow's nightmare.

"It's better than the dandy funk," said McMurray. "You know, I think they do this on purpose . . . make the food bad you know. Just the other day I saw Pete hung over—he likes to visit the Tenderloin district."

McMurray's mouth turned to distaste, "Well there he was stirring the morning mush. The tobacco juice was just streaming along that handlebar mustache of his right into the cereal."

"And you think he's doing that on purpose?" asked Van Horn.

Paul smiled. "Of course he is. Must be orders from the Old Man. The officers have good food—they just give all this sea butter or whatever you call it to the cadets. It's like what they did in old Sparta to their boys. They'd starve them half to death and make them eat this terrible black broth made of pig parts, salt, vinegar and blood. The idea was to make them strong and brave."

"I'm going to get a care package from home," said Felix. "My mother is sending a special delivery."

"Best be careful with that," said McMurray. "You're not supposed to be getting those. Hodges will confiscate it."

"Black broth sounds good right about now," said Charlie poking at the rice. "I think something is alive in there . . ."

Paul said, "Gentlemen, now I know why the boys of the *St. Mary's* do not fear death."

PRACTICAL SEAMANSHIP

Afternoons for New Mugs like Van Horn were filled with common school study. Arithmetic, grammar and history were things he already knew. The upperclassmen were filed off for lessons in seamanship and navigation. Van Horn was jealous.

But Van Horn did go to lessons which started his maritime training. One of these lessons was the "Rules of the Road," which was to teach how ships safely interacted with one another while at sea. The teenager took delight in flipping the pages of his textbook, *Seamanship*, to page 367 where he found rhymes entitled "Aids to Memory" by Thomas Gray:

> *If close hauled on the starboard tack,*
> *No other ship can cross your track;*
> *If on the port tack you appear,*
> *Ships going free must all keep clear;*
> *While you must yield, when going free,*
> *To ships close hauled upon your lee.*
> *And if you have the wind right aft,*
> *Keep clear of every sailing craft.*
> *When both side lights you see ahead,*
> *Port your helm and show your RED.*
> *GREEN to GREEN or RED to RED,*
> *Perfect safety–go ahead.*
> *If to your starboard RED appear,*
> *It is your duty to keep clear.*
> *But when upon your port is seen*
> *A vessel's starboard light of GREEN,*
> *There's nothing much for you to do,*
> *For GREEN to port keeps clear of you!*

What Van Horn really enjoyed was his lessons in practical seamanship. Aside from running up and down the rigging, he learned marlinspike seamanship under the watchful eye of the old boatswain, Dreilick. The more he came to know the old man, the more he and the rest of the boys came to fear and respect him. He was a cunning seaman and powerful despite his age. Van Horn had already seen him bend a silver dollar with his fingers. Even Field and Hodges were deferential to him.

About two weeks after Van Horn arrived on the *St. Mary's*, he along with the other boys of the starboard watch mizzentop crew, were being given a lesson in knot-making. With deliberate precision the old boatswain went through the complicated process of tying a four-stranded Turk's Head.

Van Horn loved knot-making and watched the old man's wide fingers delicately push the rope in and out. The boatswain then asked Charlie Williamson to tie a knot. The boy fumbled for about a minute, his tongue stuck out in concentration, before showing the result to the boatswain.

"Dis is da first time I've seen a Turk's Head become a bowline," growled the boatswain. "Vat about you, Van Horn?"

Van Horn held up his attempt. It was passable though it was uneven and had one strand instead of four. The boatswain grunted and looked to Felix.

Felix held up a perfect knot. He smiled at the boatswain, his blue eyes twinkling.

The cracks in the old man's face ruptured red. "Gawd damn you! Vat do you mean, standing here and letting me show you dat ven you knew it already?"

Felix blushed and said, "I didn't! I just followed what you did."

"Get out of here the lot of you! Gawd damn know-it-all boys . . ."

NOSEY BLUFF

The best times on the schoolship were after supper when the boys had an extended recreation period before they turned in. The ship was alive with activity as boys crowded in the gun deck or on the main deck playing games or reading.

Since it was late October and cool, Van Horn stayed on the gun deck and listened as Lou Weickum, an Old Mug from the port maintop crew, played a song on the piano that inhabited a corner of the gun deck. Some of the boys would sing along to the tune and often ad lib their own inappropriate verses.

"What next?"

"How about a sea song?" offered Van Horn.

There was a collective groan by the Old Mugs. Paul said, "I don't think so. The Captain last year got us singing lessons from Miss Stone in the city."

"Yeah," smiled Lou Weickum. "She'd try to make us sing all these old sea songs. We decided to change around the lyrics a bit. She nearly fainted after we sang *our* version of "What Shall We Do with a Drunken Sailor?""

Then suddenly, all the older boys started to sing as one. Lou started pounding at the piano. As Van Horn heard the lyrics, he laughed, but grew red. He could only imagine how Miss Stone would have reacted.

The laughing subsided.

"What next?"

"How about Van Horn sing us a song?" It was Dahl's friend, Sheridan.

"I don't sing."

"Don't matter," said Dahl, coming up by Sheridan. "You can either sing or have your head bumped against a wall." He patted a bench by the piano, "Now up you get."

Van Horn, crimson-cheeked, walked up to the bench and stood on it. He didn't know what to sing. Lou whispered, "You know 'The Bowery?'"

Van Horn nodded. Lou started to play the tune.

As Van Horn opened his mouth, Fred McMurray came running onto the gundeck, his face full of surprise.

"He granted it!"

The music stopped. Van Horn hopped down from the bench.

"Granted what? Who's he?"

"Iv . . . errr Lieutenant Hodges," said McMurray breathlessly.

"What is it?" The boys were growing more anxious.

"Permission to play cards!"

There was a cheer and applause. All through the gun deck, as if by magic, decks of cards materialized in the hands of the cadets.

Charlie Williamson then motioned to Van Horn to join him at a table with some of the other boys.

"What shall we play? How about poker?" asked Charlie, shuffling the cards.

"Nah," said Paul. "We ain't got money to bet with. What about Nosey Bluff?"

"What is that?" asked Van Horn.

"Oh it's simple," said Paul. "It is like poker—you know poker, right, Van? Well, since we ain't got much money we bet in whacks. You lose, you get a certain number of whacks with the deck of cards right on the nose."

"Sounds fun," said Charlie. He looked at Van Horn, "You in?"

"I don't think I'm . . ."

"He's in," said Felix sitting down next to Van Horn. "And me. How many whacks a hand?"

OVER THE RIGGING

By the time the game was over, Van Horn's nose was purple, and the yelps of pain emanating from the gun deck could be heard as far as the Bellevue morgue. Van Horn went out to the maindeck with Felix, both boys rubbing their noses. The temperature had dropped and the wind picked up. Van Horn's breath misted over the East River. The cold air felt good and took the pain away from his nose.

"I don't think cards are going to be legal for long with that noise," said Felix. "Paul should have called it Noisy Bluff."

Van Horn laughed, but was cut short as a thick hand shoved him into the rail. Van Horn turned about and saw the leering faces of Dahl, Sheridan and two other Old Mugs.

"Don't suppose you think I forgot about you?"

"No," muttered Van Horn, the thought of his sore nose all forgotten.

"That's 'No, *Mister* Dahl,'" said Dahl. "Soon to be *Chief Boatswain's Mate* Dahl. All right. I need some pipe tobacco. Hand it over."

"Ain't got any," said Van Horn.

The blow to his stomach was a complete surprise. It was like a lead ball being dropped on him from a two-story building. He doubled over.

"That's 'No, *Mister* Dahl.' Now bend over."

Felix tried to intervene but Sheridan grabbed him. Van Horn remained silent.

Blows came one by one, landing on his back, sides and buttocks. They were slow and deliberate. Van Horn chewed his lip, commanding himself to silence, since the last thing he wanted was to show a reaction.

Dahl said to Felix, "What about you? You got any?"

Felix shook his head.

"Bend over."

Felix got the same treatment. Dahl smirked and said, "Well boys, time to go over the rigging."

They led Van Horn and Felix forward in the ship and pointed up to the mast.

"To the topmost shrouds with you."

Van Horn set his foot on the line. Sheridan grabbed his shoulder and said, "Off with the shoes and jacket. Barefooted and barehanded."

Felix made a sign of protest and one of Dahl's friends clubbed him in the back with a blunt wooden belaying pin that was lying loosely about the railing.

Jackets, hats, shoes and gloves came off. They both climbed up. The rope bit into Van Horn's hands and feet. The cold air swept about them. The minutes ticked by as Dahl and his friends watched Felix and Van Horn shiver in the cold.

"Just what is going on here?" said a calm and clear adult voice. "Who is that up there? *Avast!* Get down now."

Van Horn and Felix scrambled down. On deck were Lieutenant Hodges, Captain Field and a woman. Hennessey, the captain's dog, sniffed behind them. Dahl and the other boys were gone. The captain looked at Felix and Van Horn with stern eyes and a curled lip. Hodges was impassive, and he first spoke, "What are you two doing here? Skylarking? Out of hours? Where is your gear?"

"We . . ." said Van Horn.

"What dear little boys," said the woman. "Do they always climb through the ship at night?"

"No madam," said Hodges. "As your husband may attest, these 'dear little boys' are actually tough-handed brats, active and full of mischief, and as responsible as a forest full of monkeys."

"Susan," said Captain Field. "The boys of the *St. Mary's* have strange ways of welcoming its new students. In this case, I believe we have an incident of hazing." He looked at Felix and Van Horn, "Who made you go over the rigging?"

Van Horn was silent. It would be worse for them if they told. Felix, red-faced and shivering said, "We just decided to go up on our own."

"At night?" asked Hodges. "Without gloves, jacket, or hat?"

"We . . ." said Van Horn, "We didn't realize it would be so cold."

The captain frowned, "Very well, both you boys are quarantined to the ship for this weekend—and be warned. If I find that you are not entirely truthful, then you will be expelled. Down below with you."

The captain then took his wife, and disappeared in the dark, heading to his cabin.

Hodges spent a moment studying the two boys. Felix and Van Horn backed away, and sped off to the gun deck, leaving their hats on the railing.

Only the heat cast by the steam boilers on the gun deck reminded Van Horn of how cold he was. Felix cursed under his breath and said, "Damned if we do, damned if we don't. We should have told the captain."

"And have Dahl and Sheridan beating us up every night?" asked Van Horn. "There is no way out. And even if they don't beat us up they'll start reporting us and give us seams. Ivan never believes New Mugs. There is no way out."

"Well, I guess we can just desert the ship," said Felix.

"And then where would we get sea biscuit?"

There was a long moment of silence as the two looked at each other then smiled. A private understanding of alliance and friendship had been forged. Without a word, Felix slumped into his hammock and fell asleep before Van Horn could even lie down in his hammock.

Van Horn pulled his blanket over him. Sleep was finding him quickly when suddenly his blanket was yanked right off him. He looked up with red eyes and saw it disappearing quickly around a corner as if by itself.

He got up and chased after the blanket. There were giggles coming from down the corridor. He caught up to the blanket and found a long string attached to it. There was nobody to be seen.

He tucked it under his arm and marched back to his hammock. He once more slung himself onto it. He slowly drifted toward sleep.

With a THUMP he landed on the deck. More laughter. He looked up at his hammock. Somebody had cut the hammock rope off its post.

"Who did that?" he hissed into the dark.

He heard only the *baaaaa* of the mascot goat, who was doing his business under Felix's hammock. Van Horn threw a shoe at the goat. It just glared at him. Van Horn grabbed his blanket and pillow. He found a place in the corner by a locker where he spent the rest of the cold night.

THE LUCKY BAG

In the week that followed, Van Horn quickly discovered that Dahl was not the only Old Mug who treated the New Mugs roughly. It seemed like the entire First Class was conspiring to drive the younger boys off the ship.

Sometimes, Van Horn would seek privacy in the head. The head was located in a cubbyhole over the bow and beneath the bowsprit of the ship. There were two cubbyholes, over a brass trough. The trough sloped sharply downward from one cubby to the other as water poured through to clean it. The upper cubby was reserved for Old Mugs and the lower cubby for New Mugs.

After a long period of holystoning, that is scrubbing the deck with bits of sandstone, Van Horn went to use the head. He squatted and relaxed. Here, he was out of sight from the watching eyes of officers and the First Class. Dealing with the smell of the head was worth even a minute of privacy.

Then, from the corner of his eye, he spied a flash of flame rushing down the trough from the upper cubby. It was a fireball of tissue paper aimed at a spot where Van Horn would least want to get burnt. He leapt up to his feet, the fireball missing him by half a second. He heard sniggering from the upper cubby.

Even those Old Mugs who were nice, such as Fred McMurray, were still strict and took their duties seriously. McMurray was a true believer in naval discipline and tried to instill it into his crew by working them as hard as possible.

The officers and crew were even tougher. The standards of the school were high. One by one friends who Van Horn had made either dropped out, simply left the ship without saying a word, or were expelled for what seemed to him petty offenses.

Hodges took delight in a once a week muster before the mast where offenses were read and punishments pronounced. Called the Mast, it was meant to emulate the tradition of trial before the mast where a member of the ship's crew could receive a hearing in front of the officers and his mates.

It was at one of these musters, a week after his run-in with Dahl, that Van Horn was caught by surprise when he heard, "Cadet Van Horn!"

Van Horn stepped forward toward Hodges. The Lieutenant looked severely at him.

In front of Hodges, on a table was set a thick tome whose cover read, "Conduct Book of the New York Nautical School."

One of the Old Mug's passed to Van Horn a navy-blue woolen cap. On it was stenciled Van Horn's name and number. It was the hat he had lost the night he went over the rigging.

"Two seams," said Hodges. "Item in the Lucky Bag."

"Good luck for you that we found it," said the Old Mug.

"Enough," said Hodges. He eyed Van Horn and said, "Do you have anything to say?"

"No, sir," said Van Horn looking straight ahead, eyes blank. To say anything was pointless. The entire Mast was a kangaroo court. It was expected that he just took his punishment. It didn't matter that it wasn't his fault that his hat was lost. Besides, he would have to accuse Dahl of hazing which would have just brought on more hazing. He would just have to take two hours of extra duty.

The muster was not a complete loss. Rates were given out to the students, and to Van Horn's complete surprise he found that he was assigned to the detail of Assistant Store-Room Keeper.

"Lucky bastard. Whose strings did *you* pull?" asked Charlie Williamson after the formation was over.

"Why is that?" asked Van Horn. "Sounds pretty boring to me—watching tubs of soap and racks of holystone."

"AND cases of ginger ale," said Charlie. "You are going to be the most popular cadet on this ship. Maybe you need some help cleaning the storeroom some time?"

"What did you get?" asked Van Horn.

"Assistant Ship's Writer," said Charlie brightly. "My old man pulled some strings. He went here you know . . . He wants me to learn some of the business of how a ship is run."

"Sounds dull," said Van Horn.

"Probably," said Charlie with a frown. "But it does take me off of the holystoning."

"It would be nice to get one of the cadet officer jobs," said Van Horn. "Like a captain of a crew, or the Chief Boatswain's Mate. I don't believe Dahl actually *got* that rate."

"Yeah," said Charlie. "He's going to torture us and we ain't eligible for a cadet-officer rate till the end of our first cruise. I'd like a fine rate. You know, get out of the stupid gun deck with all those idiots and get a berth on the half deck. Like going to heaven."

"I just got Ship's Librarian," said Felix walking up to the pair. "I guess it's fine . . . though I really wanted to get Mail Orderly so I can take a walk out in civilization some time."

"They give the Mail Orderly position to an Old Mug," said Charlie. "I think Lou Weickum got it."

"At least you'll get some extra sleep," said Van Horn. "There is some space in the library for you to stretch out—and the officers don't go down there that much."

"What did you get?" asked Felix.

"You are looking at the new Assistant Store-Room Keeper," said Charlie making a flourishing motion with his arm at Van Horn.

Felix's eyes glinted like a pirate's. "Tell you what Van," he said. "I'll let you come down and get some extra sleep if you let me help you do some cleaning in the store room. Maybe I can trade you some cookies for ginger ale."

"Cookies?" whispered Charlie, "You got the package?"

"That's right," said Felix. "Mother sent it this morning. I intercepted it from the Mail Orderly. I'll show you while everybody is still up on deck."

Felix led the pair down into the ship to the level where the student lockers were. The blond-haired boy opened the door to his locker with a flourish.

Van Horn's eyes widened, "Look at all those jellies!"

"And the juices!" said Charlie licking his lips.

"And mouth-watering condiments," smiled Felix.

The locker was stuffed with glass jars of all sorts of food. None of it was the hard tack or plum duff that had been eating away at Van Horn's stomach lining.

"Felix," said Van Horn, "you can't keep that in there. Ivan will give you five seams per jar if he catches you."

"Don't worry," said Felix with a wink. "I have a plan."

BIBLE STUDY

It was as Charlie said. Boys that Van Horn had never met before were coming up to him requesting to help him in the store room.

But the final decision as to who could help clean the store room rested with Paul, the senior student who was the Store Room Keeper. Most of the time, the job entailed taking inventories of the stores on a long list. At the end of every shift, the two boys would take a couple of bottles of ginger ale and drink them in the storeroom. Paul and Van Horn sank the bottles into a wash bucket of soapy solution. Then they brought the bucket to the ship's side and dumped it over. The bottles sank as fast as the plum duff.

"I think frequent cleanings of the store-room will be necessary," said Paul.

"Yes," laughed Van Horn. He felt giddy from the ginger ale. "Good for hygiene."

The late fall air was clean, and the tide was flowing out. Both boys looked out over the river.

"What is the cruise like, Paul?" Van Horn asked idly.

"Hard work," replied the older boy. "Up at 5:30 for some black coffee and four hour watches. We do watches now—sure. But that is practice for when we're at sea. Everything is much more intense. I hated when I had a watch at night. Since hammocks are stowed at 7:30 there was no place to sleep except for an oak bench."

Van Horn whistled, "How many hours of work a day?"

"About 17," said Paul.

"Why did I want to sign up for this?"

Paul laughed, "It ain't all bad. Best part are the ports and nights on the ship."

"Nights?"

"Oh yes," said Paul. "We hear stories and sing songs as the water rolls along. Sometimes, when everybody is really worked up we'll pick up our swabs and sticks and dance about in a parade."

"Sounds sentimental."

Paul didn't hear Van Horn, or chose not to, "If you're lucky you'll hear some of the Boatswain's stories. He's been in the China seas you know. Even Old Man Field will call him to identify a ship, or for his advice on how to set the sails in a storm."

"The cruise also weeds the school," he continued. "Many Mugs sign up for the cruise thinking it's going to be a pleasant voyage. But it is rough, and once we get into our first port, many boys jump ship. You see, you New Mugs have never been to sea and don't know. Why there was a time last cruise that we were becalmed in the horse latitudes . . ."

"What are they?"

"Oh hell, Van," said Paul. "You are such a landlubber." He then cleared his throat and recited as if by rote, "Those calm latitudes between 30 and 35 degrees. It is called the 'Horse Latitudes' from the circumstance that the vessels formerly engaged in carrying horses from New England to the West Indies, found it so difficult to cross this zone. They would often be detained in the calms for many days, during which time the large cargo of horses would exhaust the stock of water, become frantic with thirst, and to save a part, the rest would be thrown overboard."

Van Horn raised his eyebrows. He didn't think of Paul as a scholar.

"We were becalmed and it was hot," said Paul "It was out of hours and all was quiet. None could sleep in their hammocks. One of my chums, Claude says, 'Why don't we go for a swim?'"

"Weren't you afraid that you'd lose the ship?" asked Van Horn.

"Nah," said Paul. "The ship wasn't moving. No wind. So Claude, Art and me head over to the side, strip down and jump in the water. Well, the noise was heard by the boatswain and the next thing you know there are calls of 'MAN OVERBOARD.'"

"We were hauled aboard and taken straight to the captain. He was so mad that we were shaking. Ivan, who was there, took out the conduct book and writes down the charge: 'Attempting to go swimming naked without permission at 11:30 p.m.' We all got 5 seams for that, put in the brig for the rest of the night *and* made to toe the line for two hours."

"Toe the line?"

"You haven't seen that one yet?" laughed Paul. "Ivan really likes that. You stand at one of the seams on the deck at attention for hours. You are not to speak or move. Of course being a New Mug some of the Old Mugs had some fun with me."

"Claude was dismissed for excessive demerits," continued Paul. "He didn't have a clean record. And Art, well he was going to graduate, but he was so mad over what happened to Claude that the night before graduation he made off with one of the ship's gigs. Don't know what happened to him, but he never did get his certifi . . . What the hell is that?"

Paul pointed to the flowing tide. Floating in the water was a flotilla of books, slowly drifting out to the East River. Van Horn looked at one whose title was visible, "HOLY BIBLE."

"Are those what I think they are?" asked Paul. Van Horn nodded following the trail of gospel to their source. There, just above the water line was a port. A bright hand emerged from the porthole holding a book. With a *plop* it was dropped in the water. *Where was that porthole?* In his mind, Van Horn traced the corridors and decks of the ship—then turned pale.

"Excuse me," said Van Horn, hurrying off.

He rushed down the steps and went two decks down. He turned a corner then came to a secluded area of the ship sealed off with a lattice door. Above the door, hung a sign that said, "LIBRARY." He tried opening the door but found it locked. He shook it for a moment then knocked.

There was a long silence before a soft voice answered, "Who is it?"

"What in the name of hell are you doing?" hissed Van Horn.

The door opened a crack and Felix's bright blue eyes, filled with suspicion, looked at Van Horn.

"Come on deck, quick!"

Van Horn grabbed Felix, who was still holding a Bible, and yanked him up to the main deck. He took him to the rail and pointed to the Bibles. Felix, his eyes wide, took off his cap and stroked back his blond hair. "My God, Van! I thought they would sink."

"I wouldn't bring up God right now, Felix," said Van Horn. "Keep an eye out for an officer. If they find out . . ."

"I needed to do it," said Felix red-faced. "I had to hide my mother's package. The only place I could find was in a locker in the library."

"Where the Bibles were . . . Don't you think they'd be missed?"

"Well no," said Felix. "They haven't been used in years, see?"

Felix handed Van Horn one of the holy books. Van Horn looked at it. It was musty and shabby.

He creaked it open and the pages cracked. It smelled of mold. He saw a dedication stamp and read aloud, "To work watch and watch to save the souls and uplift the morals of the boys of the St. Mary's–New York Society for the Prevention of Crime, 1877." He shut the bible. "I don't think it was ever opened."

"There were fifty of them," said Felix watching the Society's holy books float away on the East River. "For twenty years sitting in that locker . . . Do you think I'm going to go to hell?"

"We might be there already," said Van Horn.

The boys laughed.

WASH DOWN

That Saturday was wash-down day. Van Horn stayed busy holystoning the wooden deck while working on the corners with bits of broken stone called prayer books. He was then called to the gun deck by Fred McMurray who had his crew roll the old piano to one of the gun ports.

"Van, go run a hose up here," said McMurray. "And where is Felix?"

"Don't know," said Van Horn.

"Well, if you see him send him up here. Tell him if he doesn't hurry I'll give him two seams for shirking duty."

Van Horn went out to the old steam pump and uncoiled the hose. He fed this up to Charlie then headed back to the gun deck.

When he returned, Van Horn saw that McMurray had fed the large hose into the innards of the piano. Water gushed from it, and with it a torrent of cockroaches and contraband: dime novels, playing cards, cigarettes and an occasional whiskey flask.

"We'll just let her dry out for a day or two and she'll be as good as new," said McMurray tapping on one of the keys. It sounded like warped lead being struck by a mallet. "The quartermaster told me that Lillian Russell gave it to the school a few years ago. Now back to work!"

Van Horn left the gun deck and headed toward the store room, where he was to meet with Paul. He was looking forward to it—well at least the ginger ale. As he turned out of a starboard door that ran near the railing, he saw Dahl's crony, Sheridan, on the lookout. Yet in order to get to the storeroom he had to pass by him. Something was up. The lookout system meant that they were hazing somebody. Van Horn took a gulp and proceeded, hoping that they would ignore him and let him pass.

As he drew near he saw that Dahl and Sheridan were there with two other older boys. They had a smaller boy lying on his belly on a stool. As the boy pantomimed swimming motions his cap fell off revealing blond hair. It was Felix.

"Oh here's the other one," said Dahl. The insignia of the foul anchor and three chevrons indicating his rate of Chief Boatswain Mate glowed on his right shoulder.

"Stop doing that!" cried Van Horn.

"You got something to say, Mug?" growled Sheridan. "Maybe you could take a swim like your friend here?"

"I'm Chief Boatswain Mate," said Dahl his ape-like bulk drawing close to Van Horn.

"Get over yourself Max," said Sheridan.

Dahl and Sheridan glared at each other.

"Psst!" hissed one of the boys on lookout. "Ivan!"

All the boys stood up at once. Even Felix, who quickly tucked his hair under his cap, managed to get himself to attention. From around the bend came Hodges.

Hodges drew out his pocket watch and said, "Five minutes to muster. What are you boys doing here?"

Dahl was about to say something, but Sheridan interjected, "Inspecting the railing, sir."

"You are not on duty for that Sheridan," said Hodges after consulting a list he pulled out of his right pocket. "One seam for each of you. Skylarking no doubt. Van Horn, why is your face so red?"

"The cold sir," replied Van Horn. The day was mild.

Hodges looked carefully at Van Horn and then at the other boys, "Is that all?"

"Yes, sir," said Van Horn.

Hodges was silent for a moment before he said, "Very well. And two more seams for you. . . ." He nodded at Felix, "Dirty clothes and unkempt. Everybody to muster."

MUTINY

At muster the entire student body assembled for the change of watch. The boys stood on the seams, two long lines forming the starboard and port watches. This was a daily ritual that was in preparation for the long shifts of four hours on, four hours off when the ship was at sea. Van Horn was coming off his watch, more than ready for his hammock below. Rain made the early evening experience more miserable.

As the names were called, Van Horn yawned. Charlie Williamson elbowed him to keep him awake. The officers were almost done taking the roll.

Then there was a terrified squeak, "Yip! Yip!" Hennessey, the captain's fox terrier ran onto the deck, a slush pot tied to the dog's tail.

The silence deepened. Captain Field, who was on the quarterdeck, heard the cries and descended to the muster. He picked up the pot as his face turned an impossible shade of purple.

A gurgle of anger poured from the captain's lips after which came a flurry of curses—some of which Van Horn had never heard before.

"Mr. Hodges," growled Field. "Hold fast the muster."

The captain stalked the boys lined up at the seams.

"Who is responsible for this act of cruelty?"

Silence. A bell struck. The time to change the watch was due.

Captain Field left the boys standing. For a moment, he had forgotten about Hennessey, but the dog's whimpering renewed. He handed the pet to a cabin boy who brought him below, still tied to the pot.

As the captain's back was turned, the line of boys coming onto watch grinned. The other line, Van Horn's, glowered.

The minutes clicked by. Field occasionally made a soft remark to Hodges but otherwise kept an eye on the muster as he climbed back up to the quarterdeck.

More time dragged on. The captain's intent was clear. He was going to keep the boys toeing the seams until a party (guilty or not), came forward and confessed. After a half hour, even the grins on the faces of the Port watch faded. Darkness deepened so that only glints of rain shined off the boys' uniforms.

As two bells 9 o'clock drew near soft whispers spread down the line.

"He doesn't have the right to do this. This is a public school!"

"Will somebody just step forward?"

"You do it, Weickum."

"I didn't do it! I *like* Hennessey."

Van Horn had enough. He took a deep breath and whispered, "When two bells strikes, we go below." There was whispering and nudging. All the Starboard Watch was with him. Felix even smiled.

"All or none! When two bells strike go below."

Clang! Clang!

"Now!"

With a rush of feet the boys surged for the main and forward hatches, eager to get out of the rain no matter what the consequences.

The yell from the quarterdeck was unmistakable, "Great God! Mutiny!"

"General stations! Spring the rattle!"

The CLACK CLACK of the rattle pierced the air. Officers and crew rolled up from beneath decks and every other part of the *St. Mary's*. Pistols were strapped upon their sides.

The boys raced down the hatches.

A stern call from above, "Batten down hatches!"

The mutineers were to be trapped below. Already strong arms were securing the main hatch with gratings.

Van Horn realized that any boy trapped below was likely to be liberally punished, if not expelled. But the captain did not know who were the boys who ran below—it was too dark. Only after, when they were picked off, could they be brought before the mast. They had to get back on deck. The main hatch was blocked.

"The forward hatch!" cried Van Horn. "All hands up before they lay the gratings!"

Like mad, fifty boys rushed forward under the decks.

"Forward!" cried the voice of Ivan the Terrible. "Hold them down! Rap their knuckles!"

Adult men of the regular crew were already over the forward hatch attaching the coaming. Boys from below grabbed it and tried to push it out. The seamen took pins from the rail and cracked at their fingers. All was lost.

Just then, in the dark, some of the larger boys of the Port Watch appeared. They pulled the seamen off the hatch before retreating back to the main deck. Van Horn with the other boys of the Starboard Watch poured out. Only the last boy out of the hole was caught. It was Dahl, held by the scruff of the neck by a triumphant Hodges.

The boys were reassembled and stood for another hour before the captain finally sent them below. He had caught his scapegoat, suppressed the mutiny and could sleep in peace.

THE GLOVES

The next day after supper there was silence at the table of the mizzentop mast crew who were studying. Van Horn's resolve to stay aboard the ship was weakening. How could he possibly survive all the way to the start of cruise in May when it was only early November?

Van Horn was finishing the fourth chapter of *Luce's Young Seaman's Manual* in which he needed to memorize the names of ropes. He was having trouble understanding the difference between a Crotch Rope and a Guess Rope when a shadow loomed over him. It blocked the faint light of the oil lamps. It was Dahl.

Dahl sneered and said, "How about it? The gloves, you know?"

This was serious. Calling somebody to box was a sign of scores that needed to be settled. Van Horn's face flushed, "I didn't say anything to Ivan."

"Don't matter," replied Dahl. "I got quarantined to the ship for the next month because of your pigeon-brained idea to run below decks. The Old Man even threatened to take away my rate! You are an arrogant son-of-a-bitch that needs to be put in his place."

The fight was on.

The makeshift boxing ring of the *St. Mary's* was set on the maindeck, just forward of the temporary schoolroom that the school raised for the winter term. At the direction of several of the more athletic officers, it had been made into the correct legal dimensions. At times, the officers even refereed bouts.

Boxing was wildly popular on the ship and the Tops would at times set their champions against each other. It was the only sport that the boys could consistently play on the confines of the vessel, though they often formed teams to play baseball and track and field events against other schools. On cruise, the boys delighted in racing their whaleboats against cadets from other schools in foreign ports. Yet boxing was the favorite sport by far, and it was well known that Max Dahl was champion since he had put down an older boy the previous year.

Most of the time the fights were friendly. They were used mostly to teach the New Mugs their proper station in life, but also it was used to settle serious disputes.

Van Horn's bout was set for Tuesday during the afternoon recreation period. Word that Dahl was going to beat up Van Horn had passed quickly among the boys. Some of the more cheeky students took to measuring Van Horn for a coffin.

Most boys would give unwanted advice.

"Make sure you keep moving."

"Keep your fists tight. Punch and cover, punch and cover."

There was also a good deal of illegal gambling on the upcoming match. The word was that Lou Weickum was giving 20 to 1 odds on Dahl. When Van Horn heard about this at dinner he nearly choked on his salt horse.

"What's so bad about that?" said Charlie. "When you beat him you'll make me a rich man. I put a dollar on you. That money will come in handy when we go on cruise."

"Sure will," said Felix, gnawing at some stale bread.

"You bet on me too?" asked Van Horn.

Felix shrugged, "Just fifty cents. I mean come on—you have to support your chums."

"Ahoy Felix," cried a voice from the table of Forecastletop. "Do you have any Bibles for Van to pray with?"

Van Horn left the table and went out to the taffrail looking back into the gloom towards shore where the city morgue sat. Just then a rough hand was placed on his shoulder. "Hey Mug."

He turned about and saw Dahl's friend, Sheridan.

"What do you want?" asked Van Horn, spinning around. "I've had enough of this. Your friend is going to be turning me to mincemeat on Tuesday—I don't need more shit from *you*."

"Easy Van Horn," said Sheridan, his clear eyes cat-like in the gloom. "I'm here to offer you some advice."

"What? To get off the ship? I don't think so."

"Nothing like that," said Sheridan. There was a long pause before he went on, "Listen, I think you got guts. Especially for what you did the other night when the Old Man was going crazy. I don't think you're responsible for Dahl, that's just bad luck."

"Wish he'd see it that way."

"Look," whispered Sheridan. "The rough treatment is all part of tradition. I went through all the same shit you did. It makes you stronger. But it ain't right for Max to be picking on you so particular. He needs to come down off his high horse—Chief Boatswain Mate . . . phaw!"

Sheridan spat and said, "He also thinks himself a good boxer. Well he's just a bruiser—a brawler. And I've fought him too."

"Did you win?"

"Yes," said Sheridan. "It was all unofficial. Max won't fight me anymore. But what you got to do is hit him in the gut. He can't take it."

"How can I trust you?"

"What choice have you got, Mug?"

Tuesday's recreation period came faster than Van Horn wanted. By the time he got to the boxing ring a large crowd had gathered. There was a great deal of cheering for Van Horn.

"Take him down Van! I don't care if I bet on Dahl."

Dahl was already in the ring, his shirt stripped off and his thick arms flexed.

Van Horn stripped off his own shirt showing his lean muscles. The air was cool, but he did not feel it. He climbed into the ring, trying to avoid Dahl's glare.

Felix helped Van Horn get the gloves on. Van Horn's hands were clammy. He drew himself up eyeing Dahl who, though shorter than him, was much thicker.

A senior student stepped into the ring and motioned to the two fighters. He inspected their gloves and said, "A clean fight in three rounds of three minutes. Shake hands."

Van Horn tentatively reached out his gloved right hand. Dahl struck it with casual arrogance. They parted to their respective corners. Then the referee said, "Fight!"

Van Horn came up quick. He was faster than Dahl. He kept his hands up to his face, but this did not protect his gut. Dahl faked a right jab to the face but unloaded on Van Horn in the stomach.

Van Horn's guts felt like they had exploded. He staggered a step back, then Dahl charged after, slamming a punch into Van Horn's mouth.

The watching teenage boys *oohed* as Van Horn staggered back. Then there was a silence. Van Horn felt his lips swell. He swished his tongue about his teeth. They were all still there.

Van Horn's heart thumped, and he found it difficult to breathe. Panic accelerated all his senses.

Dahl charged again. There was no subtlety or strategy to his movements. Van Horn was too easy prey to waste thought on. This time he threw a wild left hook. Van Horn dropped, the punch flew over his head and he delivered a right then a left short punch into the stomach.

OOF!

Dahl doubled over. Sheridan was right. Van Horn sent a right short punch to the ribs.

CRACK!

Dahl felt that. He took a step back.

Success drove Van Horn on. He sprung forward and dealt two more blows to the stomach before a right hook to the head. Dahl looked surprised. He hadn't even put his guard up, believing that the New Mug couldn't hit him at all. Blood streamed from Dahl's left eyebrow.

Another blow from Van Horn. Then another. The boys watching the fight were stunned into silence. Glassy-eyed, Dahl stumbled and fell. Van Horn stood over him.

Dahl was a knocked-out mess. His face was a pool of blood. Sheridan took a bucket of water and threw it on him.

Van Horn never needed to box again.

CHAPTER 6

"The Only Pebble on the Beach"

"The captain of the Newport would frequently begin the day by coming on deck in his pajamas. . . ."
—The Marine Journal, March 18, 1909

EVERHART TAKES COMMAND

Lieutenant-Commander Lay Everhart, in his photographs, looks lean and aristocratic—holding an air of arrogance that only those who have absolute command of their surroundings possess. This attitude served him well when the Navy assigned him to be the St. Mary's executive officer from 1900 to 1902. Everhart was dedicated to the Navy, but forced to retire due to budget cuts. He yearned to be at sea again.

His chance came in 1908. Admiral Henry Erben, the schoolship's second superintendent, was approached by Richard Aldcroftt, the Chair of the Nautical School Executive Committee, and asked to recommend a new captain for the schoolship. Erben went to Everhart and asked him if he was interested. Everhart jumped at the chance and promised the Admiral that he would serve for at least three years. He took command on April 1, 1908 and began the process of instilling his brand of discipline upon the cadets of the Newport.

"AIMLESS AND USELESS"

Everhart's experiences, and the headaches that any superintendent faced aboard the old schoolships, can be summarized in the story of Franklin Tighe and the cruise of 1908.

This was Tighe's second voyage as a cadet. In his first year aboard, he had been punished 74 times for breaking the rules. Among the more interesting entries were:

- "Sleeping on berth deck and denying it"
- "Under the influence of wine"
- "Shirking work continually"
- "Stowing away in steam launch"
- "Aimless and useless"

If Tighe was an early 21st century high school student, his peers would call him cool.

Why Tighe returned or was even welcomed back for a second year was due to his father, a retired New York City police captain who was friends with the *Newport*'s executive officer, Christopher Marsden.

As Franklin Tighe saw it, being a senior at the New York Nautical School had one saving grace; he was an upperclassman who, with appropriate prudence, could take his aggressive energy out on underclassmen. Yet the boy was not circumspect. He got into trouble immediately by returning late from winter break. By the time the *Newport* arrived at Glen Cove in May, 1908 to stage for her annual cruise, he had stacked up 24 more violations. This time his offences included "throwing food on the gun deck," forcing an underclassman to stow his hammock, "leaving class without permission," "skylarking in class," "smoking out of hours" and "taking apples from box on spar deck." Tighe was given extra duty, quarantined to the ship and put in solitary confinement. None of this reformed the boy. He only got angry at Everhart.

The superintendent wanted a taut ship and clamped down on the boys whenever he could. For his part, Tighe suspected that Everhart was specifically picking on him because of his father's relationship to Marsden; Everhart did not get along with his executive officer. Tighe convinced four other boys to desert the *Newport* with him when they reached Plymouth, England.

On June 30th, the five boys jumped ship and headed to Southampton. There, they found an inn named the "Sailor's Rest," rented a room and pooled their money. It wasn't much, even by 1908 standards–$25. It is unclear what they had planned to do with their newly won freedom. The most likely design was that they intended to board a New York bound ship; but the $25 was hardly enough to buy one ticket in steerage.

While the boys pondered the situation, Everhart sent out search parties and interrogated Tighe's classmates. He confirmed that they deserted and decided not to waste any more time on them. He ordered the *Newport* to sail on for Cherbourg, relieved at getting rid of five rotten apples.

Meanwhile, at the "Sailor's Rest," one of the deserters, a boy named W.A. Hollenbeck, celebrated Independence Day by stealing all his comrades' money in the middle of the night. He boarded the liner, *St. Louis*, bound for New York. When the remaining boys awoke, they were enraged at Hollenbeck, but they were also angry at Everhart. If the ship had been decently and fairly run, they would not have deserted. Still, Tighe and the others decided that the only way home was to return to the *Newport* at Cherbourg.

The boys went to the nearest American consulate where they begged for help. The consulate cut them short and told them that he had received a telegram from Captain Everhart who advised him not to help the boys in any way—and especially if they came for money—since they were dishonorable deserters. They were dismissed.

Penniless and homeless, the boys decided that the best thing to do was to seek help in London—over 60 miles away. They arrived in the city on July 6th, just two days after Hollenbeck abandoned them.

In London, the truants went to the British and Foreign Sailors' Society, a Christian organization that provided care to seafarers. There the boys met with the secretary, Edward W. Matthews, and told him that they lost their ship due to a missed train. Matthews believed them and gave them money for transportation. What is more, he paid for their lodgings at the *Hotel l'Angleterre* in Cherbourg. After the boys left, he sent a letter to Everhart: "Feeling sure there was no intentional wrong doing, and for the sake of their families, themselves and the ship, we extend to them this courtesy and kindness." He also requested reimbursement totaling 6 pounds, 13 shillings and 10 pence. When Everhart received the letter, he wrote back telling Matthews that he had been duped and that there were no funds to reimburse the Society. In addition, Everhart sent him the names and addresses of the boys' parents and told Matthews to contact them directly for the money. Everhart then dispatched the ship's doctor, Keran O'Brien to fetch the truants.

When O'Brien arrived, he found Tighe and the other boys upset. They were particularly concerned that Everhart would restrict them to the ship until they returned to New York. They declared that the captain did not have the right to do this, and that Everhart was not "the only pebble on the beach."

If the captain wanted to play rough and try to confine them, they would desert again. Tighe added that he would "not hesitate to steal the money [taken by Hollenbeck] or its equivalent for his own ends at the first opportunity."

Tighe and the boys were brought before Everhart. The superintendent was in a quandary. If he refused to accept them aboard it would create a political mess in New York with outraged parents complaining that Everhart was abandoning their sons overseas. He could imagine what the newspapers would print. Everhart decided that the best thing to do was to offer them a "clean slate." In return, the boys promised to "turn over a new leaf."

But a few weeks later, while on liberty in Gibraltar, Tighe found himself in a drunken brawl with a local. When the police intervened, he fought them too. Tighe was arrested and brought to the local jail house. O'Brien and one of the ship's officers, Albert Dorey, were sent to retrieve Tighe. When they arrived, O'Brien found that the boy was so drunk and insubordinate that the doctor appealed to the "police force present to quiet him."

In the meantime, Dorey feared that Tighe would be brought up on charges and negotiated with the police. They agreed to hand the boy over so long as he was not allowed to leave the *Newport*. Tighe was still drunk when Dorey and O'Brien returned him to the ship. He was ordered to the sickbay.

Everhart expelled Tighe and wrote a letter to the boy's father listing all 112 of his son's violations culminating with being "drunk and disorderly in the streets of Gibraltar, resisting a police officer, using profane language and fighting to the disgrace of the uniform of the school." The father sent a quick reply stating that that he could not thank Everhart "for such a brutal statement. But will thank you to send 'Franklin' home here to his mother as soon as you receive this." He enclosed a dollar for the train fare.

When the boy arrived home sometime in mid-September, his father heard a different account of events. In October, Tighe's father formally accused Everhart of favoritism probably because the boy reported how Everhart was not getting along with Christopher Marsden and expelled his son because of it.

The Board of Education opened an investigation and stated that although Everhart should have found a way to reimburse the British and Foreign Sailors' Society, he was right to expel Tighe. In the end, Tighe went home and slipped into obscurity. There is no record of what became of the worst-behaved boy of the schoolship. As for Everhart, it was clear that he was the only pebble on the beach—the *Newport* was his command.

THE PURGE

Everhart had a forward-thinking, national vision of the role of the merchant marine that echoed Luce. He believed that merchant marine training was a federal function and thought that the various nautical schools should be controlled by the national government. A federal system would increase the supply of merchant officers, make training more consistent and create a reserve force for the U.S. Navy that had a "national spirit." Everhart submitted a letter sharing his views to the Secretary of Commerce and Labor. Though his suggestions were not adopted, they foreshadowed the growth of federal involvement in merchant marine training that would come later in the century.

For Everhart, the cruise of 1908 reinforced the idea that a training ship needed to be run by the Navy. Right after the *Newport* returned to New York, he purged the schoolship of the merchant marine officers of the Hanus administration. In particular, Christopher Marsden and Senior Instructor Charles E. Littlefield were targeted.

Everhart branded Marsden and Littlefield as "unsafe to sail with" and "incompetent," despite both men being highly recommended by Hanus. Everhart gossiped in a letter that Marsden had threatened to "make trouble for the school." Suggestively, Everhart had dismissed a cadet by the name of Roland Marsden, a possible distant relation of Christopher, for "inaptitude."* He asked the two men for their resignations. Marsden complied, but Littlefield made a fight of it. But Everhart got the Board of Education to directly intervene and force him to resign. Everhart replaced these two with Annapolis graduates. By 1909 he had an entirely new staff of officers, with the exception of the ship's doctor Keran O'Brien.

"ON DECK IN HIS PAJAMAS"

Complaints about the purge caused the New York Marine Society to investigate the affair. Aldcroftt defended Everhart stating that the superintendent had the freedom to select his own officers. No legal action was made by the Society, but a report was published that gave support to Marsden and Littlefield followed by a resolution that endorsed their abilities. One

---

*The exact relation of Roland to Christopher is unknown. According to, Captain George Marshall, a descendent of Christopher Marsden, Roland Marsden is not in the genealogy but may be a distant relative.

prominent member of the Marine Society, Captain George Norton, took the matter personally. Norton was the owner and editor of the trade magazine, the *Marine Journal*, which he used as a platform to denounce Everhart's policies. Norton emphasized that the school needed to be controlled by men in the merchant marine instead of the Navy. He published a series of articles that condemned Everhart, culminating in a libelous piece that used an anonymous graduate as a source:

> The captain of the *Newport* would frequently begin the day by coming on deck in his pajamas, roaring and blustering and use undignified language to the boys who were about their work, usurping the place of the officer of the deck in his detail duties, such as was never before known on the schoolship.

In addition, the article stated:

> ... the commander of the *Newport* is evidently one whose prejudices against a merchant mariner are so great ... that he made the [1908] cruise of this vessel a very disagreeable one for these officers and a much less profitable one to the schoolship boys than their trips on the *St. Mary's* had been ... the discipline of the ship in comparison with that under her former commander was practically ruined.

Also, the *Marine Journal* referred to Everhart as a "condemned naval officer" insinuating that he was retired early because he was unfit.

Everhart's problems did not end there. In May, 1909, while the *Newport* was at New Haven preparing to sail into the Atlantic, Keran O'Brien got into a fight with Everhart. The two had had run-ins before; one over the physical fitness of a boy entering the school. O'Brien declared the boy unfit, but Everhart vetoed him. Later, Everhart recalled that when the doctor asked him why he did this, he responded that it was none of his business. Everhart never stated why he vetoed the doctor.

The 1909 brouhaha was over aspirin. The evening before the ship was to sail, O'Brien noticed that he did not have any aspirin in his medical supplies. He asked Everhart if he could purchase five dollars' worth. The captain said no since they were to sail from New Haven in the morning. Everhart said he would buy some in England adding, "If we have been without for three weeks we can surely do without it for two weeks more." O'Brien argued the point and Everhart cut him short, stating the conversation was over since he was the doctor's superior officer.

The doctor lost his temper, wrote a hasty resignation and fled the ship. The captain's headaches (for which he had no aspirin to cure) were compounded since he could not go to sea without a surgeon. He immediately delayed departure, travelled to Washington and brought his case to the Secretary of the Navy who assigned a Navy doctor to the ship.

In the meantime, O'Brien went to New York City and gave a rambling account to the newspapers. The doctor described Everhart as "savage" and that his duty as a doctor would not allow him to "start on a cruise of many thousand miles involving the lives of one hundred and sixty persons when I am convinced that the commanding officer is suffering from delusions."

O'Brien declared that Everhart was "very peculiar mentally" with "peculiar disabilities. . . ." O'Brien stated that when Everhart suspected that O'Brien knew something was psychologically wrong with Everhart, the captain used the aspirin incident as a pretext to get rid of him. As a parting shot the doctor stated, "I think that Captain Everhart is about to embark on his last cruise as commander of the *Newport*."

Chairman Richard Aldcroftt investigated the fiasco. As before, he supported Everhart saying that O'Brien's reasons for leaving "were trivial and the inference is that the doctor resigned for reasons of his own which are not expressed." He condemned the doctor's statements which "embarrassed the ship" and asserted that the school was "in a much higher state of efficiency than it has been for many years." This was all because of "the efforts of the captain and his staff."

Aldcroftt's stance is not surprising since he was the chair of Nautical School Committee and Everhart was his own pick. Still, it is accurate to state that O'Brien did not resign over the aspirin. He was the last of the civilian officers from the Hanus administration and felt alienated. In addition, O'Brien's brother had died leaving the care of their mother to him. The stress of these factors drove the doctor to a breakdown. As for Everhart, he wrote that in 1909 "there was much less sickness on this cruise than on that of the previous year."

By the fall of 1909, Everhart had the personnel he wanted but at the cost of creating powerful enemies. Some, like George Norton, actively continued to work against the school with the intent of carrying off a *coup*.

Norton reported that after the Everhart scandals "several captains of our coastwise steamers" decided "to employ no more boys from the schoolship" since they were receiving Naval instead of merchant marine training. But Norton is highly suspect as a source. He had been actively working against the school and its Navy element—it is likely that he and those working with him influenced companies not to hire *Newport* graduates.

"GIVING A CHILD TO A FOSTER PARENT"

As Everhart promised to Admiral Erben, he stayed on for three years then retired in 1911 stating that the job was too "arduous." One article reported that his resignation may have been linked to parents' complaints over the captain's promotion of excessive boxing matches aboard the *Newport*. Even though he had made plenty of foes, Everhart was popular among the cadets. The students wrote a testimonial to him (with no mention of boxing) that was published in the *New York Times*:

> We feel that we are losing the one who has kept up, with such success, our spirit and interest in our studies; the one who, with unselfish interest, has sought to assuage our grievances; and it is the earnest wish of every cadet on the training ship *Newport* that you leave us knowing that you take with you our thanks, esteem and respect as a right and honorable Commander and Superintendent.

Now that he was a private citizen, Everhart's first action was to seek justice against his chief opponent, George Norton. Everhart sued the *Marine Journal* for libel to the sum of $35,000. He won $1,186.67.

The departure of Everhart coincided with fresh attacks on the school. In 1910, the New York City Department of Finance cut funding and forced a reduction in personnel. Yet there was hope for a reprieve by the federal government when an updated version of the 1874 act was passed by Congress in March, 1911. In this law, Congress expanded the number of ports that could host nautical schools and pledged up to $25,000 support for each institution. But the cash became "pigeon-holed" in Congress. With no additional monies and attacks mounting against the *Newport*, Chairman Aldcroftt resigned in October, 1912.

After Everhart and Aldcroftt left, Captain Harry Dombaugh took command. In response to the budget cuts, he advocated limiting cruises to the

Atlantic coast. He also clamped down on students to suppress an epidemic of hazing. In his one year as superintendent, he dismissed 17 students. Once, when Dombaugh expelled a boy for hazing, the student's entire class came to his defense, insisting he was innocent. In a brazen show of unity, they purposefully disobeyed a call to muster by Dombaugh. The captain expelled 8 to 10 of the disobedient boys on the spot before the rest submitted. Dombaugh's resigned in 1912 due to illness. His replacement, Edwin Tillman, was a capable officer but was inexperienced in the vicissitudes of New York City politics.

Meanwhile, Mayor William Jay Gaynor appointed anti-Nautical School men to replace Aldcroftt and other vacancies at the Board of Education. Of these, Michael J. Sullivan and Dr. Ira Wile were the two most outspoken. Sullivan was appointed Chairman of the Nautical School Committee.

On May 6, 1912, Sullivan contacted Jacob W. Miller, the chairman of the Chamber of Commerce's Nautical School Committee, and told him to come to a closed meeting for an important announcement. At the meeting, Sullivan reported it was doubtful, if the city could continue the nautical schoolship on account of its cost.

Miller, aside from being a prominent member of the Chamber of Commerce, was influential among the New York elite. He was a retired Navy Officer, helped organize the New York Naval Militia and was the son of a former U.S. Senator. On the business side, he was general manager of several steamship companies, as well as involved in canal survey work, including the construction of the Cape Cod Canal. He was a member of several important trade societies, and he had connections throughout the shipping industry.

Miller realized that the only hope for the schoolship would be to obtain the pigeon-holed federal money. He sought the help of the Maritime Exchange and the Alumni Association. They sent a group to Washington to meet with the New York congressional delegation. Miller reported that they "seemed friendly, but no appropriation was made...."

In January, 1913, Sullivan went public and moved to disband the school. He called the *Newport* a "luxury" that never achieved its original purpose of preparing boys for life as mariners. He cited a study which stated that of 769 graduates, only 134 went to sea. To Sullivan, the city was being taken advantage of since it was paying tuition, free board and lodging and providing a summer sea voyage.

Ira Wile agreed, stating there was little indication that the school had helped the merchant marine grow and the public still viewed it as a reformatory, or at least a public boarding school. Also, a number of the students were not even city residents. Wile noted that if the merchant marine wanted a special school, then the maritime industry should support it. When Wile was asked why the school was not closed earlier if it was such a failure, he stated, "There used to be too much politics in it."

As discussed, the Nautical School was costly for the small number of students it graduated and never stimulated growth in the merchant marine. How could it? The training of merchant sea officers does not increase the demand of tea from China nor stimulate the building of ships. Sullivan and Wile's arguments were persuasive. But their figures were inaccurate as to how many graduates went to sea. Wile and Sullivan's source for their data was Superintendent Tillman who wrote:

> I have been at times asked to furnish a list of graduates of the school who follow the sea, and because such a list only contained a few hundred names the conclusion is jumped at that the others do not follow the sea. The Superintendent has no practical means of keeping track of pupils after they leave the school.

Tillman argued that going or not going to sea was not a measure of student success. He wrote, "that the pupils from this school do not all follow the sea for a livelihood is not an argument against the school; all graduates of law or medical colleges do not follow the profession for which they were educated." He ended by asserting that the school should continue as a state-controlled institution.

Tillman's call coincided with the efforts of Norton and other shipping men to undermine the school. This leads one to think that Tillman was directly influenced by Norton and Miller. Their plan was to create a Nautical School that no longer excluded the "maritime fraternity" but was independent, financed by the state and run by the merchant marine.

Jacob Miller became the main organizer of the transfer plan. With him, the two most active organizers were John Hatzel* and 1886 graduate Reginald Fay. Miller's committee met with New York's Maritime Association, the National Board of Steam Navigation, the Marine Society, the Navy League and New

---

*This is the same Hatzel who donated the money for cadet uniforms.

York's Board of Transportation and Trade. From the meetings, Fay led a delegation to Albany to appeal to the New York Legislature for the transfer.

They argued that a state-wide institution would be more in line with the spirit of the 1874 law and provide a greater pool of candidates. They pointed out that the purpose of the school was still valid—to have native-born Americans as officers on American ships—besides, it was good for the economy. The Panama Canal was about to open, which would surely provide a boost to American shipping—and the demand for merchant sea officers.

Generally, the major newspapers favored the transfer. The *New York Herald* wrote on March 22nd that the problem with the schoolship was "limitation of the training and subsequent employment in seagoing ships to lads presumably living within the municipality." While the *Herald* recognized that the Board of Education had "tried to do its duty," the enterprise would be better in the hands of "men of tried maritime experience and that its support should be borne by the whole state." The greatest advocate of a state transfer was naturally George Norton's *Marine Journal*, where in weekly articles, all through early 1913, he strongly advocated a state takeover. He even changed the masthead of his publication to "Official Organ of the New York Nautical School."

Norton, later admitted that the whole effort to transfer the school was a conspiracy in response to the Everhart "scandals." When Aldcroftt backed Everhart over the firing of Marsden and Littlefield, Norton asserted that he and his associates had lost faith in the city's ability to administer the school. Because of this, he and his cabal "began a campaign in favor of change." Norton wrote that Everhart's libel suit was a part of the ploy. The lawsuit "broke the ties that held the Board of Education together, caused them to desire to be rid of that which had become a troublesome burden and later voluntarily 'give up the ship' and aid the *Marine Journal* and its associates."

It seems ridiculous that Norton, alumni and shipping interests would concoct an intricate plan to instigate Everhart to sue the *Journal* with the idea that it would lead to a transfer of the Nautical School to New York State under merchant marine administration. This was just Norton taking credit after the fact and trying to explain away the attacks against Everhart as having a higher purpose. It is hard to believe Norton anyway since he was a convicted libeler. Still, Norton was accurate when he pointed out that the Board of Education backed the transfer plan. This proved to be an easier way for the city to get rid of the schoolship than trying to sink it altogether. So, by January, 1913, when Sullivan motioned to disband the school, everything was arranged.

After Sullivan's motion, the Board of Education and merchant marine interests worked in sync. The legislation proceeded like clockwork with little to no debate. Fay's committee found political allies in Albany, including Speaker Al Smith, Governor William Sulzer, State Senator George A. Blauvelt and Assemblyman Ralph McKee. Blauvelt and McKee were both chairmen of the public education committees in the New York State Senate and Assembly, respectively. They coordinated the necessary legislation which was signed by Sulzer on April 17, 1913. At the signing, Sulzer enthused, "The time is at hand to place the American flag again where it was before the Civil War, on every sea and in every port. We must have more ships; they must be manned by and owned by Americans."

Attached to the legislation was $100,000 to help re-found the institution. Yet the law made clear that the New York *State* Nautical School was a continuance of the old institution:

> It is not the purpose of this act to duplicate the New York Nautical School . . . but to perpetuate and insure the continuation of that institution and extend its privileges to young men throughout this state. . . .

The formal transfer of the school occurred on the *Newport* shortly after eight bells on November 1, 1913. Thomas Churchill, president of the Board of Education, directed the ceremony with Jacob Miller, who was named the Chairman of the school's newly established Board of Governors. Miller remarked:

> It will be our aim to broaden the scope of the school. There's the Panama Canal about to be opened, and we wish to make our mercantile marine what it was before the Civil War. We hope to have the State Nautical School do as great work as the Naval Academy has done for the Navy in making our country the second largest naval power in the world.

Churchill represented the city: "We are giving a child to a foster parent, but it must be remembered that we do this with the kindliest sentiment and realize that it may be for the best for this creature of the educational service. After the matter had been debated, it was realized that under the state the school would have a wider field, and hence the divorce was contemplated."

The city's control of the schoolship was over. Now the state was going to see what it could do.

CHAPTER 7

"We are All Dirty in Consequence"

> *"The State Nautical School must be to New York a miniature Annapolis, preparing young men for marine positions during peace, on the same lines as the country educates them for war."*
> —Jacob Miller, 1913

"A MINIATURE ANNAPOLIS"

On August 5, 1913, Jacob Miller bounded with enthusiasm as he made his way through the warrens of lower Manhattan. His mind was not on the crowds of people that milled about on Liberty Street, but on the victory that he, with other businessmen, had achieved for the merchant marine. Just before he turned to enter the Chamber of Commerce at number 65, the implications of what he had done rushed through his head. Just the previous month, in Albany, Miller had been elected Chairman of the New York State Nautical School's new Board of Governors. The schoolship was now his to sink or sail.

Miller entered the Chamber of Commerce, found a board room and met with some of his co-conspirators who helped transfer the school to State control. There were nine men on the Board, most named to the body by Governor William Sulzer. George Norton of the *Marine Journal*, and the libeler of Lay Everhart, was present as was John Hatzel, the alumnus who donated the first set of cadet-officer uniforms to the school. Also of note was Frederick Dalzell, the tugboat company owner who tried to help rescue the meningitis-stricken Albert Ruffin several years earlier. Miller called the meeting to order.

"The State Nautical School must be to New York a miniature Annapolis," said Miller to his fellow governors, "preparing young men for marine positions during peace, on the same lines as the country educates them for war...."

Despite Miller's grandiose statement, he gave credit to the city's handling of the school which was "perfected by the experience of 37 years through the wisdom of the Board of Education coupled with the marine knowledge of a long line of distinguished naval officers."

Yet Miller had no plans for future Navy officers to run the *Newport*. Miller and the rest of the Board did not want another Everhart. The New York State Nautical School was to be an institution run by and for the merchant marine. The governors advocated eliminating any common school course and focus exclusively on maritime training with military elements. Instead of learning history and English, the cadets were to be taught, "elementary military instruction such as formation, the handling and use of small arms and rapid fire guns."

The military instruction was inserted to appease the Navy, which still lent the ship to the school. In addition, despite Miller's desire to focus on merchant marine training, he advocated the appointment of Nautical School cadets to Annapolis in order augment the school's prestige.

But the most important decision that the governors made was who was going to be superintendent. Miller reasoned that considerable nautical *and* teaching experience were "rarely united" in one person. They decided that the best man for the job was an "*alumnus* proud of his *alma mater* and who will work for her future." What is more, the officers under the superintendent would be alumni too. Miller enthused, "With a graduate Captain and graduate officers, ambition will bring us recruits from all parts of the State." The Navy would no longer have a leadership role in the school.

JAMES DRIGGS AND THE CRUISE OF 1914

The first *alumnus* superintendent was James Driggs who relieved Edwin Tillman on February 1, 1914. He had graduated from the *St. Mary's* in 1882 and was a pure merchant mariner having extensive experience in the Far East trade. In fact, he had received the job offer from Miller by telegraph, while commanding the ship *Ajax* in Manila. When Driggs's appointment was announced, George Norton gloated: "This is a red-letter day for the *Marine Journal*, as those who know and read us are aware that ever since Capt.

Hanus resigned from the *Newport* four years ago and the merchant service officers under him were forced to resign, we have continuously worked for this change."

The reborn schoolship stimulated new enthusiasm. In one of the few moments in its history, applicants outstripped space available on the *Newport*. Miller used this as bait to negotiate with Washington for a larger ship. As it had been several years before, the *Hartford* was eyed as well as the cruiser, *Buffalo*. In addition, the Board of Governors, with the Alumni Association, intensified the campaign to wrest the pigeon-holed $25,000 from the federal government.

When neither a new ship nor federal money materialized, Miller tried to bring more positive attention to the school by ordering Driggs to sail the *Newport* up the Hudson River on a publicity cruise. The 200-foot gunboat unfurled its sails and wound its way up the Hudson. They were greeted by the people of the Hudson Valley with cheers, salutes and parades before arriving at Albany on May 14, 1914.

The cadets marched through the city to a dignified ceremony. The *Newport* shot its guns in salute, the cadets stood at attention. A local committee headed by Charles Bissikummer, a member of the Board of Governors, paid a formal visit. That evening, a dance was hosted by the Albany Yacht Club followed the next day by a procession to the Governor's mansion where Sulzer made a speech followed by an inspection of the *Newport*. The Governor announced that he was donating 125 volumes for the ship's library as well as money to form a band. More feting of the schoolship followed at several banquets before the *Newport* departed. The prospects of the school never seemed brighter.

After leaving Albany, the *Newport* touched briefly at Poughkeepsie and Newburgh for more pageantry. Parades were held honoring the cadets of the schoolship. Then Driggs steamed the *Newport* south out of Hudson River, and after a brief stop to prepare for the voyage, across the Atlantic. The outbound cruise was without incident, and they reached Tangiers safely. Then Driggs leisurely sailed to Naples before bringing the schoolship to Marseilles in late July.

The tranquility of the cruise was broken as the *Newport* lay in Marseilles. Austria-Hungary declared war on Serbia over the assassination of Archduke Franz Ferdinand, and alliances among the European nations were activated. On August 3rd, Germany declared war on France. World War I had begun, and the *Newport* found herself in a war zone.

The officers and cadets of the schoolship were not the only Americans in Marseilles. There was also a delegation led by Samuel M. Conant of the Rhode Island State Harbor Improvement Commission who had come to France to witness the launching of a new Fabre Line ship.

Conant met Driggs at the American Consulate just as the political situation in Europe crumbled. He invited Driggs and his officers to attend the launching. Then they met again on August 1st. At this meeting, they came to the realization that the *Newport* had the unique distinction of being the only American-flagged ship in the Mediterranean.

France mobilized for war. At night, mobs of citizens and soldiers marched the street singing "La Marseillaise." By August 4th, it was virtually impossible to buy provisions. Cash became scarce. Everything from men to automobiles was being confiscated by the government. Luckily, the *Newport* had finished taking on coal before the French government seized the entire supply in Marseilles. The American Consul, Alphonse Gaulin, begged Driggs to bring food for his family since there was none to be bought in the city.

Driggs sent the ship's commissary to scour Marseilles for provisions. The commissary obtained 2,000 pounds of potatoes which he loaded into an automobile. But just before he reached the *Newport*, the police stopped the vehicle and confiscated it, potatoes and all.

As a last resort, Driggs obtained from the French government an automobile for half an hour. The captain took the American flag, lashed it to the car's side and drove to Gaulin's home in order to deliver some supplies they scraped together. Again, the car was stopped by the police, but this time Driggs pointed to the flag and explained that the supplies were for the American Consulate. He warned that they better not interfere lest they create an international incident. He proceeded unmolested.

Later, Driggs met again with Gaulin and Conant. It was decided that Driggs would evacuate Conant's delegation with their families to the neutral port of Genoa where they could find a steamship home. Saying farewell to Gaulin, the *Newport* steamed to Italy on August 6th with 13 unexpected guests who stayed in the officers' quarters. They arrived in Genoa the next day.

Driggs reported that Genoa had the "appearance of a . . . dead port, some three or four hundred vessels filling the anchorages huddled together inert and silent." Transportation was completely paralyzed. There was no way for Conant and his party to return home. That afternoon, the American Consul in Genoa presented Driggs with a letter that formally requested he transport the Americans home.

On August 8th, Driggs left Genoa and laid a course for Funchal, Madeira. He proceeded ahead to the Straits of Gibraltar, but not before being intercepted on multiple occasions by British cruisers and torpedo boats. The *Newport*, being a gunboat, was easily confused for a military vessel. On August 9th, the French cruiser, *Ernest Renan* stopped them. After an inspection they were released, and the ship headed to the United States via Funchal. But as a last reminder of the war, a British cruiser gave chase to the ship just 150 miles from the American coast. After using her searchlights to identify the school-ship, she steamed away and left the *Newport* unmolested.

The training ship arrived in New England, and in the process she became the first man-of-war to pass through the Cape Cod Canal. Driggs debarked Conant and the other refugees in Providence, Rhode Island. He narrowly avoided trouble with the federal government since he landed them without officials coming aboard first. However, no report was filed because of the service the ship did for the United States. Conant, grateful for Driggs' assistance, attended the graduation ceremonies that year and presented gifts to the officers and crew on behalf of the refugees.

While the public record shows that the cruise of 1914 was a success, despite the near-miss moments, there were problems with Driggs. He was unhappy. His wife wanted him to "quit the sea altogether and go into business ashore." Also, Driggs had unspecified problems with Miller and the Board of Governors. After Driggs returned to New York, the Board did a great deal of firing and rehiring, with many of the personnel decisions superseding Driggs' wishes. His successor, Frederick McMurray, later wrote that the Board was "all excited over the mess of things made by Driggs." The mess was never specified, although suggestively, a great many cadets deserted the *Newport* when she arrived in Providence, only to be reinstated later by the Board of Governors. This may be because of the harrowing cruise or because of the way Driggs treated the cadets. The record does not say either way.

In the end, Driggs was probably burnt out by the micro-managerial style of the Board of Governors. While at sea, Driggs was the absolute master of the *Newport*, and it was hard to comply with the wishes of a group of men giving orders from a board room. In fact, Driggs could not sit in on meetings of the Board without their permission. Also, being the superintendent was a stressful job—the lives of over 100 boys were in his hands. Burn out was common among the heads of the New York State Nautical School. Whatever the reasons, Driggs resigned on October 31, 1914.

"TRASH ABOUT THE SEA"

Driggs was replaced by Frederick McMurray who graduated from the *St. Mary's* in 1896. McMurray had been raised without a father since the age of two and had been "inoculated with the desire to go to sea" since the age of six. As a youth, he spent his time reading illustrated books of the sea which included William H.G. Kingston's *Shipwrecks and Disasters at Sea* and Charles Nordhoff's, *Sailor Life on Man of War and Merchant Vessel*. He laboriously assembled a cardboard jigsaw puzzle of a clipper ship, memorizing discs that labeled the various parts of the vessel.

According to his own embellished accounts, McMurray repeatedly ran away from home, even as a toddler. He claimed that at the age of two he tried to escape through an upstairs window. Before McMurray could harm himself, the neighbors found the boy on the roof. A couple of years later, in another escape attempt, he tried to flag down a moving train and got so close that he was knocked to the ground by the rush of air as it whizzed by.

As a pre-teen he "had several talks with seamen ashore," and while living at New Bedford, Massachusetts, visited the whaling ship, *Sunbeam*. He climbed the rigging of the whaler and reached the main royal before he was "ignominiously" ordered down. He even attempted to recreate a hammock in his attic by sleeping on a ladder that he hung horizontally. He refused to wear an overcoat and overshoes in order to toughen himself for the sea.

His mother, Charlotte, did not know what to do with him. But one day, when her son was an early teenager, she came across an old *Harper's Weekly* article that profiled the New York Nautical School. She thought that perhaps she could get her son under control and out of her hair by sending him there.

In 1893 she visited the *St. Mary's* Superintendent, John McGowan. She was shown the ship. Then the captain asked her, "Why do you wish your boy to go to sea?"

"He seems to desire nothing else," she replied. "He reads trash."

"What sort of trash?" McGowan asked.

"Trash about the sea."

"That is not a bad sort of trash." The captain smiled. "What type of problems are you having with your son?"

"I cannot get him up in the mornings."

"Madam, do you have a garden hose at your place?"

She curiously looked at the captain and replied, "Yes."

"Turn it on him," said McGowan.

Won over by McGowan's approach, McMurray's mother enrolled him in the school the next year under the guardianship of an uncle in Brooklyn.

McMurray travelled to New York and found himself face-to-gangplank with the *St. Mary's* which was sitting on the south side of the pier at East 28th Street. He was examined by the school's doctor and "pronounced fit in wind and limb." Then he was given a test in general studies which he easily passed since he had already done the coursework at the Wilbraham Wesleyan Academy. He was fitted out with three working uniforms of white duck canvas, watch cap, hammock, mattress and blanket. All of these items were stenciled with his number, 690. He had begun his first year on the *St. Mary's*.

McMurray was a good student, but like many boys aboard the old schoolship he was no angel. When the *St. Mary's* visited Ponta Delgada in 1895, he and a friend wandered the town. They visited a wine shop where they proceeded to drink port liquor. When they got up to leave, McMurray's friend, instead of going through the door, crashed through the window. The shop's owner demanded to be compensated for the damage. McMurray's friend turned out his empty pockets, having spent all his money. McMurray only had a dime. The shopkeeper called the police.

But before they were arrested, a large party of his shipmates rounded the corner. When they saw the situation, they seized the two drunken boys and hauled them away. In a daze, McMurray and his friend returned to the ship where they slept off the alcohol before going on deck for drills.

After he graduated, McMurray had his first major adventure aboard the *St. David*, in which he journeyed under sail around Cape Horn. After several other voyages, he eventually returned to his *alma mater* as a junior officer under Superintendent Hanus. From 1903 to 1904, McMurray taught arithmetic and navigation courses specializing in Rules of the Road. But he grew bored and wanted to accelerate his career. In 1905, he left and became an officer and navigator for the Navy dry dock, *Dewey* as it was towed from the United States to the Philippines on a voyage of many months. Then in 1910, he became a master in his own right on the brigantine *Carnegie*. During all this time he remained in touch with his acquaintances at the Nautical School, and at one point he almost took a job as Driggs' executive officer. But McMurray preferred to command, and he only returned to the schoolship in 1915, this time as her commanding officer.

A BULLY TIME: THE PACIFIC CRUISE OF 1915

When McMurray became superintendent, the immediate question was what to do about the annual cruise since war raged in Europe. The decision was to send the *Newport* on a cruise to the Pacific. It would be good publicity, a great opportunity for the students to see the newly opened Panama Canal and attend the Panama-Pacific Exhibition on the West Coast.

The *Newport* departed New York on May 4, 1915. After stopping at Saint Thomas in the West Indies, the ship reached the Canal Zone on May 26th. There, the schoolship lingered as cadets looked at wonder upon the locks which dwarfed the *Newport*. Slowly, the vessel wound its way through the narrow passage, and on May 31st, for the first time, New York's training ship entered the Pacific Ocean. McMurray sailed directly to Hawaii, another first since no ship until that point had made the transit from Panama to Hawaii without stopping at California first.

Along the way, the *Newport* was suddenly hit by powerful gales. The rain came in violent sheets. Many of the 103 cadets aboard fell violently seasick. Despite their condition, McMurray called all hands to reduce sails. This did not prevent the outer jib stay from being carried off by the wind. Throughout the night, the cadets remained up and on watch as they battled the storm. The next morning, the weather moderated, and on June 30th the *Newport* reached Hilo, Hawaii.

After the exhausting voyage, all hands eagerly anticipated visiting the islands including Executive Officer Charles Littlefield,* who had been to Honolulu aboard the *San Mateo* but had never gotten off the ship. When interviewed, Littlefield explained, "The day the *San Mateo* dropped anchor here in 1888, the skipper put off in his gig, and they gave him such a good time on shore for a week that we never had sight of him again until an hour before we sailed.... I've been waiting to see Honolulu ever since."

The Hawaiians eagerly welcomed the schoolship. The cadets toured the islands, visited a sugar plantation and saw Mount Kilauea. McMurray allowed all the cadets to go to the famous volcano, even those who were being punished due to poor behavior or grades. "I thought no one should miss it," he wrote in a letter to his mother. "It is much better than *Dante's Inferno*."

---

*This is the same Littlefield that was removed by Superintendent Everhart. In 1915 he returned as McMurray's Executive Officer.

McMurray thought Hawaii was a delight. "We found the sights more splendid than anything we ever saw in our European trips." One newspaper reported that the cadets had a "bully time." The Outrigger Club at Honolulu taught the cadets how to surf at Waikiki Beach, and in exchange, islanders were given tours of the ship.

After Hawaii, McMurray turned the ship homeward and stopped at the ports of San Diego and San Francisco, where the cadets visited the Panama-Pacific Exposition. This world fair was meant to salute the completion of the Panama Canal as well celebrate the 400th anniversary of Balboa's expeditions to Central America. As in Hawaii, people came aboard the *Newport* for tours. In fact, the schoolship's stay excited efforts to create a California nautical school. After the *Newport*'s visit, the *San Francisco Call* wrote, "The wind calls, the sea sings, the tide of courage and the love of adventure rises high in the heart of youth—California needs the merchant marine and the merchant marine needs California." The *San Diego Union* wrote, "When one considers all the advantages from such an institution, it appears strange that California has not done as New York and Massachusetts have."

McMurray was optimistic about the success of his cruise despite three cadets deserting at Cristobal, Panama. He wrote that two of them were expected to desert and that the ship was "better off without them." He was also encouraged by an article Norton wrote in the *Marine Journal* which was "decidedly friendly" so he expected no "trouble with the Board in consequence." In a letter to his mother, McMurray confided, "I think the Board as a whole has more confidence in me than ever before. I hope so at any rate. I have made a very economical cruise of it so far, and we are still way ahead of our expenditure allowance."

To keep costs down, McMurray stopped the ship at the Navy shipyard on Mare Island off San Francisco for inspection and free repairs. This cost the *Newport* precious time. When McMurray brought the ship to the Panama Canal on September 20, 1915, they found that landslides had choked the waterway just a week before. The *Newport* was stuck on the wrong side of the Canal at Balboa. McMurray waited to see when it would reopen.

Boats dredged the canal, but it only caused more material to slide into the waterway. On October 13th, George Washington Goethals, the canal's Chief Engineer, reported that the canal could be closed for up to a year as the Army Corps of Engineers dealt with the landslide. Goethals recommended that ships find other routes. There was little McMurray could do. He might have taken the ship around Cape Horn, but this would have been too dangerous for the cadets. Instead, he proposed to the Board of Governors that they send a class of new students to Balboa so he could repeat the Pacific cruise. His idea was rejected, and he was told to wait. McMurray sent the senior class by train across the Canal Zone then by steamer to New York where they graduated at the New York Maritime Exchange, instead of on the ship as was the custom. The junior class remained on the ship with McMurray. Nobody blamed McMurray for the delay. He wrote, "The Board has evidently taken the matter of our delay philosophically, for I hear no word of complaint against me in the matter."

As the months passed, McMurray kept the remaining cadets busy:

> They are constantly at some work or other. Boat work and drills with the sails loosing and furling after drying, for it rains nearly every day. . . . Painting ship is going on all the time somewhere, the interior not yet being done, and there will be a couple of weeks' work at that alone.

When not toiling on the ship, the students formed a basketball team and played in a Canal Zone league where they placed third. One cadet said, "We could practice one day and play the next—play against boilermakers and railroad men and all kinds of big guys. We were in pretty good shape from the hard work on the ship."

The Panama Canal incident reinforced the view that the school needed a more modern ship. "We have no cold storage system and our fresh water supply is far too limited," McMurray wrote. "Conditions at sea are not so hard now as they used to be, and these boys are made to undergo hardships on this ship that they are not likely to encounter later. That is unnecessary."

It was not until two months later, on December 20th, that dredging boats had cleared just enough of the landslide that the *Newport* could pass with some other small vessels. He got underway, leading a string of other ships through the canal. They returned to New York on January 3, 1916, having travelled a total distance of 15,400 nautical miles. They had been gone for nearly eight months.

THE CLOSURE CRISIS OF 1916

After the extended cruise, the cadets were given three weeks of vacation. During this break, the shadow of abolishment loomed as the new governor,

Charles Whitman, denounced the Nautical School. "In view of other and more pressing educational needs of the State," he wrote in his annual report, "it does not appear good public policy to feed, clothe and maintain pupils of this school at the cost of $100,000 for approximately 100 pupils."

It had been only three years since the school was transferred to the state. Now, all of the organizers behind that effort remobilized. Of these, Reginald Fay wrote that it was "incredible" that the governor would call for a closure "when the prospects for the development of the merchant marine of the United States was never greater."

Whitman's position was also weakened by anticipated American involvement in World War I. Merchant mariners were now expected to serve as an auxiliary to the U.S. Navy, and in May, 1916, after a lapse of nearly thirty years, the U.S. Navy supplied the ship with small arms and cutlasses for military drills.

The backlash against Whitman came from all sides. Editorials panned the Governor's suggestion with hard hitting articles in Norton's *Marine Journal*. The alumni, as well as the Chamber of Commerce, the New York Board of Trade and Transportation, the Merchants' Association and the Security League gathered to protest. A delegation from the school was sent directly to the Governor. Frederick Dalzell, who accompanied the delegation, reported that the Governor told him: "If you can create sufficient public opinion to carry this through then I shall not be opposed." To do that, the Board of Governors hired 1903 graduate, Louis Weickum, as a publicist for a fee of $244.

Weickum organized a campaign in which hundreds of individuals wrote letters directly to the Governor. The chief argument of the schoolship's supporters was that it was necessary for national defense. Justice Harrington Putnam of the Appellate Division of the Supreme Court wrote, "In a close and direct way the Nautical School affects the commercial interests, and even extends to the national defense." The Sons of the American Revolution, the National Board of Steam Navigation, Isthmian Line, United Fruit Company, American Steamship Association and the Naval and Military Order of the Spanish American War were among the many groups that aided the Nautical School. Weickum, a talented artist, drew political cartoons for New York newspapers showing the *Newport* being attacked by a Whitman-manned submarine.

McMurray asserted that the school should *expand* rather than be abolished. He said that on the 1915 cruise, the *Newport* encountered foreign training ships that put the New York State Nautical School to shame:

The Japanese laughed at us with our one little ship when we steamed into the harbor at San Francisco as they rode by in their majestic vessel. . . . Little Belgium has two ships, each of them larger than the *Newport*. The city of Bremen, Germany, has five such ships. Great Britain has eighteen training ships for her young men. . . .

At a hearing of the New York State Senate's Ways and Means Committee about the issue, only one person showed up in favor of shutting down the ship while Nautical School supporters made up the remainder.* The bill to abolish the school died in committee.

By March 11th, Governor Whitman had backtracked completely. He told the Bronx Board of Trade that he realized, "clearly the necessity of having nautical training schools. I wish there were more. . . ." Even so, Whitman charged that merchant mariner training was a federal, not state, function. "It must be clearly understood that in the near future they [national government] will take over the school, and if necessary establish new ones."

"WE ARE ALL IN THE SAME BOAT"

After the closure crisis, two legislative developments occurred which heralded good news for the schoolship. First, the United States Steamboat Inspection Service lowered its licensing age from 21 to 19 for junior officers. This had enormous implications for graduates. With the lowered age, the waiting time for graduates dropped and made the option of going to sea more attractive.

Second, in 1916 Congress finally released the $25,000 it promised to the state nautical schools. This included a retroactive payment for all the missed years to total $125,000. It seemed that the attention drawn to the Nautical School during the closure controversy finally helped win the backing of Congress.

Flushed with cash and optimism, the Board of Governors continued to press for further professionalization and expansion of the school. Miller and the rest of the Board turned to the federal government for more support and prestige. They pushed for a bill that would allow the President to give the Nautical School automatic appointments for graduates to the U.S. Naval

---

*The one person was Dr. Abraham Korn, who represented the United Real Estate Owners of New York. He contended that the school benefitted only maritime industries and kept men from joining the Navy who would otherwise do so.

Academy. They resumed the fight for a larger ship and advocated raising wages to competitive levels so they could retain competent employees.

Despite the good news, melancholy settled on McMurray. After just two years, he was burnt out. In 1916, the *Newport* cruised to the Azores, avoiding Europe due to the war. On this voyage, the ship lost her propeller and tail shaft while en route to Fayal. The rest of the voyage was done by sail and in stormy weather.

In April, 1917 the United States entered World War I, and the *Newport* was restricted to Long Island Sound and the Hudson. McMurray had difficulty keeping a competent crew since the war was driving up wages. He complained that the pay of commercial mariners was 50–200 percent greater than what was paid to the *Newport*'s crew. He warned that "the additional necessity for men for instruction purposes has reached an acute stage."

In a letter to his mother he complained, "We are constantly hiring men here and they are as constantly leaving the ship. The Board went up to Albany and saw the Governor in an attempt to get our wages raised, but were told that absolutely nothing could be done." McMurray was further annoyed when the state legislature accidentally allotted him a salary of $2,000 instead of $3,000.

Without a full crew, most of the preparations for the annual voyage fell on the cadets. McMurray was frustrated, as were the cadets' families. "Parents are complaining at the dirty work put upon their boys in cleaning ship, but no one else is here to do it and we are all in the same boat. We are all dirty in consequence."

McMurray was also fed up with Miller and the rest of the Board. They were concerned with image and did not take negative news well. What is more, he learned that Miller was "working separately from the rest of the Board, and to their great indignation, in an effort to have the ship taken over by the federal government and operated as a federal school with him established on a salaried position as a member of its controlling committee."

McMurray attributed this to a downturn in Miller's private career in shipping. At one point, McMurray even heard that Miller was trying to get the position of superintendent, but "finding out something about its peculiar attractiveness, he promptly changed his mind."

In May, 1917 McMurray wrote his mother: "Am getting tired of this job as there is so much trouble connected with it which I am not responsible for and which I cannot help." Later that month, he made the decision to leave, writing that he was "disgusted with the present position of the Nautical

School and if I can do so to advantage will leave this job as soon as I can get something else to do." He also lamented about his and the school's future. "There are no prospects here and no immediate prospects of better conditions. I sent in another letter urging increases of wages for the crew and the members of the Board are going to Albany shortly to try to get them as it is now absolutely necessary that something be done."

But McMurray was filled with pessimism. "I do not look for their success, and believe that the school will die a natural death under present management. It seems as if everything was going wrong with me lately. Everyone seems dissatisfied on board. . . . I have no doubt that Nautical Schools will come in time as there is an effort being made for them which is better than anything either I or our Board can do."

Miller ended up suddenly resigning from his position on the Board in June, 1917 due to reported "growing outside interests." John Hatzel took his place. Miller died of pneumonia the next year. In the meanwhile, McMurray escaped the Nautical School by joining the Naval Reserves to help the war effort.

Despite McMurray's pessimism, the school lived on and entered an era dominated by some of the schoolship's strongest egos. Personal reputation dominated their psyches, and the chief of all these men was McMurray's classmate and friend, Felix Riesenberg.

CHAPTER 8

The Age of Riesenberg

"My two years in command of the Newport seemed like twenty. . . ."
–Felix Riesenberg

"THE SEA IS SELECTIVE"

For Felix Riesenberg, August 1, 1917, was one of the hottest days he could remember. By the afternoon, the temperature soared to 98, and a record 108 New Yorkers died in the heat wave. Hospitals were swamped with heat-related cases, and the only newspaper story bigger was the American entry into World War I. In the *New York Tribune*, the German Kaiser, Wilhelm II, was quoted as saying, "New nations continue to enter into this war against us, but it does not frighten us. We know our strength and are determined to make use of it." The United States Congress had passed the Selective Service Act that May which allowed the government to conscript men. But by that summer, hardly any of the American Expeditionary Force had gone to Europe. The country was still switching to a war footing.

Felix Riesenberg wasn't thinking about the war. He was wearing a dark blue wool uniform as he approached the starboard gangway of the schoolship *Newport*. He was suffocating, but he didn't mind. It was all a part of a formal ceremony which was to culminate in him being installed as her captain.

As he approached, he became spellbound at "one of the great commands of the sea." In his autobiography, he recalled:

> I loved her. A genius had designed this craft of a thousand tons. Her clipper bow flowed gracefully into the slight stave of her bowsprit and the droop of

her sheer made a gentle sweep aft to her perfect oval counter. Her sides had a slight tumble home that caught the light caressing her curves, accentuating her lovely lines.

As he came aboard to relieve his friend, Frederick McMurray, side boys saluted, the boatswain's pipe shrilled and pennants changed. He later wrote, "Imagine, if you please, what such ceremonies mean to a man bred to the sea."

But Felix Riesenberg had grown up about as far from the sea as possible. He was born in Milwaukee, Wisconsin in 1879, but at an early age, his family moved to Chicago where the climate was (in his words), "suited to the incubation of restless active lives." His father, William, was a German immigrant who had voyaged around the world in the China trade. Strange as it may seem, Felix's father did not speak much about his adventures, and when he did "he would look far away and seem to dream." At the insistence of his strong-willed wife, Emily Schorb; he gave up the sea. According to Felix, "Getting married cut his [father's] cable and sent him adrift among the reefs." As Felix knew him, his father was "a man of another sphere, a man unable to adjust to his shore surroundings." On land, William tried to go into business, but failed.

Riesenberg loved his father but pitied him. He would say that the family would have been better off if his mother was the head of the family. The shadow of William Riesenberg loomed over Felix's life. He wrote, "Often, in moments of peril, I have felt his presence when only luck has saved me from disaster."

On visits to the Chicago wharves, Felix Riesenberg was drawn to the ships. As he climbed the rigging of old sail vessels, he knew he was meant for life at sea. In 1896, the blue-eyed, blond boy enrolled at the New York Nautical School. He satisfied the residency requirement by living with his aunt and uncle in Harlem on the weekends. Riesenberg took well to the rough discipline aboard the *St. Mary's*. He became a cadet officer, overseeing a crew of boys and served as coxswain of the captain's gig, a position of honor.

During the 1897 cruise, Riesenberg went ashore at Tangier with two shipmates under the protection of a man named Abdul Mus, who promised "on the Koran, to look after the small boys and see that no harm came to them in the city. . . ." After making Riesenberg and his companions count out their money, Mus took them aboard a steamer filled with "exhausted whores" that he was transporting back to Tangier. They got a tour of the city before Mus put the boys up in a brothel. Riesenberg claimed to have resisted his "erotic impulses" due to ". . . the smells—I have always been warned by odors. Credit my nose, not my morals." At least one of his companions contracted a venereal disease that "ruined his life." Riesenberg mused, "We were seventeen, could swear like sailors and little remained to be known except the burn of ruin."

As a *St. Mary's* boy, Riesenberg came to believe that the seafaring life weeded out those who were not ready for it. To him, the sea chose its own: "The sea is selective, slow at recognition of effort and aptitude but fast in sinking the unfit." This was to become an adage that students at the institution memorized. He graduated in 1897.

Being young, adventurous and not a little foolish, Riesenberg wanted to sail in deep water. He was advised by the *St. Mary's* boatswain, William Dreilick, that he should sail around Cape Horn. The old mariner saw the coming of steam and said, "It won't last much longer." Riesenberg signed on as an ordinary seaman on the clipper *A.J. Fuller*. The voyage was a four-month trek which Riesenberg dramatized in his book, *Under Sail* (1918). This would become the first of twenty-six books he authored. Most of these works were nautical fiction based upon his own experiences and were described by the *New York Times* as "salty and racy" providing "delight to many readers." His most successful work was non-nautical. *East Side, West Side* (1927), was a fictional story of New York City, which was made into a silent film. He also published several non-fiction history books and a textbook on seamanship that became the standard in its day.

After his first voyage, Riesenberg worked on a variety of steamers and involved himself for a year with the U.S. Coast and Geodetic Survey. During this period, he even applied for admission as a cadet to the U.S. Revenue Cutter Service, now the U.S. Coast Guard. He was accepted and began training but resigned on a "hunch." Riesenberg yearned to be on land and "taste the homemade bread that Mother made."

He returned to Chicago in 1905, unsure and restless. One day, he read in a newspaper about Walter Wellman, a journalist from the Chicago *Record-Herald* who was famous for exploration. Arctic discovery was in vogue, and the North Pole was yet unattained. Wellman suggested that since men could not achieve the pole by ship or foot, then they should try by air. He proposed to fly an airship over the North Pole. Riesenberg thought that "the scheme was crazy enough to seem workable." He contacted the newspaper and met with

Wellman. The journalist was impressed by Riesenberg's geodetic credentials and hired him as a navigator. Riesenberg spent the winter of 1906-07 in charge of a group of men above the Arctic Circle. When the time came, he was aboard the airship manning the instruments. The mission failed, however, due to equipment malfunction and ferocious gales. They were forced to land on a glacier.

Riesenberg returned "not a hero, not a bit the wiser" and seeking direction. Under the advice (and partial financial backing) of his New York uncle, he entered Columbia University where he earned a bachelor's degree in Civil Engineering. He served on several building projects including the Catskill Aqueduct and the Columbia-Presbyterian Medical Center. During this time, he married Maud Conroy, an Irish woman who gave him five children. To bring in money for his growing family, he wrote books and invented a compound lever for compressing the sac in a fountain pen. It netted him $1,000.

But longing for the sea struck once more at Riesenberg's heart. He joined the U.S. Shipping Board and was chief officer of the interned German liner, *Prinz Eitel Friedrich*. Though he was not at sea, but only preparing the ship for it, he was happy to feel a deck once again under his feet. This strengthened his desire to be on open water. When he found out that the superintendent position aboard the schoolship was open, he applied.

Since Riesenberg had been president of the Alumni Association from 1912 to 1914, most of the Board of Governors knew him. Also, Riesenberg's fame as a writer and explorer were all good press for the schoolship. Hiring him was an easy decision for the Board.

"THE ARMS OF MORPHEUS"

Riesenberg's first major action after taking command was to find a new shore facility for the *Newport*. The ship, which had been berthed at the East 24th Street pier, was forced to move since the Navy commandeered the site due to the war. As a result, the schoolship was forced to relocate far uptown at a wharf on the Hudson River at 129th Street.

The new berth had its good points and bad points. On the positive side it was close to Columbia University. Riesenberg pulled some strings and brokered a deal where his cadets could use Columbia's swimming pool, gymnasium and a classroom in exchange for allowing the university's students to take courses on theoretical navigation and seamanship aboard the *Newport*.

On the negative side, the winter of 1917-18 was colder than usual. In early March there was a sudden thawing, and some ice sheets made their way down the river. One ice floe was particularly nasty, poking eight feet out of the water and spreading outward below the water line, invisible to sight.

The sheet careened down the Hudson at night, narrowly missed a ferry boat and took aim at the *Newport*'s pier. It slammed into the dock and carried a good chunk of the wharf away.

Riesenberg wrote, "I was in the cabin, near midnight, at some work, a shock sent tremors through the ship, and as I looked out of a cabin port I saw the end of the pier begin to weave." Then a cadet's voice rang "clear as a clarion, warning the sleepers in the bowels of the ship."

The *Newport* avoided being crushed through the use of hawsers to pull the ship out of the way. Riesenberg said immediately after the incident: "One shudders to think of the fate awaiting the 200 helpless seamen who, all unconscious of the danger, lie locked in the arms of Morpheus on board the imperiled ship. "

In the morning, to the surprise of all aboard the *Newport*, the wind and tide had shifted the ice back upstream, and it was ready to make another go at the schoolship. This time it struck dead on. The floe "hit the spars and snapped them like toothpicks." The ice rammed into the pier causing the *Newport* to heel over. All hands "heard loud cracking reports coming up from her hull" as the ice crunched into the pier's fender piles. Even in the bitter chill, Riesenberg was bathed in clammy perspiration. The crunching continued for a few minutes then the ice floe shifted back out into the Hudson. Upon inspection, Riesenberg found that the *Newport* was lucky. Although her copper bottom had been stripped off in sheets, there was no other obvious damage.

That December, Riesenberg brought the *Newport* to Pensacola, Florida with the intent of instituting a two-cruise curriculum. The ship would sail in warmer latitudes during the winter months and then in the summer, due to the war, sail in New York and New England waters.

It was a good voyage. Remembering the awful food of the *St. Mary's*, Riesenberg introduced to the *Newport*, in February of 1918, Lewis M. Weber, the "shortcake king of the North Atlantic." One newspaper wrote, "He has been on the *Newport* three weeks now and every soul aboard, from the skipper to the ship's cat, has gained anywhere from one to eight pounds." But Weber was an Army deserter. When his name was publicized in the press, the U.S.

Army arrested him. He had been a private in the Pancho Villa campaign and did not realize his obligation to serve in the reserves for three years. He ignored a mustering. Riesenberg vowed to get Weber back, but there is no evidence that this occurred.

Meanwhile, after arriving in Pensacola, Riesenberg found residual damage to the rudder due to the ice incident. It had to be replaced. This created delays, but the *Newport* managed through her cruise of the Caribbean.

Riesenberg stayed on through the next year slowly burning out. Despite the protests of the Board of Governors, he resigned on May 1, 1919, to take a position as an editor of the journal, *National Marine*. He later wrote of his time as superintendent:

> My two years in command of the *Newport* seemed like twenty, the crowding together of a lifetime of incidents, of activity, of days and nights during which the ship sailed me, drove me—me, the nerve center of a creature built of steel and wood and filled with the flesh and blood of men and boys.

THOMAS W. SHERIDAN

When Riesenberg returned to shore, the Board of Governors, now under the chairmanship of Marcus Tracey, turned to the services of Thomas W. Sheridan. The policy of naming alumni superintendents was still in place, and Sheridan was a 1906 graduate of the *St. Mary's*. A gifted navigator, he was hired by the schoolship as an instructor after graduation. Sheridan, a devotee of traditional seamanship, once said in an interview, "There is nothing in the world like sail to instill into a boy the will to do things that must be done at sea if a man is to succeed. Nothing can produce in him the sea zest, the feeling for the sea that sail can."

Sheridan was also an exponent of fitness and an able amateur boxer. It was reported that he had once trained with and fought prizefighter Luis Angel Firpo who was taking passage on a ship he worked on; it is unknown who won. Sheridan was no exemplar of love and kindness, but rather dedicated to discipline. With a Vandyke beard and steely sharp eyes, he presented a formidable figure. Take the case of Cadet Paul J. Eilman, who encountered Sheridan as an instructor under Superintendent McMurray.

Eilman was a hard case who had been written up multiple times for serious rule violations such as stealing, lying, being away without leave and disobedience. The school attempted to punish him into compliance by restricting him to the ship and placing him in solitary confinement. But Eilman only commented that the brig did him good.

In April, 1917 Eilman tormented an underclassman and forced him to do his work. He was stopped by Executive Officer Charles Littlefield. Afterwards, Littlefield mentioned the incident to Sheridan. Sheridan flew into a rage and ordered the teen into his cabin. He had enough of Eilman.

Later, Eilman insisted that Sheridan beat him, hitting him in the face at least five times. He testified that Sheridan ordered him to lower his pants then struck him several times with a small red cane. When Eilman did not remove his pants fast enough, Sheridan tore them off, ripping buttons in the process. After the beating was administered, Sheridan told him to keep his mouth shut or it would be worse for him.

Sheridan insisted that Eilman was lying. He admitted that while he did strike the cadet, it was out of anger when the boy commented that he had all the officers on the ship "bull-dozed" and tried to push past him out of the cabin. In the process, Sheridan asserted that Eilman scratched at his face and bit his hand. He also insisted that he did not order Eilman to lower his pants.

After the incident, word got back to McMurray who ordered the cadet to write a statement. Before Eilman could bring the statement to McMurray, he was intercepted by Sheridan and Littlefield. In their testimony, they claimed that Eilman admitted the statement was false and tore the paper up.

Eilman left the ship and informed his guardian, who brought the case before the Board of Governors in 1917. A hearing was held that May and the governors expelled Eilman from the school. As for Sheridan, the Board was divided, but in the end they decided not to fire him but order him to apologize to the Board of Governors. Eilman never got an apology.

While it is impossible to determine the truth, Sheridan's account smacks of lies. It is easy to imagine Eilman's destruction of his statement as a result from fear of Sheridan. At the hearing, Eilman's guardian questioned Sheridan, and the officer admitted that he begged the guardian to forget about the affair.

With a cloud over him, Sheridan left the schoolship and worked on private vessels for a few years. When Riesenberg resigned, the Board of Governors, pressed to find somebody quickly for the summer voyage, hired him. They were nervous enough about Sheridan to place him on six-month probation.

Sheridan immediately suggested administrative changes, the chief of which was to break up the two-class system in favor of a four-class one with two graduations per year. Sheridan said that this would create smaller classes that would be "easier to handle and instruct." This was adopted by the Board of Governors and the cadets were broken into first, second, third and fourth classes. They also adopted his recommendation for the schoolship's first cruise to the Great Lakes. The *Newport* proceeded north to Canada where it passed into the St. Lawrence River, stopped at Quebec, then entered the Great Lakes and navigated their locks. After visits to Montreal and Buffalo, the *Newport* sailed on to Bermuda. It was a great success, except for one notable episode.

During the cruise, two cadets, Carl Reugge and James Kelly, were caught stealing food. This was not a rare violation of the rules. The meals served to the cadets on the schoolship were notoriously bad, and the students often tried to steal better food from the officers' mess. The two met with Sheridan. He wrote that they were

> informed that the occurrence would be made known to their parents (this being a custom in the past). Both requested that it be kept from their parents, and made the further request that instead of the report being made they be given a thrashing on board, which both stated would happen to them at home. This I did.

Sheridan quickly added that he deeply regretted the incident and that it would not happen again.

Marcus Tracey and the rest of the governors investigated the legalities of the matter. Maritime and educational law had become more progressive by 1919. Corporal punishment and mistreatment of crew, not to mention public school children, was illegal. An Assistant U.S. District Attorney advised them that Sheridan could receive three months to three years in prison. He added that if a formal report of the incident reached the office of the Attorney General, there was "nothing that would prevent them from prosecuting the case." The attorney advised the Board to take care of the problem and make sure that such a thing could not happen again.

Sheridan caught wind of this and tendered his resignation in late October. Tracey refused it, and the Board fired him. The scandal was covered up. In fact, in the annual report of 1919, there were only positive comments about Sheridan as a "capable young officer of exceptional ability. . . ." Sheridan left with as much dignity as he could and entered a successful career with the American Lines.

"ALL LIFEBOATS ARE BROKEN"

To men like Sheridan and Riesenberg the importance of reputation cannot be understated. For hundreds of years, merchant sea officers and sailors were not respectable. Yet by the 1900s merchant sea officers had become an honorable caste. The men who commanded the great liners like the *Titanic* and the *Olympic* were heroes. Those who graduated from the decks of the *St. Mary's* and the *Newport* were deeply concerned with maintaining their images as gallant officers and gentlemen.

The greatest example of courage by an alumnus during this period was in 1925. On October 11th, the *Ignazio Florio*, a small Italian freighter, departed Montreal. The ship was en route to the port of Avonmouth, England, loaded with grain. The *Florio* was manned by a multi-ethnic crew of about 30. There was also a black and white cat named Mirone and a black dog named Mirus. The vessel's commanding officer, 39-year-old Aniello Lauro, was an experienced hand at crossing the fickle North Atlantic.

The weather had been fair until the late afternoon of October 17th, when it began to blow from the west with high seas. By the morning of the 18th, the *Florio* was caught in a storm of hurricane proportions. Gusts of 90 miles per hour slammed against the freighter. Lauro, who was on the bridge, watched in horror as the sea suddenly broke into the forward hatches.

Lauro left the second mate, Luigi Leboffe, in charge of the bridge as he went to inspect the damage. While Lauro was gone, the sea continued its onslaught, and suddenly a huge wave washed over the bridge and took Leboffe with it. It was impossible to launch a life boat. The seas were too terrible. It would have been smashed to pieces. Besides, the crew of the *Florio* could not even make out what direction the lost officer had been swept due to the haze and flying spume.

By the next morning, the storm hadn't abated. Gear was washed away and the engine room flooded. The grain in the holds shifted, and the ship tilted nearly to its beam ends. The deluge decimated all in its path. Ladders were broken and derricks crashed through the deck into the storeroom. Lauro sent out a desperate SOS.

About 150 miles away, the liner *President Harding* steamed toward Hoboken with 314 passengers. She also had to contend with the storm and was running at a reduced speed of eight knots. The *Harding* handled the storm better, being larger and more stable than the *Ignazio Florio*. This did not prevent heavy sea sickness among many of the passengers.

George Kohle, the ship's radio officer, was sitting at his station with his earphones on, a cigarette dangling from his lips. A telegraph came through the receiver:

SOS . . . SOS Lat 49:55N. Long. 38:16 BROKEN STEERING ENGINE.

Kohle took the message and hurried to the *Harding's* captain, Paul C. Grening.

In a way, Grening was the ideal person to come to the *Florio's* rescue. Born in Brooklyn, he was sea-crazy from a young age despite not having the air of a salty mariner. One source characterized him as "more like a man of leisure with an assured income whose sea life had been confined to the shelter afforded by a first class cabin in an executive liner." Another described him as being short and husky, looking more like a banker than a sea captain. But from the time he could read, Grening immersed himself in sea stories of heroes and rescues.

Grening, by his own account, was an "independent spirit," who wanted to join the merchant marine. His father, who was in real estate, did not readily agree, but the boy threatened to drop out of school and run away. His father relented and encouraged his son to join the Navy. The younger Grening would have none of it; his heart was set on becoming a merchant mariner. It offered "greater freedom."

A compromise was made. Paul Grening would go to school, but aboard the New York Nautical Schoolship, *St. Mary's*. His parents thought that the *St. Mary's* would tire their son out of his maritime mania. It proved to have the opposite effect. Nicknamed "Spider Grening,"* he cultivated a burning desire to display his courage when the sea was at its worst.

Grening graduated with Felix Riesenberg in 1897, and then he went to San Francisco serving on the old Cape Horn square riggers. After, he worked for several steamship companies, almost all in the Pacific. When World War I broke out, he took the job of reconditioning the interned German liner *Vaterland*. Grening had her so shipshape that the Navy commissioned her in the transport service as the *Leviathan*. To Grening's disappointment, he did not get to command the *Leviathan* because he "looked like a capable business man" rather than a master of a great ship. This was more than Grening could stand, and he joined the Navy on the transport *Rondo* and later the battleship *New Jersey*.

---

*A nickname probably derived for how Grening climbed the rigging.

After the war, he was employed by the United States Lines, the company that owned the *Harding*. By 1925, he had been the captain of the *Harding* for three years, and his love of the sea was still strong. "The sea is my life," Grening said. "I have very little time on shore, and what time I have is spent on sea matters. Golf, games, sports—such things are not for me."

Although several ships received the *Florio's* distress signal, Grening's *President Harding* was the nearest and fastest. He altered course and sent signals to the *Florio* that they were on the way and would be there in the morning. At 10:00 that evening, Lauro telegraphed him: "We trust only in you, as we cannot remain a long time on ship. All lifeboats are broken. SOS."

At 11:30 on the morning of October 20th, the *Harding* found the *Florio*. The seas were forty to sixty feet high and the wind blew at 75 miles per hour with gusts up to 90. Grening was only able to maintain his position via radio compass. Meanwhile, the *Harding's* 314 passengers were bumped around incessantly; three women were injured by falling onto the deck. A successful rescue was a dangerous prospect.

Grening ordered the ship to back away from the *Florio* to avoid a collision. Lauro radioed Grening, "Are you abandoning us? We are ready to come to you." Grening replied, "We are standing by you. Do not worry. Courage."

Grening ordered the rescue efforts to begin. They tried discharging oil to calm the sea, but this proved useless in such harsh conditions. He next tried shooting cables to the *Florio* using a Lyle Gun, essentially a mortar that launched projectiles attached to heavy white lines. The first shot frayed the rope, and the second shot plunged deep into the water missing the target. Meanwhile, the *Harding* drifted dangerously close to the *Florio*. Grening decided to try his luck with an empty Lundin lifeboat. It was lowered into the ocean with a line attached to the *Harding*. Grening had his men drift it toward the crippled ship. The boat got so near that Lauro radioed the *Harding* asking what they were supposed to do with it. The reply was to the point: get on.

But even as the lifeboat neared the bow of the *Florio*, the sea reared and drove it away. The boat capsized, and was ripped off its line. It was just as well that the men of the *Florio* stayed out of the lifeboat.

The afternoon wore on, and there was still enough light for one more rescue attempt. Volunteers on the *Harding* offered to row to the *Florio* but Grening had given strict orders against it, as it was too dangerous. Instead, he brought the *Harding* as close to the *Florio* as he dared and shot another line with the Lyle gun. This time the *Florio's* crew got a hold of it. The *Harding's* crew attached their end of the line to a lifeboat and took a second line and attached that to the *Harding*. This created a daisy chain to draw over the boat to the *Florio* and load her crew. The *Florio's* crew managed to pull this boat across and get it ready. However, they had already seen one lifeboat capsize, and the seas were so high and rough that it was suicidal to risk jumping into the boat. Lauro, encouraged by a slight rise in the barometer, assured Grening that they could stay afloat through the night, and he would not order his men to board the lifeboat.

That evening, the *Harding* could do nothing but circle the *Florio* and hope that the freighter would not sink. The liner's passengers remained awake to watch events unfold. Grening could not see how a rescue could be achieved without a lull in the storm. At last, he decided that when the *Ignazio Florio* was in its final death throes, he would run the *Harding* "bow to bow" with her and throw over anything that would float in order to save as many lives as possible.

The next morning brought, as Grening called it, "an act of Providence" as the storm suddenly abated. The seas were just as high, but there was no wind to break the waves. Grening ordered a party to be sent over to rescue the *Florio's* crew.

A Lundin lifeboat was manned by Grening's chief officer, Giles C. Stedman. He set out with six men and an interpreter, Salvatore Brocco, who had been translating the radio messages throughout the whole affair. According to Stedman, the danger he had to "contend with was to prevent my boat from being carried on top of a big wave" and being "landed on the side of the *Florio* as the water roiled over her."

They drew close. This was the critical part in which a sudden wave could smash the lifeboat to pieces against the *Florio's* side. "Sometimes we were within twenty feet and then the men at the oars had to put their backs to it and pull for their live," Stedman recalled. "Two or three times we had six men at the oars."

Stedman made it and evacuated the worn out crew of the *Florio*. The ship's cat, Mirone, was rescued although he clawed at the sailors who tried to hold him. Sadly, as they rowed back, Mirus, the *Florio's* dog, jumped out of the lifeboat and tried to swim back to the sinking ship. He disappeared into the sea. Aside from the dog, and the earlier loss of Luigi Leboffe, the rescue was a complete success.

Grening steamed to Hoboken with the survivors. Even before he arrived, the radio was jammed with messages of congratulations. More than a thousand radiograms were received. As he travelled along the New York waterways, factories along the shore, other vessels and crowds of well-wishers saluted the heroes with cheers and whistles.

Grening, Stedman and the crew were celebrated in a ticker tape parade in New York's "Canyon of Heroes." The cadets of the New York Nautical State School proudly came to salute one of their own. One writer commented, "Those thirty-six hours of heavy weather rescue work seemed simple compared with the ordeal of being showered by ticker tape and torn paper."

Grening soon jumped up the corporate ladder to become the Assistant Director in Europe for the Fleet Corporation. Stedman rose on his own path of fame and became the second superintendent of the United States Merchant Marine Academy at Kings Point. The crew of the *Harding* received medals from the Italian government and were even feted by dictator Benito Mussolini. Fortunately for Stedman and Grening's reputations, neither were present to meet *Il Duce*.

JOHN S. BAYLIS

After Thomas Sheridan's ignominious departure, Marcus Tracey hired John Baylis. He graduated from the decks of the *St. Mary's* in 1903 and afterward found a home with the Revenue Cutter Service, the forerunner of the Coast Guard. He was the first head of the institution associated with that service. He was not as salty as Riesenberg nor as brutal as Sheridan, but a dignified man who sought to increase the school's prestige.

His administration introduced collegiate customs such as the first yearbook, *Eight Bells,* and the school's *alma mater*, "The Bells of St. Mary's."* He sought to make the training cruises more cultural for the students. When he brought the *Newport* back to Europe for the first time since the end of World War I, he made a point of stopping at Antwerp. There, they observed the 1920 Olympic games and visited World War I battlefields. To Baylis, the New York State Nautical School was less of a trade school and more of a college.

In addition, the school became more academically focused, especially in the engineering curriculum. This was due to the contribution of Baylis' chief

---

*The song was a modified version of a 1917 song of the same name by Douglas Furber and A. Emmett Adams.

engineer, 1912 graduate, Arthur M. Tode.* He introduced to the engineering cadets tours of modern factories and brought engineering company representatives aboard the *Newport* to give lectures to the cadets.

Baylis maintained the four-class system instituted by Sheridan, but the two-cruise per year experiment was eliminated due to cost and time lost. To compensate, Baylis introduced miniature cruises around New York Harbor to instruct the students in local waterways.

In 1921, Baylis faced an abolition crisis when Governor Nathan Miller called to eliminate the school due to cost. Miller's proposal was easily quashed since the forces that stopped the attempted closure in 1919 were still active. These made the same, persuasive arguments. Baylis, with the Board of Governors, visited Miller providing figures that countered claims that graduates did not go to sea. They reported that of 1,300 men who graduated since the school was opened, 95 percent took to seafaring. This was an unbelievable number,** but with incessant lobbying, their strategy worked and the matter soon vanished.

Baylis said he wanted to "obtain a suitable site ashore in order to conduct the winter term with some comfort and better facilities for instruction." He originally suggested a berth at Quarantine, Staten Island, but what he got was better. After negotiating with the U.S. Army, he was granted permission in 1922 to use the military facilities on Bedloe's Island, better known as Liberty Island. Baylis was thrilled to dock the *Newport* at, what he called, a "dignified place" in the shadow of the Statue of Liberty. Baylis wrote, "This location is particularly desirable for the training of our future merchant officers as they can see all shipping passing in and out of New York Harbor, thereby learning the different types of vessels, house flags and funnel marks."

A CHANGE IN COMMAND

In 1922, Governor Nathan Miller lost his re-election bid to Al Smith. Smith was one of the politicians that supported the transfer of the Nautical School to New York State in 1913. The Board of Governors expected a friendlier

---

*Pronounced "Toe-Dee" or "Toe-Day" depending on the source.
**See Chapter 3. Ninety-five percent was far too high if they were counting from the beginning of the school's history.

administration than Miller's. However, when Smith assumed* office in 1923, he set out to reorganize the state government. The Nautical School, independent of any other state agency, was a rogue elephant in the jungle of the New York State government. Smith targeted it as one of many departments that needed to be merged and simplified in order to create more efficient government.

Smith also had problems with the Board of Governors. He criticized them for paying excessive rent for their office in the Cunard Building at Bowling Green, and he suspected that they were guilty of taking graft. Smith said that the schoolship should no longer be administered by an independent board but come under the jurisdiction of the New York Naval Militia. When Marcus Tracey found this out, he immediately sent Baylis to Albany to negotiate with Smith.

There wasn't much bargaining with the Governor, and the Board's argument for independence changed to a plea that they be transferred under the umbrella of the State Education Department. The Board feared that being run by the Naval Militia would squelch their control of the school, while the Education Department was more amenable in allowing them to continue managing the institution. Smith agreed to the change.

The law, signed in May 1923, was to the Board's liking insomuch as they made a gentleman's agreement with the Education Department that there would be limited oversight on how the school was run. Baylis claimed credit for the transfer, asserting it was for the good of the institution, and Smith had won a victory in streamlining the State government. But the long term implication of the legislation was more meaningful, since the ultimate authority over the New York State Nautical School passed to the Education Department.

THE DETERIORATION OF THE *NEWPORT*

Since New York State took control of the school, the *Newport*'s condition had been deteriorating. A 1917 Navy inspection found a considerable amount of corrosion on the vessel. Repairs, however, were difficult since the *Newport*'s design gave it many nooks and crannies where machinery blocked access for repair and maintenance.

---

*More properly described as reassumed since Smith already served as Governor from 1919 to 1920 before he was unseated by Miller.

After the 1917 inspection, the Navy recommended that since the life of the ship was limited to a few years, that repairs should be restricted to those areas "that would put the ship in serviceable condition for continuing her present duty until such time as she can be replaced by a more suitable vessel." As a result, the Navy did minimal work. This became a pattern as the Navy and the Board of Governors believed that the school would soon acquire a new ship.

Arthur Tode asserted some years later that the Navy had, in fact, condemned the ship in 1921, but Baylis managed to convince the Navy to put in enough repairs to keep the ship afloat. "The paid crew on board the *Newport* had always been too small for the proper upkeep and preservation of the vessel," Tode recalled. "Due to lack of funds, the other desirable repairs requested by the Commanding Officer of the ship were eliminated." This deterioration was furthered by Baylis's policy which did not allow cadets to do physical maintenance in favor of academic study.

In the official records of the Nautical School there is no mention of structural problems with the ship. It is possible that Baylis hid this information from the Board of Governors in order to maintain his position as superintendent. In other words, he did not want to be the bearer of bad news. In December, 1923, Baylis wrote to Tode noting the "good points" of his administration which included, "getting the Navy to keep the ship afloat for two years longer after it had been condemned" as well as "getting repairs, supplies and surveys from the Navy thereby saving the State thousands of dollars."

But the *Newport*'s problems were removed from Baylis's hands when, in early 1923, he was recalled to active duty. The Coast Guard, vowing to stamp out the rampant smuggling of illegal alcohol, needed as many veteran commanders they could get. Baylis went to hunt rumrunners.

This left the Board of Governors in a quandary. They wanted to hire 1907 graduate John H. Boesch, but the position needed to be filled immediately. Boesch was out of the country. Just then, Felix Riesenberg, "tired of the shore," made his interest known. The Board snapped him up for a second stint as superintendent. Boesch became his executive officer. Little did the Board of Governors know that Riesenberg's return would set off a firestorm.

"THEY HAD PULLED HER PRETTY TEETH"

When Riesenberg reassumed command on May 15, 1923, he might have expected some changes, but what he found completely demoralized him. The schoolship was in the Brooklyn Navy Yard, where it had been laid up for two months, undergoing repairs and maintenance. With all the work crews aboard, the ship was filthy. Riesenberg was especially upset that the *Newport*'s guns, which he called her "teeth," were removed:

> The old girl, as I remained on board of her for the first night, seemed to whisper to me, to ask why I had been so long away. I walked the quarter-deck for hours that night. A moon was out; she seemed to glow with her former beauty. They had pulled her pretty teeth. . . . In the cabin . . . were a brace of pink-eyed white mice, abandoned pets of the former commander [Baylis]. They ran about on the mahogany sideboard. I put them ashore—perhaps they were drowned.

He arranged for a full inspection of the *Newport*. He approached the Navy's Captain John G. Tawressy and Commander Ivan E. Bass, called "Lord High Executioner" by Riesenberg. The years of minimal repairs had now reached a critical point. The worst were the ship's boilers. These the inspectors condemned.

Without the boilers, the *Newport*'s engines were useless. According to Riesenberg, he was unofficially informed, "that unless there was improvement, the Navy Department would recommend the taking of the schoolship away from the State of New York."

It is hard to reconcile how this could have been a surprise, especially since the Navy had inspected the *Newport* regularly from 1913 to 1923. Regardless, Riesenberg was furious. He did not blame the Navy. Rather, he condemned the prior administration.

"There were quite a few on board who needed to be fired."

In the hostile work environment that followed, almost all of the Baylis-era officers resigned or were demoted by Riesenberg. He undid some of the administrative changes, such as the four-class system. Riesenberg wanted to make a clean sweep:

> If the *Newport* had been any other ship, I would have abandoned her then. After all, a sailor cannot take up with a slattern. But I once knew her, and

she had served me and had been faithful, and I loved her. I made up my mind that I would clean her up, shine her, polish her, make her new and fresh and beautiful—if I had to do it with my bare hands.

Tode, the Chief Engineer, might as well have had a bull's eye on his forehead. Riesenberg scoffed at Tode's curricular changes, "Two-year cadets were to be made to look like six-year scientific students and would be about as useless at sea."

Riesenberg coerced Tode into resigning on July 25th. In response, Tode enlisted former and current engineering students to petition Riesenberg and the Board of Governors. They wrote of Tode's competence, and they begged for his reinstatement. Riesenberg smelled a rat:

> A concerted movement was started among the cadets, with the knowledge of the Chief Engineer and forwarded to me whereby the senior engineering cadets threatened to leave the vessel. . . . Mr. Tode had already tendered his resignation when this condition took place and the letter signed by the entire first class of the engineering department was forwarded without his signature but with his knowledge in an attempt to coerce us into asking him to withdraw his resignation and stay on board.

Tode was replaced by Cyrus E. Davison, called by Riesenberg one of his "ablest shipmates."

THE CRUISE OF 1923

With the boilers out of commission there was little hope for an annual cruise. But Riesenberg requested that the Navy unship the *Newport*'s propeller and allow him to make the voyage entirely under sail. The Navy had no objection nor did the Board of Governors. When the work was complete, there was only one small boiler left for the auxiliary machinery and equipment. They were as engineless as the *St. Mary's*.

Meanwhile, the press started howling about the ship being allowed to sail without a working engine. The newspapers' main source was Henry C. Anderson, who had worked temporarily on the ship. Anderson was quoted as saying, "If they return I'll be happy. But I'm afraid they will not return." Riesenberg suspected that Tode was responsible for cajoling Anderson into talking with the press as well as "circulating malicious slander about the vessel."

Tode was doing exactly that, although he would not have called it malicious slander. He wanted to make sure that if there were problems on the schoolship, he was not going to be the scapegoat. He wrote to anybody he could think of, including governmental agencies, warning about the condition of the *Newport*.

Worried parents contacted the Board of Governors. The Board wavered, but finally assented to the cruise because of the Navy's support, and because Riesenberg announced that he would bring two of his sons on the cruise, ten year old Felix Jr., and eight year old William.

A cruise completely under sail was a challenging prospect. In 1916, Frederick McMurray sailed the *Newport* under sail alone for a good portion of the annual voyage since he lost his propeller and tail shaft while en route to the Azores. But to purposefully sail a complete summer training cruise without a working engine had not been accomplished since the *St. Mary's* last voyage, 15 years prior. To make matters more difficult, only a handful of the crew had worked on sail-only vessels. Riesenberg wasn't daunted: "I'll bring her home clean and I'll work the discontent out of the ship and have her manned by sailors."

On July 17, 1923, Riesenberg had the *Newport* towed to her traditional staging ground at Glen Cove where he tasked all hands. "I drilled the lot of them," he wrote. ". . . at loosing, hoisting and sheeting home sails, reefing, furling, boxing about the head yards and learning the ropes. Those who had made the previous cruise were little better than the green hands." He wrote that this was the "hardest grind" he ever worked aboard a ship. But he believed it was worth it as the *Newport* "seemed to whisper her delight as the clean salt water of the Sound lapped along her side."

After two weeks of training, the *Newport* made for New London, Connecticut, where final safety checks were done. Riesenberg, one last time, assured the Board of Governors that the schoolship was safe. On August 8th, the *Newport* weighed anchor. For the last time in the institution's history, the schoolship made a cruise under sail power alone.

Riesenberg headed for Funchal, Madeira, over 3,000 miles away. The 25-day passage was uneventful, although Riesenberg's sons did make a nuisance of themselves by fighting, climbing over the rigging and pulling pranks. Eventually, Riesenberg asked two supernumeraries, William Schneider and A.A. Bombe, to babysit and keep the boys out of trouble. They were a handful, but luckily the weather got rough. The children became seasick and stayed in their bunks.

As the ship neared Madeira, the wind shifted against them. Due to the poor condition of the *Newport*'s rigging and sails, the ship could not be brought effectively into port. For a week, Riesenberg tried to approach Funchal, tacking constantly. Privately, he questioned himself. "Doubt, of the most depressing depth, surged through me. I feared some accident aloft, feared I might lose a boy or two. I drank gallons of black coffee; my nerves were rubbed raw." Then, it was discovered that the foremast had rotted. With all hands worn out, Riesenberg gave up on Funchal and altered course to Tenerife in the Canary Islands.

They made it there without incident. When they arrived, Riesenberg wanted a protected berth, well inside the harbor. But since the *Newport* was under sail, the port authorities would have placed the ship well outside of the center of the harbor.

When the harbor pilot came aboard, he saw the *Newport*'s steam stack issuing smoke from the auxiliary machinery. He did not realize that the ship was under sail even though the vessel had the black ball sign at the foremast to signify it. Riesenberg allowed the pilot to message the "engine room." When a signal from "Stop" to "full speed astern" was given, Riesenberg slyly issued orders to maneuver the *Newport* to mimic a steam ship. The ruse worked. The pilot left the ship still assuming she was under steam power. The *Newport* acquired a "pretty mooring."

The time at Tenerife was one of recuperation from the failure to reach Madeira. Work was done on the *Newport* and supplies were replenished. They departed on September 6th. During the homeward voyage, Riesenberg had the entire wardroom condemned for a bedbug infestation (he had all the officer bunks thrown overboard), and they encountered a hurricane which speeded their homeward voyage. The *Newport* reached New London on October 3rd. Riesenberg then sailed the ship to Glen Cove, exulting that he had not "spent a cent on towage."

Back at home, the ship got the care she needed. For the first half of 1924, the *Newport* was taken by the Navy for refitting. The boilers were fixed, as well as most of the other recommended repairs. The cadets, in the meanwhile, were housed on a cruiser, the U.S.S. *Pueblo*. Reginald Fay, now Chairman of the Board of Governors, happily reported that, "the *Newport* has been thoroughly overhauled at the expense of the Navy Department and is now in very good condition and will probably not need any extensive repairs for several years."

IRREGULARITIES AND MALADMINISTRATION

While the *Newport* was away on the cruise of 1923, Arthur Tode had not been idle. He and another former officer, Charles H. Clarke (class of 1876), prepared charges against the school. The final report Tode submitted to Governor Al Smith consisted of 147 pages of thirteen separate allegations against the Board of Governors and Riesenberg. There were also testimonials citing Tode's abilities and character. Clarke, for his part, sent a separate letter to the governor complaining of irregularities at the school.

Most of Tode's charges were petty and focused on his desire to reclaim his reputation. But the whole affair divided the alumni into Riesenberg and Tode factions. Tode and his supporters made such a stink, that in February of 1924 the Education Department called a hearing to settle the matter.

At the hearing, Tode used hearsay, rumor and innuendo to accuse Riesenberg and the Board of Governors of favoritism and harassment. Tode nitpicked, and though some of his charges were true (such as Riesenberg's purging of Baylis-era crew) most were regarded as frivolous.

Clarke's accusations were more substantive. He served as a logistics administrator for the schoolship and had access to financial records. He identified problems regarding the "Clothing Fund."

This fund was an account where students deposited $130 to pay for uniforms and other necessities before entering the school. Yet the cost of all these items amounted to $107.50. The balance of $22.50 allowed the account to build up over time. In addition, students were entitled to a refund of their money upon graduation. Students who did not graduate were not given the refund, thus allowing the account to build up even more. By 1924, the accrued money allowed the Board of Governors to hire a new secretary and to commission paintings of the *St. Mary's* and the *Newport* for $250 each.* Clarke thought these were unnecessary expenses, and that the Board was using the money as a slush fund.

Clarke's second charge was that the school bolstered graduation rates by granting diplomas before students completed the two year course. Riesenberg insisted that it was only one or two months early and the students were not "graduated until they had passed our examination and qualified."

---

*These paintings, by Charles Robert Patterson, are housed in the administrative offices of Fort Schuyler.

The hearing led to a confidential investigation by the Board of Education. Tode wanted to know what was going on and sent repeated inquiries to Governor Smith and the Department of Education. He wrote to the Chairman of the Ways and Means Committee of the New York State Senate and the Speaker of the New York Assembly, insisting that no funds should be given to the school. He also wrote to the Secretary of the Navy to inform him of the school's "maladministration."

In late March 1924, Tode received a letter from the Education Department. It stated that as a result of the investigation there would be a closed hearing that Tode could not attend. Tode typed off an irritated letter. The Education Department assured Tode that no charges regarding him were to be taken up: "It seems to have reduced itself merely to a question of administration and not to one of specific complaints about individuals."

It is hard to say if the Board of Governors was acting as improperly as Clarke and Tode charged. Certainly, there was a lack of control over the school, and the Board of Governors was not subjected to any regulatory body. It would be easy for them to graft money. But it seems more likely that Tode's charges were trumped to create a brouhaha and shift blame for *Newport*'s condition as far away from himself as possible. Clarke's motivations were unknown. He had respect for Riesenberg, describing him a gentleman. Maybe Clarke was just an honest man.

Tode meticulously preserved all his correspondence on the matter. He had a great love for his *alma mater* and resented how he was forced to resign. He felt exiled but made the best of it by focusing on accomplishment. In 1926, he became the first marine engineer to be granted a Professional Engineer's license. He helped found the U.S. Propeller Club, whose purpose was to support the Merchant Marine. He served as the Marine Superintendent in New York for the Texas Company from 1926 to 1931. Tode also wrote numerous technical publications. Eventually, with dignity in hand and a slew of shiny certificates, he reconciled with the school and headed the Alumni Association in 1929. The next year, he joined the Board. We have not heard the last of Arthur Tode.

As for Baylis, he became Captain of New York Port during World War II and was eventually promoted to the rank of Commodore in the Coast Guard. He also became associated with a terrible tragedy when he was the captain of the destroyer *Paulding*. On December 17, 1927, while searching for rumrunners near Provincetown, Massachusetts, his ship accidentally collided with the Navy submarine, *S-4*. The submarine quickly went to the bottom, and Navy divers found six men alive (out of a crew of 40) in the forward torpedo room. Yet any rescue effort was hampered by a powerful storm that nearly killed two divers in the wreckage. The Navy had no choice but to stop rescue efforts until the storm abated. When it did, the six men aboard the submarine were dead having run out of breathable air. A Navy Court of Inquiry blamed Baylis and the late submarine commander jointly for the disaster. Baylis, with his career on the line, was defended by the Coast Guard and eventually exonerated.

The sinking of the *S-4* dominated national news at the time. Baylis received all sorts of letters from fellow alumni and friends offering their support. One of these was from Felix Riesenberg. The raw feelings of 1923 had faded.

Riesenberg stayed on as superintendent through 1924 claiming to have never again put the ship through "more than ordinary jeopardy." The 1924 cruise was without incident, except that Doctor Herbert L. Bridgman, journalist and member of the board of Regents, died while observing the schoolship for the Education Department. Upon their return to New York Riesenberg resigned because, as one alumnus wrote, he "had enough trouble with Tode and the Board." He continued writing until he died of a heart attack in 1939.

THE FALL OF THE BOARD OF GOVERNORS

Riesenberg's replacement was Edward V.W. Keen, a decorated naval commander from World War I who graduated from the *St. Mary's* in 1900. He brought back the four-class system and two yearly graduations. However, more fundamental change was ushered in by the state legislature which strengthened the Education Department's control of the school, probably due to fallout from the Tode-Riesenberg affair. Most of the Board's powers were transferred to the New York Education Department's Board of Regents. The Board of Governors was renamed the Board of Visitors and was, by law, responsible for advice.

In 1925, the Education Department dealt with some of Clarke's charges. It placed a representative on the Board of Visitors and instituted changes. These reforms required monthly audits, students attendance for a full two years and proper educational credentials for instructors.* The reforms also

---

*This left Riesenberg's executive officer, Boesch, who had assumed temporary command and wanted the superintendent's job, out. Boesch had a limited education, and the Commissioner of the Education Department would not appoint him. There might have been personal tension as well, since the Commissioner would not appoint Boesch even after he promised that he would take the required courses.

facilitated communication, since the superintendent was now required to be present at Board meetings when not at sea. He also had to sit for monthly meetings with the Board's secretary.

The end result of these changes were that it weakened the Board's influence, strengthened the position of the superintendent and made the Education Department the ultimate arbiter in the administration of the school. The Board of Visitors, while it still exerted considerable influence in the school's affairs, was no longer directly responsible for the day to day administration of the New York State Nautical School, this fell to the superintendent.

In addition to the Education Department's influence, the Navy began to insist that the superintendent had to be an active or retired Navy or Coast Guard officer and not just a member of the reserve force. They argued that since the ship was the property of the Navy, then the vessel needed a commanding officer associated with that service. The Board resisted the request and insisted that the superintendent should be an alumnus merchant mariner. They took up a resolution on June 10th, stating that they will not consider the appointment of a Naval Officer.

Keen was recalled to the Navy in 1927. However, he remained active with the school and became a member of the Board of Visitors. Thomas Sheridan, the cadet-thrasher, tendered his application, and the Board of Visitors recommended him on May 6, 1927. But the Navy insisted that a Naval or Coast Guard officer must be appointed. The State Education Department sided with the Navy. Grudgingly, the Board resolved:

> That this Board, while it holds its position to be correct, sound and for the best interest of the school, yet, rather than hamper the work of the School, and delay the cruise, is willing to acquiesce in the appointment of a satisfactory Navy Officer at this time, and will use its best efforts to have the policy of the Navy Department changed or declared unauthorized.

Keen's replacement was not the Board's choice. He was neither a merchant mariner nor an alumnus which broke the policy set by Jacob Miller's Board of Governors 14 years earlier. The new superintendent, James Harvey Tomb, was a retired Navy captain who was to become the most transformative head the institution ever knew.

CHAPTER 9

Coming Ashore

"We haven't time for sails anymore. . . . Sails just get in the way."
—Captain J.H. Tomb, 1931

In 1927, flappers were in fashion, and Prohibition was lax. New York was a burgeoning center of commerce and culture. The Holland Tunnel opened connecting New York to New Jersey bringing in a swarm of visitors to the city. Many of the first generation bridge-and-tunnel set found themselves going to the newly opened Roxy Theatre, a 5,920-seat movie house mecca on 50th Street between 6th and 7th Avenues.

Everything in New York seemed bigger than life. That May, Charles Lindbergh flew his famous non-stop flight on the *Spirit of Saint Louis* from Roosevelt Field on Long Island to Paris. Then that September, Babe Ruth hit his 60th home run on the last day of the baseball season at Yankee Stadium. Ruth and the rest of the Yankee's so-called "Murderers' Row," went on to crush the Pirates in the World Series 4 games to 0. Lucky Lindy and the Babe were toasted all through the town. Business dominated, and few foresaw the economic collapse that would strike at America's soul two years later.

"A SEA-DOG OF THE DOGGIEST TYPE"

To those aboard the *Newport*, the city seemed to swell around their ship as she was docked near the Statue of Liberty at Bedloe's Island. It certainly felt that way for the portly, cigar-chomping man who made his way to the schoolship on June 29, 1927. He looked like a bulldog with a puffed face and squinty eyes—and he was just as tough. James Harvey Tomb was joining the *Newport* as her superintendent.

Chairman Reginald Fay and the rest of the Board of Visitors did not welcome Tomb. He was an outsider from the Navy who had no previous connection to the schoolship. Tomb was born in St. Louis to a father who was a prominent Confederate Navy engineer. He followed in his father's footsteps (albeit not for the Confederacy) and graduated from Annapolis in 1899. After a lengthy career in which Tomb took part in the Spanish-American War, the Filipino Insurrection and the Boxer Rebellion, he retired from the Navy in 1926. He then briefly served as the Marine Superintendent of the Panama Canal before becoming the head of the New York Nautical School. At age 50, he was starting a second career, and he soon proved his value to the Board of Visitors.

Though he was not a merchant mariner, Tomb embraced his new position with gusto. "He's a sea-dog of the doggiest type . . ." one newspaper reported, "tall, heavy-set, red-cheeked and with a voice like a fog horn. He went through Annapolis and did his stuff in the Navy, and he's the fightingest enthusiast for the merchant marine you ever saw."

Tomb also had patience and an ironic sense of humor. It was a good fit for nautical education. Cadet Edward "Nick" Carter referred to him as "Blubby."

> . . . several of us were detailed to remove [a] safe from the skipper's [Tomb's] office. . . . We got the [safe] up on the spar deck via the cabin skylight and a tackle on the spanker boom and were waiting for the new one to be delivered. Amusing ourselves while waiting, one of the boys played 'Jimmy Valentine' with the combination dial, and to the surprise of all, the tumblers fell and the door could be opened. Just at that instant 'Blubby' came on deck and while we shivered at the thought of what would happen to us, he merely commented, 'That proves that I needed a new safe.'

"SAILS JUST GET IN THE WAY"

Tomb was not attached to tradition. He wrote, "American merchant marine literature is rich in the splendid exploits of our sailing vessels and decidedly scant in steam or motor, thereby creating a tendency to live too much in the past and to stick to obsolete training. Our marine schools have never been abreast of the times."

To bring the school up-to-date Tomb had three goals. First, he wanted to make the name of the school sound more elite. Chairman Fay thought this was an excellent notion since it would "eliminate the reformatory idea which still clings to the . . . schoolship. . . ." Fay and Tomb pushed the matter through to the State which passed a law which renamed the school in 1929 to the New York State Merchant Marine Academy (NYSMMA).

Second, Tomb wanted a new training ship. The *Newport*'s design was obsolete. In a newspaper interview Tomb said, "We haven't time for sails anymore. We have to teach our young men too many things in addition to seamanship. We have to teach them ship's business, maritime law, economics, a whole general education. Sails just get in the way."

Governor Franklin D. Roosevelt proved to be an indispensable ally in acquiring a new vessel. He sent a letter to Charles Francis Adams, the Secretary of the Navy, stressing the poor condition of the *Newport* and the need for a modern ship. The Navy responded by offering the *Procyon*.

The *Procyon* was built in response to a shortage of merchant vessels during World War I. The ship, like others in her class, was a "hog islander" which was slang for where it was built—in a shipyard set up at Hog Island, outside Philadelphia. She was a modern vessel in all senses, entirely powered by steam, and much larger than the *Newport*.

But then the Navy got cold feet and became reluctant to assign the ship to a state institution instead of a federal one. To placate the Navy and get the ship, Roosevelt got a law passed that allowed out-of-state boys to attend the school provided that they pay tuition and board. This satisfied the Navy, and they agreed to refit the ship which was given to the school in 1931. It was renamed the *Empire State*.

Tomb's third and most important goal was to acquire a permanent shore base for the school. When he first saw the *Newport* on Bedloe's Island, he was "much impressed with the lack of modern facilities available. The schoolship [was] berthing at an old wooden pier badly in need of repairs."

In fact, by 1929 the pier at the island had become "shoaled up," preventing the *Newport* from docking. Tomb relocated the schoolship to the Brooklyn Navy Yard. In the meantime, a stopgap measure in lieu of a shore facility was made with the $6,000 purchase of a schooner hulk named the *Guilford D. Pendleton*. The vessel, renamed the *Annex*, was converted into a floating classroom and dormitory. Tomb thought the *Annex*, was a "godsend but inadequate." Conditions were unhealthy, ". . . colds, flue [sic] and pneumonia were common. . . ."

Furthermore, Tomb firmly believed that a land base was critical toward the success of the school. He wrote:

> Modern life at sea is different from that of the old days. Food is now good, living quarters are ample and sanitary, discipline although strict is fair and humane, and pay is four times what it was in 1900. American boys are now attracted to the sea. No longer, therefore, must we depend on foreigners to officer and man American ships. To meet the changed conditions, however, requires much more than a modern training ship for this academy.

Tomb began a search for a location that could serve the NYSMMA. The site had to be cheap as well as have land and sea facilities. To find a large lot of cheap waterfront property in New York City was no small feat. But there was one promising candidate, the federal property of Fort Schuyler on the Throggs Neck peninsula in the Bronx.

FORT SCHUYLER

Fort Schuyler was an obscure location with a little-known history. The site was selected by the Army Corps of Engineers as part of the "Third System" of coastal defenses in the wake of the War of 1812. They recognized the tactical value of placing a fortification at Throgg's Neck, where the East River met Long Island Sound. With another defense at Willet's Point in Queens (the future Fort Totten), they believed it would provide adequate crossfire against enemy ships approaching New York City from its northern approach.

The plan to buy the property at Throggs Neck after the War of 1812 was not without debate. One opponent to the project was New Jersey Senator Mahlon Dickerson. He argued that to build a fort at Throggs Neck would "throw away our money," since any enemy fleet attacking New York from that direction would be stopped by "the whirlpools of Hellgate." He said a small battery of guns could be quickly put in place near Hellgate to check any approach. Dickerson may have been right, but the desire to construct coastal fortifications was strong enough that the government approved the plan to buy the property.

Colonel Joseph Totten of the Army Corps of Engineers negotiated the purchase of the property. This was not without incident as local landowners insisted on selling for higher prices than the assessment value. By 1828, he bought the last piece of the property from Charles H. Hammond for $15,000 ($4,500 more than the appraisal price). However, Totten had forgotten to purchase the right of way onto the property. The government paid Hammond $2,000 more for the right.

The Army Corps of Engineers began construction in 1833. Due to supply problems and labor difficulties, work was slow. The fort, which was named after New York politician Philip Schuyler, was not ready for occupation until 1856 at a total cost of $740,000.*

During the early years of the Civil War, the fort was used as a staging area for Union troops. Regiments like the New York Volunteer Infantry Regiment, known as Duryee's Zouaves, mustered at Fort Schuyler for training before heading to battlefields in the South. Later, a Union hospital, named McDougall General Hospital, was built on the property and the fort was reconditioned to house up to 500 Confederate prisoners of war. After the war, the fort eventually became a backwater post that spawned little interest aside for an urban legend about a tunnel running from it to Fort Totten under Long Island Sound.** The fort was never fired upon in anger, and the soldiers spent more time getting into trouble at local saloons than waging war. By 1911, the post was obsolete and the garrison reduced to eleven men.

For these eleven, Fort Schuyler was a dream assignment since the sergeants in charge and the soldiers under them had complete access to the beach and private residencies. The guns were still operational. One of the sergeants commented, "They are ready right now for any emergency. The only thing being missing is the gunners." A private who was interviewed by the *New York Times* said that Fort Schuyler was the most popular post in the army. The only things they were lacking were a lawn mower (since there were not enough men to cut the grass) and a brass band.

It was in this half-abandoned state that the deteriorating fort became a favorite outing destination. Day-trippers would make their way to the village

---

*There is a rumor that the fort was designed by Robert E. Lee, yet there is no primary evidence to support this. There is stronger evidence that he had more to do with the construction of Fort Totten.

**There is a great deal of speculation about the supposed tunnel in local newspapers and among those associated with the school. There is no evidence of its existence outside of rumor. The supposed tunnel was probably a sewer drain or a tunnel to control an electric minefield across the sound. In either case, all tunnels stopped at or just beyond the water's edge.

of West Chester and take the "most beautiful three-mile walk in the vicinity of Manhattan" to the ruins. The dilapidated fort also attracted the attention of the motion picture industry which used the location in the 1910s and 1920s to film movies that starred Mary Pickford, Gloria Swanson, Charles Ruggles, and Norma Talmadge. Scenes for *The Hummingbird*, *The Girl Habit*, *Wages of Virtue* and *Her Love Story*, were the beginning of a long tradition of film making at Fort Schuyler that in recent years has seen Martin Scorsese's *The Departed* with Leonardo DiCaprio and the 2014 *Spiderman* movie.

The army, however, had no practical use for the property, and in the late 1920s they contemplated putting it on the abandoned list. When word spread that some cheap waterfront property may become available, vultures gathered.

Fort Schuyler was brought to James Tomb's attention in 1928 by David Collins, an acquaintance he knew through the New York Yacht Club. Collins introduced Tomb to his father-in-law, railroad executive Leonor F. Loree, who happened to be the president of the New York Chamber of Commerce. With insider knowledge, Loree told Tomb that the Army planned on putting Fort Schuyler on their abandoned list.

The Board of Visitors, excited about the possibility of acquiring Fort Schuyler, wrote that it was an "ideal site" for a shore base. Fort Schuyler made good sense. Not only was it near to New York Harbor, but they would be able to get it for a fraction of the price compared to privately held properties along the waterfront. This was a serious consideration, since the budget of the school did not allow for real estate purchases.

Yet before negotiations began, the War Department removed Fort Schuyler from the abandoned list, planning to convert it into a military prison. With the property unavailable, the school continued to hunt for other locations. They examined sites in Queens as well as on Long Island at Lloyds Neck and Cold Spring Harbor, but these did not work out.

In 1931, the Army dropped its plan and once again placed Fort Schuyler on the abandoned list. According to Robert Caro, author of the monumental biography of Robert Moses, *The Power Broker*, this was done at the behest of Franklin D. Roosevelt, who prodded "the army to close the base and turn the land over to the state." The academy was one of his pet projects. In 1929, he wrote to the Secretary of War requesting that the Army grant a revocable license for the use of a portion of Fort Schuyler. The situation, however, grew more complex when the New York City Parks Department, under Moses, decided to try to obtain the entire property and convert it into a public park.

The reason for the Parks Department's interest was linked to the general expansion of parks throughout the city under Moses. When Fort Schuyler was listed as abandoned, the Parks Department was already negotiating to purchase and convert the property at Ferry Point, about a mile distant from the fort, into a marine park. The New York Parks Association, headed by Nathan Straus, Jr., got his marching orders from Moses, and in late December 1931 he identified Fort Schuyler as an excellent supplement for the Ferry Point project that could be obtained for minimal cost.

THE BATTLE OF FORT SCHUYLER: ROUND ONE

On June 4, 1932, the War Department notified Congress that they were ready to give up Fort Schuyler and issue a five-year lease. The War Department recommended dividing the property between the NYSMMA and the Parks Department. The academy would receive twenty acres at the tip of the Throggs Neck peninsula, including the actual fort, and the Parks Department would receive the other thirty. Tomb accepted the War Department's proposal, happy to get any cheap shore side property. Yet Moses, via Straus, rejected the proposal and laid claim to the entire property. The fight was on.

Some business interests, such as the Bronx Board of Trade, sided with the NYSMMA. It stated, "By having the academy located there, the Bronx would gain worldwide fame and at the same time will provide the State Merchant Marine students with a suitable site for their land activities." The Bronx Chamber of Commerce, which was initially in support of the academy, changed its stance when it acquired a new head in George F. Mand. He explained that to share the property with the academy would be, "depriving residents of this needed park space—when there are so many sites for the academy and none that are suitable for parks." Besides, he said the NYSMMA was "being offered the best portion of the land . . . ," right at the end of the peninsula.

Shortly after Mand's comments, Straus started a campaign to win public support for a park. On June 24, 1932, he went to Fort Schuyler and addressed a meeting of representatives from 36 civic and welfare organizations:

> A few well-meaning, well-intentioned people want to take these fifty-two acres, the finest waterfront peninsula in the greater city, to train a few boys to become officers and sailors in the merchant marine. They want to take this land from the people of one of the most rapidly growing sections of the

city to be used by from 300 to 400 boys a year. If this land is made a park it will be used by from 300,000 to 400,000 people every week-end during the summer months.

Straus stated that building a park would correct the "City Fathers of past generations, who left the children of sections of the lower east side to bake through the summer months in parkless miles of pavement and stone."
Tomb felt that Straus's argument was disingenuous:

> The campaign was not fair as Mr. Straus concentrated the attention of the public on the lack of park facilities on the Manhattan lower east side, where parks for the poor were badly needed. The distance from the slums of the lower east side to Fort Schuyler is 17 miles via subway and bus, round trip fare 20¢ per person, taking 3 hours for the round trip. Transportation to the large Pelham Bay Park, reached by the subway, costs only 10¢ round trip. One-sixth of the total area of the Bronx, including streets, was in parks, an area out of all proportion. . . .

Meanwhile, Mand wrote a letter to Roosevelt noting that the Bronx Park Commissioner came out in support of Straus's proposition. According to Tomb, Mand's letter was taken by Roosevelt's secretary, without his knowledge, and brought to Robert Moses. Moses drafted a letter of reply that was favorable to the parks. Roosevelt then signed this as a matter of course without realizing what content was in the response. The letter read:

> I agree with you that this would be a most desirable location for a shore-front recreation area and that it is much more important to use this area for municipal recreation purposes than to make it the headquarters for the New York State Merchant Marine Academy, which can be well taken care of with a smaller and cheaper piece of land somewhere outside of the city limits.

Park proponents used this letter to bolster their cause. When Roosevelt found out what happened, he ordered his secretary to give all Fort Schuyler correspondence to the State Education Department. The matter became muddier when Roosevelt then announced his support of the compromise as originally proposed by the War Department where the Parks Department would share the property with the NYSMMA. Roosevelt did not disclose the details of the prior letter mishandling—it was too embarrassing.

In the summer of 1932, maritime interests vigorously argued for the academy. Emmett J. McCormack, the president of New York's Maritime Association, cited the necessity of a well-trained merchant marine:

> . . . the value of our merchant marine, for defensive purposes in case of war, is largely conditioned upon the efficiency of its officer personnel, and it is only through such institutions as the New York State Merchant Marine Academy, properly equipped and maintained, that this can be provided.

Mand retorted:

> . . . it is not clear to us why [the Maritime Association has] not heretofore interested themselves in that neglected institution, but we believe the people of the Bronx will resent having the [Maritime] Exchange tell them what their public recreational need is or should be. No community can have too many parks, and we only have to look around Manhattan to verify this statement.

Straus supported Mand by stating:

> The Merchant Marine Academy has an enrollment of 135 students. The total appropriation for the Merchant Marine Academy in the New York State budget for 1932 is $85,365. The United States Government contributes $25,000 . . . Moreover, the expense of keeping in repair the *Empire State* . . . amounted last year to approximately $70,000. The total cost, therefore, to maintain the academy for one year is in excess of $180,000. This means that the cost to the taxpayer of graduating each student after a two-year course is more than $1,200.

Straus added that there were limited job opportunities for merchant mariners. He cited the U.S. Shipping Bureau: "[the] number of licensed merchant marine officers available exceeds the maximum possible number of jobs in the ratio of two and one-half to one."

As an alternative for the NYSMMA, Straus suggested Clason Point, just to the west of Ferry Point. He noted that it could be obtained for $220,000 with a down payment and the rest paid when the funds became available. But neither party was willing or able to obtain Clason Point. Tomb wrote, ". . . the State would not assume the great expense for such a purchase."

Some newspapers took sides, and those that did usually supported the Parks Department. The *New York Times* wrote, "It can hardly be disputed that the city needs the Fort Schuyler reservation for a park. . . . There is very little land left for parks within the city. . . . The waters are as yet free from pollution, which cannot be said of some of the municipal bathing beaches."

The *Daily News* wrote, "Something similar to Jones Beach, on a smaller scale, could be worked out there."

The newspaper that gave the most consistent and ongoing support to Moses and the Parks Department was the *Bronx Home News*. In July, 1932, it editorialized:

> Fort Schuyler is the best possible location for a marine park in the Bronx. If the entire reservation is turned over to the City for park purposes, Bronxites will not have to go to Westchester County where . . . they are not welcomed any too cordially, nor will they have to travel to far-away beaches on Long Island.

Then important alumni from the school argued against a shore base. Chief among them was Thomas Sheridan and Felix Riesenberg. Sheridan stated:

> I think that those who favor an academy ashore do not fully comprehend just what kind of a career they are about to prepare the sea-seeking youth who would attend it. . . . The training and education should be done aboard a cruising ship, and therefore I think that if any governmental agency is going to do this the State training ship should. . . .

Sheridan added that by obtaining a land base, it would continue to increase the costs of the academy which might eventually lead to the dissolution of the school. These published views hurt the NYSMMA's cause and were used in editorials to question the assumption that a land base was even necessary.

According to Tomb, opinion swayed in favor of the Parks Department during the summer of 1932. Tomb blamed this on the fact that he was not in New York because of his responsibility to command the schoolship for the annual cruise.

THE BATTLE OF FORT SCHUYLER: ROUND TWO

Upon his return from the cruise, Tomb carried on the fight for Fort Schuyler, but increasingly the War Department was getting frustrated by all the local

Stephen Bleecker Luce (1827–1917), was an important advocate for the professionalization of maritime and naval training. His lobbying efforts resulted in federal legislation that enabled the creation of schoolships. Photo taken circa 1865.

Students of the New York Nautical School training in a boat. Circa 1900.

The sloop of war *St. Mary's* had a storied Naval career before being turned over to New York City to found its Nautical School in 1874.

The students of the *St. Mary's* wore traditional sailor uniforms often leading to trouble ashore. Circa 1903.

Ross Gilmore Marvin (1880–1908), shown wearing heavy gear for Arctic exploration. He joined Peary on his two expeditions to reach the North Pole.

The caustic Boatswain William M. Dreilick (1859–1932), taught generations of boys aboard the *St. Mary's* and the *Newport*.

Wells Field addressing the boys and public on the deck of the *St. Mary's* prior to the 1895 cruise.

Students of the New York Nautical School being inspected by Executive Officer Christopher Marsden, circa 1906. The new uniforms were donated by alumnus J. Hatzel and viewed as a sign of the growing dignity of the school.

The *St. Mary's* beached prior to its burning in 1908 at Point of Pines, Massachusetts.

Students running up the rigging of the *St. Mary's*. Circa 1903.

A student being taught how to use a sextant aboard the *St. Mary's*. Circa 1903.

The students of the *St. Mary's* used the gun deck as a place to eat, study, and sleep. Circa 1903.

The *Newport* was the New York Nautical School's second training ship. A gunboat, it served in the Spanish-American War.

Captain Lay Everhart (right) showing Richard Aldcroftt, Jr., the Chairman of the Nautical School Executive Committee, the *Newport* circa 1909.

Frederick S. McMurray and his officers. Left to right: Clarence D'alton (surgeon); C.E. Littlefield (executive officer); Thomas W. Sheridan (navigating officer); Frederick McMurray (superintendent); F.R. Nichols (instructor); C.H. Matthews (Chief Engineer). Circa 1915–16.

Desperate Plight of the New York Nautical School

In 1916, Louis Weickum drew this political cartoon to fight against the move to close the Nautical School by Governor Charles Whitman.

Felix Riesenberg (1879–1939), was an 1897 alumnus who became famous as a writer. He served as the superintendent of the school on two separate occasions. Circa 1920.

John Baylis (1884–1971), was a dignified superintendent who first introduced collegiate customs to the school and brought it to berth at Liberty Island. Circa 1922.

James H. Tomb (1876–1946), revolutionized the school through his successful efforts to obtain a land base at Fort Schuyler. Circa 1938.

The *Empire State I* at Fort Schuyler's pier with the *Annex* circa 1937. The *Empire State*, the former *Procyon*, was the institution's first entirely steam-operated ship. The *Annex* was a converted schooner used as a dormitory before the school came ashore.

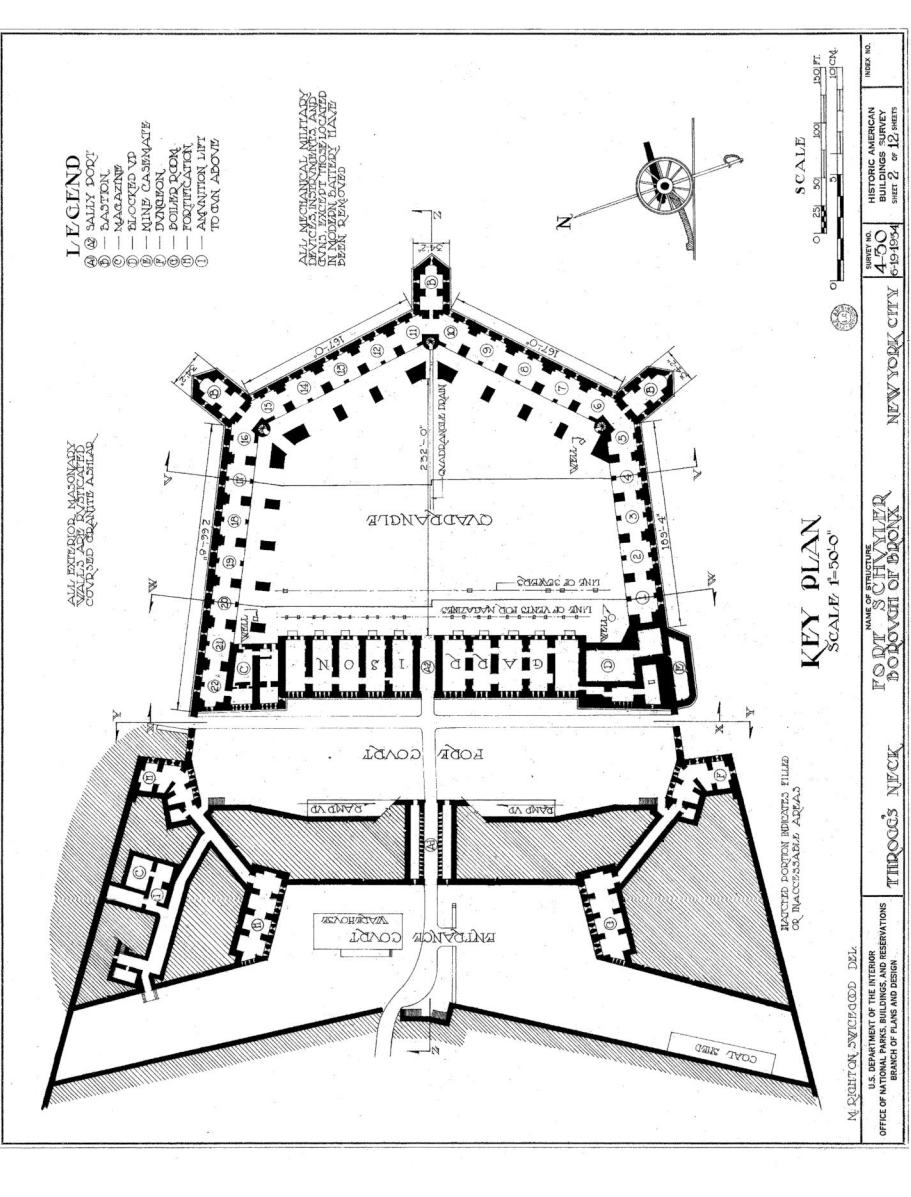

Fort Schuyler was built as part of the "Third System of Coastal Defense" in order to guard the northern sea approaches to New York City. Construction began in 1833 and the fort was ready for occupation in 1856.

Fort Schuyler was rebuilt for the school through New Deal agencies such as the Works Progress Administration. Circa 1937.

Fort Schuyler was dedicated for the school's use on May 21, 1938, the day before National Maritime Day.

Admiral T.T. Craven (1874–1950), was the first flag-ranked officer to head the school. He led the school during the World War II period.

Oath of Acceptance being administered to candidates for the October, 1946 class. Cadets of the NYSMA went through an accelerated 18-month program.

Arthur M. Tode (standing) and Lewis Wilson seated third from left, were the main forces behind the push for college status. Telfair Knight of the U.S. Maritime Service (seated 2nd from left) looks on. John Baylis far left, second row, seated. Circa 1940s.

Admiral Leary with Governor Thomas Dewey. Arthur Tode and Captain Olivet walking in background. Dedication of the *Empire State II*, 1946.

The *Empire State II* was the former *Hydrus*, an Artemis-class attack cargo ship. It served as a training ship from 1946–1956.

politicking. On August 19, 1932, the Secretary of War, Patrick J. Hurley, announced that his department did not have a preference as to who controlled the property, but wanted to know in advance what was to be done. New York, Hurley said, "was looking a gift horse in the mouth." Then Hurley warned that if they did not settle the affair, the War Department might take the land back.

In the fall of 1932, the NYSMMA's backers intensified their efforts. McCormack of the Maritime Association sent an open letter to Hurley writing that training the merchant marine had grown more complex since the 19th century, and that a land base was essential to instruct in engineering and terminal operations among other subjects. McCormack noted that private funds would be solicited to build up the school, "It is planned . . . with private endowment to provide these facilities. . . . This shore base is in line with marine school bases established in Germany, England, Japan and other countries where the necessity for such education is recognized."

Tomb, meanwhile, sought to enlist the support of the Navy by publishing an article in the *U.S. Naval Institute Proceedings*. He defended the need for a land base and advocated for the expansion of merchant marine officer training. Tomb likened the New York State Merchant Marine Academy to the federal military institutions, writing that no person would "dispute the value of the Naval Academy at Annapolis." Tomb wrote that well-trained officers were needed to "operate their ships with maximum economy and efficiency in the battle for foreign trade."

In November, a delegation of park proponents, including New York City Mayor, Joseph McKee, went to Washington for a conference with the War Department. The meeting went so badly that right after it, a representative from the War Department telephoned Tomb and asked if the academy could use the entire site. Tomb jumped at the offer and sought the Education Department's approval.

In mid-December, Hurley informed Mayor McKee that a five-year lease giving the grounds to the NYSMMA had been drawn up, approved, and sent by the War Department to Roosevelt for his signature. Yet the controversy was hardly over.

Roosevelt, now President-Elect, was a lame duck governor. Tomb was told to wait for Herbert Lehman, the Governor-Elect, to sign the lease. The new governor wanted to hold a public hearing on the matter. Tomb attempted, but failed, to arrange a meeting with him. It did not help that Lehman's brother was married to the sister of Nathan Straus.

Unexpectedly, and for reasons that are still not clear, Roosevelt signed the lease on December 29, 1932. Lehman grumbled in *The Bronx Home News* that "The signing by Gov. Roosevelt . . . was due to a misunderstanding, but all this can be straightened out."

There are two possibilities as to what happened. Roosevelt may have simply signed the lease in error, as he erroneously signed the letter that Robert Moses had drafted supporting the Parks Department the previous summer. Or, he could have signed it to spite Moses, who had become a major antagonist, a more likely scenario.

Regardless of why Roosevelt signed the lease, Lehman was determined to fight against the NYSMMA acquiring Fort Schuyler. To make matters worse, the State Education Department told Tomb that the lease Roosevelt signed was void since the New York State law which established the school, stipulated that it had to operate on board ship and did not provide for a shore base.

With the lease invalid and with the new governor's family connections to a leading park advocate, the outlook for the NYSMMA looked grim. But Tomb doggedly fought on. He realized that in order for him to win the fight for Fort Schuyler, he would need to stay in New York during the annual cruise. It was for this reason, that during the voyage of 1933, command of the ship on fell to the newly created position of Assistant Superintendent.*

THE *GUMERSINDO* INCIDENT

The first of these Assistant Superintendents was Lucien B. Green. Short-tempered, he was described by Tomb as "arrogant when administering discipline to subordinates." Even though Tomb was unhappy with Green, he was a good enough sailor that Tomb felt comfortable enough to stay in New York during the cruise of 1933—the first time that the Superintendent did not directly command the schoolship during an annual voyage.

Green's cruise started quietly enough. The *Empire State* sailed to Bermuda, then crossed the Atlantic with stops at Plymouth and Le Havre. At Le Havre, the ship was freshly painted and set out on a leisurely route to Gibraltar, doing circles to eat up time. They stayed off the major shipping routes.

On August 3rd the ship was still travelling its circuitous route, when warm wind from the west brought in rain and heavy seas. While the cadets

---

*This position would evolve to become the Commandant of Cadets.

conducted their drills, one of the watchmen spied a bulky, listless shape wallowing in the water. It was a ship's hulk with haggard men peering at the *Empire State*'s cadets in surprise.

Green hailed the ship. She did not have a radio, but the men signaled themselves as the *Gumersindo*, an 80-ton Spanish fishing trawler. There were twelve young bachelors aboard the vessel, all out of the fishing village of Bouzas, near Vigo, Spain. As was the practice, the ship had gone out with another vessel that was equipped with a radio, the *Maria*, on an eighteen day fishing voyage in Irish waters. But the weather became heavy, they separated, and the *Maria* radioed the *Gumersindo* as missing. As the lost trawler tried to make its way back to Bouzas, the sea tormented her. Deep swells tossed the ship about, and as the vessel took a deep dive the stern was lifted and the propeller fell out. Without a means of propulsion, wind and current blew the ship into isolated waters. When the crew of the *Gumersindo* attempted to anchor, they could not find a bottom and the anchor snapped off.

Since they had no radio, the *Gumersindo*'s crew could not call for help. They attempted to create ad hoc sails with their sleeping blankets but these were ripped away by the high, contrary winds. Then the fresh water they had grew foul. All they had to eat were the fish they had caught. To the crew of the *Gumersindo*, the appearance of the *Empire State* was an act of Providence.

Since the seas were heavy and the wind fierce, Green would not risk lowering his boats to rescue the *Gumersindo*'s crew. Rather, he decided to take the vessel in tow and make for Vigo. This was no easy operation and was educational for the cadets. First, the *Empire State* discharged oil that "served to quiet the sea to a great extent." This calming effect had a price since the strong wind blew it back onto the *Empire State*'s starboard side. The new paint job was ruined. The second part of the operation was more intricate:

> A small messenger line, supported at intervals by floats and about 100 fathoms long, was trailed over the stern of the *Empire State*, which then circled the *Gumersindo* close aboard and the *Gumersindo*, on drifting over the messenger line, picked it up and hauled over a towing hawser from the *Empire State*. This whole maneuver was made particularly difficult by the heavy seas running, the wind (which was blowing a gale), and the slowness of maneuvering the *Empire State* with its high sides. Also the heavy seas caused the *Empire State* to yaw considerably, preventing the ship from answering her rudder properly, even with the rudder hard over.

Despite the difficulties, the towing line was attached and they proceeded to Vigo. Meanwhile, water, food and other provisions were delivered via the messenger line. The *Gumersindo*, in thanks, sent back enough fresh fish to feed the cadets and crew of the *Empire State* for two days. Many years later, Cadet Frank Bell recalled that the fish dinners were some of the best seafood he'd ever eaten.

When the *Empire State* brought the craft into Vigo they received three "lusty" cheers of *vivas* from the rescued. To the surprise of the *Gumersindo's* owners, Green did not demand any salvage payment. Suitably impressed, the Presidents of the Spanish Federation of Fishing Vessel Owners sent a thank you note to President Roosevelt that stated "their heartfelt thanks for the disinterested assistance and rescue that the brave Commander, students and crew *Empire State* afforded our fishing vessel." In conclusion, they offered their respect to "the Honorable President of the United States and formulate their wishes that God may grant him long life for the good of North America."

THE BATTLE OF FORT SCHUYLER: ROUND THREE

Meanwhile, in New York, James Tomb carried on the fight for Fort Schuyler. He met with a sympathetic Bronx Board of Trade. That organization enlisted local support from William Peters, one of the major property owners of Silver Beach, a residential community next to Fort Schuyler. Through Peters' influence, the Throggs Neck Civic Improvement Association declared itself, ". . . definitely opposed to any move to convert [Fort Schuyler] into a public park." Mass meetings in support of the academy were held in Throggs Neck.

The people of Throggs Neck favored the academy for two reasons provided by Mayor McKee while he was arguing against the NYSMMA's position in 1933. McKee said the first cause was that, "Property owners in the immediate vicinity have expressed alarm at the prospect of huge assessments on adjoining property." The mayor's second reason was "that establishing a park . . . will lead to the intrusion of a lot of undesirable people."

Meanwhile, Peters' friend and New York State Senate majority leader, Democrat John Dunnigan, approached Lehman. He suggested creating a new law that would allow the NYSMMA to operate ashore, but not necessarily at Fort Schuyler.

But the legislative session dragged on and no action was taken to draft a bill. With only ten days left in the session, Tomb headed up to Albany. There, he met with Dr. Lewis A. Wilson to figure out what to do.

Wilson was a professional in the State Education Department with a long connection to the school. He started his career in 1911 as a vocational specialist and worked his way up to becoming an Assistant Commissioner of Education.* A warm and outgoing man, he was widely respected in his field. Wilson was especially known as a supporter and advocate for vocational and special education. He was the primary point of contact for the NYSMMA with the New York State government.

They decided that Tomb should draw up the bill that would allow the NYSMMA to operate ashore. Tomb did so with the assistance of the State Law Department and submitted it to a State fiscal review. By the time they gave their approval, there was only one week left in the legislative session.

Since time was so short, to introduce a bill to the legislature required a special message from Lehman. This was duly written. Tomb then asked Dunnigan to approach the Governor giving him the bill with the special message. He then warned him not to introduce it without Lehman's approval. Tomb then told Wilson what happened and assured him that "the bill would not be introduced without the Governor's approval and with [the] special message included."

Time dragged on. With four days left in the session, Dunnigan introduced the bill, but he did not confer with the Governor. It passed the State Senate and went on to the Assembly. The Assembly, however, halted the bill since they did not receive a message from the Governor regarding it. They telephoned Wilson and asked him to come over to clear up the matter. When Wilson arrived and was told what was going on, he said that the Assembly could proceed since the special message was on the Speaker's desk, attached to the legislation. Wilson had assumed, based on his earlier conversation with Tomb, that Dunnigan had gotten the Governor to approve the bill. The Assembly, not bothering to check, passed the bill.

Tomb wrote: "On learning of this situation the Superintendent wrote to the Governor giving him all the facts and assuming full responsibility." There is a question of the truth of Tomb's account. There was obviously some political gamesmanship over the bill, but the only detailed record we have of it

---

*Wilson would become the New York State Commissioner of Education from 1950–55.

is from Tomb, written a decade after the fact. In any event, Lehman, furious at being out-maneuvered, threatened to veto the bill. In late April, 1933, he called a public hearing to discuss the issue. At the meeting Straus made a strong case to a sympathetic governor.

Meanwhile, Tomb campaigned throughout the Bronx in a series of speaking engagements. Tomb, who never wrote a speech but spoke off-the cuff, found he had a talent for connecting with his audience. He spoke at American Legion Halls as well as other local civic groups. The Throggs Neck Property Owners Association gave firm support to the NYSMMA. Tomb was modest, and wrote a year later: "I am not much of a politician, but this work certainly has compelled me to get in the political game."

According to Tomb, it was R.J. Baker, the president of the American Steamship Owners Association, who finally convinced Lehman to sign the bill. Under Tomb's urging, Baker sent a long telegram to Lehman, Roosevelt and Dunnigan insisting that the Governor sign the bill. Baker emphasized that the bill only enabled the school to search for a shore base *somewhere*, not necessarily at Fort Schuyler. Lehman signed the bill.

Lehman was clear that he was not giving up on the idea of a park at Fort Schuyler, "This bill is merely permissive. It does not specify any particular site or lease. It does, however, place the State in the position of securing a shore base for the Merchant Marine Academy. . . ."

All that remained was for the War Department to compose a new lease since the Roosevelt one was invalidated. Park advocates used this opportunity, one last time, to lobby the War Department to compose a lease that was favorable to them. But the War Department, thinking in terms of national defense, and because the new Secretary of War, George Henry Dern, was a Roosevelt appointee, drew up a pro-NYSMMA lease. The school was allotted the entire property, and New York State could sublease about 30 acres for public purposes. By September, 1933 an agreement was reached after conferences with Lehman in which it was decided that a park would be built on the 30 acres. Robert Moses gave his approval to Lehman stating that it was, "a reasonable solution to the problem." The Governor gave his support to the school and executed the lease on March 22, 1934. Lehman took credit for resolving the controversy. The NYSMMA had a home for only $600 a year.

Popular historical memory has the Roosevelt lease as the charter that brought the school to Fort Schuyler, but it was really the Lehman lease.

Perhaps it is a fitting mistake. Roosevelt had always been a friend to the NYSMMA, while Lehman was, at best, a grudging supporter.

THE RECONSTRUCTION OF FORT SCHUYLER

With the land issue settled, Tomb's attention turned to the reconstruction of Fort Schuyler. From the start, all plans were hampered by a stipulation in the lease which declared that any changes to the Fort Schuyler property must be temporary—even the removal of trees was prohibited.*

Also, an inspection by Tomb identified several problems. Army buildings in the center of the fort had to be destroyed or relocated. But moving buildings was a problem since the entrances and exits into the fort were too narrow. But Tomb's chief concern was the need for a pier. The original reconstruction plan called for having a new dock in the same location as the Army's original, at the very tip of the peninsula, but this was impractical. Not only was the old wooden pier too small and flimsy to handle the *Empire State*, but building a larger dock at the tip of the peninsula would make it stick too far into Long Island Sound. It would endanger ships rounding Throggs Neck Point.

To build a pier would cost over $75,000. This sum would devastate the academy's budget—$117,200 in 1934. The NYSMMA could not get additional money from New York State for the project. Work stalled before it began.

But help came from an old friend and the Great Depression. With Franklin Roosevelt's ascension to the presidency in 1932, the federal government swiftly enacted the legislation of the New Deal. These programs, meant to avert and reverse the Great Depression, offered grants that could help develop Fort Schuyler. In this way, Tomb began reconstruction using the "Transient Division" of the Temporary Emergency Relief Agency (TERA). TERA surveyors and architects made formal plans that included converting the fort's casemates into dormitories and constructing a pier, classrooms, machine shops and heating plant.

As construction began, most of the direct supervision of the work fell to Tomb's Assistant Superintendent, Captain George W.R. Hughes, who replaced Lucien Green in 1934. Under Hughes, TERA cleared the fort of debris

---

*The lease literally stated that, ". . . the lessee shall cut no timber, conduct no mining operations, remove no sand, gravel or kindred substance from the ground, permit no waste of any kind, or in any manner substantially change the contour or condition of the demised premises."

and took down an old outwork stone wall that hindered the passing of moderate-sized equipment. In addition, workers began to remove the earth from the roof of the fort so that it could be waterproofed. The work was slow and laborious since heavy machinery could not be used. Laborers shoveled dirt by hand and loaded it onto trucks. Meanwhile, a temporary arch was made in the casemates so that some machinery, albeit not the large equipment they really needed, could enter.

The pier was a nagging issue. Despite the terms of the lease, Tomb worked to build a permanent dock. He wrote: "As it was to be a reinforced concrete pier there was nothing temporary about it." The War Department knew about his plan but helped the school anyway. Piles were driven in June, 1935 with an estimated completion date for that September."*

Progress was slower than anticipated. There was a lack of skilled workers and there were "weak sister supervisors." This alluded to a problem of work being done by the Transient Division of TERA. Most of these personnel were unemployed seamen who complained that they should not be constructing a school that would train competition. This issue was taken up by seamen's unions and protests were carried to Washington, DC. Administrators there dealt with the problem by removing the Transient Division. This had an immediate effect; by March, 1935, Hughes reported that the men were working at a 75 percent efficiency rate.

In the autumn of 1935, the work on the old fort was transferred to the federal Works Progress Administration (WPA) under a $1,752,270 grant. They began work in early December, 1935. Their workers completed the pier and the repairs that TERA started before moving to new construction they had planned.

As this construction was going on, Tomb asserted that there was a conspiracy to undermine reconstruction efforts. "The magnitude of the work at Fort Schuyler also disturbed WPA headquarters . . . ," he wrote. "A secret board of Army engineers investigated and recommended that the project be abandoned." Tomb suspected the local WPA coordinator, Victor Ridder, of conspiring against the reconstruction when he attempted to have the S.S. *Leviathan* assigned to the school instead of continuing the Fort Schuyler

---

*The actual completion of the pier took far longer due to the inefficiency of TERA, the takeover of the WPA, as well as ice floes during the winter of 1935–36. Work on the pier had progressed far enough by January 19, 1937 to allow the *Annex* and *Empire State* to dock at Fort Schuyler.

project. The *Leviathan*, a huge ocean liner of over 54,000 gross tons, would not have been able to pass under the East River bridges and more dredging would be required near Fort Schuyler to dock the ship there. Tomb estimated that to convert this ship for the NYSMMA's use would have cost more than $6 million up front and over $600,000 in yearly maintenance. Tomb dismissed the notion as that of a "landlubber," and all it did in the end was slow down the entire project.

Tomb received support from Colonel Brehon Somervell, the New York Head of the WPA, who wanted the project to proceed. Somervell removed Ridder from Fort Schuyler and conducted a new survey. In addition, new Bronx Borough President, James J. Lyons, co-sponsored the project and the WPA grant was increased to $2,972,272. With additional money and a friendly WPA on August 1, 1936, "real work started."

It was a huge project that employed over 1,000 men. At the height of reconstruction, up to 330 men worked in three shifts. Despite these efforts, progress was hampered because of the lease stipulations. The War Department refused to approve the removal of a spur of land close to the new dock and certain outworks of the fort because of their historic value.

An appeal was made directly to President Roosevelt by Governor Lehman. Roosevelt responded sympathetically but wrote, "In spite of my desire to help in every way I can, I find that the War Department has done everything that it is legally authorized to do, and I find myself without authority to direct any further concession."

Even so, Tomb had an academy to build and grew increasingly frustrated with the War Department. All construction moved at a crawl due to the necessity of obtaining permission from the War Department at every step. His frustration peaked in the fall of 1936 when he requested permission to cut through an outer curtain wall so that a road could be built for the use of needed equipment such as fire trucks and garbage wagons. He asked the War Department for permission to remove the wall. When they refused, Tomb dynamited the wall.

This was reported to the War Department by a dismissed employee. A firestorm erupted in which even Roosevelt wrote a letter to Tomb warning him not to blow up Fort Schuyler. There were conferences and inspections by the federal government. According to Tomb, "there was the deuce to pay." Yet the controversy gradually ebbed, and he stood doggedly by his actions: "Things had to be done in spite of the terms of the lease to enable construction work to be accomplished, and the Superintendent had to accept responsibility for authorizing the same regardless of the law."

LEASE RENEGOTIATIONS

The controversy over the wall, restrictions in the lease and a growing concern for future expansion compelled the NYSMMA to seek more space and acquire the grounds permanently. Tomb's fear was that a growing school would be too constricted within 20 acres. Specifically, Tomb wanted to have open space for drills and athletics.

The Department of Education approached Robert Moses and requested that the Parks Department cede 10 acres of land. According to Tomb: ". . . as soon as [the] request was made a most insulting letter was sent by . . . Moses to [Lewis Wilson] refusing the request." This letter is no longer extant, but it can be imagined what the contents were.

In the spring of 1937, Lehman pushed for Congressional legislation that would hand ownership of the site to New York State. This did not come to pass, however, since Roosevelt did not give his support. Probably under the advice of the War Department, Roosevelt wanted to retain the land as federally controlled. Also, the War Department had additional considerations since other states were monitoring the situation at Fort Schuyler, with an eye towards obtaining similar federal lands in their respective states. Instead of a transfer of ownership, Tomb managed to negotiate an extended lease. In the new terms, the wording was revised so that the purpose of the Fort Schuyler grounds "were for nautical purpose" rather than "chiefly for nautical purpose." Tomb wrote:

> If this is not eliminated the whole problem will be thrown into politics with Park Commissioner Moses of the City of New York stirring up political trouble. . . . As I understand it, the War Department is vitally interested in national defense and is strongly interested in national parks, but is not interested in municipal parks where the locality is supposed to set aside its own park area. Local parks are not a national problem but national defense is. . . . The claim would be made that we have the chief part of the reservation due to the fact that the fort is located on the academy area. It is considered that this question is most important and that it cannot be settled by throwing the matter back into politics.

The new lease was for 25 years with a 25 year renewal option and, perhaps most important, permitted new construction. This was a victory for Tomb. But he did not gloat since he knew that Moses was "very powerful politically and none of the State authorities care to oppose him." Lewis Wilson gingerly brokered a "gentleman's agreement" where the Parks Department could hold onto 20 acres at the western end. The NYSMMA took permanent control of the park territory during World War II for national defense purposes.

On Saturday, May 21, 1938, the day before National Maritime Day, Fort Schuyler was dedicated as the new home of New York State Merchant Marine Academy. The total cost of reconstruction was $4,250,000 in Depression-era grants, not including outlays made by the school in its regular budget. The struggles to obtain the site, as well as the construction efforts, were some of the most tension-fraught times in the institution's history.

In the 64 years that the school was based aboard a ship, there were at least four major closure crises. Since the move, there has been only one significant crisis that threatened the survival of the institution, and that was in the late 1990s. Fort Schuyler's stone granted the school a stability that made it a *bona fide* institution and landmark that could not be easily closed. Simply, it is much easier to sink a ship than a fort. But in choosing the shore, the school had made the irrevocable step of breaking with the culture of its past.

CHAPTER 10

The Federal Program

> *"The first and primary purpose is loyalty to America, to our merchant marine and to the academy. . . . There must be a spirit of mutual confidence imbued with the requirements of honor as exists at the U.S. Naval Academy, U.S. Military Academy and the U.S. Coast Guard Academy. Many think this system of mutual confidence of honor is of a military nature, but it is not. It is made up of ideals for service to our country whether we serve in the army, navy, coast guard, or merchant marine."*
> —James Tomb, Fundamental Principles Governing the New York State Merchant Marine Academy, 1936

FEDERAL INVOLVEMENT IN MERCHANT MARINER EDUCATION

When the NYSMMA occupied Fort Schuyler in 1938, it was the largest merchant marine academy in the nation. Captain James Tomb, flushed with success, wanted Fort Schuyler to be mentioned in the same breath as Annapolis and West Point. He anticipated and even wanted a federal takeover of the NYSMMA.

Since at least the time of Stephen B. Luce, there had been proposals that merchant marine training was a federal function. A 1930 questionnaire of various shipping companies and interests showed 80.9% of respondents in favor of a federal training system.

But until the 1930s, establishing a national training program was not possible since such training was popularly viewed as a state function. But this outlook changed, not least because of the Great Depression. The Depression saw an unprecedented expansion of the federal government through the creation of regulatory agencies and relief programs to deal with the economic crisis. Even Fort Schuyler was rebuilt for the NYSMMA through these programs. Attitudes changed. There was a greater acceptance of federal involvement in those tasks that were once reserved for the states. This included the training of the merchant marine.

In the battle to obtain and convert Fort Schuyler for the NYSMMA's use, Tomb had argued that merchant marine training was a federal function for national defense purposes. He expected that the government would use the ready-made academy at Fort Schuyler to be the centerpiece for a federal training program. In 1936 he circulated a memorandum entitled "*Fundamental Principles Governing the New York State Merchant Marine Academy.*" In it, he described how the institution was taking on the same status before the American public as the federal academies for the Army, Navy and Coast Guard. He introduced regulations that matched their honor codes, uniforms and rules of behavior. At about this time, cadets began to be referred to unofficially as "cadet-midshipmen," a term tying the students closer to federal service academies like Annapolis. The Board of Visitors, then under the chairmanship of Milan L. Pittman, unanimously adopted Tomb's principles. To further enhance the NYSMMA, Tomb and the Board of Visitors instituted a plan to expand the curriculum to three years with an eye on eventually offering college degrees. This was enacted in 1940.

Tomb had good reason to anticipate a tighter relationship between the NYSMMA and the federal government. He had worked closely with government authorities on the Fort Schuyler project, and President Roosevelt was a known friend to the school. In addition, the academy, in order to acquire the *Empire State* from the Navy, had to change its admission policies to officially accept out-of-state cadets.

Milan Pittman showcased the NYSMMA as a national entity. He wrote to the other state academies and suggested they adopt the same regulations as the NYSMMA. He recommended that they reserve half the berths at their institutions for out-of-state students and lobby for a $500 monthly federal subsidy per student. But it soon became apparent that the government's plan was not to adopt Fort Schuyler as a federal academy, but to create a separate program.

Congress passed the 1936 Merchant Marine Act. The new law built on preceding legislation which had begun to regulate the maritime industry since the early 20th century. Among its many provisions, the act created the five-man U.S. Maritime Commission which was charged, among other duties, to create a comprehensive training system for the merchant marine. To fulfill this, the U.S. Maritime Service (USMS) was created in 1938.

THE CREATION OF THE USMMA

The USMS began a wide-spread training program for both unlicensed and licensed mariners. Federal stations to train seamen in abbreviated three-month courses were established throughout the United States with some in New York. These non-officer schools, such as the training centers at Hoffman and Swinburne Islands, were organized in 1938 and complemented the NYSMMA. The next year, men were trained to be licensed merchant officers in a crash-course program at Fort Trumbull in New London, Connecticut. Since these seamen had no livelihood while enrolled at the station, they were given stipends of up to $125 per month.

In that same year, three federal Cadet Corps were created in San Francisco, New York, and New Orleans. Each federal cadet was paid $65 per month with uniforms, textbooks, and transportation provided by the government. The New York Corps brokered a deal with the NYSMMA in which they borrowed space at Fort Schuyler.

The authority of the national government over the merchant marine was accelerated by World War II. In 1940 there was increased anticipation of American involvement in the conflict. On June 30th the Maritime Commission was placed in charge of the state academies as a regulatory body acting as a liaison with the Navy. This was not to the liking of the state schools, which had previously maintained independent relationships with the Navy. Matters became more complicated as World War II approached. The Maritime Commission commandeered the *Empire State* in February, 1941. The ship made one last cruise and touched various Caribbean islands before returning to Fort Schuyler. In June, the ship was renamed the *American Pilot*.

Then the Maritime Commission disrupted the academies by issuing a memorandum entitled "Minimum Regulations" in September, 1941. It set graduation schedules, dictated the number and composition of men assigned to the schools' governing boards, established curricular standards and insisted that all communication between them and the U.S. government had to go through it. As part of its practice to achieve standardization, the Maritime Commission required the names of the various academies be changed to a similar format. As a result, in November, 1941, the New York State Merchant Marine Academy was renamed the New York State Maritime Academy (NYSMA).

After the United States entered World War II, the Maritime Commission was tasked to meet unreasonable personnel quotas for the merchant marine. According to Telfair Knight of the Maritime Commission, the entire training system was to turn out 100,000 unlicensed seamen and 25,000 officers to man 3,000 new ships. The NYSMA was given an initial yearly quota of 400 graduates. In order to meet the quotas, the Maritime Commission ordered a reduction in training time, eventually settling on 18 months, with two graduations per year. The three-year program at the NYSMA was over.

To Ralph Leavitt, the Chairman of the Maine Maritime Academy's Board of Visitors, all these changes were heavy-handed. They "virtually ignored the authority of the states to have anything to say relative to the running of their schools."

New training stations for seamen were opened at places like Sheepshead Bay, Brooklyn, commanded by *Newport* graduate George Wauchope. But the Maritime Commission's crowning achievement was moving the federal cadet corps from Fort Schuyler to the former Chrysler estate at Kings Point, Long Island. With that move, the Commission established the United States Merchant Marine Academy (USMMA) in February, 1942.

The state academies complied with all of the Maritime Commission's wishes since they were beholden to federal subsidies and due to the war emergency. Yet their support was tentative and soon turned hostile when the state academies realized that the Maritime Commission favored the federal training program over the states.

ADMIRAL CRAVEN

After the United States joined the war, the Navy placed Tomb on its active duty list. The Maritime Commission got the Navy to detach him from his duties at the NYSMA and order him to cross Long Island Sound to become the first superintendent of the fledgling U.S. Merchant Marine Academy.

Tomb did not go willingly. While he was an avowed advocate of federal merchant marine training, he had become a fixture at the NYSMA. In April, 1942, Telfair Knight wrote to Lewis Wilson, the Assistant Commissioner of Education who had been a key player in obtaining Fort Schuyler for the

NYSMA. Knight wrote that even though Tomb's "first loyalty" was to the NYSMA, the Maritime Commission "pointed out to [Tomb] that during the war time period the national consideration was of primary importance. . . ."

Tomb served as the USMMA's superintendent briefly and only during the development of the grounds at Kings Point. He retired in October, 1943 due to vision problems. Tomb served the rest of his career as a court martial judge before dying on September 23, 1946. He was buried in Arlington National Cemetery.

The USMMA named an athletic field after their first leader. At Fort Schuyler, a memorial plaque was hung within the Sallyport. But NYSMA's true monument to the head that brought them into the modern era are the walls of Fort Schuyler itself.

With Tomb gone, Telfair Knight tried to force the NYSMA to accept the Maritime Commission's choice for a replacement: Commander Charles Daniel Schutz, a former Superintendent of the Pennsylvania Maritime Academy who had worked at the New York Nautical School. He was also the Assistant Superintendent of NYSMA since George Hughes was stricken with a heart attack. Notwithstanding any opinion about Schutz, Tomb and the Board of Visitors, which was now headed by Arthur Tode, were sick of federal meddling. Tomb wrote a letter to the Board recommending that the NYSMA be headed by a retired flag officer since the academy was growing and a Navy Indoctrination Center was being built on the property. The Center, which was to train Navy Reserve Officers, was initially placed under the command of the superintendent. He provided a list of potential candidates—all admirals.

Tode wrote back to Knight telling him that the NYSMA would not accept a Commander as its head. "It was felt that the prestige of the Academy required a high ranking officer to be in command," Tode wrote. If the USMMA had Captain Tomb, then the NYSMA would accept no less than an admiral.

The Board consulted Tomb's list and tapped Vice-Admiral Thomas Tingey Craven. Born in Vallejo, California, Craven came from a venerable Navy family and graduated from Annapolis in 1896 where he was active in football and crew. He fought in the Spanish-American War before coming to the New York Nautical School where he worked as an officer aboard the *St. Mary's* in the early 1900s. After this stint, he served in a number of commands at bases and aboard ships. By the time he retired in 1937, he had earned a host of medals including the Chinese Double Dragon, French Legion of Honor, the Navy Distinguished Service Medal and the Italian War Cross.

At 68, Craven was elderly for a superintendent. But getting a more youthful head was impractical while the country was at war. The Board planned to have Craven serve for the duration of the conflict and then replace him. Lewis Wilson said that they could "later seek a younger man to take over the strenuous duties."

The age bias against Craven was unfounded. He was highly active and energetic and nicknamed "Tough Tommy" and "Turn To." Whenever he took up a command, he would tell his new supply officer, "You feed 'em. I'll work 'em." He told the Board, "I do not prefer to be idle in times like these, and I definitely want to be of service, where best I can be. I would be glad to go over to your Academy at Fort Schuyler and do what I can."

Due to Craven's age and rank, the position of Assistant Superintendent was transformed into the Commandant of Cadets. The commandant was given direct charge of the students. The first commandant was none other than Charles Schutz, the man who Knight originally recommended for Craven's job.

The white-haired Craven had a commanding demeanor which compensated for his uninspiring height. His true strength was in his relaxed, but humorous, disposition with a genuine commitment to improving life for the students. He pushed for the development of extracurricular activities at the NYSMA. He helped organize a glee club, sports teams and a school newspaper called the *Boson's Pipe*.

Cadet Phylipp Dilloway was in the campus tailor shop at the old armory when he spied the Admiral's uniform lying about. The temptation was too great for Dilloway, so he tried it on. Just as he was admiring himself, Craven walked in. The admiral asked, "You like that, son?" To this, Dilloway replied in the affirmative. Craven commented, "Well maybe one day you'll get to wear one."

"ENTIRELY INADEQUATE"

During World War II, obtaining a new training ship proved to be impossible since all resources were mobilized for the conflict. Training vessels were shared by the academies. The Maritime Commission assigned to the NYSMA the older *Keystone State*, a 1,100 ton steamer that was a former training ship of the Pennsylvania Maritime Academy. The NYSMA cadets, in their 1942 yearbook, expressed their opinion about the ship when they first saw her:

None of [the cadets] had ever seen [the *Keystone State*], but hopes were high even though they knew 'she was a little smaller than the [*Empire State*].' With eager anticipation, one by one, they stepped from the bus and saw their coveted craft. Ugh! Oh! No! 'it couldn't be ours' rose the chorus. But alas! She was, and the best had to be made of it.

The *Keystone State* was only temporary. At Baltimore in August, 1942 the cadets transferred to the *Allegheny*. The NYSMA cadets likened the new ship to ". . . a snail leaving its shell for the wider expanse of a clam's crustacean enclosure."

Craven called the *Alleghany* "entirely inadequate" since the vessel did not have proper facilities to train deck cadets. In addition to these difficulties, the ship was used to train enlisted men of about the same age as the cadets. "That does not make for contentment," Craven said.

The Maritime Commission assigned the *American Pilot*, the former *Empire State*, to the school. But the NYSMA had to simultaneously share the ship with the Massachusetts and Maine academies. Craven said that although the cadets from the different schools got along well, there was "looseness and lack of coordination." Craven acknowledged that although the ship sharing plan was not "entirely satisfactory," the war prevented changes. Telfair Knight expressed his regret for the situation but asserted that it could not be helped. He said that the Maritime Commission's extra ships that could have been used as training vessels had been sunk by U-boats. As the war continued, the ship-sharing formula was amended once more so that each academy would take turns using the ship.

At the outset of the war, the U.S. Army planned to take Fort Schuyler over as a deployment point, much as it had done during the Civil War. However, after negotiations, the U.S. Navy was allowed to take over the public park area of the grounds and convert it into a Naval Officer Indoctrination Center. Naval Reserve officer candidates flooded in and shared space with the NYSMA cadets at the fort. However, conditions became so crowded that within a few months, the WPA erected new buildings for the reservists that were used by the Navy for the duration of the war. Although the center was on the same grounds as the NYSMA, there was little interaction between the two and some cadets did not have much respect for the center. Phylipp Dilloway referred to the indoctrination center as the "90-Day Wonder School."

THE COAST GUARD DEBACLE

The arrival of Craven coincided with a confusing period for the state academies. In March of 1942, the entire training division of the U.S. Maritime Commission, which included the federal and state academies, was transferred to the Coast Guard in order "to expedite the prosecution of the war effort." Instead of having the Maritime Commission act as a liaison between the academies and the Navy, the Navy was removed from the equation altogether.

This was troubling to Craven who thought that the Coast Guard was going beyond its bounds. "It would be very unfortunate for the academy to lose its contact with the Navy," said Craven at a meeting of the Board of Visitors, "The Coast Guard is wrong in trying to look out for distant overseas affairs. The Navy has always considered it their duty to take care of the Merchant Marine Service."

Furthermore, the Coast Guard's administration was working against the state academies. The Commandant of the Coast Guard, Russell Waesche, had no great love for the state schools. In May of 1942, he circulated a policy statement which read that merchant marine training was "properly a Federal and not a State function."

The Coast Guard could not legally dissolve the state academies, nor could the federal government. But the government was still providing the state schools with training ships as well as a yearly $25,000 subsidy. The federal government could, theoretically, withdraw this additional funding if the state academies did not comply with its wishes.

A livid Lewis Wilson declared that the federal government was purposely discriminating against the NYSMA in order to grow the national program. The federal cadets were being subsidized by direct payments of $65.00 per month while the state cadets received nothing. "If the Federal Government is going to pay the young men at the [United States Merchant Marine Academy]... and provide instruction without cost," Wilson declared, "we might just as well consider that the New York State Merchant Marine Academy will go out of business."

The Coast Guard recognized the immediate short-term need. They promised state cadets $65 per month plus 75¢ per day for subsistence for the duration of the war and as long as they served in the Coast Guard Reserve. After the war, all bets were off, and the state academies could be subject to closure.

Yet this never came to pass. The state academies were unanimous in their opposition to being controlled by the Coast Guard, and the entire issue was reexamined. The academies found an unlikely ally in the Maritime Commission which also did not want to be under the thumb of the Coast Guard. The commissioner and the academies petitioned President Roosevelt, who on July 14, 1942, shifted control of merchant marine training to the War Shipping Administration (WSA).

This did little to placate the academies since the federal government was still advertising for and paying their cadets while the state schools were not. Due to this, and the perception of rough treatment on the part of the Maritime Commission, a meeting between all the academies was held in January, 1943 at the WSA's offices. There, it was agreed that state cadets would receive the $65 payments and $195 for clothing and books. The schools themselves would get $300 for every out-of-state student in attendance.

These payments were the first direct subsidy by the federal government to the state cadets. Establishing financial support was a significant precedent because it gave the federal government control over the state schools through money. The issue of federal dollars would be at the center of several controversies between the state academies and the federal government over the following decades.

Nor did the agreement relieve any tension between the representatives of the state schools and the Maritime Commission. At the 1942–43 American Merchant Marine Conference, much of this frustration was vented when Ralph Leavitt of the Maine Maritime Academy declared that the state schools' morale was "all shot to pieces, because they never knew what the decision was going to be from Washington, except that they could generally predict that the decision was going to be unfavorable." Craven, who was there, pointed out that the state schools "can't compete with the federal institutions in equipment, because they haven't the resources, they haven't the money, and can't establish the plant that they have at the federal institutions, and if the cadets that we graduate are going to compare in training and knowledge and experience with those turned out from federal institutions, and don't measure up to their standards, of course we are going to be discredited."

Telfair Knight assured the state schools that the federal training program had "no intention in peacetime of having more than 1,200 men at any time." These assurances were generally accepted, and since there was a war going on they agreed to cooperate.

With an accord reached, the state academies and the federal government cooperated under the WSA for the rest of the war. During this time, Navy personnel dominated the school. Craven noted that in 1942 the staff was composed of one Navy officer and six state officers; by 1945 there were 35 Navy versus six state officers.

There were other administrative problems. Craven complained that the state academies had to deal with the extra burden of dealing with more than one government. "I can't get enough typewriters or enough stenographers to handle the correspondence with the State and the different departments of the Government." His worst problem was finding "sufficient and proper instructors and assistants." Yet despite these hiccups, a remarkable program had been established at the NYSMA for the common war effort.

CHAPTER 11

Eighteen Months Before the Mast

"We shall be the first class from this Academy to be graduated into this, World War II. We have been rushed through a highly accelerated course and have not had the full advantages of extended cruises or an abundance of time to absorb the intricacies of much of our work. . . . The job that faces us isn't exactly an easy or comfortable one. We are going out to take supplies and troops to all parts of the world, and to bring back much-needed raw materials. We are proud of our heritage and way of life and mean to keep it just as it is."

—John C. Frothington, *Eight Bells*, 1942

CRAVEN'S HAVEN?

The once-abandoned fort bustled with activity. Young men clamored to enter the NYSMA's 18-month program in numbers that put the old Nautical School to shame. As the demand for merchant mariners grew, so did applications. In 1942, Congress lowered the draft age from 21 to 18. Worried parents seeking to shield their sons from war tried to send their kids to the NYSMA where they received a deferment from the draft during training. Parents hoped that sending their sons aboard vessels to transport war supplies was safer than entering the other services. Those who graduated the program received a commission in the Navy Reserve. Those who were not physically qualified to enter the Navy were given Coast Guard commissions.

In July, 1944, Admiral Craven reported how the NYSMA had been "overwhelmed with applications for entrance. Political as well as parental influences have kept us fully occupied, and naturally there has been dissatisfaction among those who were not accepted."

Between 1941 and early 1946, 920 cadets graduated from the NYSMA, which was greater than the total number of graduates during the entire interwar period. One source reported that the school was nicknamed "Craven's Haven for Draft Dodgers."

Parents who thought that the merchant marine was a safe option were mistaken. From a pre-war total of 55,000 American merchant mariners, training programs increased their number to over 215,000 by the war's end. Of this number, estimates vary from 5,662 to upward of 8,000 killed as a direct result of enemy action, reported missing at sea, collision, foundering or died in prison camps. In addition, there has been an estimated 12,000 wounded. Unfortunately, the government did not track the number of merchant marine dead as thoroughly as they did other service branches. Still, these numbers surpass the per capita death rate of any service branch with the possible exception of the Marine Corps. The job was by no means safe although the public was slow to recognize it. It was only in 1988 that merchant mariners were retroactively granted veteran status.

OFFICERS (IN A QUALIFIED SENSE)

The young men of the World War II generation were nicknamed the "Greatest Generation" in journalist Tom Brokaw's memorable book. The NYSMA graduates of this era formed some of the strongest bonds to their school of any period in the institution's history.

Aside from avoiding the draft, the NYSMA cadets learned a trade. Charles Strommer, an October, 1946 graduate, commented that the NYSMA's "program offered the best long term possibilities for after the war, because common sense said that if you did something constructive during the war, you would benefit after the war."

Young men like Strommer as well as his classmate, Phylipp Dilloway, often stumbled upon the program at Fort Schuyler. Dilloway first looked into the V-12 program which was a Naval officer candidacy course, as well as the V-5 program for Naval Aviation. He took the admissions tests for them but before he proceeded, a representative from the NYSMA came to his school.

Dilloway, who had grown up near Fort Schuyler and as a boy was a Sea Cadet, was attracted to the program, applied and after extensive interviews and testing was accepted.

Dilloway, along with all the other soon-to-be cadets, made a deposit of $250—no small sum at the time—and was given a list of gear to buy including two blankets and white shoes. Some items were rationed, so cadets were given stamps to obtain the harder-to-get items.

Even though the NYSMA cadets avoided being drafted into the service, they still entered into a boot camp and received military training with the expectation that they would be entering the war zone upon graduation. Dilloway and his fellow cadets came to Fort Schuyler and were hustled into *St. Mary's Pentagon*, the interior courtyard of the fort. They stenciled all their gear with their names as indoctrination began.

Dilloway's training occurred while the upperclassmen were away on cruise, which was limited to Long Island Sound due to the war. Rumors spread as to what would happen to the underclassmen when the ship returned. Dilloway noted that hazing, while not encouraged, was prevalent. One of his classmates, Leonard Weiss, confirmed this and added that there was "major hazing" and that the discipline was "strict as hell."

One 1945 graduate, with some pride, remarked many years later that the boot camp sequences in the movie, *An Officer and a Gentleman*, were "what we would call a 'fine young lady's Swiss finishing school' by comparison of what we had to do."

Hazing though was harsh only when compared to later practices, and it took the form of personal service and harassment. Since the Tomb administration, hazing had been controlled. When Charles Strommer spoke to his father-in-law, who was a cadet during the 1920s, the older man thought the hazing was acceptable compared to the physical abuses he had gone through.

Also, there was buy-in to the hazing by the cadets. The NYSMA was meant to train officers for a war situation and wanted to put their charges under serious stress. One 1945 graduate remarked, "If we were going to crack, it ought to be here, on land." Another said, "I didn't realize [the hazing] had a value because here we are 18 months through a rather intensive training program and you were dumped out there to actually be an officer, third in charge. The hazing taught you something . . . how other people look at you when you're beating on them. It was a valuable lesson."

Students dropped out because they couldn't take it. One alumnus commented that this was "good because you don't want them out there responsible for people's lives." Another graduate concurred. "We were fairly highly selected and we wanted everything to be shipshape, both upstairs and your body."

To get by, a cadet might choose to become a "cozy Mug." Generally, this term was for a cadet who flew under the radar by avoiding eye contact when possible and saying nothing but "yes sir." Dilloway thought of the expression as pejorative and

> ... lessened the importance or character value of the individual to whom it referred. A Mug who catered to the whims of an upperclassman in exchange for being 'left alone' was considered 'Cozy.' My observation was that the coziest of my classmates became the 'mug beaters' as first classmen.

Dilloway added that, "to cozy-off usually meant to find a place to hide from a work detail."

A different definition is offered by Robert Barr who was a self-admitted "cozy mug." Barr went through his entire third class period without a demerit. Barr said:

> This was my opportunity to break away and be something and get some great training. I was not going to be put on report and earn demerits and maybe lessen my opportunity to graduate. A cozy mug was a person who simply followed the rules, was quiet, didn't sound off, managed to get through the weeding out process, took a lot of demands and followed the discipline.

The hazing was mixed with the practical, physical training that had been the hallmark of the school. In addition, true military induction was added. Calisthenics were followed by close order marching.

Daily routine for the cadets was rigorous and demanding. Infractions were punished, as they were in the days of the schoolships, through extra duty, which took the form of all sorts of busywork. They were sometimes given the assignment to weed dandelions using a multi-tool. One cadet commented that such extra duty was "more or less of a degrading occupation for an officer (in a qualified sense)."

Fear was instilled upon the cadets by their drill master, George Riser. Riser was a short man (he wore platform shoes to compensate) with a rasping voice that demanded attention. Professor Fred Hess remarked that due to Riser's immaculate appearance and dress, he was a "model of sartorial splendor." He was also known for the idiosyncratic and salty mannerisms that he imparted to the cadets like a twisted Zen master. One cadet was advised by Riser before climbing a mast, "Now listen to me or you'll be splattered all over the deck." Another, recalled Riser saying, "A sailor without a knife is like a whore without a . . ." Riser left the statement unfinished. He'd chastise lazy cadets with, "If you bunch of lolly-gagging cadets don't get a move on you, I will tie yer tails into knots that even six whores couldn't undo with a fid."* If he really wanted to insult you, he'd call you a "farmer." Robert Barr remarked that Riser would put a cadet on report without hesitation. "If you smiled or even smirked in his presence, you were on report for insubordination." In one instance he castigated the class of 1947 for marching like a bunch of "scissorbills."** The name stuck, and that class has worn it as a badge of honor ever since.

By lunchtime, and especially after Riser was through with them, the cadets were exhausted. As they digested their meals, the officers played typical military educational movies. Dilloway said, "there was everything from Naval orientation on how to salute to getting on and off the ship to a lot of V.D. movies that put the fear of God into you and some things on elementary gunnery and seamanship and navigation." The cadets were so exhausted that they would fall asleep—even during the V.D. films.

Harsh discipline was not always universal. Arthur Murray told about how he and engineering cadet, John Green, were in charge of the underclassmen who cleaned the mess deck head. One morning, an underclassmen reported to Murray and Green that there were crabs in the toilet bowls. Green knew how to take care of the problem. He left and came back with a jar of gasoline. He poured it into the toilets, lit a match, and then tossed it in.

The resulting explosion was, ". . . a spectacular sight. A mushroom cloud of flame went up. . . . The toilet bowl, which was porcelain, went up."

---

*A fid is a conical tool made of wood or bone used in marlinspike seamanship.
**According to Bob Barr the term scissor-bill referred to a "lazy seaman." There are several definitions which are offered by dictionaries of slang which include "A nagging, gossiping and otherwise objectionable woman." (Partridge, Dictionary of Slang) as well as being the equivalent of a "scab," complainer, contemptible person, disreputable person, traitor, etc. (Berrey, American Thesaurus of Slang). The *Oxford English Dictionary* defines it as slang for "a foolish, incompetent, garrulous, or objectionable person." Which of these definitions Riser applied to the class of 1947 is unknown, but they are all amusing.

Fragments of porcelain scattered across the deck accompanied by ill-favored brown splotches.

General quarters was called. Obviously a bomb had been detonated. When it was discovered what happened, Murray and Green were put on report by Commander Guy DeSimone for destruction of government property. However, when they came before the mast and charges were read, DeSimone burst out laughing and the cadets joined in. Murray and Green were only given weekend restriction.

On the weekends, students would file into buses and go home to find out news about their friends who were fighting abroad. Often they were subject to looks and pointed questions. "Why are you around so much?" people would ask Phylipp Dilloway. Another cadet reflected on the guilt of being home.

> We've been exempted from war. This is a difficult situation to be in when all of the nation's men are called to fight for their country. You find it easy to spend your pay every Saturday night on Broadway, but the real payoff comes Sunday afternoon when the neighbors start talking about their boy in the Pacific or in Germany, and somehow you wonder why you aren't over there too.

The cadets were being trained for war, but their deferments gave them time that their friends did not have. That same cadet also said that the training had a purpose. It was to "help you be a better fighter" and to "lead men in battle." It was with those thoughts that cadets found it easier to justify their deferments.

The cadets suppressed these mixed feelings with entertainment. On the weekends they would go to hotspots in Manhattan such as "Amen Corner" at the Fifth Avenue Hotel on 9th Street. Its grand piano relaxed the cadets as they sat back in large easy chairs, played cards and sipped the barkeeper Tony's excellent drinks. Other places included the "Janet Roper Club" on 67th Street, which was more family friendly. There was also the American Theatre Wing for Merchant Seamen on 43rd Street which proved to be a good gathering place to "shoot the breeze." If dancing was preferred, cadets went to the J.W.B. Club at 65th Street where they could dance with "pretty hostesses as congenial partners."

More local to Fort Schuyler was Westchester Square, which often received cadets on liberty. There were bars as well as a frequented diner called

"Jacks." A glimpse of what liberty was like is shown in a 1945 parody of "the Whiffenpoof Song" written by cadet Jim Weston. It is entitled "Liberty at the Square":

> *To the tables at Three Corners,*
> *To the place where NYSMA dwells,*
> *To the old Westchester Bar we love so well;*
> *Stand the Midshipmen assembled,*
> *With their 'Bowditches' on high.*
> *And the magic of no musters casts its spell.*
> *Yes, the magic of no 'one hand' calls*
> *No 'turn to' and the rest,*
> *No calisthenics in the Inner Gorge;*
> *We will listen to the juke box*
> *While the dimes and liberty last.*
> *Then we'll chugalug and be bilged with all the rest.*
>
> *We are poor underclassmen who have lost our way–*
> *Ba, ba, ba,*
> *We are cozy upperclassmen who will show you the way–*
> *Ha! Ha! Ha!*
>
> *Gentlemen-Midshipmen 'in a qualified sense!'*
> *Damned to restrictions for ever hence,*
> *Commander have mercy on such as we–*
> *Ba! Ba! Ba!*

In their spare time, cadets bonded by cutting each other's hair. As reported in 1945: "Every afternoon in the room next to the paint locker, you'll find Cadet Dick Yanni doing more than his bit towards keeping up the good looks (and morale) of the Cadet Corps. With his clippers and scissor he can work wonders with the most unruly head of overgrown hair. Dick tells us that on the next cruise, he'll have a pretty blonde manicurist on board to help him out. Gung Ho Dick. It's great work if you can get it."

As far as social life at For Schuyler, there were formal dances and student run-shows such as "In a Qualified Sense: A Three Act Farce." This particular show was a satirical look at the NYSMA's routine through the eyes of a fictitious Cadet named "Egor." As part of the variety, Cadet Eugene N. Starbecker "appeared as a mess man doing a tricky boogie-woogie tap dance."

But there was always an undercurrent of reality. The summer, 1945 issue of the student newspaper, *the Bosun's Pipe*, had one such letter:

> Dear Sir:
> Theodore Scharpft of the class of 1940 to whom you wrote in connection with a subscription to the 'Bosun's Pipe' has been missing since January, 1943 following the torpedoing of his ship off the Azores and is presumed to be dead.
>
> Inasmuch as he took a great deal of pride in the fact that he graduated from the New York State Maritime Academy and I am sure would be very much interested in your paper, I am enclosing a check for one dollar as requested.
>
> I am certain that the paper will be very much appreciated by the many fine young men who have graduated from the Academy in the past and have survived the terrible holocaust in which our country is presently involved.
>
> Very truly yours,
> Margaret Scharpf.

The cadets of the New York State Maritime Academy graduated and went to war.

CLARENCE HOLM

Clarence Holm, class of 1936, worked for the Moore-McCormick line as an officer aboard the *Mormacdove*. When the war broke out, his ship was requisitioned by the Navy and renamed the *Alchiba*. He sailed to Bora Bora where he helped to establish a fuel depot, carried troops as part of a convoy to New Zealand and brought marines to the battle of Guadalcanal.

"The first night at Guadalcanal, Japanese ships attempted to sink our transports, but were intercepted by American Cruisers, one of which, the *Astoria*, was damaged, burning and sinking."

Holm's ship was ordered to tow the *Astoria* away. They approached, and he left the ship in a whaleboat to rescue survivors. Then suddenly, the *Alchiba* was forced away by an alarm warning of enemy submarines.

"There I was with just my little .45 waiting for the sub to come up."

Fortunately for Holm, American cruisers drove off the submarines.

After Guadalcanal, the *Alchiba* carried high test aviation gas, ammunition, grenades and 100- to 1,000-pound bombs. On November 28, 1942 at 0616, the ship was struck with a torpedo in a hold filled with gasoline. Holm said that it caused, "such an explosion that it ruptured the bulkheads between numbers one, two and three holds. The ship took an immediate list of 17 degrees."

Fire spread to almost all the holds. In desperation, the captain ordered full speed ahead until the ship hit the beach. This righted the vessel. But the inferno was spreading rapidly, and the captain ordered the crew to abandon ship.

After everybody was off the ship, Holm gathered a group of volunteers, boarded the ruined vessel, and discharged the bombs all through the night and into the morning. After that, a skeleton crew went aboard and extinguished the flames. The ship was saved but badly damaged.

Then on December 7, 1942, while Holm was inspecting the holds for fire, another torpedo struck the ship. This time, he was overcome by gas fumes. His shipmates rescued him and he was evacuated to the New Hebrides for treatment before being sent to New Zealand on a hospital ship.

When Holm returned to the United States, he came back to his *alma mater* and became an instructor at the NYSMA in the fall of 1945.

THE MURMANSK RUN

Walter Hesse graduated from the academy as an engineer in 1940. Young, patriotic and looking for work, he signed aboard the SS *Mormacrey* in April, 1942 as Third Assistant Engineer. The *Mormacrey* was of World War I vintage and constructed by orders of the U.S. Shipping Board. Hesse's training at the NYSMA was thorough enough to familiarize him with this kind of craft, but it is hard to imagine that it would have prepared him for the contingencies of World War II Arctic convoys.

Supply routes were established to bring goods to the Soviet Union through their northern ports of Murmansk and Archangel. The *Mormacrey* was bound for Murmansk, the largest city north of the Arctic Circle. Ice and high seas were constant threats, but not as dangerous as the German U-Boats and *Luftwaffe* which relentlessly hunted the convoys.

The city was so far north it was only accessible by sea during the warmer months of the year. As a result, the convoys had to sail when it was light out longest. This meant the convoys were easier to find and sink by Axis forces. These supply fleets sustained horrific losses, with the most notorious being the ill-fated PQ-17* convoy to Archangel, of which only 11 out of 35 ships survived.

In Baltimore, the *Mormacrey* was refitted with two anti-aircraft .30 caliber machine guns. These were set on the wings of the bridge. To counter U-boats, she was also armed with two .50 caliber machine guns and a four-inch surface gun. Navy personnel were assigned to man the weapons.

After the refitting, the ship was loaded with mixed cargo. There were food items, such as butter, powdered milk, dried fruit and beans, as well as war materials, including jeeps, howitzers, cannons and small arms. Even tanks were lashed onto the deck. There were also three hundred tons of explosives in the forward hold. According to Hesse:

> One commodity not listed on the cargo manifest was present. Fear. We were unaware of its presence until later in the voyage. However, at this early stage, an undercurrent of apprehension pervaded the crew. The prospect of U-boat attack, of being cast adrift in an open boat for an extended period, or being hurled into the frigid north Atlantic waters was a major concern.

The *Mormacrey* hurried along from Baltimore to Halifax running at its maximum speed of ten knots. The ship arrived without incident, and in Halifax a number of other vessels had gathered to prepare for the more dangerous North Atlantic crossing. A Navy commodore was put in charge of the convoy to escort them to Reykjavik, Iceland, via Oban, Scotland.

The convoy sailed in a tight 48-ship formation to the northeast, sailing as fast as the slowest ship—about seven knots. Three destroyers protected the convoy's front and flanks. There were no destroyers behind them. U-boats could not maintain the seven knot pace for long distances and especially not while submerged. A U-boat's best chance was to come head-on or attack the convoy's flanks.

At night, the ships went into total blackout to make it difficult for the enemy to find them. Even smoking was not permitted on the deck. Since the ships could not see each other in the darkness, it made it difficult to maintain the convoy's formation. To counter this problem, the ships towed a small float that

---

*The letters "PQ" designated ships that were inbound to Murmansk or Archangel; outbound convoys were given the designation of "QP."

created a tiny wake that was visible at night. Radar, a new invention, was limited only to the commodore's ship, which assisted in maintaining the formation.

According to Hesse, the captain of the *Mormacrey* was tireless. He never left the bridge, ate his meals there and slept short naps on a cot he kept nearby. Aside from threats from enemy attack, the captain felt mentally and physically stressed due to the risk of collision in the tight formation. Hesse wrote, "During a storm or foggy night, all points of reference were lost."

The convoy arrived in Reykjavik without incident. However, Iceland offered no comfort to Hesse. The neutral government would not permit the men from the convoy to go ashore. For a week Hesse "saw no more of Iceland than could be seen leaning against the rail of the ship."

At Reykjavik, the convoy was reorganized into a new formation and assigned the number PQ-15. It departed Iceland with at least 26 other ships in a squared pattern. What chilled Hesse most about this part of the voyage was how *much* protection they were given. They had added two British cruisers and four trawlers to "pick us up if we get knocked off."

As PQ-15 sailed north, the day lengthened and the danger of detection grew. Sure enough, at the northern cape of Norway four *Luftwaffe* planes dove out of the sky. Hesse recalled scrambling out on to the deck to ". . . chaos. Gun fire erupted from the ships. Germans darted in from every direction."

The *Luftwaffe* attacked the corners of the convoy's formation. The *Mormacrey*, inside the square, was better protected, although one fighter managed to get through to Hesse's vessel where, to his horror, he saw how "ineffective our fire power was." The .50 caliber guns malfunctioned and were useless. Yet somehow the combined fire of all the ships drove the Germans off and resulted in a stalemate. No ships were sunk and none of the fighters were downed. This was the first of 150 air raids that Hesse survived.

With this first taste of violence, rumors began to spread in the *Mormacrey*. Men told each other that the convoy was being used as bait to draw out German forces. Below decks, it was whispered that the German pocket battleship *Tirpitz* was lurking in the Norwegian fjords and that behind PQ-15, a British carrier and an American battleship were just out of sight ready to hunt her down.

These unsubstantiated rumors affected the men's morale. The crew and officers became withdrawn, such as the second mate of the *Mormacrey* who, "shunned social contact" and "spoke to no one except in the performance of his duty on the bridge."

The slightest sound, a dropped hammer, the sound of running feet, sent shivers of dread through each man. We slept with our clothes on, never undressed except to shower. Mealtime was no longer leisurely nor a time for conversation. We deserted the officer's mess as soon as food was bolted down. Four hours in the engine room was an eternity. . . . Conversations were whispered. We became introspective as events forced us to consider our own mortality.

By the time the Soviet Navy met PQ-15 on May 30th and escorted them into Murmansk, three ships had been lost.

Murmansk was about 30 miles from the front line and subject to constant air raids. While Hesse was aboard, three German *Stuka* dive bombers targeted the ship.

"The rattle of gunfire, the whine of the diving planes and the scream of the falling bombs were nerve-racking," Hesse hid in the officers' mess and thought, "I wonder what it's like to be dead?" He wouldn't find out that night. There was no severe damage upon the *Mormacrey* as she had been "bracketed" and not directly hit.

According to Hesse, within ten days the cargo was unloaded. This was done mostly by Soviet women. During this hiatus, he met his counterparts in the British and Soviet convoy services. More importantly, he wrote home to his wife. He was alive despite the constant air raids. When it was time to go, he was inured to the bombings. Everything became surreally routine.

The *Mormacrey* attached herself to a new convoy (QP-13) and departed Murmansk on June 26, 1942. They headed back the way they came, running the gauntlet of North Cape. For the first five days, there was no action. The only sounds of gunfire were from attacks on *inbound* convoys. The Germans were less interested in homeward bound ships that had little cargo.

On the sixth day, a German reconnaissance plane saw QP-13 and gave her location to a "wolf pack" of U-Boats. With only a day away from Iceland, the *Mormacrey* steamed into a German ambush. The high seas made it difficult for the U-boats to aim, so they shot their torpedoes in a wide spread hoping that some would strike. As Hesse was coming off watch, chaos erupted. "Ships behind us up-ended and going down," he wrote. Four more ships went down. The convoy scattered and rushed into Reykjavik. Hesse wrote, "The convoy is in disarray. It's every man for himself."

The next day, QP-13 reassembled at Reykjavik and began the last leg home. Hesse's ship had little food, problems with the boilers and shattered nerves. The convoy abandoned the *Mormacrey* because she was unable to keep up. As the ship limped alone into Long Island Sound, Hesse and his shipmates felt the tension ebb. "Men who hadn't spoken to each other in months laughed and joked together." They were glad to be home and even happier to be done. Even though the men of the *Mormacrey* had been bound together through war, none wished to be aboard any longer.

"As soon as the relief crew arrived we quit the ship without a backward glance. Each man went his separate way."

PEACE

After the Japanese signed the articles of surrender on September 2, 1945 the war ended. With it, the accelerated curriculum ceased and the NYSMA shifted to a peace-time footing. Then, at the end of the year, Admiral Craven retired.

For the cadets, there was a sense of dislocation but also optimism. One cadet wrote:

> Suddenly one summer evening while we were aboard the *Pilot* the news broke. The war was over and with it seemed to go all thoughts of duty or responsibility. The war was over, college would be opening, the draft closing, everything would be back on a peace time tempo. Gradually though it becomes apparent that such reasoning is a fallacy. Armies of occupation remain in Europe and fleets still patrolled Pacific waters while we occupy Japan. The draft still functions. Returning veterans tell of the tremendous amount of work still to be done. Strangely enough those old questions begin popping up again as you realize that your neighbors' kids are still being sent over—this time to fight a war of occupation, and again you wonder what you can do.

For the NYSMA, its next battle was to become a college.

CHAPTER 12

The Annapolis of the Merchant Marine

NYSMC is a College now,
Or nearly so at least.
What was a "Mug" is now a Frosh
No more "Heave-to" but "Cease."

No more do Mugs sound off when called,
The Rules and Regs are short,
A sneer is now the answer to
The Power of Report.

English Lit, Psychology,
Eco, Law and Gym.
Next we'll have a Dancing Class
To keep the Freshmen slim.

Ah, to bring back the good old days,
When men were men, not boys,
And Rates were issued side arms
For protection—not for noise.

But don't get too collegiate Mugs,
Your Seniors don't abuse.
Remember only God can help you
When once we start the cruise.

—James Betts, *Porthole*, February 24, 1950

"A SOVIETIZED FORM OF GOVERNMENT EDUCATION"

"We are facing a sinister thing," said Captain Henry Blackstone. The large and dour-faced administrator from the California Maritime Academy looked across the table to the other officials from the state schools. He had come a long way to join his colleagues at the Waldorf Astoria hotel in October, 1944, and he was going to tell them what he thought.

World War II was winding down. As the Allies pushed back Germany and Japan, at home, the merchant marine academies were vying for power. During the war, the state academies had complied with the wishes of the Maritime Commission. But now with the war's end in sight, they feared that Telfair Knight, the head of the Maritime Commission's Training Division, was plotting to usurp all American merchant marine training and dismember the state academies, including the NYSMA. To organize themselves against this threat, the leaders of the state maritime academies called for a meeting in New York, right before the annual American Merchant Marine Conference. Blackstone was livid.

He accused Telfair Knight of treating merchant marine training as a purely federal function and ignoring the efforts of the state academies. Blackstone stated that Knight told his school that "after the war, there will be no place in the Merchant Service for the graduates of State Academies." He then went on to state that Knight told him that the Maritime Commission would not give the state academies their federal subsidies. He added, "This seems to be a very definite indication of a desire on the part of the present administration to Sovietize the United States." Yet much of this animosity was personal. Blackstone said, "Knight is trying to perpetuate himself, make a big organization and make himself look important."

Telfair Knight had, in fact, told some academies one thing and others something else. Claude Bassett of the Massachusetts Maritime Academy was surprised at what Blackstone said, "Knight told us that he was going to include the state academies in all his recommendations to the Congress for funds. He said that we had vested rights." Yet other officials told how messages from the Maritime Commission were delayed and how the Commission was reducing their quotas.

The outcome from this was that Telfair Knight and the Maritime Commission were not to be trusted. The state academies' officials decided to press Knight on the issues the next day at the American Merchant Marine

Conference. There, Knight denied Blackstone's accusations but said that the Merchant Marine was subject to the regulations of the Maritime Commission.

"It [the merchant marine] does not go from one state to another," Knight said, "but goes to all foreign countries and is the concern of the nation as a whole."

The state academies heatedly disagreed. Michael Sweeny of the California Maritime Academy said, "The Government's function is to provide the army and navy. No simile can be drawn between them and the merchant marine." He argued that the merchant marine, since they worked for business and commerce, was a private function and naturally fell to regulation by individual states.

Yet Knight and the Maritime Commission had built up the USMMA and other federal training programs during World War II. The USMMA was better funded and publicized than the older state schools. With such daunting competition, it is no wonder that the state academies were defensive. As for NYSMA, it decided that it needed to make fundamental decisions to change the course of the school for a prosperous future.

A meeting was held by the Board of Visitors in early 1945. Dr. Lewis Wilson and Arthur Tode were worried about what the federal training program was going to do to their school. They decided to adopt the stance that a nationally-run training was bad for the nation. Lewis Wilson said that "it would be a sorry day for this country if education was run by a central government agency in Washington." Arthur Tode stated with a dose of Cold War rhetoric:

> Why should the federal government have a national academy for training seamen or officers any more than it should foster and support a national engineering school, a national forestry academy, a national agricultural school, etc.? Education is a function of the States. Possibly there is a group or individuals in our country who believe in a sovietized form of government education, and this is the first step.

Yet this ideological stance was only because of the imminent threat to the NYSMA from the federal government. For years, the school had lobbied for greater federal support. All the training ships of the school had been provided by the national government, and the reconstruction of Fort Schuyler was conducted by grants through the federal Works Progress Administration. The truth was that the state governments were running merchant marine training in *partnership* with the federal government and private industry. What all the state academies feared was the closure of the state academies and a monopolization of training by the federal government. On this account, Tode and Wilson were justified in their concerns since, at the end of the war, there seemed to be nothing that would prevent the growth of the federal training program.

Tode and Wilson steeled themselves for the expected withdrawal of federal support and direct competition with the USMMA. Wilson asked, "How are we to mobilize our strength to compete with the Federal Academy?" The answer would dictate the history of the institution for the remainder of the century and beyond. It was going to become the pre-eminent degree-granting maritime college in the nation.

THE VISION OF AN EXPANDED PROGRAM

Expanding the school's program had been proposed as early as 1913, when Jacob Miller's Board of Governors wanted to lengthen the curriculum. In 1932, James Tomb came to a similar conclusion after comparing the curriculum of the U.S. Naval Academy to the New York State Merchant Marine Academy. He asserted that the two year course failed to "embrace the whole field of education in the merchant marine profession." He recommended expanding the program to a three-year course eventually moving to a four-year program.

However, at that time the school needed to have a land base in order to provide the physical plant necessary to support a longer course of study. Tomb's proposal was deferred as the work on Fort Schuyler commenced. Meanwhile, in 1940, the California Maritime Academy began granting unaccredited bachelor degrees in Maritime Science in a three-year program. The pressure was on New York to do the same because as Tomb put it, "the insistent demands of the maritime interests" who wanted to have graduates who would be considered experts in their fields.

By October, 1940, Fort Schuyler had been physically prepared for an expanded program. The academy introduced the new course of study where cadets took a common set of classes in the first year and then specialized in deck or engineering for their final two years. But before the first set of cadets under the program graduated, the United States entered World War II, and the program was abbreviated by fiat from the federal government. But now the war was ending and the federal training program was threatening the state academies' existence. They had no choice. The NYSMA had to excel or die.

But Arthur Tode, who became the main driver for the NYSMA's elevation into a college, had been planning this move since he became the Chairman of the Board of Visitors in 1942. The key was not just being able to grant college degrees, but to form an academic niche that was different from the USMMA and the other state academies. The business of shipping, combined with traditional merchant marine training, was something that none of the other schools offered:

> Should we not plan for the post-war, a College of Maritime Training, where young men would learn not only to be a ship's officer, but could as well be prepared for executive positions with our country's great steamship companies, studying export and import trade, economics, maritime law, foreign languages to equip them as ship's agents in foreign posts and graduating these men with Bachelor of Nautical Science, or Bachelor of Nautical Arts degrees?

Selling such a proposal was easy. The school had a great sense of the upward trajectory of its own history. Cadet Felix S. Vecchione, in the summer of 1945, drew a cartoon that showed a person carrying the school's banner, trudging up a river with stops at "Saint Mary's," "Newport," "Empire State" and "Shore Based Academy." On the horizon, emblazoned by the setting sun, there read, "The Annapolis of the Merchant Marine." The editor of the student newspaper, Cadet Walter V. McNiece wrote, "The aim of all concerned, the graduates past, present and future, acting as a united force must be to stamp our men with the mark of quality, one which will make them stand above the rest as NYSMA trained, graduating from the New York State Maritime Academy, the 'Annapolis of the Merchant Marine.'"

BUILDING A COLLEGE CURRICULUM

The architect of the soon-to-be college's curriculum was Dr. Lewis Wilson. With his connection to New York's Education Department, Wilson effectively spoke for the quality of the curriculum while at the same time ensuring that the essential mission of the institution, to train merchant sea officers, remained in place. He gave the Board of Visitors wide latitude to recommend what was needed to create a prestigious maritime college.

The core of the new academic structure focused on the business of shipping. Wilson viewed this as a valuable niche where ". . . young men could be trained, not only as officers, but as executives for the various steamship companies and as ships' agents in foreign ports." Admiral Craven agreed that there was a market for this field since "for the most part they [American businessmen] are satisfied to leave their affairs in the hands of a foreign agent."*

The course of study that Wilson presented to the Board of Visitors in 1944 was similar to the aborted three-year course. Students were exposed to both deck and engineering instruction and then specialized in one of the two areas based on preference and officer recommendations. To meet the state's higher education standards, Wilson inserted general education courses, such as history and foreign languages. To widen the appeal of the college to the "finest young men in the State," he proposed expanding the annual cruise destinations to ports in South America and China. To further elevate the status of the school, cadets began to be called Cadet-Midshipman.

Wilson's efforts were buoyed by the passage of the GI Bill in 1944. The law, which provided educational funds for war veterans, was seen as an opportunity. "I expect there are a lot of things we would like to do for these boys," Wilson said. "Courses in economics, international law and trade, etc., things that would make them more valuable."

THE DEED TO FORT SCHUYLER

One immediate roadblock to establishing the college was Fort Schuyler itself. Wilson cited that the school needed a machinery building with the "finest diesel and electric shop that we can build" and a health and recreation center that would contain a gymnasium, drill hall and swimming pool. But major construction projects could not take place since New York State would not finance any future development unless it obtained the deed to Fort Schuyler from the War Department. The War Department maintained that to transfer the property to New York would require a special act of Congress. To make matters more complex, New York State needed to pass corresponding

---

*Craven worked separately on his own curriculum until early 1944 when he handed it over to Wilson. Wilson had his staff integrate it into his version. It is unknown what parts of Craven's curriculum were retained.

legislation to accept the property if it were ceded. Therefore, beginning in 1944, passing the needed laws to obtain the deed to Fort Schuyler became a paramount objective.

The NYSMA enlisted the aid of William E. Matthews of the Bronx Board of Trade. He lobbied New York Assemblymen Murphy and Brown who introduced the required state legislation. At the federal level, Representatives Emanuel Celler and Peter Quinn introduced the appropriate bills.

But the transfer of the property was delayed. While the War Department's tone seemed to be favorable toward the handover, the U.S. Navy wanted to maintain a training center on the grounds. To satisfy the Navy, the NYSMA brokered a deal in 1946 that allowed the Navy to retain control of the northern part of the property while the rest would be turned over to New York State. It was not until 1950 that Congress ceded the land with amendments following in 1952 and 1957. It was sold to New York State for a dollar. The deed stipulated that the grounds were to be used by New York State as a maritime school with the provisos that the federal government could reclaim the property in times of war, if Fort Schuyler was not maintained as a historic monument or if it were used for other purposes.

Due to the delay, and later a lack of desire by the State to invest in new construction, the NYSMA was forced to make permanent what were supposed to be temporary war-era structures. These were augmented and converted for the academy's use: an armory/drill hall to the north of the fort, a seamanship building to the south, as well as wooden barracks on the Navy portion of the property.* Fort Schuyler became the academic heart of the campus.

"QUIETLY GOING NUTS"—LEARY AND THE *HYDRUS*

After World War II the nation demobilized, putting to an end the intensive training program at Fort Schuyler. The two-year curriculum was temporarily restored as the school prepared for the expanded course of study. On campus, there were massive personnel changeovers since the Navy withdrew most of its staff and Admiral Craven retired.

Craven was succeeded by Vice Admiral Herbert Fairfax Leary, a boisterous man from a Navy family who, during World War II, was commandant of the Eastern Sea Frontier. He also headed the combined naval forces of the

---

*The barracks were used as dormitories starting in 1949 when 200 students moved in.

Australian-New Zealand area. Among various honors, Leary was awarded the Legion of Merit and the Silver Star.

Leary was tall and austere with a florid complexion and forceful energy. Graduate Donald White commented that, "He strode across the pentagon, or anywhere, with a long gait that taxed anyone trying to keep up." Faculty Fred Hess described Leary as "inspirational" and having a "foghorn voice." Hess wrote that he "felt it was an honor to salute him." Harold Parnham, a 1948 graduate, recalled how difficult it was to look Leary straight in the eye. Leary also had considerable connections with the U.S. Navy and even recruited Admiral William "Bull" Halsey to swear-in the cadets at the 1950 graduation.

Leary took advantage of post-war military surplus. Much of this took the form of additional equipment, such as motorized whaleboats and two 110-foot long sub-chasers, which the school leased in January, 1946. These were used for weekend cruises and gave students experience with up-to-date marine technology. In addition, the school obtained from the Navy, for a dollar, the destroyer-escort *Balfour* which they stripped as a "valuable source of engineering material."

The most revered piece of surplus was a new training ship. On March 9, 1946, the Maritime Commission turned over to the school the 4,087 ton Artemis class attack cargo ship, the USS *Hydrus*. The *Hydrus* was built during the war and served in the Pacific theater, taking part in the invasion of Okinawa and the occupation of China. For her actions, the ship received one battle star.

The *Hydrus* needed to be reconditioned into a training vessel and the War Shipping Administration allocated $50,000 to do it. The *Hydrus* was put into dry-dock where her capacity was expanded and modern equipment installed. On May 13, 1946, she was brought to Fort Schuyler and renamed the *Empire State II*. New York Governor, Thomas Dewey, presided at the vessel's dedication.

Despite the rebuild, the *Hydrus* was a troubled ship. In 1946, the first post-war voyage, the ship went south to Panama and Peru. But the vessel kept breaking down. Donald White, in a letter to his parents, complained that the engineering plant was "arranged so that when one part of it goes off kilter the rest of it reacts in a similar manner." The ship broke down several times during the voyage resulting in all aboard "quietly going nuts." White asserted that it was only because of Commander "Salty" Bill Muir, a rough and profane engineer, that that the voyage was a success. Muir, who was a chief engineer aboard a destroyer during the attack on Pearl Harbor, told the cadets that the *Hydrus's* boilers had a similar design. He knew how to handle them.

Leary lauded the *Empire State II's* first voyage and praised the "exemplary" conduct of the cadets with "no cases of drunkenness and only one case of venereal infection." However, Leary admitted the ship was "very hot" and needed "awnings and many additional air ports." To add to the inconvenience and discomfort, Leary cited inadequate toilet facilities, poor berthing facilities and fresh water supply problems. Alfred Olivet, the captain of the ship, concurred but cautioned that it would "take a great deal of time and money to make her suitable as a training ship.

Over several years, enough modifications were made to the vessel to make her adequate. In 1948, wooden top decks were installed and the lower decks were covered in magnesite to reduce heat. But the main problem with the *Hydrus* was that she was designed to Navy specifications which did not match Coast Guard regulations. This would later prove to be a major problem.

"A NUCLEUS COMPOSED OF GRADUATES"

On April 6, 1946, Governor Dewey signed into law a bill which authorized the school to grant bachelor degrees in Marine Science under a three-year program. Despite years of planning, there was a scramble by the new college to adapt. It found that the incoming class was ill-prepared for a college curriculum, and they gave them a five-week intensive remediation course in that fall on "certain fundamental academic courses in conjunction with an indoctrination and orientation program." During this period, classes were conducted six days a week in mathematics, history, theoretical seamanship, naval science and tactics, practical seamanship, small boats and physical training. Leary admitted that even though it was "a very heavy program," the cadets had ample time since they were "restricted to the station."

Almost immediately, there was a problem with teaching qualifications. Until 1946, the cadets were mostly taught by industry professionals or Navy men who often did not meet the state's collegiate-level faculty qualifications. Leary, who professed that the school's objective was to produce "educated gentlemen thoroughly imbued with honor, uprightness and truth, with practical rather than academic minds," was faced with the practicality of having to obtain academic minds to meet state standards.

Men who had the requisite degrees, the necessary experience and the desire to teach were difficult to find. The school, as it had done throughout its history, relied on many of its own graduates to come back and teach. Leary sought to create a faculty which had "a nucleus composed of graduates." Leary said he wanted this to "carry on the heritage and traditions of the school," although in reality it was necessary because of the lack of qualified personnel.

Those instructors who graduated from the school prior to the college changeover were put on probation. They were allowed to continue to teach, provided that they obtained a baccalaureate degree by taking classes at night. These instructors, as well as those former graduates who returned to take additional courses to earn a college degree, were handled by a new "Academic Department" that organized them as day students apart from the regular cadets. This department also handled the thorny issue of how to integrate general education requirements into the curriculum.

To head this department and to handle staffing issues, Leary hired Dr. Ralph E. Page, the Dean of Men at Bucknell University. Page worked on a tentative general education curriculum for the school and hired faculty, but he soon left the school for a higher paying position. His successor, Dr. Albert Ogden Porter, was a Harvard graduate and assumed the title of Dean. He became the first true head of the academic side of the college.

Faculty Fred Hess noted that one of Porter's most interesting traits was his enthusiasm for railroads. "He had memorized the timetable of virtually every rail line in the United States. When staff members needed rail transportation they went to him to plan their itineraries and found him to be completely accurate."

Under Porter, faculty pay was made equitable to other state colleges which, according to Leary, "breathed new life" into the institution. Some of these early appointments stayed at the college for years and brought stability. The Marine Transportation department found solid leadership under Guy DeSimone who remained with the school until 1974. New academic departments were formed. The Social Sciences department (which later morphed into Humanities) was headed by George M. Gregory and the Science department, led by Dr. Meir H. Degani, made its debut. In addition, athletics were organized under Roger Reinhart, and a college library was established under Terrance Hoverter. This faculty had no connection with the school prior to coming aboard. This was a significant departure from past practices that would result in continuing tension between the academic and practical sides of the campus.

Of these, one of the most significant appointments was that of Alfred F. Olivet in 1946 as the Commandant of Cadets and Master of the Training Ship. Olivet had much practical experience that ranged from working as an able-bodied seaman, to commanding supply vessels in both the European and Pacific theaters of World War II. The respect given to him by graduates of the school for his paternal, although draconian, leadership abilities was nearly universal. Yet even Olivet, a graduate from the class of 1921, had to take courses at the college in order to earn a baccalaureate degree.

As the academic program matured, Olivet and Leary came down hard on the rougher hazing practices of the past. Alumnus Craig Smith recalled inspections by the pair:

> [Leary] and Olivet took two companies each along with the battalion and appropriate company rates. Together they made a terrifying inspection team. I doubt the likes of it has been seen at Schuyler since. I think we all agree that the good Captain was as volatile as nitro—you just never knew what would set him off. Leary, on the other hand, I remember for his thundering voice. When lifted in anger, it would echo off and around the walls of the Inner Gorge.

Both Leary and Olivet worked to make the students stakeholders in the new college's success. One of the chief markers of this occurred in September, 1946, when the first Student Association was founded. Members, selected by Leary, were assigned responsibility for generating revenue to augment student life. By 1951, the Association formed an eight-cadet board and operated various revenue-making ventures on campus including a barber shop, laundry and canteen. This core of student activity outside of the regimental structure would, within a few years, blossom into a full-fledged student government that did not always abide by the administration's wishes.

Along with empowering students, sports and clubs grew throughout the period. The college's teams all had different names, such as the "Harriers" for cross country, "Nimrods" for rifle, "Marauders" for basketball and "Mariners" for baseball. In December, 1952, an editorial in the student newspaper suggested changing the name to "Privateers" since the designation more accurately reflected the merchant marine. It was adopted and the name stuck.

The athletic program was buoyed by the hiring of Matthew Twomey in 1946. A Georgetown graduate, Twomey had played five years for the Washington Redskins football team before becoming a boxing manager/trainer. His most notable protégés were Steve Mamakos, a middle weight contender, featherweight Lou Gevinson and heavyweight Marty Gallagher.

A 1950 article stated that Twomey "devotes himself religiously to keeping his boys in shape but never a harsh word, only encouragement coming from his lips, never a rebuke only praise."

Twomey was a coach of multiple sports, but achieved his greatest notability at the college by organizing, in 1946, the first inter-regimental "Golden Gloves" boxing tournament. Seven weight divisions were defined and each class sent boxers to the ring. These tournaments, in their day, were wildly popular, not least because it gave the Mugs an opportunity to beat up the upperclassmen. The tournaments lasted until 1957 when "cadets could no longer devote the time needed and boxing declined as a college sport." There were over 500 bouts total. Twomey retired in 1971.

As part of the effort for the institution to become a college, more extracurricular activities were made available. An assortment of clubs was founded, including a student branch of the Propeller Club. In 1954, the Pershing Rifles established a company at the school. This organization performed rifle drills and competed nationally. Fort Schuyler's unit, P-8, was the first maritime unit of all Pershing Rifle Teams. It was rather like a fraternity within the fraternity of the institution by having pledges and conducting separate hazing. By 1956, nineteen clubs were listed in the yearbook including radio, pistol, rifle, French and Spanish clubs.

THE FOUR-YEAR PROGRAM

Despite the best efforts of Leary and his faculty, it was obvious that the three-year curriculum was not working. For one thing, the USMMA had a four-year curriculum. The federal government ruled that students of four-year programs could obtain second mate licenses; graduates of three-year programs could only obtain third mate licenses.

Second, Dr. J. Hillis Miller, the New York Associate Commissioner of Education, examined the college in January of 1947. He found that the "extreme military discipline" often interfered with students' studies and faculty work. Students were required to do chores, ship maintenance and watch standing. In addition, the academic workloads of the students were very heavy. The cadets at Fort Schuyler typically took course loads of eighteen to twenty semester hours per week while the average at a traditional college was fifteen. The faculty too was expected to take part in regimental activities, depriving them of time to develop into effective teachers.

Miller specified that although the college had the legal right to grant degrees, it was different from having the curriculum appropriately registered with the state. In Miller's opinion, the school was "operating under legal terminology and not educational terminology." Until the problems he outlined were addressed, students could not transfer credits out of the college to other institutions. This did not prevent students from transferring credits *into* the school. It was in this way that engineering cadet, Eugene N. Starbecker, became the college's first recipient of a bachelor's degree in October of 1947.*

As the school was forced to focus on its academics, it was impossible to maintain all the new equipment that the school had obtained as war surplus. The two sub-chasers and most of the motor whaleboats were returned to the Navy. In addition, the indoctrination period was shortened, and practical work was reserved for the training cruises.

Despite the difficulties, Leary noted that the students were performing well, with an entire cadet corps grade point average of 78.4%. Nevertheless, in January of 1948, Leary wrote, "We are still struggling with our readjustment to the new degree-granting program. It is evident that in order to cover the requirements, the Academy must go on a four year program. This is the unanimous opinion of our faculty. . . . This will reduce the size of classes and provide for better instruction."

A revised four-year curriculum was submitted and accepted by the State in 1948. The strain of the change reverberated through the student body. That May, Leary wrote, "The past year has been a hard one in readjusting our students to the new and increased standards of a college course, and the attrition has been unusually heavy. We have about 25 students who have dropped at the end of this year for academic failures."

The new four-year course was quickly implemented. In January, 1949, the school was inspected by the State Education Department and found satisfactory. The next year, the college's curriculum was formally registered with the

---

*Starbecker, who became an award-winning scriptwriter, director and producer, transferred in credits from New York University.

State of New York allowing course credits to transfer to other state colleges and universities.

During this process, other changes in New York higher education were occurring. In 1948, New York established the State University of New York (SUNY), and the NYSMA entered as a founding member. To highlight this metamorphosis, on April 1, 1949, the NYSMA adopted the name of Maritime College. As Leary explained, the reason for the name change was prestige:

> ... the term 'Academy' is usually and popularly applied to boys' or girls' high schools and preparatory schools, or to the few schools of higher learning training young men specifically and solely for a military career. Since the elevation of Fort Schuyler to collegiate status, every effort has been made to publicize this change in status, and to sell the school as one of higher learning.... While proud of its military tradition, and zealous of preserving its nature, Fort Schuyler essentially educates its students for civilian maritime careers.... Therefore, it is considered desirable to distinguish it from service colleges whose aims and purposes are not entirely similar and, above all, to distinguish it from preparatory schools.

Leary's title changed from Superintendent to President, although he, and all the subsequent presidents by common custom and rank, have been colloquially referred to as "Admiral." In 1950, Leary bragged about the college's success, particularly that of the engineering department headed by Jeremy Blood:

> Events have proved the wisdom of our four year curriculum. Our graduates who have been admitted to graduate schools on the basis of this work here are doing well at Harvard, Columbia, and M.I.T. Three engineers have been employed by Westinghouse for research on the atomic energy marine power plant for submarines, and another engineer has recently been hired for a responsible position by the New York Port Authority.

By 1956, the engineering program had gained such prominence, especially under the direction of Blood's successor, John J. Foody, that there were rumors that the college was going to become a pure engineering school.*

---

*Faculty member and alumnus Jose Femenia recalled that Foody was "... a gentlemen and very stern. Very proper, a no-nonsense person. He was the kind of person where you did your work or you didn't. You knew exactly where you stood with Foody. There was no gray." Foody was nicknamed "God."

INTEGRATION

The creation of SUNY coincided with the first steps toward true diversity in higher education. In 1948, President Truman ordered the desegregation of the nation's military. At the state level, greater progress was made with New York leading the way. In the immediate post-war years, there had been an increase in discrimination at New York colleges against Jews and African Americans. After several years of agitation by activists, the New York State Legislature passed the Educational Practices Act. Also known as the Quinn-Olliffe Law, it was signed into law by Governor Dewey in April, 1948. The new law made it illegal to discriminate in admissions at non-sectarian colleges in New York State.

It was in this context that the first African Americans enrolled at the school. Carl F. Burnett was the first and graduated as an engineer in 1950. Walter Womack Branford was the second and he graduated in 1952. Both went on to become successful business executives with Branford even founding an early minority-owned steam ship company, Double Eagle Lines.

What discrimination these two early pioneers may have gone through is unknown. Both Burnett and Branford died before their stories could be recorded. From our primary sources, there is no record of the discrimination that they probably faced in trying to join the ranks of merchant marine officers.

Despite the breaking of the color barrier, the school would remain racially homogenous for decades. Admission practices targeted the white suburbs of New York City, and until the late 1960s, there is little to no mention of race or racial problems at the college, nor were there any official data kept on racial demographics until the 1970s. Officials at the college may have assumed that since they were taking in a handful of African Americans, they could not be accused of discrimination.

As for the cadets of the period, race was not talked about except in the larger context of the nation. In this regard, the students held tolerant views. After the 1954 landmark decision of *Brown v. Board of Education*, the issue of racial integration was discussed in the pages of the student newspaper. Students were critical of segregation, but considered it a problem confined to the South. Cadet William G. Bullock, commented, "... a true American never judges a man by his race, color, or creed but only by the person himself. This segregation in certain Southern States is definitely against the American principle and should be corrected as soon as possible."

Another student, Richard Seel, urged a more gradual approach citing that "the way of life down south is different than it is up north." Cadet David Baker, stated that, "southerners should accept the fact that we are all human beings and we must live together if we ever expect to have a democratic world." The cadets could afford to be tolerant. Race was not and could not be a problem for them due to the campus' demographics.

THE GROWING CURRICULUM

After the war, there was greater enrollment of engineering students at the college. This and the elevation of the program led to demands to implement a separate engineering degree since it was reasoned that an engineer with a degree in Marine Science would not be taken seriously by industry or graduate schools. The college gained this right in 1949 and began offering degrees in marine engineering.

The college also sought to acquire nationally recognized accreditation. In 1949, the school began negotiations with the Middle Atlantic States Association of Colleges (commonly called Middle States) to become fully accredited. Middle States found that the curriculum was satisfactory, but declined to grant accreditation until 1952, when the first cadre of students under the four-year program graduated.

In the interim, the college intensified its efforts to broaden its course offerings. Classes such as Western World Literature, Drama, Creative Writing, and Contemporary Fiction and Poetry were offered for the first time. By the time Leary retired in 1951 to, as he put it, "baby-sit with my grandchildren," the college had a broad swath of courses in the humanities.

There were still fundamental problems. The relationship between the college and the federal government had not been resolved, and the physical limitations of Fort Schuyler were blocking the institution's progress. Over the next two decades, these problems became key issues in the growth and development of Maritime College.

CHAPTER 13

"But Men and Officers Must Obey"

"It was a college, but it felt like a prison."
—1957 graduate

"A CIVILIZED MIND"

The 1951 term was coming to an end. The *Empire State II* was about to depart on her annual cruise. That year's first stop was to be Miami followed by an Atlantic crossing to Europe. All hands eagerly anticipated the voyage.

But on campus at Fort Schuyler, there was anticipation of another kind. The rough-and-ready Admiral Leary was retiring, and a new president was coming to lead the college into the post-war world.

Word was passed to the faculty to gather on Newport Field, the college's athletic ground. When instructors arrived, to their surprise, they found the Admiral had set up the grounds as if for a military review. There was a contingent of eight ceremonial side boys, the faculty and newspaper reporters. Admiral Leary had planned something special.

The breeze blew as silence fell upon the field. Then, from the sky, came a swiftly growing noise: WHUMP-WHUMP-WHUMP—quick staccato beats of a craft in the air. Then, from above, they could see a flying machine silhouetted against the sky. A collective *ooh* went through the crowd. It was one of Igor Sikorsky's helicopters.

The helicopter was still a novel invention. Although there had been successful flights for decades, the machine was not put into full production until

World War II, and even then there was only a limited number. In 1951 they were still a rare sight.

The helicopter circled the field and softly floated downward, kicking up dirt and grass as it touched down. The cockpit opened, and out stepped a man in his late fifties who carried the distinguished look and aristocratic mien of a movie star. Cameras flashed, a boson's pipe whistled and the side boys saluted. It was the new president who had come to join Admiral Leary for lunch. He stepped onto the field, saluted Leary, and smiled. "I didn't expect this," he said. But Vice Admiral Calvin T. Durgin surely enjoyed the attention.

Always sensational, always adventurous, Durgin was naturally attracted to derring-do. After graduating from Annapolis in 1916, he became a pilot when naval aviation was in its infancy. Durgin was so attracted to this sexy new mode of travel that he decided to make it his specialty. He earned a master's degree in aeronautical engineering from MIT and became a recognized authority in naval air combat. Because of this, during World War II, he became the head of naval aviation training and commanded an aircraft carrier squadron. In the process, he was decorated with medals and honors such as the Distinguished Service Cross, the Commander of the British Empire and the French Legion of Honor. Durgin once declared that his "most thrilling and self-satisfying duty" was the command of the aircraft carrier *Ranger** during the Allied assault on Vichy-French Morocco. His work after the war as head of Naval Air Operations proved dull enough to lure him into what he imagined to be a quiet retirement at Fort Schuyler.

Durgin, as a character, was more complex than Leary. He was aristocratic with refined tastes. He had more than just a passing interest in the humanities. He loved literature, opera and history. One professor wrote that this was a reflection of his "civilized mind and personality." But there was another side to it. Durgin was "no angel and could be capricious, unpredictable, and occasionally ruthless." This tendency was coupled with an "aristocratic disdain for details and minutiae, for the routine and commonplace."

---

*Faculty member Fred Hess provided one anecdote of Durgin's time on the Ranger:
". . . he once unexpectedly ordered a sharp turn to the right. Just as the ship came about, the crew spotted two torpedo trails approaching the ship, but because of the turn they were missing the ship . . . [Durgin] insisted he had no idea that an enemy submarine was about to fire on his ship. . . . The officers and crew gave him full credit for saving the vessel with a sensational act of seamanship." (Hess, 40)

Durgin drew to him many prominent acquaintances both in and out of the Navy. Aside from a personal relationship with Igor Sikorsky, his correspondence reveals friendships with Herman Baruch,* Frederica the Queen-consort of Greece and opera singer Maria Callas. Durgin also had connections with almost every important flag officer in the U.S. Navy. He used these contacts for the college's benefit to hold public lectures or dinners with important guests for graduating students and select members of the college community. Through his friendship with Ambassador Mohammed Ali of Pakistan, Durgin introduced the first foreign student exchange program to the college in 1952.

The new president did not expect much out of his second career. In early 1952 he wrote, "When I took this job, I had an idea that it would be very interesting but not too strenuous." He was particularly happy about having free rein. "I find that it keeps me just as busy as any job I ever had," he wrote, "but with one big advantage. I am completely my own boss, come and go and do as I please. So far we have had no orders or control of any kind exerted from Albany. The result is a busy job but a very pleasant one and I am very happy about the whole setup insofar as the College is concerned."

Durgin immediately introduced his own brand of aesthetics to the college. He ordered the repainting of the *Empire State II* from battleship gray to peacetime white. "At first there was a bit of opposition," the Admiral wrote, "but now I think we are unanimous in the thought that it was a good idea. It looks more like a yacht now and, as a result, when we go into a foreign port we stand out as a thing of beauty and not just as another freighter or cargo vessel."

Durgin was equally willing to change school traditions. Since the 1930s, an excerpt from George Francis Robert Henderson's biography of Thomas "Stonewall" Jackson, had hung in the Sallyport. Henderson's writing became known as the "Sallyport Saying," an adage that all cadets had to memorize:

> But men and officers must obey . . . no matter at what cost to their feelings, for obedience to orders, instant and unhesitating, is not only the life-blood of armies but the security of states; and the doctrine that under any conditions whatever deliberate disobedience can be justified is treason to the commonwealth.

---

*Herman Baruch was an American diplomat who was the brother of the famous financier, Bernard Baruch.

Durgin thought the saying was inappropriate for the college, since Jackson was an army figure. "I think that since this college is a maritime college, the Sallyport should bear the words of a man from our profession."

Durgin opened a contest in 1952 to change the saying and offered $10 to the cadet who supplied the winning entry. Yet there was not much enthusiasm for the change, and the matter faded away. Cadets are still memorizing the quotation today.

"I SHALL KICK YOUR SHINS GOOD AND HARD."

Durgin had a knack for getting himself into troublesome situations. The first major issue of his administration had to do with the subsidy that the students received from the Maritime Administration (MARAD), which had replaced the Maritime Commission in 1950.

In the post-war world, the demobilization of the armed forces meant budget cuts. Support for federally sponsored merchant marine training slipped, particularly among influential maritime labor unions whose membership consisted of men who worked their way up through the hawse pipe. The Maritime College's graduates competed for their jobs. Since the hawse pipers made up most of the membership of the unions, they used their position to influence Congress to drop support from federal training programs.

It started in early 1952, when MARAD received a budget cut. MARAD didn't like the cut, but they decided that they weren't going to let it impact the federal training program at Kings Point. They maintained the same $1,020 a year subsidy for the USMMA cadets and reduced state cadet subsidies to $455. To aggravate the situation, even these lower payments were delayed due to bureaucratic changes.

While tuition at Maritime College was free, there were other associated costs such as textbooks and uniforms which the federal money paid for. Many of the Maritime College students came from working class families. The loss of funding was a financial blow that they could not make up since the regimental system and annual training cruises dug into any available time the students had for work. One article in the student newspaper reported that some cadets, for lack of funds, sold their blood to purchase books.

To Durgin, the situation was unfair since Fort Schuyler cadets were "under the same obligations as the boys at Kings Point." Graduates from both academies received commissions in the Navy Reserve and were required to serve if called. Since the money for all the cadets was given as a lump sum to the college and administered by it, the admiral ordered that the full amount, referred to as "federal scholarships," be given to the upper two classes while underclassmen would go unpaid. Even then, there was not enough money to go around. Payments were given only to the highest ranking students in the sophomore, junior and senior classes.

In January, 1952, Durgin enlisted the help of the cadets' parents and held a meeting in the old armory.* From that meeting, a Parents Association was formed. The group was soon involved in many aspects of student life that included material improvements, "creature comforts," and the creation of a student loan fund.

The Parents Association's original charter stated that its purpose was to "bring the home and college closer." The Student Council made the parents strike out this line. The student newspaper reported, "The cadet evidently feels he has enough trouble without having his mother fixing things up for him at school."

Meanwhile, Durgin took personal action and wrote to all the Congressmen on the relevant committees to restore the payments. He reasoned that state cadets fell under the provisions of the Holloway Plan, the forerunner of the Naval Reserve Officer Training Corps (NROTC).** Response to this suggestion was lukewarm at best, and even Congressmen who were sympathetic to Maritime College did not agree with him.

The strongest opponent to extending federal aid was Texas Representative Albert Richard Thomas who headed the sub-committee that controlled the funding. Thomas believed that no maritime school, including the USMMA, should receive any funding since the graduates worked in the merchant service, a private industry. In fact, Thomas told Durgin that the federal academy "should have been folded up as soon as the war was over." When Durgin brought up his idea of the Holloway plan, Thomas rejected it, stating that graduates from maritime schools were required to serve only if called. Thomas pointed his finger at Durgin and said, "That *if* makes all the difference in the world."

---

*The Armory was a World War II structure that sat on the tip of the peninsula outside Fort Schuyler. It was used as an athletic hall and for assemblies until it was demolished in the fall of 1965 after the construction of the new athletic building, Riesenberg Hall.
**NROTC was formally brought to the college on October 1, 1973, when the Naval Science Department was changed to NROTC by the Secretary of the Navy. Under the initial program, 40 students could join, and after training were commissioned as ensigns in the U.S. Navy.

Rebuffed, Durgin changed tactics and argued that the state academies were cheaper than the national program on the order of $153,000 to $198,750. Durgin said that the state schools, with their training ships, had better, more consistent instruction than the apprentice system practiced by the USMMA.

Durgin's figures were debatable. A 1954 Senate investigation found that costs were roughly the same. Even so, it brought a fresh wave of contention between MARAD and the state maritime schools. Durgin teamed up with Ralph Leavitt, the President of the Maine Maritime Academy's Board of Visitors, and presented to Hollie J. Tiedmann and E.L. Cochrane, the heads of MARAD, a plan to reduce aid to *all* maritime schools. By Durgin's estimation, it was the fair thing to do. Cochrane was indignant and commented half-jokingly, "Kings Point is my college and if you do anything to affect that I shall kick your shins good and hard." The relationship between the Maritime Administration and the state academies became so strained, that at one point Durgin contemplated the possibility of trying to get the state schools federally administered by the U.S. Navy.

In October of 1953, MARAD was faced with more budget cuts, but this time there was a new Maritime Administrator. Louis Rothschild, who had little maritime experience, was charged to reduce costs. He informed Durgin and Leavitt that in 1955 there would be no federal assistance to the state schools, and that there was a good chance that the USMMA was going to shut down.

Durgin and Leavitt gave Rothschild their budget data showing how much cheaper the state schools cost. Rothschild immediately became sympathetic and referred them to the Undersecretary of Commerce, Robert B. Murray, Jr. A friendly conversation ensued. Durgin reported that Murray "pointed out that no definite decision had been made, but that he felt the federal government should get out of maritime training and that there was no more reason to keep Kings Point than there was to establish federal schools for farmers, doctors and others."

Durgin and Leavitt did not attempt to defend Kings Point. They assured Murray that the state academies would continue with or without federal aid. In addition, they maintained that if the federal government decided to close the USMMA that the individual state schools would expand admission to be more inclusive nationally. The meeting ended with nothing decided, but Durgin reported that it stimulated inquiries and investigations into the operating costs of the federal school versus the state schools. Later, meetings were held by the representatives of the governors of the four states operating maritime schools, in order to ascertain the permanency and flexibility of the state operations.

News of what was going on leaked to the Kings Point Alumni Association who promptly sent a telegram to Governor Dewey and accused Durgin of plotting against the USMMA. This was picked up by the newspapers, and the matter became toxic. When questioned by the press, Durgin said, "I am quite sure that when interested people take the time to study the facts, a true perspective on this unfortunate telegram will be gained." The Kings Point Alumni Association issued a statement that said that the closing of the USMMA would be a "national tragedy" for the merchant marine if "officer training were left to the mercies of the inferior operations of the state schools."

Durgin angrily fired back stating the Alumni Association was only trying to "stir up an emotional defense of Kings Point, thereby clouding the basic issue of economy." Durgin declared to the College Council, "Early determining upon a course of dignified silence, I am quite sure . . . that by refusing to descend into the arena for mud-slinging and name-calling, the Maritime College added to the dignity it has earned as America's oldest and best maritime training school."

One notable result of all this was that the rivalry between the state and federal academies intensified. More significantly, the clamor galvanized support for Kings Point, which resulted in a 1956 law that made the USMMA a permanent institution.

The feud got a reprieve in August, 1958 when President Eisenhower signed into law the Maritime Academy Act. The new legislation increased the state schools' subsidies to a maximum of $75,000 per institution and increased annual state cadet payments from $450 to $600. Credit was given to the efforts of the Maritime College's Alumni Association for helping to promote the law. Payments began in July of 1959. Still, the hard feelings over these issues filtered to the cadet level.

"OPERATION RAM"

The students at Fort Schuyler referred to the USMMA as the "trade school" and started raiding the campus at Kings Point as early as 1951 when they hoisted their school flag up the federal flagpole. The USMMA cadets would repay the Maritime College in kind. Both sets of cadets would take boats, cross Long Island Sound, then invade and vandalize each other's campuses. Usually, the pranks were handled in a sportsmanlike fashion, but at times incidents grew especially ridiculous such as in 1952's "Operation Ram."

Kings Point and Fort Schuyler regularly played one another in sports. Competition was promoted by everybody, and naturally the cadets of each school wanted to out-prank the other. One group of Maritime College cadets, dubbing themselves the "Jollyboys," dedicated themselves to the abduction of "Neptune II," the mascot ram of the USMMA.

The Jollyboys, William Weiss, John Turi, Roger Wessel and David Oaksmith, first tried to reconnoiter Kings Point. They drove to Long Island and brought "Morgan," a beagle that was Fort Schuyler's mascot, in order to smell out "the ram, if all other means of locating him failed." Unfortunately, they could not get close to their quarry so the Jollyboys returned to Fort Schuyler "empty-handed and temporarily depressed." They realized they needed to have a better strategy in order to pull off the caper.

After some consideration, Weiss telephoned the Kings Point Athletic Department's business manager, Jim Camerata, and impersonated a faux sports reporter named Joe Ferrara of the magazine *Tru-Sport*. "Ferrara's" scoop was to interview the personnel at the USMMA about college mascots. Camerata was open to the idea and made an appointment to meet with Weiss.

Yet before Weiss could go to the meeting, he got written up and was restricted to the campus. Undeterred, he called the USMMA again, and this time spoke to another officer, Richard J. O'Connell. Weiss said to O'Connell, "I'd like to make it up there Monday but I've got to interview two great Negro touchdown twins, Rog Oaksmith and Flash Turi. You've heard of them of course, played for the Jollyboys back in '27."

A new appointment was made but before Weiss hung up, O'Connell said he was glad to get the call since he wanted to make sure everything "was on the up and up." Weiss promptly replied, "Yes sir! That's *Tru-Sport*, everything is on the up and up."

Weiss's role in "Operation Ram" ceased at this point, and the field work was left to the other Jollyboys. Donning trench coats and wielding cameras, Turi pretended to be reporter "John de Santo" while Wessel and Oaksmith were photographers "Ignatz Jones" and "Joe Glotz." When they arrived, they met Camerata and two male USMMA cheerleaders. Nobody questioned them as they were led to the ram. The cheerleaders then brought the mascot out for their inspection. The Jollyboys were aghast when they saw the "limping, wheezing and thoroughly under-nourished poor excuse for a ram."

Despite the lackluster condition of the animal (the Jollyboys "wondered if all their effort was worthwhile") they proceeded. They took photos of the mascot posing with the cheerleaders (which were duly published in the student newspaper)* and then asked questions.

"How much does he weigh?"

"Has he ever been stolen?"

"Is the fence around his pen in good condition?"

After the interview, the Jollyboys returned to Fort Schuyler and started to plan how to steal Neptune II. To the credit of the officials at Kings Point, they were suspicious of the reporters' youth and line of questioning. They contacted Durgin, who promptly put a stop to the plot. The Jollyboys insisted that if the Admiral had not stopped them, they would have carried out the kidnapping. To placate themselves, at the start of the next basketball game against Kings Point, the cadets dressed a Mug as a ram and led him onto the court—his head in a hangman's noose.

It was not a total loss for the Jollyboys. They received a fair amount of local attention. Aside from the student press, Turi, Weiss and Oaksmith, were accompanied by Athletic Director Roger Reinhart to an interview by local television journalist, Jimmy Powers, on his show, "The Powerhouse." Powers dubbed the cadets "ram-nappers."

"FELT LIKE A PRISON"

While many of the cadets adhered to the tenets of the "Sallyport Saying," others did not. Often, there was shock at being brought into the boot camp-like discipline of Fort Schuyler. One student recalled, "I felt confined by the walls of the school the moment I entered the gates. It was a college, but it felt like a prison."

This student applied to Maritime College because the brother of his best friend went there. "If my friend's brother had been going to Queens College, I would have applied there." But, after visiting the campus, he was impressed by the spectacle of "phalanxes of bright cadets in spanking clean uniforms." He didn't know anything about marine transportation, and he didn't care.

---

*Photos in the newspaper are a bit dark, but the ram sort of looked like a goat.

He was only going because his father forced him too. He wanted his son to be the first in the family to earn a degree, and he wanted his son to give up his dream of becoming a ballet dancer.

Being known as a ballet dancer at a place like Fort Schuyler was an invitation to bullying. He knew he'd have to be tough. So the cadet dedicated himself to athletics. Boxing coach Matthew Twomey was so impressed that he invited him to join the team. He soon became the college's junior welterweight champion and also won a letter on the varsity baseball team.

But he remained dedicated to his art. He grew frustrated and secretly joined a dancing school at Carnegie Hall. Lessons were three nights a week. The questions were how he was going to get off the campus without getting expelled, and how he was going to pay for the lessons.

He used any means necessary. He walked along the seawall until he could climb over an unguarded fence. He volunteered for any work that would get him off the campus. He had a friend who was on liberty hide him under a blanket in the backseat of his car or in his trunk to get him out. When it proved impossible by any other means, he forged a pass.

To pay for the lessons, the cadet bought cases of beer and snuck them onto campus in his laundry bag. He sold beer to cadets by going from dorm room to dorm room, charging 25¢ per can. He also worked at the post office during the Christmas and Easter breaks.

Looking back on the experience he recalled, ". . . it's hard to believe how rigidly the rules were enforced at the school in the 1950s. It was very much a reflection of the times."

Edward Villella graduated in 1957. He then joined the New York City Ballet, dancing for George Balanchine. Of his time under Balanchine, the *New York Times* wrote, "In his two decades with the New York City Ballet, from 1957 to 1977, Edward Villella was one of America's great ballet stars, perhaps the only one to have made virile masculinity synonymous with grace and beauty in the same fashion as Rudolf Nureyev." He then went on to become a choreographer and founded the Miami City Ballet. Among many honors, he was presented with the National Medal of Arts by President Bill Clinton in 1997.

When asked about the impact of the college on his career, Villella commented that it gave him confidence and pride. He was the first in his family to achieve a college education. He found that the experience was enlightening, especially when compared to the insular world of ballet. "It gave me a sense of myself. It was terrific to have a formal education beyond the world of dance."

MASTER AND COMMANDANT

Still overseeing the cadets at this time as Master of the Training Ship and Commandant of Cadets was Captain Alfred F. Olivet. Draconian and short-tempered, he had become a college legend due to his various encounters with the students.

Len Sutter of the class of 1953 provided one story of the Captain's inspections:

> One of the cadet battalion officers was a bright, friendly fellow, with a taste for art. He had found an attractive piece of driftwood that . . . occupied a place of honor on the bureau in his room. During an inspection, Captain Olivet discovered the driftwood and said, *'What is that?'* The cadet replied it was a piece of driftwood. Captain Olivet then asked, *'Why is it there?'* The cadet said that he liked to look at it. Without further comment, Captain Olivet threw it out the open window, awarded the man a couple of demerits and went on with his inspection.

Other students had repeated run-ins with Olivet.

Dan Lynch had earned dozens of demerits resulting in weeks' worth of restrictions and extra duty. As Lynch recalled many years later: "I was just a misplaced South Bronx youth who didn't realize that I wasn't attending an advanced high school but a military boot camp. . . ."

Lynch was punished for having an unmade bed, reading the Sunday comics while on duty, sneaking off campus to see his girlfriend and writing a nasty note to an upper classman. Of this last offense, Lynch was innocent, but Olivet made all the Mugs provide handwriting samples. He decided Lynch's handwriting matched. Olivet fumed at Lynch's cowardice for writing a note calling an upperclassman a "Mary." Lynch objected and said to the captain that he should get a handwriting expert to examine the sample. Olivet dismissed the idea stating that he knew it was him, and he didn't need an expert.

This was just in Lynch's first year—which ended with him failing out. He recalled:

> I drove my car into the Sallyport one Saturday morning to take all my clothing, books and other gear completely forgetting that the Captain would be having his inspection in the inner gorge as he did every Saturday before the cadets went on weekend leave. When I backed out I found myself locked in by all the cadets. . . . I blew my horn for them to get out of my way.

That included the Captain himself. He flew into a rage and I just smiled and continued to proceed at one mile per hour, beeping my horn, through the throng. The Captain came to my window furious. "Lynch what are you doing?" I replied "I'm out of here for good, Captain" as I proceeded through the archway and on my way home.

But Lynch, by some miracle, returned to Fort Schuyler that fall for more encounters with the Captain. During the 1956 cruise, he was one of the operators of a boat ferrying cadets from the ship to Bermuda. Lynch handled the engine. He could not see a thing from his position, nor could he hear verbal orders because of the noise from the motor. He relied on the coxswain to ring a bell to provide commands. As they raced across the water:

> The last bell order I had received was "full speed ahead" and I had the engine wide open rushing across the water. To my surprise I saw Otto, a 2nd classman, over the gunnel with a look of shock. I turned to look at the coxswain, and he too had a look shock on his face as he was yelling, unheard, in the engine noise. I stood up to see, too late, that we were about to crash into the back of the Captain's gig. I attempted to stop the engine, but the forward momentum took control in that last few feet.

At the hearing, the coxswain insisted that Lynch was innocent. But Lynch distinctly heard Olivet mutter, "Lynch again."

As a cadet-ensign, a position invented by Admiral Durgin to give the senior students more privileges and responsibilities, Lynch got his own stateroom. On the first morning of the 1957 cruise, he decided not to wake to reveille, but sleep in. Olivet's executive officer, James Maley, woke him and reported him to the captain. Lynch lost his stateroom and was tossed into a compartment with sixteen cadets.

Then, when they arrived in Bilbao, Spain, Lynch's luck began to turn. He met an American girl who invited him to a party at a yacht club. After the party she wanted to go to a restaurant and bar. Lynch's curfew was at midnight, but the place she wanted to go was obscure, albeit close. It was on a mountain overlooking the ship. More importantly, he knew the cadets on the deck watch and was certain they'd cover for him.

Lynch decided to risk it:

> When I arrived at the restaurant I had had a few drinks already and was feeling lightheaded when I entered. The young lady was wearing my hat on

the back of her head. As I entered, there was a group of four men sitting at a table, and one of them pointed to the girl I was with. I asked him if he thought she was cute. We sat down . . . and immediately a cadet came to my table with a grim face. He said, "Dan, the Captain wants to see you." It seems that one of the men, in civilian clothes, was Captain Olivet and the person I spoke to was the mayor.

Olivet was furious. Lynch's wisecrack to the mayor and his date wearing his hat were grave offenses to the dignity of the college. It was 11:52 p.m. With eight minutes until the end of curfew, Lynch seized his hat from the girl's head, ran down a spiraling road, leapt through backyards and hurtled over fences to get to the *Empire State III* before midnight. As he panted up to the ship, eight bells rang. He shouted, "Lynch is returning!" He was logged in.

Two hours later, Olivet summoned Lynch and all the cadets of the 8-12 watch. He could not imagine him getting back on time. He thought the watch was covering for him. The captain glared at Lynch and asked him how he did it. He replied, "I ran fast."

Olivet wanted to hang Lynch from a yardarm. He then said, "We'll see you do it again tomorrow. I'll personally drive you back to the restaurant and time you getting back to the ship. Then I'll have proof that all of you are lying."

Lynch, who was in the band, arranged to have them play thrilling music from the fantail for the race. He didn't think he could do it again, but he was going to have fun trying.

But it was not to be. The next day at the appointed time, Lynch was told that the captain was ill. He was saved.

Olivet was nicknamed "Botts" by the cadets. At that time it was a pejorative coming phonetically from Italian slang meaning "crazy." Yet in later years, it transformed from an insult to a sign of affection. Lynch recalled, "This man was responsible for the lives of some 700 young men under the most stressful conditions. He had to be a hard disciplinarian. We knew that. While we referred to him as 'Botts' we respected his position and responsibilities." Olivet remained at the college until 1965.

"JOHNNY COME LATELY"

In 1955, SUNY replaced the 19-member Board of Visitors with a nine-member College Council. The Council, like the Board, was essentially advisory in nature and created by SUNY in an effort to standardize advisory boards across campuses.

The change to a council structure was unremarkable except that Arthur Tode once more became the center of a political fiasco. When Durgin came to office, Tode was still the Chairman of the Board of Visitors. When the change to the new structure was declared, he submitted a list of names to Durgin advising who he thought should be on the Council. Tode omitted his own name assuming that he would be automatically nominated as Chairman of the Council. Durgin, took the list, swapped one of the recommendations for his own, and never included Tode. This new list was then sent to Governor Dewey who approved it.

When Tode found out that he was not only not Chairman, but completely off the Council, he exploded. He denounced Durgin as a "Johnny come lately" who through machinations ousted him from the college. One of Tode's friends tried to mollify him: "The Governor might have thought that since you did not include yourself for appointment that you might not want it as it has become common practice for incumbents to ask for their own reappointment." But there was nothing Tode could do. He was out, and the first Chair of the College Council was former admiralty lawyer Carl Vander Clute who had served as Tode's Vice Chairman. Tode remained in contact with the school until his death in 1966.

The truth of whether or not Tode was manipulated off of the College Council will never be known. Durgin might have had some cause to want to oust Tode. Tode was forceful, and wielded his position as Chairman as almost a second president. It is easy to see how a self-willed man like Durgin could have wanted meddlers removed. Also, as demonstrated from his relationship with Felix Riesenberg, Tode knew how to make enemies.

"AN INDEFINABLE INSTITUTION"

Admiral Durgin wanted Maritime College to become the most elite school of its kind. Yet in order for the college to enter the top ranks, there was general agreement that new buildings were required. There was no room on the campus. The cadets had been kicked out of Fort Schuyler and into the World War II era barracks in order to make room for academic programs. Also, if the college was to be taken seriously as an engineering school, it needed a separate building with appropriate labs.

But Durgin and the college were stymied all throughout his tenure in getting the money that was needed for new construction. At first, it was because the state did not own Fort Schuyler. Yet even after the property was transferred to New York in 1957, the State was unwilling to further invest in SUNY. In that same year, the State promised Durgin a $4.7 million grant for construction. It never materialized.

Durgin, seeing the trend, took matters into his own hands and made some phone calls to solicit money for the college. He had some measure of success with individual donors—such as Herman Baruch sending some shrubs and tobacco magnate Richard J. Reynolds, Jr. giving money to build a domed planetarium atop Fort Schuyler. Durgin also obtained a new ship, the *Mercy*, which was renamed the *Empire State III* in 1956. This was especially needed since the old *Hydrus* was not passing Coast Guard inspections due to her being designed to Navy specifications. One graduate likened the new ship to a "luxury cruise liner" when compared to the *Empire State II*. But the *Empire State III* was generally disliked by all hands, and within a few years was exchanged for the *Henry Gibbins*, which became the *Empire State IV* in 1959. Yet everybody on the campus knew that if the college was to become an elite institution, it needed more than a ship. It needed a commitment from the State.

But New York State had other plans that promptly disrupted the entire campus. Robert Moses, who had long planned to build a bridge to Queens over the property, got permission from Albany to begin construction. Durgin protested, and Moses, who remembered the trouble he had over Fort Schuyler almost three decades earlier, disregarded the Admiral's pleas. When it became apparent that Moses was going to build the bridge no matter what the college wanted, Olivet suggested renaming it the Fort Schuyler Bridge for advertising. Moses dismissed this idea and began the construction of the Throgs Neck Bridge.

The construction of the bridge made the campus a noisier place. No longer would cadets listen to just the wind, ships and sea. But the inconvenience of rumbling traffic also brought new opportunity, since ten acres of land were added to the campus by landfill dredged during the bridge's construction.*

The building of the bridge coincided with the election of Nelson Rockefeller as Governor of New York in 1959. Rockefeller was a strong

---

*The bridge, until it became more restricted, became an excellent place for graduating students to surreptitiously paint their class year.

proponent of public education. Under him, the State began a systematic and large scale investment in SUNY. The long-sought funding to construct new buildings was at last realized, and over the next decade the campus blossomed. New dormitories were built. These were critical additions. In 1960, the barracks were in such bad condition that the college moved the cadets aboard the training ship. This was a smart move since on March 25, 1962, a fire destroyed the barracks. The cadets moved into the new dormitories the next year.

In addition to the dormitories, the college built an athletic building, a waterfront facility and a building dedicated to Science and Engineering. All the new buildings, which were described by writer Neil Steinberg as "square and charmless" stood in stark contrast to Fort Schuyler. But they allowed the program to expand and flourish as never before. The building efforts were so significant that it led one student to write, "The graduate of the future will not think of his Alma Mater in the compact, solid and clear cut terms of our rather austere ship and fort. Rather, he will know a vastly more complex, more inscrutable and more indefinable institution."

The faculty took the lead and established new programs and majors. A nuclear engineering program was established under Drs. Meir Degani* and Salomon Liverhant. Through their efforts, the Atomic Energy Commission gave a grant in the form of a subcritical nuclear reactor that was built on campus by the cadets. By 1962, the college had expanded beyond its traditional programs into new majors that included Nuclear Science, Meteorology and Oceanography. Then, in 1968, a masters degree in Marine Science was introduced. In the following decades, program expansion continued to pile on new majors, so that by 1980, students could select among nine different fields of study.

Yet the beneficiary of the Rockefeller boom was not Durgin but his successors starting with Coast Guard Admiral Harold Moore.** The students honored Durgin as the "Robert Moses of the Maritime College" when he

---

*Degani had a great nuclear resume and was said to have been involved in the Manhattan Project. This rumor, however, was untrue. In an interview with the student newspaper, Degani said that while he was invited to join the project he declined. He remarked, "At the time it was so secret that I couldn't see what responsibilities I would have or what connection it had to World War II, so I turned it down . . . It wasn't until after Nagasaki that I found out that this work had such tremendous importance."

**Moore, a graduate from 1924, was the first alumnus to head the school since E.V.W. Keen left in 1927.

retired in 1959, not knowing that the fruition of his building plans was yet to come. Durgin himself commented that the climax of his presidency was the full accreditation of the college, but this was something that was mostly achieved during the Leary administration.

"VISSI D'ARTE"

But Durgin possessed style, grace and melodrama. He reminded everybody about this one last time during his retirement, in 1965. He and his wife had decided to visit New York City because his friend, the legendary soprano Maria Callas, was performing Puccini's "Tosca." The opera world was tittering. After the premier, the *New York Times* commented, "New York had been thrown in a tizzy ever since the announcement about the performance was made, and last night only served to bring everything to a boil."

Durgin and his wife made their way to the old Metropolitan Opera on Broadway between 39th and 40th Streets. The Admiral, still resplendent at age 72, took an 18th row aisle seat.

The curtain drew open, and the audience's attention was drawn to Callas. His seat provided him a wonderful view of his friend, who played the jealous and talented Tosca.

As the curtain descended ending the first act, the audience was moved. Callas' voice had not weakened. The second act began. Callas began to sing the major aria: "Vissi d'arte."

As Callas's voice hovered over the audience, Durgin stood up. Some thought he was going to salute Callas for her remarkable performance. Instead, he clutched his chest and collapsed. Another attendee understood what was happening. There was a call for a doctor. They took Durgin out to the lobby. But it was too late; he had died of a heart attack. Even in death, the Admiral had style. The Durgin era was over, but at Fort Schuyler, the days of the Dome were beginning.

CHAPTER 14

The Dome

What is this madness?
Why won't it stop?
The Maritime College
Is a dead total flop.

It offers us nothing.
It does us no good.
Let's make it a place
To be understood.

These creatures above us
Where are they at?
They're dead men and old men
With more gold on their hat.

They fight and they kill
And they'll shout what they know
That nothing's as holy as
Beloved Status Quo.

All honor and valor
And yes be most brave
But eternal damnation
To them that make waves.

Brothers! Enough!
The time has drawn near
Now they are afraid
And we have no fear.

The changes are needed!
Good must be done!!
Violent or peaceful
REVOLUTION WILL COME!!!!

—Anonymous Maritime College cadet,
  circa 1970

THE METAPHOR OF THE DOME

America in the 1960s and 70s was marked by social and political upheaval associated with the growth of the civil rights movement, the development of the counter-culture and the controversy of the war in Vietnam. In a decade that began with Freedom Riders fighting for desegregation in the South and ended with the first successful lunar landing, the years from 1960 to 1970 were a crucible that redefined American society—a crucible that Maritime College fought to avoid.

Of course there were some changes at the college, but these were mostly to accentuate the academic side of the school. Top down, military-style administration prevailed. The institution, at its heart, was a regimental experience. But the students at Fort Schuyler were not immune to the happenings of the world outside. As the decade grew to a close and massive political demonstrations prevailed, Maritime cadets could see what their peers at other colleges were doing. A growing minority of students on campus began to question how things were done at the college and likened themselves to being in a domed enclosure.

This spawned a new nickname for the college in 1968: *The Dome*. Yet it didn't become really popular until the next year after the *Empire State IV* glanced off the rocks by the Stepping Stone Lighthouse, listed to port and sustained damage to the tanks beneath the engine room. Luckily, there were no injuries and they managed to get the ship off the rocks. The vessel, in fact crossed the Atlantic twice before the full extent of the damage became apparent. Afterward, a student named Steve Cernik had tee shirts designed that depicted the training ship on the rocks, a cadet twiddling his thumbs and the name "Domer" underneath. The term was here to stay.

For decades, this subversive term was as synonymous for Fort Schuyler as the Yard was for the U.S. Naval Academy. If you asked a cadet from Kings Point who a "Domer" was, they would as easily identify a Maritime College student as a West Point cadet would identify a "Mid" as a U.S. Naval Academy student. But many of those who bandied about the nickname, years later, never realized its true origin as a watchword of protest.*

---

*There are many variations as to the origins of the nickname that have been thoroughly debated by the alumni. The likely origin of the term comes from a pun on the name of a television show called "Hippodrome," which featured circuses. The nickname started as *Maridrome* then, *Maridome*, then just *Dome*. While the actual origin is debatable, all sources point out that the term was pejorative of the institution.

"FASCIST TACTICS?"

Presiding over the Dome at this time was Rear Admiral Edward J. O'Donnell. He had been head of the college since 1967, when Harold Moore retired and was named President *Emeritus*. A World War II veteran, O'Donnell was notably the commanding officer of the Navy base at Guantanamo Bay during the 1962 Cuban Missile Crisis. After, he administered the Naval Postgraduate School in Monterey before retiring from the Navy to administer Maritime College.

O'Donnell, who was in failing health and hard of hearing, was not a charismatic figure like Leary or Durgin. His tendency was toward benign neglect or vacillation. This is not to say O'Donnell was completely insulated from the pulse of the campus, since he issued orders through the cadet-officers. Professor Fred Hess wrote that he offered "constant encouragement" to the cadets and was an "inspirational factor in the development of . . . emerging naval and maritime officers who would become business and technical leaders in the maritime field." But Hess's characterization is eclipsed by the picture of a stodgy career officer who could not relate to students.

One 1973 graduate, Charlie Munsch, recalled O'Donnell inspecting the students at "Pass in Review." Slowly, the Admiral marched up the line of cadets, made even slower by his old basset hound, Gunner. At one inspection, Gunner, for lack of a tree or fire hydrant, decided he couldn't hold it in anymore and did his business on the Admiral's shoes. "Pass in Review" was quickly morphed by the cadets into "Piss in Your Shoe." Professor and 1964 graduate Jose Femenia probably got it right when he mused, "Heck of a nice guy but he came here at the wrong time."

As testament to the generational gap, O'Donnell suspected (probably rightly) that the students were using drugs on campus. He authorized unannounced inspections. The students were quick to realize that these were covert drug searches. One notorious incident occurred on March 6, 1969, when examinations of four rooms were conducted in the middle of the night. In one of these cases, the inspectors dismantled an underclassman's room and did not put his things back in place. A student newspaper editorial complained:

> I realize that the Maritime College is militarily orientated, but does that give it the right to resort to fascist tactics? Is there no respect for personal property here? To remove any article from someone's home without notifying them, or worse yet when they are not even present, is burglary. And yet, here at the Maritime College, such acts of burglary are committed with the approval of the administration!

The student newspaper condemned the administration as heavy-handed and was so critical that O'Donnell formed a fact finding committee. The cadet-officers who were involved in the fiasco submitted a 40-page report to the admiral where they pledged to "meet and carry out their responsibilities, no matter how distasteful or controversial. . . ." Despite vociferous complaints, searches would continue.

This episode demonstrated that a twofold division on campus was emerging: between the administration and the students, and groups of cadets who strongly supported the regimental system and those who did not.

INDOCTRINATION

The regimental system by the 1960s had been liberalized compared to the practices conducted during the institution's schoolship and academy days. But it was still rough. Mugs underwent an indoctrination period. They shaved their hair, they memorized a variety of military minutia* and they went through exhausting physical exercise. Hazing was relegated to affairs called "brace parties," in which the cadet-officers would call the Mugs out of their beds and make them stay up through the night doing exercises such as "front leaning rest," which was to maintain a pushup in the up position, or to sit in an imaginary "green chair." When not performing exercises, they held an exaggerated form of attention called a "brace" where the chest was puffed out and the chin tucked. Also, Mugs were forced to carry items for upperclassmen: a coin to make a phone call, a match to light his cigarette and a woman's nylon or sock to shine his shoes.

Jose Femenia said, "I thought the indoctrination period was a mixture of being yelled and screamed at, having fun and doing some silly things. I remember the first class having us go around picking up dandelions and presenting them to teachers. It was comical. I don't think it was malicious. To me it wasn't a big deal." And most of the graduates of Maritime College agreed except for a small and vocal minority that complained not only about indoctrination, but how the college was run.

---

*A personal favorite of the author was provided by Dr. Richard Burke as derived from military traditions. An IDO might ask, "How's the cow, mister?" To which the proper response was: "Sir, the cow, sir; she walks, she talks, she's full of chalk. The lacteal fluid secreted by the female of the bovine species is highly prolific to the nth degree, sir!"

"ALMOST NIHILISTIC"

The primary forum of campus dissent was the student newspaper, the *Porthole*. Beginning in the 1950s, the newspaper published complaints that were almost always minor in nature and parochial in outlook. Letters repeatedly complained about room décor, television privileges, hazing, the right to sleep during free periods and bad food.

But in 1963 this changed when the staff of the *Porthole*, with the Moore administration's permission, circulated a questionnaire asking for opinions about the school and its curriculum. This was the first time anything of that nature had been conducted. The senior first class students were particularly outspoken.

While they asserted that they received an above-average education, the article reported that there was "room for improvement" in the curriculum. Marine Transportation students commented that "too much time was being wasted on unnecessary jobs." Engineering students concurred and added that time was lost "on menial tasks, on 'make work' . . . and not enough was being devoted to on-the-job training." Furthermore, a large number of engineering students questioned the value of the regimental system and thought that "Naval Science had little relevance to their professional interests."

The questionnaire was accompanied by several sharp editorials in the *Porthole* that described disconnect between the faculty and the students. One article complained about rote teaching methods and overlap of content between courses. The cadet writer asserted that the officers who taught them were "part-timers who know nothing of what goes on within the student body. . . ."

In that same issue, another cadet, after noting the college's strong points, asserted that the general attitude toward authority on the campus was apathetic and "almost nihilistic." He wrote that this was caused by inconsistency in which some rules were applied and other not. He blamed it on favoritism and asserted that the way to restore morale was not to loosen rules but to toughen them. In this way an "*esprit de corps* or honor system backed by the cadets' respect and belief in its purposeful intent" would come into being.

After the 1963 opening salvo, students became more comfortable complaining about issues other than the food. Chief on their list of gripes was the lack of personal freedom. One cadet lamented that Maritime College stifled individuality. "Is there no more room for individualistic, liberal minded, creative thinking, dissenters who dare to question orders or directives?"

Eventually, the criticism against the college grew so intense that Admiral Moore rued the day he allowed the questionnaire. In one meeting between the *Porthole* editors, their faculty advisor and the Admiral, Moore was quoted:

> Freedom of the press and free speech have no place at the Maritime College. . . . When you criticize anything about the system or anybody connected with it, you are criticizing me. You imply that I am not doing my job. You are putting down in print, with no signature, something that you wouldn't come in here and say to my face. Why do you think I sit in this chair? Because I have an interest in the college, and because I never dared criticize my superiors or their judgment.

The cry for personal liberty intensified. In February, 1968, one student wrote, ". . . it should be noted that many, if not a majority of other schools, allow their men to come and go as they please, some without even signing in or out. . . . Even girls' schools are given a higher degree of freedom than that obtained by Maritime cadets." Students could not wait for the weekend. In November, 1968, a student observed, "This longing for the weekend, to the degree in which it is found here, is totally abnormal; and I'm sure that any psychiatrist would attend to this fact. . . . If a craving for liberty, and then the fruition of this dream, make one a better, more disciplined man, then why do so many ex-convicts return to prison?"

Some cadets released their frustration through vandalism and food fights. In November, 1968, there were complaints of overturned library furniture, vandalized clocks and vending machines jammed with sticks. In 1970, car tires were being slashed, public phones tampered with and gym lockers burglarized.

"MAKING WAVES"

Some of the most vocal critics of the college were the faculty. The most infamous was Robert Sennish, an English instructor who had been at the school since 1960. One source recalled that while an excellent teacher, he was given to conspiracy theories that made "Oliver Stone look very comfortable." At the last faculty meeting of every year, Sennish, ridiculously and half-jokingly, motioned to disband the entire faculty since it was "ineffective in challenging the administration." The motion was never seconded, even in the year he retired. For these reasons, Sennish earned the sobriquet, "Commie Bob."

At a 1969 SUNY symposium, Sennish caused a stir when he advocated disbanding the College Council (since they "did nothing") and empowering faculty and students to directly administer the college. In an interview at the end of his career he said, "People spend four years of their lives with military rigors, in order, when they are finished, not to be in the military. Now, if you go to West Point or Annapolis, it makes sense . . . , but here, it's like sending someone through medical school and then asking them to become an engineer." Sennish claimed that because of his outspokenness, after 30 years of teaching, he was the lowest paid faculty member on campus with the same level of service.

One Engineering Assistant Professor stood out for a letter he wrote to the *Porthole* in 1968. In it, he decried an institutional culture where its members were afraid to "make waves." He asserted that the college community was rewarded for doing nothing and thereby voting "for the preservation of the status quo." He criticized the students and wrote that they were "still trying to get out of high school." As an example, he cited misbehavior in the classroom and accused the students of being too weak to stand up for themselves. He wrote that the students'

> . . . only form of protest about what they don't like is to sneak off campus (especially the seniors), to change out of uniform 10 yards from the gate and to use instructors for leverage against the military system. But little do they realize that it is the military system that has beaten them. They are quite bullied, their acts of defiance being not very defiant, requiring no real courage. . . .

Then, in a charming metaphor, he wrote, "As cows who have not been milked for twenty hours submit their udders to any hands, the Maritime College students submit their intellectual capacities to whoever appears on the scene; academic or military, never questioning the rationality of their instructors." If the author wanted the support of the administration, he wasn't going to get it when he called them "either near-sighted or foolhardy" since they "knocked the students numb when the voice of dissent has been heard."

This letter was extreme in its blanket complaints about the college, but it was demonstrative of the growth of dissent either to liberalize the college or to make the military system stronger. On either side, there was discontent. The students blamed the faculty and the faculty blamed the students, but they all said that there was a problem with the college. As morale ebbed, attendance at the college stagnated. This was symptomatic of the Vietnam War era in which a military or semi-military education was not considered as valuable.

Several years later, Gary Jobson, the editor of the *Porthole*, reflected on students with poor morale:

> There are many reasons for this including dissatisfaction with the military life at the College, poor guidance, heavy academic loads, events in the outside world, the job situation in the Merchant Marine and the reluctance of making changes.

THE PROTESTS

The first Maritime College political demonstrations were over Vietnam War policies. Opinions about the war were discussed openly in the pages of the *Porthole* since 1965 when the editor criticized protests at other colleges. "For these students to ask their country to stop fighting for freedom is evidence enough that they don't realize how serious communism really is. . . ."

Pro-war opinion was strong enough that in April, 1968, in response to student antiwar demonstrations in New York City, some cadets held a counter demonstration on campus. This event, organized by first-class cadets, was called "Students for Victorious Peace—Support Our Allies Day." Cadet Howard Merkel, one of the organizers, stated that the gathering was to "counter left wing demonstrations held throughout the world which were basically for a sellout or immediate withdrawal of troops from Vietnam." The regiment hoisted the colors, the National Anthem was played and three volleys were fired by the Pershing Rifle Guard. The demonstration took a collection of $225 for the surviving relatives of a soldier killed in action. Only fifteen cadets did not to participate. Meanwhile, Admiral O'Donnell asserted the administration's neutrality toward the demonstration and insisted that attendance was completely voluntary so that it did not appear that the students were being coerced to attend.

While the majority of the college's students were pro-war, there was some antiwar dissent which coalesced in 1969. Robert Sennish with Oscar Goodman, the chairman of the Humanities department, led a small group of faculty and students in the Vietnam War Moratorium movement. The Moratorium urged a work stoppage on October 15th to demonstrate for an immediate end to the Vietnam War. Nationwide, thousands of individuals gathered at multiple rallies. However, at Maritime College, turnout was modest, between 100 to 200 people.*

Maritime College, with its military ties, was a conservative institution. Work did not stop, and the Moratorium demonstrators gathered for only an hour. One cadet was so angry at the demonstrators that he wrote:

> I am sure that we are all proud of our fellow 'Americans' who took part in October's Peace Moratorium. I know of no other group who could have incited Hanoi and the Viet Cong to fight even harder for their goals. I imagine that this display of dissatisfaction for the President's policies is just a way of showing their appreciation for all they have received here in America. To show their gratitude, they turn around and stab their country in the back.

In fact, there was a counter petition circulated by those in support of continuing the war. This petition, while recognizing the rights of Moratorium activists, read: "As loyal Americans we are against war but we are also against enslavement by communism. We believe the Moratorium demonstrations will aid the enemy by giving support to the view that the American people are not supporting their president in his efforts." A majority of the student body, 497, signed the petition.

The O'Donnell administration, following the precedent it set for the 1968 pro-war demonstration, took no action either for or against the Moratorium or the counter petition. In fact, no policy regarding political demonstrations

---

*The administration claimed there were 100 people in attendance. The organizers claimed 200.

was expressed by O'Donnell, although he stated his worry of "continued and future activities of divisiveness."

In the months after the Moratorium, nationwide antiwar protest intensified, especially over President Nixon's policies in Cambodia. At Maritime College, Nixon's policies were generally favored by the cadets. In March 1970, an opinion poll was conducted by the Moratorium organizers and found that 54% of Maritime students favored Nixon's policy of 'Vietnamization,' which meant slowly turning over the conduct of the war to the South Vietnamese, while only 27.4% of the cadets favored immediate withdrawal. Meanwhile, the cadets' antiwar peers outside the Dome were demonstrating. The most notorious incident occurred on May 4, 1970, at Kent State University resulting in four students being shot dead by the Ohio National Guard.

Simultaneous to the nationwide antiwar demonstrations, the students at Fort Schuyler intensified their protests against local conditions. The pressure for change was strong enough that by the late 1960s new rules and regulations were implemented that allowed for greater personal freedom. By 1969, food, civilian clothing and even radios were allowed inside the dorms. Alumni who visited Fort Schuyler were astounded by the changes.

Sensing that things were going their way, in February, 1970, the students ran a non-binding referendum on proposed changes to the college. Results showed that the majority of students wanted better food service, more liberty, an optional naval science curriculum and to overturn the college's honor system. They also voted to replace the six-day class schedule with a five-day one.

This last point was a sore subject. Saturday morning classes had been introduced during the early years of the college due to the intensity of the curriculum. Sessions ran until 11 a.m. then followed by inspections. It was a major inconvenience for the students. Aside from having to go to college six days a week, cadets griped that such a schedule did not leave any time for them to work on the weekend. This was important, since they had trouble obtaining traditional summer employment because they were, more often than not, training at sea. The whole issue caused much consternation among the cadets.

The faculty reacted to the student referendum in late March. They passed a resolution to do away with Saturday classes and made optional the Naval Science curricula. This resolution was not acted upon by the administration. When asked by a student reporter if Saturday classes could be eliminated, the

Admiral replied, "No. It is a very important part of your training to be here until Saturday as it prepares the individual for the discipline he will need to exert upon himself and others following graduation." The administration refused to meet with the student government over the issue and as a result further alienated it.

Then student underground publications took this issue and ran with it. The school, in fact, had a long tradition of seditious newspapers going back to the 1920s. The most ubiquitous at this time was the *Periscope: The Underwater Porthole*, which began publication in the late 1950s. Thomas Clark, one of the original editors of the *Periscope*, admitted over fifty years later his involvement in the publication. He said the administration enlisted the aid of the Humanities Department to analyze the writing style so they could find the miscreants. They only got away with publication through the help of Pat Dunphy, a secretary, who let them use the mimeograph machine.

In 1970, *Maritime Voice*, which was about as radical a broadside as Maritime College cadets would ever produce, gathered steam and denounced the administration for ignoring the referendum: "We, the students, ask the faculty to stand by us in our fight to stamp out the infestation of apathy and hypocrisy so long the controlling factors of this college." The publication then demanded that the college's governance be restructured and the referendum results implemented. What effect this publication had on the student body cannot be measured, but the matter soon came to a head.

The Admiral finally promised to meet with the cadets to talk about the matter, but this information was not widely disseminated except for the fact that demonstrations were prohibited. The Student Council became divided with the student President announcing that demonstrations would not be supported by the student government while the Vice President actively exhorted the cadets to action. Finally, using the campus's public announcement system, *ad hoc* protests were organized by the cadets on May 5th and 6th. They assembled a sit-in of about 200 cadets on the Admiral's lawn. They did not carry signs, chant slogans, nor give any other signal as to why they were there. They were, at first, confused for war protesters.*

---

*There is an apocryphal story that "Commie Bob" Sennish witnessed the protests and was delighted, thinking that the students had finally woken up. The Kent State Massacre occurred right before the Maritime protest, so Sennish would naturally have been confused. But, the cadets merely wanted off on Saturdays.

Among the demonstrators was James DeSimone. He was an unlikely figure of dissent since his father was Guy DeSimone, a long-standing and highly regarded faculty member who was a prominent leader of the college's Marine Transportation Department.

DeSimone had been aboard the training ships since he was a child, grew up on campus and knew from years of observation what to expect at Maritime College. Also, he knew how dissent was unwelcome there. Despite this, DeSimone displayed some of the iconoclastic sentiment of his generation. As the freshman class Vice President, he signed off on the request to hold the Moratorium assembly.

In the meantime, on the Admiral's lawn, 200 cadets milled about in nervous silence. DeSimone looked at the Admiral's house. He said it was like a "doll house," where the protestors could easily see through the windows into the rooms. He and the other demonstrators could clearly observe the Admiral and his wife eating lunch at a large dining room table, oblivious to the students on their lawn. After a long interval, O'Donnell and his wife noticed them. O'Donnell picked up the phone. In short order Staff Duty Officers arrived at the scene.

The cadets did not resist. In fact, once the officers arrived, the cadets fled as quickly as possible. O'Donnell, filled with outrage, summoned some of those involved and subjected them to alleged "threats of dismissal . . . irregular interrogations and . . . extraordinary measures. . . ."

The cadets who were involved were indignant and believed they were going to be subjected to reprisals, especially during the summer cruise. Oscar Goodman came to their defense and wrote a letter to O'Donnell on May 12th charging him with "repression and . . . interference with the academic freedom and constitutional rights of the students. . . ." Goodman sent copies of the letter to, among other parties, the American Civil Liberties Union.

In the meantime, John Foody, the Engineering chairman, formed an *ad hoc* committee to investigate the affair. Before the end of the month, the committee reported that Saturday classes could be "eliminated at present and that all the required military activities of the cadets could be managed during a five-day week." O'Donnell, faced by discontented students and faculty, adopted the resolution, and Saturday classes were eliminated the following year. The protest was a resounding success.

BEER AND POOLS

Flushed with victory, the students pressed for more change. The next year, due to an unclear attendance policy, the Student Council petitioned the administration to remove punishments for cutting classes. The Council reasoned that it would instill discipline, show maturity and "improve the teaching techniques of the instructor. For if there are consistent absences, he will realize that his lecture must be improved." The faculty Student Policies Committee supported the proposal and stated that it was vital to every cadet to make his "own decisions in regard to his own academic advancement." The faculty passed a resolution supporting this with the proviso that it could not be applied to the Summer Sea Term and that the students should realize the consequences of their actions.

Other freedoms were granted. In 1971, cadets on liberty were allowed to leave and enter campus in civilian clothes since they were harassed off-campus by antiwar protesters. Also, grooming policies were changed. Longer hair was allowed, and seniors were granted the right to grow mustaches. The mustache issue was a fairly major one to the cadets since it was in style at the time. The regulations regarding mustaches were on and off; in some years first class cadets could wear them, and in other years the right was rescinded.

In that same year, beer began to be served at McMurray Hall, the waterfront activities building (TIV). The cadets could choose between Budweiser on tap or cans of Schlitz at 30¢ each. The next year, cafeteria style dining replaced the unpopular family style during eating periods. To enliven the summer cruise, cadets William Muller, Curt Bluefeld and James DeSimone convinced Captain Gerald Nolan to allow them to install a 12' × 24' aluminum swimming pool on the *Empire State IV*. In addition, drills and inspections were downplayed in favor of making the institution appear more collegiate.

Despite or maybe because of the changes, division among the students grew. In the 1971 Middle States accreditation review, it was found that the college's morale had ebbed. The review asserted that the problem lay inherently in the system. The administratively appointed cadet officers, who had disciplinary authority over their classmates, were at odds with the student-elected government. The report read:

... in a military academy—or even a semi-military academy if the cadet regiment is to function effectively—there must be a strong *esprit de corps*. . . . The Student Council has emerged in the last few years as a focal point for the expression of student opinion and has brought about rivalry and a jurisdictional conflict between the 'rates' of the Cadet Regiment (who must by their office represent the military order and philosophy) and the Council members. In keeping with the mores of the times, the Council encourages student expression of opinion, seeks more student participation in College governance, and represents the students' interests and concerns before faculty and administration.

The report noted that the students, while wishing to enter into the maritime trade, did not necessarily want the military system. But it also failed to report how interpersonal relationships played out among the student body. Professor and 1972 graduate, Dr. Richard Burke said in retrospect that much of the trouble was due to "personalities. The guy who was the elected President of the student government . . . was referred to by some as 'Crusader Rabbit.' I guess that nickname tells it all. On the other hand, the regimental officers of that year [1971] . . . were particularly ineffective. They were academically the very lowest in their class. . . . They tended to react to everything in a knee jerk fashion."

Despite the problems, the school was still quite successful in preparing their students to enter the maritime industry. One graduate noted in 1971, "Many of you may question the value of a degree from the SUNY Maritime College on or near graduation. I did once, but after a recent job hunt I've come to the conclusion that it is worth all the work and aggravation this school seems to offer. . . ." Employers liked the practical experience that the college's graduates gained.

Also, as much as some students spoke against the regimental system, there was strong justification for its existence. In 1977, the training ship's captain, Frank English, noted that the system was required by MARAD, which provided the federal subsidy and the ship. English asserted that this was required because "it is the only proven way through the ages, to exercise control over large groups of people . . . and prepare them for life in the Merchant Marine." English's interviewer noted, "As he sees it, the sea hasn't changed since the days of the tall sailing ships and probably never will. There is need for a leader or a master aboard ship. A dictator and his word is law."

English's sentiments were echoed by James DeSimone, who returned to the college almost two decades later as the Commandant of Cadets and Master of the training ship. He asserted that "the most important thing is to convey to the cadets that the purpose of the system is to facilitate the safe and effective operation of the training ship. That's its primary function, and I think that if you sell that to the cadets they accept it a lot better. . . ." DeSimone said that beyond just adhering to regulations, there are "side benefits" to the regiment such as self-discipline, teamwork and leadership.

By 1972, Admiral O'Donnell was burnt out by the protests and headaches. The Admiral retired, but not before one last contentious debate on the role of women at the college.

CHAPTER 15

"The Way It Is"

> *"The introduction of the co-educational system in SUMC would solve any social problems. For instance, if there is a dance in the mess deck and you need a date, all you would have to do is restrict a blonde or two."*
>
> —Porthole, February 17, 1956

"THAT'S AWFUL"

Philomena Magavero put on her coat, boots and hat, taking pains not to stain her clothing with ink-blotched hands. She marched out of the library at Fort Schuyler, her boots echoing through the Sallyport as she made her way to a detached building that had the only women's washroom on campus. As she stood over the basin scrubbing away the grime, she pondered how much time she had wasted walking all this way to wash her hands. 15? 20 minutes? How much time had she spent over the years in this pointless ritual?

Magavero began working at the college on March 1, 1949. She was well-educated with degrees from Hunter College and Columbia University. After graduating, she took librarian jobs at Kings Point then Hunter College. She was happy enough at Hunter, but Terence Hoverter, the Head Librarian at Fort Schuyler, had lured her away for greater pay. Before she even signed the contract to work at Maritime College, she noticed that she was being placed on a clerk's budget line instead of a librarian's. She confronted Hoverter about it. It didn't make any sense that she, who was better educated than most of the faculty at Maritime College, should be a clerk. He shrugged and said, "This is the way it is."

She found that the college was inundated with a macho culture. In one instance, an instructor tossed a piece of paper at her and demanded that she type it up. "I shouldn't even call them professors," she later commented. She hated it but stayed for the money.

Yet over time, she found that she loved working with the library's archives. She would process, sort and identify all sorts of historic documents. Much of the job was with old newsprint and deteriorating ledgers. It was dirty work, and she needed to wash her hands several times a day. So she would put on her coat and leave Fort Schuyler.

Finally one day she had enough. Her hands were covered with ink, and she was tired of marching over half the campus just to wash her hands. This time, she stomped out of the library and into Admiral Durgin's office. She held up her hands in front of the Admiral.

Durgin looked concerned but said, "You know we don't have a washroom in the fort for the women."

"That's awful," Magavero replied. The conversation was over, and she returned to the library.

But the next day, the Admiral presented himself at the library. He took Magavero and led her to one of the men's washrooms.

"What if we covered the urinals?" the Admiral asked.

Magavero, who was somewhat embarrassed to get all this attention from Durgin, responded, "I don't care what you do. You could leave them just the way they are, just put a latch on the door, and when I'm in there, I'll lock myself in."

To his credit, Admiral Durgin ordered the construction of Fort Schuyler's first ladies' room.

Some progress, but a washroom did not take Magavero off the clerical line. It was only in 1959 that she was listed among the faculty although she officially remained a clerk until 1962 when she was promoted to a Readers' Services Librarian. In doing so, Magavero became the first female faculty member of Maritime College. It was a rocky start to a relationship that lasted over 40 years. After she retired in 1995, she mused, "In a way I think I did an injustice to the profession. . . . I wasn't an activist. I really didn't know how to handle those guys."

"BELIEVE IT OR NOT"

The dominance of men at the college was not surprising, given that the seafaring profession has traditionally been a male job. This was compounded by an American culture that was filled with gender bias. In the immediate postwar period, examples of male chauvinism at the college abound.

In 1945, the student newspaper advertised, "NYSMA men have always had the most beautiful women on the leash. Sort out your picture files and send us the best shot of your best girl. The 'Lassie' winning this contest will be crowned 'NYSMA GIRL OF THE MONTH." These monthly contests had themes. In December, 1945, Frances Rhinesmith won Miss NYSMA under the motif "Demure." Joan O'Rourke won February, 1946 for "Intrigue."

By the 1950s, these contests became weekly features in the newspaper. The name of the column would change from "Drag of the Week" to "Campus Belle" to "Ms. SUMC." The column would solicit and post photographs of cadets' girlfriends (i.e. "drags") and provide information concerning them.

The sexualization of women extended to staff. In the fall of 1956, the *Porthole* published an article entitled, "Seventeen, Hot Rod Queen." This article was about a new female staff member. "Miss Dunphy, who we have all seen, is seventeen years old, five feet five inches tall and weighs 120 pounds. Nice round figures." The article reported that Dunphy liked "her men tall, dark and handsome but will consider them tall, light and handsome."*

As greater numbers of colleges and universities went co-ed during the post-war period, the idea of Maritime College doing the same seemed laughable. In 1954, while the New York State Legislature debated whether to outlaw gender discrimination at state institutions, the *Porthole* commented on how supportive the majority of cadets were of such legislation:

> Although several minor adjustments might be required to handle the influx of accepted female applicants, they could easily be assimilated into the present structure of student life. . . . However, there seems to be a feeling of reluctance on the part of some students in regard to the fact that the presence of young women on the campus might rob them of a portion of the time they so eagerly devote to study in their monastic quarters. These few dissenters are greatly outnumbered by others who are anxious to see this democratic piece of [legislation] made part of the law of the land.

An article in 1956 discussed the benefits of having women on campus:

---

*Pat Dunphy was the secretary who clandestinely helped the writers of the *Periscope* publish their work. See chapter 14.

Imagine the dorms, pretty in pink and white curtains on the 'ports'? Doilies on the dresser and desk, yellow slide rules . . . telephones in every room to call their girlfriends and gossip. . . . The introduction of the co-educational system in SUMC would solve any social problems . . . for instance, if there is a dance in the messdeck and you need a date, all you would have to do is restrict a blonde or two.

As late as 1967, cadets could not conceive of a female enrolling at the college. The *Porthole* wrote that the admissions office was receiving letters from females requesting information about the school's oceanography program. The reporter wrote, "Believe it or not, there are some girls who would really like to come here." The situation only made sense when it was explained that the women in question were unaware that the school was an all-male, semi-military institution. The writer commented, "I'm quite sure that the cadets here wouldn't mind making a few sacrifices to change that situation."

EARLY FEMALE FACULTY

Even though Magavero was recognized as faculty in 1962, the college was not yet ready for female professors (aside from one or two intern instructors), much less female students. Yet the institution found itself swimming against a strong current of change.

In 1961, President John F. Kennedy established a Commission on the Status of Women. The Chair, Eleanor Roosevelt, reported substantial discrimination against women in the workplace. In 1963, Betty Friedan published the highly influential *Feminine Mystique*, which addressed the dissatisfaction of middle-class American housewives. Then the 1964 Civil Rights Act banned discrimination in the workplace and established the Equal Employment Opportunity Commission to enforce the law. In 1966, the National Organization for Women (NOW) was founded, the largest and most active of American women's civil rights group. In 1967, President Lyndon Johnson expanded affirmative action policies to cover gender discrimination. In 1969, in a bellwether for the merchant marine, Helen Bentley was appointed by President Richard Nixon as the first female commissioner of the Federal Maritime Commission.

Two years later, the college hired its first female teachers. They were Dr. Janet Pomeranz, a mathematics professor, and Beatrice Braude, a humanities instructor who had been blacklisted by the federal government in the 1950s as a security risk. Another of these early female professors was Dr. Karen Markoe, a historian who joined the college in 1974.

Markoe recalled her first meeting with the interviewing committee headed by Humanities Chair, W. Dwight Todd. She was ready to talk about her approach to teaching history, but instead was asked repeatedly about how she dealt with men. Frustrated, she was about to walk out on the committee when she mentioned she had a junior high school teaching license, taught in public schools and had never had any discipline problems. This pleased the interviewers. The college then made an offer that she later learned was at a significantly lower salary than male professors with the same level of experience.

When Markoe arrived for her first day of work, she found her desk locked. She asked Todd for the key but was told, "You won't need it since you won't be here that long." There were still many on campus who did not want female instructors. While substituting for another professor, a male student asked her, "Why are you here? Where are your children?"

Yet like Magavero, these early bumps were the beginning of a long career at the college. In an interview, Markoe said that, on the whole, she was treated well by the faculty and students. She stayed on, and in 1992 was named Chair of the Humanities department, the first female head of any academic department at Maritime College.

MARJORIE MURTAGH

In 1971, a young woman named Marjorie Murtagh was finishing coursework in engineering at Rockland Community College while working at General Food Technical Labs. One of her instructors, an adjunct named Aaron Kramer, had a full time job at Maritime College. He recognized her ability as an engineer and told her to look at the program at Fort Schuyler.

Murtagh liked the idea of being a marine engineer. She wrote up her application, submitted it and then scheduled an interview with the Dean of Students, William Toran. At the meeting, he commented that the only women who were allowed aboard ships in his day "designed the drapes for the mess deck." She was rejected in a polite, but unequivocal letter that stated that the college was a male-only institution. Murtagh, under the urging of Kramer and her friends at General Foods, approached the New York Civil

Liberties Union (NYCLU) who agreed to take the case. She sued the State of New York with Barbara Shack from the NYCLU as her attorney.

In court, the State first claimed that the college was an all-male institution, and Murtagh could obtain an engineering degree at another state college. Shack countered that this was impossible since Murtagh wanted a degree in Naval Architecture, and Maritime College was the only school in New York that offered the degree.

The court agreed with Shack and said that the reasons for Murtagh's rejection were not strong enough. The State then argued that the college did not have the facilities to support women at the college. This argument proved critical to Murtagh's case.

After World War II, the college had instituted a program for non-regimental students that gave former graduates and instructors the opportunity to earn a college degree. During the 1950s, the program was discontinued, and for several years the college was composed entirely of regimental students. But in 1969, Admiral O'Donnell, in the face of anemic enrollment, introduced "Operation Day Student." The program was open to older men with some college work and a record of service in the merchant marine who wanted to earn a college degree. These students wore civilian clothing and were not part of the cadet corps. In 1971, the program changed somewhat allowing people to enroll who could not pass the physical requirements for a license but still wanted a degree. This group was referred to as "Not Physically Qualified." It was for this classification that Murtagh applied.

Since Murtagh was not asking to be in the regiment, but be a civilian transfer student who wouldn't live on campus, the only facility she required was a ladies room—something that Philomena Magavero had won for her two decades prior. With no other recourse, the college accepted Murtagh. She started classes in the fall of 1972.

While Murtagh insisted that the faculty supported her and most of the students tolerated, if not accepted, her on campus, there was a small minority of cadets that were overtly hostile. Hoaxes started soon after her arrival. Since her number was publicly listed in the phonebook, it was easy for pranksters to make repeated, mean-spirited telephone calls. It got worse. On one occasion, she found sand in her car's gas tank.*

---

*Like a true engineer, Murtagh's first thought was that she was glad it was sand and not sugar, since sugar would have completely destroyed the engine.

Even to those who were friendly toward her, Murtagh was a curiosity. Any time she raised her hand in class to answer a question, all eyes turned to her. She was under a microscope.

But this strengthened her resolve. "I felt that if I failed, there would be the perception that women didn't belong—that people were right [when they said] that only males belonged aboard ships." Despite the problems, Murtagh remembered her days at the college fondly and loved her classes.

When Murtagh graduated in 1974, she was the first woman at any maritime school to earn a degree—a groundbreaking achievement. After the graduation ceremony, she received an irresistible offer from then-college president, Sheldon Kinney. He wanted her to work at the college.

Between the time Murtagh entered the college and her graduation, MARAD changed its policies toward female admissions to regimental licensing programs. In 1973, the California Maritime Academy admitted women into its licensing program. This was followed in early 1974 by the USMMA and the Maine Maritime Academy.

With the precedent of admitting women to the licensing programs established, Maritime College brought in its first cadre of female cadets in September, 1974. Kinney wanted Murtagh to head up the transition effort as an Assistant Dean. She took the position, not only because it would help to open the door for women, but it would also let her work aboard the training ship and earn the sea-time necessary to sit for a Coast Guard licensing exam. Her appointment was not without controversy as it was rumored that Dean William Toran, who interviewed her for admission, resigned because of her return and the inclusion of female cadets.

After accumulating sea time, Murtagh sat for her Coast Guard license and became the first woman to receive one in 1975. She left the college that year and went on to a variety of positions in the Coast Guard, the Military Sea Lift Command and the shipping industry before becoming a director in the National Transportation Safety Board.

"ALMOST NOTHING BUT HARASSMENT"

As for the new group of female cadets, opinions differ as to how well they adapted. Professor Fred Hess wrote, "They were assimilated into the cadet corps with a minimum of difficulty, at least as far as we on the faculty knew."

This was untrue. Dr. Richard Burke recalled that their experience was "almost nothing but harassment." Marjorie Murtagh agreed.

The first female cadets were tough, and several had connections to the college. Two had fathers who were alumni, and one was the niece of Fred Hess. There were seven total, and one dropped out before they graduated in 1978. Professor and 1975 graduate, Joseph Hoffman recalled:

> If you wanted to go out and choose a group of women to be the first women on the campus we chose well. Some of them already had some college experience, and some of them actually had industry experience. Our concern was not that they weren't able to throw a bag over their shoulders; the fear was they'd be putting one over each shoulder.

Karen Magliocca was one of these first female cadets. She was the daughter of alumnus, Thomas Magliocca, who graduated in 1953. Karen, however, had a much different experience than her father.

She initially took the prospect of becoming a cadet lightly:

> I remember my dad taking me to future cadet day and seeing all those ... boys in their uniforms, hanging off the side of the ship looking forward to their summer sea term. All I was worried about was whether they would make me cut my long hair. I didn't take it seriously. Just a brief indulgence for my dad who had no sons. I thought it was over that day.

But she did enroll, and found herself with six other females who were to be the first women cadets. In fact, of the group, Magliocca was the only one going for an engineering license while the rest were deck. The college took the seven and split them up into different sections. Magliocca admits she only saw her female colleagues in the evening after classes. They were expected to do the same things as the male cadets: make a bed with square corners, get up in the middle of the night for indoctrination and learn how to handle arms. According to Magliocca, what made matters worse was that they had to wear skirts and heels. At one point, the heel gave way, and she sprained her ankle. She recalled, "Needless to say all the boys thought it was a clever way to get out of physical duties. I thought being on crutches was just one more way to stand out. Not something I needed."

Even in class, she did stand out. While taking science courses with Dr. Degani, he would always greet the class by saying, "Lady and gentleman."

She had her misgivings, but the prospect of being one of the first female graduates challenged Magliocca. She made it through and did not regret her experience at the college. "The experience . . . set me on a path to professional and personal success."

In March of 1975, the *Porthole* reported a student survey that documented the resentment of the males toward the females. Male cadets accused the women of being "scappers"* who could avoid getting demerits because they were female. Accusations were made that indoctrination was softened for females, that a shipping company had withdrawn job offers because women were admitted to the college and that female Mugs dated their Indoctrination Duty Officers.

There is no doubt that the female cadets suffered from a higher level of scrutiny than the males. It was reported that a large percentage of the male cadet body

> felt that if the girls were made to shape up and adhere more rigidly to their rates, popular opinion against them would greatly decrease. Many of the cadets realize and agree on the fact that the women are looked upon more scrupulously at Maritime just because they are women and therefore it's easier to accuse them as a whole.

In 1976, Cadet Laurence Kriv wrote about the double standard that the female cadets were subjected to:

> What no one seems to realize is that for all of the faults, whether real or fantasized, that can be found with the women, you can find an equal, if not greater, amount of men who can be accused of the same thing. . . . While those men breaking the rules are in a way camouflaged by the 800 or so others, the women are more noticeable. People are always watching them, waiting for them to make a mistake. When one does, they all get blamed.**

But some male cadets played up female stereotypes. "They'll scap out of half the work assigned. They'll be worried about breaking their fingernails, smearing their mascara and getting grease and paint in their hair." In 1976, two cadets wrote in frustration:

---

*To "scap" means to shirk duty.
**Kriv moved to Texas after graduation and became president of a local chapter of the National Organization for Women.

After living through incidents at the Maritime College, such as [third class] female cadets being invited to a [first class] party on cruise, females getting their pictures taken for the *Daily News*, getting out of work for unknown reasons, not being physically fit for acceptance into this school on a cadet status, being able to stay when their grade point average is way below the minimum allowed, taking cruises after flunking required courses and worst of all getting a job at the snap of a finger after graduation, we think that something is wrong with the system and the school. Special treatment.

The administration also singled out the women. In the fall of 1975, a specific dress code for females was instituted. It specified hair length (not below the collar) and regulated cosmetics to conservative colors that would not be "outlandishly applied." The new regulations also said, "No eccentricities or faddishness of dress, jewelry or grooming shall be permitted."

Meanwhile, the faculty took steps to help the female students. In 1976, Markoe hosted the first conference on women in the maritime industry. Entitled "College Women Today—The Generation in the Middle," it examined issues of gender in the merchant marine. She also served as advisor to the first women cadets. "We arrived at the same time, and we supported each other," Markoe noted.

Markoe learned from the female students that an instructor on the ship would not teach them. Shocked by this, she walked into the president's office to report the outrage. President Shedon Kinney was disconcerted that she had bypassed the normal chain of command, but the next semester, that instructor was replaced. The administration had made a commitment toward diversity.

There were lighter moments. Right after the first group of female cadets came to the college they were invited to be interviewed on a morning television show. On the same show, they were interviewing "ladies of the night." Just before the show cut to commercials, the announcer said, "Next, we shall meet the ladies of the night." The camera panned to the Maritime women.

The incorporation of women into the college's program was successful enough that in 1981 the Middle States reaccreditation team found that females appeared to be fully integrated into all aspects of the college. The number of female students was still relatively few, 42 in 1981. The team commented that this did not permit the college to develop many of the normal activities for women students that were found at other campuses.

The 1980s proved to be a period of growing pains for the college as it slowly accepted a mixed gender campus. In 1981, the *Porthole* conducted interviews with 22 female cadets and found that they were subject to harassment. Examples of this included being shouted at with sexually demeaning slurs and males taking over women's jobs thinking that they are being helpful but with the unspoken subtext that the females were unable to do the job. Late at night, the male cadets came onto their floors and made lurid noises, forcing the women to lock their doors. Offensive messages were taped to their doors.

In order to alleviate problems between the sexes, the administration, in the late 1980s, tightened and enforced fraternization rules. These regulations were laced with bias. In 1988, a new rule was instituted where female Mugs could not speak to upperclassmen. This only made the female students angry. One wrote, "Fraternization works several ways—but it is only when a female Mug becomes friends with a male IDO that it is unacceptable behavior."

Another female cadet wrote in 1988:

> We are branded the second we pass through the opening of the gate. Should we assume that former female graduates of Maritime were sluts who couldn't control their sexual desires? The male population around here seems to have the need to discuss the social standings of any female on campus. People feel that we attend this school for the ratio of guys to girls. If some of the male cadets would take time to look in the mirror, they would realize that this is probably not the reason. Maybe we are here for a license to sail or just to experience a better campus that enforces the idea of studying instead of partying all the time.

Yet in tandem with these problems, attitudes *were* changing. A male student wrote:

> I find it rather appalling that in this age and time we still encounter an indecent degree of sexual segregation based on male chauvinism and disrespect. I think it is about time we male cadets assess ourselves. Our chauvinistic attitudes are outmoded, and our nice and few female counterparts deserve better respect than we accord them. We ought to be proud of them and we shouldn't forget that they also represent the college in all spheres.

Female graduates became role models. Susan Janis, who graduated in 1979, obtained a job with Exxon as a junior deck officer. "The time at sea is a good time for me. I think a lot. Sometimes I miss people, and I do miss having friends I can talk things over with, but I use the time. I love being on the sea."

In December of 1988, Cadet Linda A. Malay was appointed the first female Regimental Commander of any of maritime school. In that same year, the third ranking position, Regimental Adjutant, was also held by a fellow female Naval Architecture student, Alisa B. Zimmerman.

Dr. Richard Burke, described how women helped to "civilize the place. This was kind of like the world's largest locker room. You got a locker room with 800 guys in it, and they are doing all the kinds of things you'd expect. . . . When the women came along, at least some of the men started behaving better."

The integration of women was a slow process, but by the 21st century the college had made significant headway. In 2010, Timothea Larr became the first female Chair of the College Council. Then in 2011, Rear Admiral Wendi B. Carpenter became the first female President of Maritime College. By 2011, slightly over 12% of the college's total enrollment was female. While this is still a low figure, and the recruitment of females is still a problem, it is a historic high for the institution.

CHAPTER 16

"A Very Elegant Man"

"Those classes graduating from the mid-70s to mid-80s were, as a whole, among the best in terms of competence, intellectual curiosity and camaraderie of all I have witnessed."
—Conrad Youngren, Engineering Faculty

A SECOND CHANCE

In late July, 1987, Sean Kirby and Frank Cuccio planned a trip from Rockaway to Montauk. They were to take Sean's boat, a 40-foot fiberglass Luhrs Sports Fisherman named the *Rebound*. It was fully decked out. It even had a cooler that was so big that Sean and Frank nicknamed it the "Coffin Cooler." When word of their plan leaked to relatives and friends, they urged Sean to take a group of them on a shark fishing expedition along the way. They could fish then be dropped off before Sean and Frank headed to Montauk. They set the date for the 26th.

Sean and Frank met as cadets at Maritime College. Both were active students. At different points, Sean was treasurer, president of the student council and president of his class year. Frank was a battalion commander. After their 1982 graduation, each served as the other's best man.

Sean had been around the water all his life and after graduation found work in the North Sea aboard a semi-submersible oil rig, the *Sedco/Phillips*. His job was cut short on March 10, 1983, when, while working off Norway inside an enclosed lifeboat, the boat was accidentally dropped while being lifted. He broke his back. After months of rehabilitation he recovered, but permanently carried his injuries with titanium supports in his spine. The July trip would serve as a pleasant morale booster for Sean. The *Rebound* was an appropriate name for the boat.

Frank and Sean spent the night of the 25th catching smelly bunker fish to use as bait. They washed up, woke the others and headed out at 4 a.m. A total of eight people boarded the *Rebound*. Aside from Sean and Frank, their classmate, Tony McDonald, joined them. Tony, a Marine Transportation alumnus, was their "token deckie." The rest of the "mixed up crew" were landlubbers: Sean's sister Julie and friends Christine, Ellen, Tommy Boyle and a neighborhood acquaintance, Sean O'Hagan.

By 7 a.m. and 70 miles out, they dropped their first fishing lines in the Atlantic off the coast of New Jersey. The morning went without incident until suddenly, near noon, mayday calls filled the radio. Soon enough, they saw on the radar an intense squall approaching rapidly from the west. "It looked like the State of New Jersey marching at us," Sean recalled. None of the Fort Schuyler graduates anticipated this. The water was fine with a two-foot chop and only a light breeze.

After hearing the distress calls, everyone aboard knew the trip was to be cut short. They started to reel up their lines, but the storm approached so quickly that several had to be cut. The whole sky blackened. "It was coming at us, and it was coming quick," said Sean. They battened down and headed to shore.

Sean, who was "in the bad seat that day," steered the boat. He first tried to run the *Rebound* inshore toward Rockaway and away from the storm, but found that it was overtaking them. He then navigated by the storm line looking for the least dense area on the radar. He took a parallel course with the storm which became 45 degrees as the clouds drew nearer. He then turned the *Rebound* 90 degrees from the storm to a flat-out run of 28 knots. The squall gained. Out of options, Sean turned the boat directly into the storm in order to counteract the worst effects of a roiling sea.

Frank, on the bridge with Sean and Julie, wrote that the squall hit them with the impact of a twister. Everything went dark. The winds were over 100 miles per hour, and the seas rose to 30 feet. "With no rhyme or reason, we were battered by waves in every direction," Frank remembered. Sean said that that there was so much foam and moisture in the air that "you could have drowned looking at it."

Meanwhile, the remaining five people filed into the cabin. There, they were shielded from the outside by a pair of glass panels, similar to patio doors.

Sean headed south, southwest into the squall and ran into large waves. The first one was about 30 feet high from crest to trough. The *Rebound* floated over it and then a massive wind caught the boat low on the port bow. Sean quickly steered to port to try to get the boat into the wind. The gusts held the bow and kept it from responding. The boat took on water from the starboard quarter. Sean continued to try to turn the bow to port, but there was "no hope as the wind was sustained and unyielding."

As water poured in, another large wave rolled approached. Sean steered starboard to take the wave and bring up the starboard quarter. The boat heeled to the right. He turned, the *Rebound* came up, but the wave crashed over the port side aft and "swished around the cockpit." The water broke through the glass doors and drove the passengers into the cabin's salon.

"We were awash in less than a minute," Sean said. The *Rebound* was sinking; its bow turned up and the stern, heavier because of the engine, submerged into the water. The boat bobbed temporarily, being suspended by air pockets inside the cabin. It was only by this good luck that those inside were saved from drowning.

As the boat bobbed, Sean, Tony and Frank's training at college came into play. First, there was the matter of the people trapped inside. They quickly opened the side windows to the cabin. Meanwhile, Tommy Boyle was swept through the bow hatch. Sean looked at him and asked him if he was all right. Wide-eyed, Boyle nodded. Sean cursed and ordered him to get out. Then Ellen and Christine popped out, helped by Tony and Sean O'Hagan. O'Hagan, was the only man wearing a life jacket. Even though the *Rebound* was well-supplied with 26 life jackets, not everybody was able to get one on in time. Sean tried carrying six life jackets to the others, but they were whipped out of his hands by the wind. He grabbed another—the last jacket he could find aboard the drowning vessel. But it was not for him.

He groped across the *Rebound* seeking his sister. He had to make sure that Julie was well. There she was, grabbing onto the remnants of the boat. But there was blood on her foot. A rig of a dozen 9/0 bluefish hooks, meant to catch game fish, had bitten into her foot. They were so tangled that if the *Rebound* went under, it would drag her down with it. There was no time. Sean scrambled to Julie and strapped the last life jacket on her. With a meaningful look he said one word. "Sorry." He ripped the hooks from her foot and threw her into the ocean.

The *Rebound* sank further, only her bow was above the waterline now. Sean clambered upward. There was one last task. On the bow, there was an inflatable life raft. If he could climb up there, then release the turnbuckles that secured it, they might have a chance. Hand over hand he pulled himself up, and just as he was about to touch the turnbuckles a wave washed him down. He could hardly hold on. He repeated this operation of crawling upward only to be dashed back down by the waves. On the fourth try, with the greatest sense of relief, he reached the turnbuckles. He released the raft and grabbed its sea painter line with his right hand while holding onto one of the boats breast cleats with his left. The raft opened.

"I felt triumphant for all of about a second and half," Sean remembered. Then a big wave broke across the boat. It caught the life raft with such force that it broke Sean's ring finger. The flesh swelled tightly around his Maritime College graduation ring. He held on, but the energy of the storm was so intense against the inflatable life raft that it carried it away with Sean attached.

He was pulled so hard that he felt like he was water skiing. He was being yanked away from his friends and family. He then made a decision. "I didn't want to be the only guy in the life raft," said Sean. He released the painter from his grip. As the wind carried off the raft out of reach and out of sight, he swam back. All his heroics were rewarded with a lost life raft and a broken finger. "In hindsight, it was the wrong thing to do," said Sean. "Because if I held onto the life raft, it wouldn't have blown as far away as it did."

Sean, Frank, Tony and three of their companions grabbed onto the bow of the *Rebound*, clinging to life. Sean O'Hagan, however, was still trapped in the cabin. It was his life jacket that was his undoing. As water flooded into the cabin, he became pinned despite Tony's best efforts to pull him out. O'Hagan was lost.

Then the *Rebound* finally sank, and those who clung to the bow were yanked under with the boat. "I felt my ears pop," said Sean. He and the others let go simultaneously and scrambled to the surface. They bumped and jostled in the confusion. This was the worst part. "I was pretty much devastated," Sean said. "I was totally in shock at that point. It took me a minute or two for me to get my shit back together after that."

The survivors found the water surprisingly cold. The storm winds had ripped off the top layer of warmer water and replaced it with the chill of the deep. All of them could swim, but they were in serious distress. Of those in the water, only two, Ellen and Christine, had life jackets—and Christine's was a child's vest. Tommy Boyle hung onto a bucket. To Sean's horror, there was no sign of Julie. Sean began to whistle loudly for her. Meanwhile, Tony, who had swallowed too much water, was in trouble. In a painful moment, Sean commandeered Christine's child life jacket to give to Tony.

To maintain morale, Sean told the group he got a mayday message out. He later admitted that he couldn't do this since there was no time, and the radio was jammed with distress signals. Sean said, "There were so many people panicking, so much traffic on the radio, I couldn't get anything off, and I didn't get anything off. I didn't think we were sinking and definitely not that fast."

They treaded the cold water. Frank and Sean had no floatation device and were struggling to stay up. It was then that Frank turned to an old sea survival trick taught to him by Maritime College instructor, Coach Roy Larsen. During training drills at the college swimming pool, students would jump in the water fully clothed. Then they would remove their pants, and tie the pants' legs with shoelaces before slamming the clothing's waist into the water to trap air. Frank had the long pants necessary, but no laces; he had kicked off his shoes when he went into the water.

He improvised and tied the ends of his pants legs. But the operation was far more difficult in the open sea than in the controlled conditions of a swimming pool. One of Frank's pants' legs was inside out, and after some fumbling, the trick "worked like a champ." Frank wrote, "Short of getting found, that provided us with the greatest emotional (and physical) lift. . . . For about half an hour to forty five minutes during the worst part of the storm, the inflated pants enabled us to catch our breath and rest a little."

Sean tried to do the same, but his cotton pants were ripped from his hands by the wind. "I used to like those pants," he recalled. Sean shared Frank's makeshift float and eventually grabbed a bucket from the flotsam. Yet despite this relief, there was still no sign of his sister.

To add to their misery, the sea was filled with jellyfish. Sean was naked and Frank, only slightly less so. As the stings tormented them, Sean found a woman's pair of "blue candy underwear" floating in the water. He took them and slid them on remarking that he would do anything to keep the jellyfish "off the old goolies."

As the survivors bobbed in the sea, they saw the orange life raft that had blown away in the distance. It was difficult to figure out how far it was as they treaded water. For the next two hours, the six companions kicked toward the raft. Little by little they made progress. "We had a goal," said Sean. "We weren't hopeless."

Frank added, "We said our Hail Mary's and kept on kicking."

Eventually, they grew near enough that they could see a figure aboard the raft that brought a surge of relief to the survivors. Julie Kirby was there. When Sean had pushed her off the boat, Julie found the top cushion of the "Coffin Cooler." She grabbed it as a makeshift surfboard to paddle to the raft where she expected to find her brother and friends. But the raft was empty. Later, when she heard her brother's whistles, she thought her mind was playing tricks on her. Even though those in the water could see Julie, she could not see them. In the deep swells of the aftermath of the storm, the dark shape of the survivors hanging low in the water was almost impossible to see.

Just then a boat named the *Southern Wind* arrived on the scene. This vessel had ridden out the storm, but not before seeing a terrifying funnel cloud. As the boat owner headed inshore, he sighted the orange blur of the raft, and after some debate with those aboard, decided to see what it was. He picked up Julie, who told them about her missing companions who were bobbing feet away, but out of sight. The owner radioed the Coast Guard, which sent a helicopter.

The *Southern Wind* tried to locate the other survivors. This was agonizing for the six in the water, who could see the boat that could not see or hear them. After twenty minutes, the *Southern Wind* finally spotted them and went to pull them aboard. Even this was treacherous. Though the storm was over, the sea was high and dangerous. The stern of the boat was going up and down over ten feet.

As Sean climbed into the boat, he was happy to be reunited with his sister. But he also flushed red as the candy underwear—blue—flashed for all aboard to see. About two weeks later, his sister asked, "Sean, how long have you been wearing my underwear?"

The survivors were exhausted, and as they tried to recover on the rocking boat, a Coast Guard helicopter swooped in to begin a search for Sean O'Hagan. It was fruitless. O'Hagan had drowned in the *Rebound*. Then, because it was too dangerous to transfer the survivors to a Coast Guard vessel, the *Southern Wind* headed inshore to the Sandy Hook Coast Guard Station where they were treated. Tony and Sean suffered the worst. Tony swallowed a great deal of water and had to be hospitalized for the evening. Julie was injured as well. One of the hooks that Sean had ripped out of her foot remained lodged in it and had to be removed at a hospital. Sean's broken finger was troubling, since it was jammed into his graduation ring, which was made of lustrium, a hard metal. The cutting tools at the hospital were made to cut silver and gold and broke against the ring. Eventually, Sean made the hospital personnel bring him to the building's machine shop where he used a vise, a hacksaw and oil to cut it off himself.

Sean Kirby and Frank Cuccio credited their survival to their maritime education. "It made a difference," said Frank. "It is very easy to panic when you are in the water like that. . . . You feel it rise up; you have to choke that back down. It is something that we think about probably every day. You don't get too many second chances, but we got a second chance on that one."

"Life's a gift," said Sean.

SHELDON KINNEY

Frank Cuccio, Sean Kirby and Tony McDonald were graduates of Maritime College during the tenure of Rear Admiral Sheldon Hoard Kinney who replaced Admiral O'Donnell in 1972. Kinney, from Pasadena, California, climbed to flag rank due to ability and dash. A high school dropout, he enlisted in the Navy in 1935. He became a signalman and was so impressive that in 1937 he was selected from the ranks to attend the Naval Academy. In 1941, he graduated as a marine engineer then entered combat in World War II.

After reporting for duty aboard the destroyer *Sturtevant*, he served on convoy duty. During this time, Kinney earned the Navy and Marine Corps Medal for Heroism for jumping overboard to rescue two downed pilots in a crashed plane. In April, 1942, his ship struck a mine and sank. Kinney survived the sinking by grabbing onto a floating bag of coffee beans. He was said to later remark that the war made him fond of coffee. In 1943, he became the commander of the destroy-escort *Edsall*. In doing so he became the youngest commanding officer of that class of ship.

But Kinney is best remembered for a remarkable action in March, 1944. While in command of the destroyer-escort, *Bronstein* he sank two U-Boats and disabled a third in a single night. For this, Kinney received the Navy Cross, the highest decoration given by the Navy. The ship was awarded a Presidential Unit Citation. Theodore Roscoe wrote in his work, *United States Destroyer Operations in World War II*, that the *Bronstein's* record under Kinney was one "which many a veteran A/S [anti-submarine] vessel might well envy." Kinney was a *bona fide* war hero.

After the war, Kinney served in the Korean and Vietnam conflicts in commands of rising importance. He became involved with maritime education, first as an instructor at the Naval Academy from 1954 to 1956. He returned later as its Commandant of Cadets from 1964 to 1967. He was also an editor for the *Proceedings of the U.S. Naval Institute*. A polyglot, he spoke seven languages. With this experience, and possessing graduate degrees in International Economics and Politics from George Washington University, he brought with him an ample set of credentials when he assumed the presidency of Maritime College after retiring from the Navy as a Rear Admiral.

Kinney's handsome features and courteous mien made for a charismatic and appealing leader. Sean Kirby said Kinney was an "absolute gentleman," and Dr. Karen Markoe described him as a "very elegant man," adding that he was a "poster person for an admiral and college president."

ENROLLMENT AND IRAN

Kinney was thrust immediately into an enrollment crisis. The lack of sailing jobs and an absence of enthusiasm about military education due to the Vietnam War made it hard to recruit students. One faculty member remarked, "It was hell in that period of time to get kids to come to Schuyler. Picture yourself in 1970 going to a high school and telling a kid to cut his hair, wear a uniform and pay $3,000 a year to do it."

From a high of full-time undergraduate enrollment of 722 in 1968, numbers had slipped to a low of 662 in the 1972-73 academic year. Although the decline in raw numbers was modest, for a small college like Maritime it represented an almost 10% drop in enrollment. Also, this slip was after new dormitories had been built meant to increase the size of the college. But the dorm rooms lay empty, and SUNY Purchase housed their own students at the college while their campus was being built.

To partially solve the problem, Admirals O'Donnell and Kinney increased the admission of foreign students. The largest group was Iranian Naval cadets who started arriving in 1971. By 1974, there were about 100 Iranians on the campus. In 1976, the Iranians, plus other foreign students, represented 15% of total enrollment. The relationship was strong enough that, in 1974, the Shah of Iran donated to the college 12,000 barrels of fuel oil—a most welcome gift considering the shock of rising oil prices in the 1970s. To cultivate the relationship, in 1976 Admiral Kinney and the Vice President of Academics, William Porter, visited Iran and toured its Navy bases.

As the number of foreign exchange students grew, anecdotal reports of bias were reported. In 1971, when asked about the college, an Iranian cadet replied, "At first I thought I would like it, and would become friends with many of the American cadets, but now unfortunately I find that some of them don't like to become friends." Language and culture barriers isolated these foreign students. One writer for the *Porthole* wrote that "the regiment could learn much by being friendly to these fellow students, since they are not only far from home and lonesome for friendship, but on the whole they are very nice, genuine people."

Intolerance persisted. A 1974 letter to the *Porthole* said that it was better to allow non-regimental students on the campus than Iranians. The writer then launched a tirade against them:

> But NO, instead Iranians will enter. I for one feel it very 'GROSS' to have to live with these Iranians who don't shower, cheat on tests, can't speak our language, bitch and moan about life here, and threaten the lives of cadets (literally). For the Administration to allow these 'people'(?) here is a sin and disgrace to the tax payers of this state and to the previous graduates of this school.

Another student wrote: "It seems that the administration has decided that in future years this school will be known as the Iranian Naval College. . . . Sorry will be the day when the Iranian flag flies under the Stars and Stripes, and the announcements must be made in English and Persian."

These letters, particularly the first one, produced such an outrage that the writer was ordered to meet with the Iranian students and apologize. The administration, as well as many students, strongly denounced the inflammatory remarks. One article in the *Porthole* addressed Iranian culture and how it should not be stereotyped. Humanities professor Dr. Hartley Spatt speculated that the root of the problem was envy. According to him, the Iranians were wealthy from petro-dollars and were paid a stipend from their government. "They all had much nicer cars than the American students," remembered Spatt. "Every one of them had a Trans-Am or a Camaro, or one of the nice American sports cars."

The Iranian contingent persisted throughout the 1970's, although by the latter part of the decade, they were limited to 30 as general enrollment grew. This relationship suddenly ended after the 1979 Iranian Revolution and the associated hostage crisis. After President Carter cancelled all the visas of Iranian government personnel, they were forced to leave.

THE KINNEY EXPANSION

In 1974, the college began a slow, but steady, growth in enrollment. By 1982, the total number of students at the college was 1,126, a historic high. This growth was marked by higher retention. The percentage of freshman who dropped out or were expelled from Maritime averaged at about 53% during the 1960's. Between 1972 and 1981 this was reduced to 31%. Aside from students not quitting, those who got into trouble were more likely to stay than be expelled as they had in the past. In 1973, only 14% of students who appealed for readmission were accepted. In 1977, this figure was over 86%.

By 1979, the campus was at full capacity, and admissions had become competitive. In 1980, it was reported that the college received five applications for each open space. What is more, the number of students who were accepted and then chose to enroll was unusually high, at up to 80%.

The Admiral claimed that the secret to the college's success was a recovered job market and the way the "excellent and rigorous education presented in the classroom is complemented by personal attention available to each individual student." Thomas Cerny, the head of admissions, was commended, but it really was because the cadets were happy. They praised the school by word of mouth.

There were other factors that led to the growth. Since the end of the Vietnam War, attitudes toward the quasi-military education at Fort Schuyler were softening. Also, the civilian day student program was promoted, and transfer credit policies were liberalized making it easier to apply credits from other institutions to Maritime College. In addition, there was greater retention.

Part of Kinney's success lay in his ability to unite the faculty. Socially, he helped create a strong morale among the faculty and staff. He was also credited with understanding why a strong academic program was critical for the well-being of the college. To Kinney, the college's mission was to "support the maritime field . . . in its broadest sense." In practice, Kinney left the design of the curriculum to the faculty, who were led by the Vice President of Academics, William Porter.

Faculty members were grateful. Jose Femenia remarked that when he became the head of the Engineering Department in 1974, he was given a free hand to develop the program.

By the time Kinney retired in 1982, two more majors were added, bringing the total to nine. Also, cross-over curricula were introduced whereby a student could take various majors while studying for a deck or engine license. In this way, the modern curriculum of the college was founded that allowed for various permutations of majors.

In 1977, Kinney introduced the first substantial development effort at the college with the creation of the Fort Schuyler Foundation. This organization, which sponsored America Cup title defenders, contributed scholarships and work study supplements to the student body.

Kinney also activated the first Naval Reserve Officer Training Corps (NROTC) unit at the college. Establishing NROTC was not an easy process since the staff of the Naval Education and Training Command (CNET) was opposed to it for unstated reasons.

When federal cutbacks in the program arrived, CNET suddenly blocked NROTC students from entering the program at the college. Kinney then spoke to Graham Claytor, the Secretary of the Navy and a fellow World War II destroyer-escort commander, to reinstate it. Claytor was sympathetic, and NROTC was made permanent in 1976.

Kinney also worked to increase the monthly federal cadet subsidy to $100 a month, a figure that had not changed since it was set at $50 a month in 1958. Kinney remarked, "While this new figure of $100 by no means covers the full cost of education, it should prove to be extremely helpful to all cadets and may be instrumental in allowing many to complete their education." By the end of Kinney's tenure, this subsidy became known as the "Student Incentive Payment Program" or SIPP. Those who received SIPP were obliged to sail under their licenses for at least three years.

In addition, general federal aid to the college was increased from $75,000 to $100,000. This was used to "offset tuition differentials" for out-of-state students. Even the higher figure was dismissed by Kinney as unrealistic due to the rising cost of fuel. In 1973, it cost $48,000 to fuel the ship, in 1977, $160,000 and in 1980, over $250,000. He maintained that if the federal government really was interested in promoting the merchant marine, the figure should be $1 million.

Fueling the ship wasn't the only concern. The *Empire State IV*'s capacity was too small, even when enrollment numbers were anemic. In 1968, cruises were divided into two parts to fit all the students aboard the ship. In 1973, the college identified the *Barrett,* a combination passenger-cargo ship that was used by the Military Sea Transportation Service in the Korean War, as a replacement. In a general reshuffling of training vessels, MARAD took the *Empire State IV,* gave it to the Massachusetts Maritime Academy, and the *Barrett's* sister ship, the *Upshur,* was given to the Maine Maritime Academy. The *Barrett* was reconditioned for training purposes, renamed the *Empire State V,* and delivered to Fort Schuyler on October 16, 1973. The vessel's greater capacity allowed the school to return to one cruise per year.

The Kinney-era was a high watermark in the development of Maritime College in terms of enrollment, academic growth and development. But even with its many positive points, it had its own peculiar problems. From streaking to food services, the Admiral had his hands full.

CHAPTER 17

"As Military as Mickey Mouse"

"I'm used to eating fresh fish from a creek but I think they're serving us some of those fish we see floating on top of the East River."
—Porthole, September 29, 1975

"WATCHING A WORM"

As one cadet put it, life at Fort Schuyler in the 1970s and 1980s was about as exciting as "watching a worm." The campus became a ghost town on the weekends, since most of the students lived in the New York City region. Around Throggs Neck, there was little for a cadet to do aside from going to one tavern outside the gates. Sure, a student could go to some bars on East Tremont Avenue like "Sebastian's" where "you can always pull up a stool next to an old man and discuss U.S. Foreign Policy" or go to one of the Irish bars where there were "plenty of older men" with whom you could "discuss such things as religion or the current situation in Northern Ireland." In spite of these allures, every Friday there was a massive evacuation.

Even if there was a more robust campus life, the tougher rules put in place by the Kinney administration made students want to escape. After the more liberal policies of the O'Donnell years, Kinney retrenched. He was a former Commandant of the Naval Academy and wished to extend at least some of the discipline from there to Maritime College.*

---

*Some faculty believed that Kinney, in fact, retired from the Navy after the appointment of Admiral Elmo Zumwalt as Chief of Naval Operations. Kinney, who was more conservative in outlook, did not agree with Zumwalt's more liberal policies. However, it was unlikely that Kinney would have been at odds with Zumwalt's more inclusive race and gender policies in the light of Kinney's acceptance of female cadets.

At the Admiral's command, the regiment was revitalized. Kinney ordered that the unwieldy rules and regulations be streamlined. In 1968, there were 229 lines of regulations. When he was done, there were 149, and these were meant to be enforced. This bothered the students to no end.

Take hair. The rules and regulations said that the cadets had to have a short haircut and that they must use the college's barber. But, short hair was not in fashion, and the students had found ways to get around the rule since the heyday of the Beatles.

Robert Berner learned firsthand about the importance of haircuts. He came to the college in the early 1960s knowing how to cut hair. When word of his skills got around, he found himself managing a cottage industry where he gave haircuts to his fellow freshmen in the training ship's forecastle rope locker.

One day, Berner received a summons to a room of six first classmen who were hanging out and playing cards. They asked Berner where his "stuff" was. He looked confused, and the first classmen informed him they knew he was giving haircuts. Berner denied the accusation, thinking he was going to get demerits. But the seniors just wanted to have their hair cut.

Every Friday night that year, while the seniors studied Heat Transfer Power Plant Design, Berner cut their hair with a trim on the sides to look regulation while their mop was safely tucked under their caps. All was going well, until a rival, another Mug barber, learned what he was up to and reported him. At that time, the college worked on a three strikes policy. For that incident, Berner was given 25 demerits. A second violation for the same offense would be 100 demerits. A third would be dismissal.

Berner went to a disciplinary hearing called the Mast, which was a holdover from the schoolship days. It was patterned after the 'trial before the mast' traditionally held in merchant and naval vessels. There were several kinds of Masts depending on the severity of the violation. For example, for Class II violations, offenders would often be heard before a "First Class Cadet Mast." Class I offenses, were heard by an administrator either at a "Captain's Mast" or an "Admiral's Mast." There was also a "Request Mast," by which individuals could petition officers through the chain of command.

At Berner's Mast, he saw longtime Commandant, Captain Alfred Olivet. The young man had heard of Olivet from his father and uncle, who were also graduates, and the idea of standing at a Captain's Mast with Olivet was surreal. Olivet, addressing Berner in his rough voice, informed him that he knew his father and his uncle and made it clear that if he did not clean up, he would be contacting them. Robert Berner retired his scissors.

By the Kinney period, longer hair plus beards were in style. Yet Maritime College was immune to fashion trends and it was only through hard-fought lobbying that Admiral O'Donnell let the seniors wear mustaches. After Kinney came aboard, this was rescinded in an on and off again war on facial hair.

Students tried to get around the rule by growing longer and bushier sideburns. What aggravated the situation was that some of the staff officers had lots of facial hair. One cadet wrote that it was "rather hard to take being told I need to shave by a man whose beard wouldn't meet Russian Navy regulations and who looks about as military as Mickey Mouse." Another complained, "Why should we be forced to do something and conform to the rules of something that we will never become?"

To let off steam, the cadets would act out in ways that were common at other college campuses at that time. One way was streaking, which was inaugurated in 1974 after the Maritime students heard that 26 Kings Pointers had dashed nude across their campus. Not to be outdone, the cadets started their own streaks, first across the quadrangle of Fort Schuyler, then across Admiral Kinney's lawn. Eventually, 100 students (including some of the Iranians) took part in the activity which culminated in an attempted streak across the Throgs Neck Bridge. The police intervened, but the spectacle was enjoyed by all. One student said, "It was relieving, but much more so to rack out [go to one's bunk]. It really united the student body."

"NOTHING WAS ROUTINE ANYMORE"

Student resentment over the revitalized regiment declined over time. Practically, it was hard for students to stay perpetually upset over minor issues. More importantly, Kinney was no O'Donnell. The new president had a talent for eliminating dissent while keeping a finger on the pulse of the student body without seeming repressive. Where Kinney had the most trouble was in finding a long-term Master of the training ship. Kinney's tenure started with Gerald Nolan as the Commanding Officer, who had replaced the affable Robert Phillips. The youthful Nolan was a 1956 graduate and was molded much more in the short-fused tradition of Olivet rather than the easy going Phillips.

Nolan was immediately challenged on his first cruise when first class cadet, Bill Tuthill, fell from a lifeboat onto the steel deck. The ship turned to the Azores. Air Force paramedics were rushed aboard. Yet Tuthill died as the ship was maneuvering for arrival. The sun shone bright as a silent ship watched a tiny hearse carry a wooden coffin away and up the mountainside. Norwegian tall-ship *Christian Radich* and a Russian freighter in port dipped their ensigns as the hearse drove by. One faculty member remarked that "Nothing was 'routine' anymore."

Nolan remained Master until 1977 when he was replaced by Frank English, who was named Commandant, a title that had lain dormant since Moore discontinued it in an effort to stress the academic side of the college. If Nolan was tough, then English was his opposite. He tried to find a balance between the military and academic sides of the college.

In the meantime, Kinney took a sabbatical for five months to spend time "on both American and foreign flag vessels along with visits to shipping firms, shipyards, port authorities and the union halls." Really, Kinney missed the sea. When the Admiral returned, he found that the students were upset that discipline went by the board due to English's leadership and the unfair application of punishment. English was let go and a crackdown began. Meanwhile, upperclassmen were dismissed by the academic board for disciplinary problems as the Admiral intensified militarizing the college.

Kinney hired Robert Thompson as Master and Commandant for the 1978 cruise. Thompson, while maintaining it was one of his favorite jobs in a long career at sea, chose not accept a permanent appointment since it would mean moving onto campus. Also, he had acquired considerable time and experience in his union. Thompson's replacement was Richard W. Trimble, a martinet who believed that, "Providing a sound military atmosphere is one of the best ways to train people in leadership and management." He asserted that instilling military and moral values into the cadets will improve their "appearance and way of thinking." At the same time, in the fall of 1978, Kinney appointed a tough cadet regimental commander, Bart Eckhardt, who enforced a by-the-book policy in order to improve the regiment's reputation, increase the respect of the maritime industry and improve general standards.

Cadets lashed out. The fall of 1978 saw a spiking of incidents on campus. Vandalism and food fights intensified. Resentment was focused on Trimble, and one cadet shoved paper towels beneath his apartment door and tried to set it on fire.

The unpopular Trimble did not last long and was forced to resign because of complications in obtaining his masters license. He was replaced in early 1980 by the more laid back George C. Previll. Previll also desired to run a tight ship, but was content in maintaining rules and regulations according to Coast Guard standards.

THE RISE AND FALL OF SERVOMATION

Where student anger was justly placed was over food services. One of the most ancient traditions at Maritime College was bad food. The meals aboard the schoolship were notoriously awful, and after a brief reprieve of decent federally-provided cuisine during the World War II era, tradition reasserted itself. While complaints from college students about institutional food are ubiquitous, Maritime College cadets of the mid to late 20th century had a special reservoir of hatred devoted solely to the food.

The problem with the food went back to at least 1951 when Admiral Durgin received a letter from a cadet's mother: "My son tells me the food at the college is very poor. He also states that it is not at all out of the ordinary to have the men who serve them have a cigarette dangling from their mouths or to have ashes drop into their food."

Durgin did not disagree with her but claimed that the problem was due to a budget that did not allow for better food services. In 1951, the budget amounted to less than $7 a week per student. In 1957, it was $8.54 per week, the lowest of all SUNY schools. Durgin wrote that while the college "strived to give a plentiful, balanced diet of wholesome food" there was not enough money to serve a variety of more expensive dishes. Durgin added that students would gripe anyway since they were not "at home enjoying their mother's cooking."

As the years passed, the food grew worse—or at least the students' complaints about it did. In 1968, one cadet wrote about cockroaches caused by fetid conditions in the mess deck. He wrote that the proof was in his pork chop. In March, 1969, another cadet insisted that his food had a yellow worm in it. He advised others to "chew a little more carefully in the future."

Much of the blame for the food fell upon Food Manager and Chief Steward, Charley Rey, who had been at the college since 1943. A 1969 graduate, Jerry Hasselbach, wondered, "Just what the heck was it that he put in the eggs that made them green? . . . After being on ships and places all over the world, that had to be the worst food that I have ever eaten." And 1960 graduate, Robert Vogel wrote, "Two things that one cannot over-exaggerate are the North Atlantic in the winter and the terrible food of Charley Rey. As I look back on the Mess Deck, both at the Fort and aboard ship, they should have been condemned by the Health Board and jailed for impersonating a cook."

Rey frequently served mystery meat. According to faculty and alumnus Conrad Youngren: "There were many theories about 'mystery meat' and numerous arguments over its physiology. It got its taste from the ubiquitous salty gravy it was smothered in, but the texture defied identification. Beef? Lamb? Pork? Some other 4-legged fauna? As a Watch Officer in 1972 or 3, I finally got up the courage to ask Charley. His answer: 'depends.'"

Specific dishes acquired nicknames. "Pucks" were hamburgers, since they were as tough as hockey pucks. "Elephant Tracks" were meatloaf, which derived their moniker from the fact that the slices of meatloaf resembled plaster casts of pachyderm footprints. According to Dr. Richard Burke, 'tracks' were "not too bad, but sometimes tasted like other things found behind the pachyderm." Other nicknames included "collision mats" for pancakes, "yellow/green death" for scrambled eggs and "scabs" for breaded veal cutlet"

In 1969, the Student Council issued a letter that condemned the mess deck for being below all satisfactory health standards. As a result, inspections were held, and by early 1970, it was reported that there was some improvement, at least in the cleanliness of the deck. This did little to improve the quality of the food. One student wrote, "I'm sick and tired of Jell-O that won't jell, fudge that won't fudge, green eggs on St. Patrick's Day, pucks twice a week during Lent and frequent servings of elephant tracks (which cadets, like elephants, never forget). And most of all, I'm fed up with chocolate pudding, rather than tomato juice, which plops when you pour it."

Food Services tried to defend itself by stating that the quality of meals was dictated by budget and prices. They added that student behavior caused money to be wasted, such as cadets not showing up for meals, taking more food than they could eat, purposefully stealing or destroying dishes and silverware and staging food fights. Under pressure, they tried to accommodate the students, and in early 1972 changed from the highly unpopular family-style eating to a cafeteria model.

After cafeteria style was introduced, complaints were less vitriolic, and for a time there were even compliments about better service. Cadet Gary Jobson wrote in December 1972, "Having several choices of meals, more realistic hours, and . . . hot food is the key to the success."

The praise did not last long. Within a year, cadets complained about the greenish tint in the meat and the lack of clean plates and silverware. There were problems aboard the ship too. In 1973, the college was stripping down the *Empire State IV* since the college had just acquired a new training ship. As they were clearing out items, they found "Deep in a galley storeroom . . . crates and crates of canned food. They were grey 'No. 10' cans with stenciled military codes on them and a date—1943." In 1974, frustrated students painted graffiti in the mess deck reading: "AD. KINNEY: THE FOOD IS BAD NEWS." In protest, students boycotted the food, published derogatory cartoons and held food fights.

By the next year, the food was a running joke as seen in the *Porthole*'s mock advice column called "Dear Andy":

Dear Andy,
I used to live on a farm and so I'm not used to some of these fancy city foods they serve us here at the Dome. . . . Where I come from hotdogs are usually red or brown but around here their normal color is green. . . . I'm used to eating fresh fish from a creek . . . but I think they're serving us some of those fish we see floating on top of the East River. Tell me if I'm the only one who finds fault in the food.

Sincerely Yours,
Clem.

Dear Clem,
If you think you're the only one who finds fault with the food here just look at the lines that form outside the heads after some of the better meals. Hell, if we sent some of that food in CARE packages to underdeveloped nations we'd be sure to start an international incident.

Andy.

To improve the meals, the college privatized food services in 1975. It received permission from the State to buy food from private sources and outsource food services to a company named Servomation. In 1977, privatization expanded when Dennis Calhoun and Billy Pilecki opened a new snack bar at the TIV. They added different varieties of beer and food as well as a new juke box, pinball machines and a foosball table.

While the cadets were happy with the snack bar, complaints about Servomation continued. Then on March 1, 1979, a severe epidemic of food poisoning broke out on campus. It was reported that more than 78 cadets and seven faculty suffered from severe stomach pains, diarrhea, headache and vomiting. Of these, 48 were sent to Jacobi and other area hospitals. Classes were cancelled, students were quarantined to the campus and no food (bad or good) was available since it all had to be tested.

Word leaked to the local press of "Domers' Disease," and reporters from ABC's Eyewitness News, the *New York Times*, the *New York Daily News* and WOR-TV descended upon the campus. A press conference was held near the dormitories. While this occurred, some of the more playful cadets, tired of being quarantined, hung a sign that read "Free the Maritime 900." It was a public relations disaster.

The illness ran its course, and the next day cadets were given early liberty. Servomation maintained that all the food that the students were served was fresh. In fact, in the immediate aftermath it was reported that the outbreak was caused by a short-lived viral infection and the U.S. Public Health Service exonerated Servomation. The cadets believed it was a white wash, and the food service director resigned for "personal reasons." Even so, the college renewed Servomation's contract and forced students to purchase their meal plans.

Then on November 8th another outbreak of food poisoning occurred that affected 110 cadets. Foul meatballs and egg salad were contaminated with fecal coliform bacteria. The department of health stated that it was probably due to lack of cleanliness by the food handlers. The news hit all the local newspapers. One kitchen worker told the *Daily News* that it was "lousy food management" that caused the problem. He said "cooked vegetables and chicken or beef pot pies cooked on Monday frequently are dumped into soup on the following Saturday." These practices were denied by the new food manager. There was belated appreciation for Charley Rey.

A faculty-student committee was formed to investigate the problem. Surveys were distributed. Thomas Hartley, a member of the committee, pleaded with the cadets for patience. "Food fights and threats solve nothing and just further antagonize the food service," he said. The survey results, published in May, 1980, found that 74.4% of the students wanted Servomation out and that 93.3% felt the company was directly responsible for the illnesses. The committee recommended firing the company.

Removing Servomation was not a simple thing to do. There was no direct proof that the company was the cause of the illnesses, and due to state regulations the contract had to go out for bidding. Servomation was the cheapest company. It was only because the school used the poll information about how unpopular it was that it was able to be replaced on August 12, 1981 by United Interstate.

Interstate got poor reviews as well, and by 1984 columnists in the *Porthole* were mocking the "grisly concoctions" served to them. Food service was switched again, this time to Saga/Marriott. Again, the reviews were awful. In 1988, one cadet wrote, "Unless you're one of those people who read through numerous text books on the bowl and therefore lightened your academic load (and your body at the same time), you might want to speak out against Saga/Mariott."

To be fair, criticisms were far fewer, and in 1989 there is actually a rare, positive article in the *Porthole* that while complaining about some raw chicken and hair in the food, added, ". . . it seems to be slowly improving when compared to last year. There is fresh fruit at every meal, better cereal dispensers at breakfast and a better selection of cold cuts with lunch." Saga eventually changed its name to Sodexo and was removed from their contract with the college in October, 2006 after a failed health inspection. After a brief period in which "Patricia's," a local restaurant, handled food service on an emergency basis, the school hired Chartwells in November, 2006.

THE 1981 MIDDLE STATES REVIEW

Aside from the food, the Kinney period was a time of prosperity for the campus. But the 1981 Middle States review found fault in the regimental system. The reviewers wrote that the officers of the regiment were not perceived as qualified for their duties by the students. They found that there was more of an emphasis on discipline and punishment than leadership training and noted that senior students were not directly involved with underclass cadets. They also found that the *corpus* of rules and regulations (which Kinney had ordered pared down) were still so voluminous that they were not well understood and poorly enforced. All of this had a negative impact, and some of the people the reviewers interviewed said that the system led to vandalism, excessive drinking and interpersonal problems among the students.

To address the issue, Kinney appointed a committee which reported its findings on October 21, 1982 to his successor, Rear Admiral Floyd Miller. The report explained that the demilitarization of the college during the O'Donnell years resulted in a lack of accountability with cadets coming and going as they pleased. In addition, the report charged that faculty had become passive in supporting the regiment. They found that "every cadet was looking for firm, fair consistent leadership from the Commandant's staff and in the administration of the academic program."

The report made 37 suggestions which stipulated various ways to strengthen the regimental nature of the college. It suggested instituting Friday afternoon inspections and requiring that the Commandant and his deputy live at the college. It charged that the first class should be more involved in running the regiment with the Commandant's office acting as a shadow government. It recommended eliminating non-cadet enrollment options since they "demoralize the regiment." It even went so far as to suggest a dress code for the faculty.

The criticisms of the Middle States Review were limited to the military elements of the school and did not involve the academic program, which received high marks. There was actually little to complain about. When Kinney retired, Maritime College seemed poised for sustained growth. Few foresaw that the institution would free-fall into a decline that would jeopardize the college's existence.

CHAPTER 18

First and Foremost

"The year was 1882 and Maritime County was an unhappy town. Long-haired, unregimental outlaws ruled and apathy was king. . . . Then one day a great new Marshall rode into town."
—*Porthole*, October, 1982

"HOSS"

Floyd Harry Miller returned to his *alma mater* with a mission. He was going to clean up the Dome and bring it back into line with the Maritime College he had graduated from in 1953. He knew he was the man for the job. "I felt I could offer something back to the school," Miller said. "It was a once in a lifetime opportunity."

He grew up in Freeport, Long Island, where he worked at a boatyard and listened to sea stories told by his uncle, who was a chief engineer. In making a decision about college, he only applied to Maritime from which he graduated as an honor cadet with a deck license. In his yearbook, one of his classmates wrote, "We are all sure that some day we will read the name of F.H. Miller in the annals of Marine History." Or at least in the annals of Maritime College history.

Right after he graduated, his Navy Commission was activated. Instead of getting a job in the merchant fleet, Miller was drafted. He made a career of it, and in 1977, while still in his mid-forties, he was promoted to Rear Admiral. He took command of a Destroyer Group, then later headed the Navy Recruiting Center. It was there that Miller reestablished relations with Maritime College while trying to recruit its graduates to the Navy. Never one to let go of an opportunity, he retired from the service at age 50 and began a new career as a college president.

Tough and hardworking, Miller seemed to revel in the persona of a cowboy. At some point during his Navy career, Miller's childhood nickname of "Horsie" evolved to "Hoss" after a character from the popular Western TV show, *Bonanza*. The persona also emerged in the friendly, homespun manner in which he told stories about himself and the Navy.

Miller was much more hands-on than Kinney. Thomas Cerny, the Director of Admissions at that time, reported that he came across the Admiral during the summer of 1983 in a "boiler suit with a brush in his hand, varnishing tables for the TIV. I soon learned this was just one of the many evenings spent so that all would be ready for when the cadets return."

One day, the Admiral's wife was walking in the dormitory quadrangle. Some cadets wolf-whistled at her. Miller's wife noticed which window the sound was coming from and told Hoss. Miller went to the dorm room and banged on the door. When the door opened, he said to the flabbergasted cadets, "I heard you're whistling at my wife!" Miller, besides "Hoss," earned the nickname "Flashlight Floyd" due to his alleged penchant for looking under cadets' beds during inspections with a flashlight.

Miller said of himself that he was low key. "You've got to be approachable," he said in an interview. "You've got to be able to listen." But while he could be personable and friendly, faculty accounts also called Miller a "hard ass," a "screamer," and "heavy-handed," whose attachment to maintaining a traditional regiment blinded him to other problems and opportunities. When asked about Miller, Professor Conrad Youngren commented, "What bothered me about Floyd Miller was that I think he confused nostalgia with insight. A product of the '50s version of Maritime, he sincerely believed that the evolution of the College peaked during his cadet tenure and sought to return to those halcyon days." Hoss Miller was to be a controversial figure, and often criticized; but even his greatest detractors could never deny that he loved his *alma mater*.

NYMFAF

Miller took the 1981 Middle States Review and internal committee report which recommended militarizing the school to heart. He gradually shifted resources to the training ship. He replaced personnel and introduced policies to strengthen the regiment. He inaugurated a cadet service program that required students to do work aboard the ship in order to provide a cost-saving way of providing vessel maintenance while gaining practical experience. Miller claimed this would foster teamwork and *esprit de corps*.

To the dismay of the students, he introduced a mandatory exercise period for the regiment on Friday afternoons. It was sold as a way to develop battalion competition, build cadet pride and end the week in an upbeat way. It also had the bonus of preventing students from cutting Friday classes. All these measures were introduced under a new slogan, "New York Maritime, First and Foremost," abbreviated to NYMFAF.

Naturally, there were complaints about NYMFAF and the new "Friday Afternoon Formation," since the exercises ended between 3:30 and 4:00, just as the nearest entrance ramp to the Throgs Neck Bridge closed. The resulting jam of students trying to leave the campus was compared to how "the citizens of Pompeii attempted to flee from Vesuvius' wrath." Yet there was solace in the situation that inadvertently led to greater camaraderie among the regiment—but in a way that Miller did not foresee. Since the formation ended when traffic was at its height, there was little point of going home. Instead, some cadets gathered at the TIV for beer. As 1985 graduate, Erik Johnson recalled, "The post-inspection gatherings, coupled with some Friday afternoon sailing, are some of my fondest memories of Fort Schuyler."

In those first months, Miller's tough policies and his nickname "Hoss," earned him this satirical blurb in the *Porthole*:

> The year was 1882 and Maritime County was an unhappy town. Long-haired, unregimental outlaws ruled and apathy was king. Then one day a great new Marshall rode into town. Yes, it was the famous Marshall Miller and he was disgusted with what he saw. Marshall Miller remembered how great and wholesome the town was when he lived there, and he set out to return to it the pride that had been dragged through the mud by the long-haired unregimental outlaws. The great new Marshall took away what the long-haired outlaws had considered their rights. No longer could they break windows, throw beer bottles from their saloons, turn over deputy's horses, and yes even put their hands in their pockets during morning town meetings.

Miller responded briefly in the next issue by writing that he was really sworn in as the Marshall of "Domer County." The next year was spent further strengthening the regiment. There was no arguing with Hoss Miller.

TYRANT OR SAVIOR?

Initially, Miller's programs had positive results. In 1982, the *Porthole* wrote that vandalism on campus had declined by 80% due to a crackdown on alcohol abuse. "No longer is it cool to kick down the lavatory partition or pull the fire alarm at 3 a.m." The change was so quick that another editorial remarked, "No one dreamed so many changes could take place in three months. Who in all honesty, can complain about decreased vandalism, much less drunkenness, better maintenance of the ship and a real concerted effort to improve both internal pride and external impressions of the college?" By February, 1984, the *Porthole's* editor, Martin Muniz, wrote that vandalism and alcohol issues were "practically nil," and the first class cadets were "now running the entire regimental operation in probably the most efficient and effective manner ever known in the history of the school. And most importantly, the cadets are taking more pride in the college and are establishing a sense of leadership."

There was a dark side to Miller's reforms. Inspections were unannounced, and rooms were entered without the students present. Muniz labeled these methods "unsavory" and wrote "it is an unsettling and uncomfortable experience." According to some accounts, the attitude of much of the student body toward the school abruptly changed as the college became more regimental. When the ship left on the 1983 cruise, those aboard could see graffiti painted along the seawall insulting Miller.

Most parents favored the changes. One was the outspoken, Marilyn Desborough, who wrote letters to the *Porthole* as "Maritime Mom." In 1983, she wrote, ". . . as a parent I'd like to voice my opinion in favor of the stronger Regimentation practices (did I hear a Boo, mom??)" One can imagine what Desborough's son (or his friends) thought.

An in-depth exposé of Miller was published by the *Porthole* in 1985. The newspaper wrote that Miller

> . . . has been strongly criticized by cadets and faculty alike. Many new and unpopular policies were implemented with no warning or consultation with student government. Who is Floyd Miller? Is he a tyrant, a savior, a politician, or a champion of the student body? Strangely enough, while criticism has been widespread, serious opposition has not. The Admiral's detractors blame this on what they say is fear of his autocratic style.

ACQUISITIONS AND DEVELOPMENT UNDER MILLER

The nostalgic Miller easily gave his support to a plan to use part of Fort Schuyler to establish a maritime industry museum. The effort was spearheaded by faculty Jeffrey W. Monroe and 1947 graduate, Jack Hayes. Their goal was to make the museum "the foremost collection reflecting the proud heritage of the United States Merchant Marine in the nation." Construction began in 1984 and it opened its doors in 1986. By 1989, it was the third largest maritime museum in the New York City region and became involved with various projects including the search for the HMS *Hussar* and the salvage of the wreck of the Confederate raider, *Alabama*.

Yet what Miller wanted more than anything was a new training ship. As the *Empire State V* aged, it grew costlier to maintain. By the fall of 1984, the vessel was in need of some $4.2 million in repairs.

Obtaining a new ship was a lengthy process that began early in Miller's tenure and required substantial lobbying in Washington. He was constantly contacting members of Congress and soliciting parents to do the same, even providing the addresses and phone numbers of their representatives.

At that time, the two main congressional allies of the college were Democrat Representative Mario Biaggi and Republican Senator Alphonse D'Amato. Biaggi, who was the college's local Congressional representative, was Chair of the Congressional Committee on the Merchant Marine and Fisheries. He had a long history with the school and even gave the 1972 and 1983 commencement speeches. Also important was 1946 graduate, Rudy Cassini, who was a staff member of Biaggi's Committee. Cassini was instrumental in securing the $8.5 million to purchase the *Mormactide*, a C-4 steam freighter, and convert it into a training ship. The conversion process took over a year, but finally on May 5, 1990 D'Amato's mother, called "Mama D'Amato," re-christened the ship the *Empire State VI*.

DIVERSITY

During Miller's time as president, Maritime College began to become racially diverse. Although there had been minorities at the school since the 1940s, enrollment was dominated by whites from the New York City suburbs. This was noticed as late as the 1960s. Despite policies which sought to change the racial makeup of the college, by the early 1980s there was little headway. In

1982, one potential student commented that while the college was a "pretty good school for academics," in terms of "recruiting people from different places . . . [it was] disgusting."

Yet as the decade passed, racial diversity on the campus increased so that by the middle of the 1980s over 10% of the student body consisted of minorities. At this time, the college formed a committee on affirmative action to deal with rumors of discrimination. The committee's job was to act as an advisory board, make recommendations and "sensitize students and employees regarding the institution's policy and commitment to equality of opportunity regardless of race, color, sex, creed, national origin, or handicap. . . ."

As the decades passed, the ratio of minorities grew, so that by the turn of the 21st century, the percentage of these students had grown to between 15-20%. While this is well short of the average in national demographics, the school had made some progress.

STAFFING AND DRIFTING

During Miller's first few years, there was quick changeover in personnel. In 1983, the Admiral dismissed for unspecified reasons Commandant George Previll. Miller then assigned Captain Douglas Hard to be the temporary captain of the training ship until he hired thirty-year Navy veteran, Richard Gooden.

Gooden served three years. Then Miller, believing that the stability of the regiment needed a long-term commandant, actively sought a younger person for the job. He found his answer in Saturday morning class protestor, James DeSimone, the son of Guy DeSimone, the longtime head of the Marine Transportation Department.

DeSimone and his brother were visiting the campus when they had lunch with Miller. At the lunch, the Admiral mentioned in an offhand way that Gooden had left, and asked if DeSimone would consider taking the position. DeSimone thought Miller was simply being polite and figured that the job of the training ship captain was for an "old person." However his family encouraged him to pursue it. He telephoned the Admiral to see if he was serious. Miller offered the position again, and this time DeSimone accepted. He served as Commandant and Master of the training ship from 1987 until 1996.

The personnel changeover was not without incident as 1987 saw the removal of the venerable Chief Engineer, Edward Pfleging. Pfleging had served as Chief since 1959 and had become an institution aboard the training ships. He was popular among the cadets and faculty with one former faculty member recalling that when the ship had problems everybody turned to Chief Pfleging.

Pfleging and Miller did not see eye to eye. The Admiral changed the personnel rules of the ship so that Pfleging had to choose between being faculty on land or Chief Engineer at sea. Meanwhile, the administration also implemented a policy where Fort Schuyler graduates could not serve as watch officers on the ship because they were thought to be too close to the cadets. As a result, new officers were brought aboard, mostly retired Navy personnel who were not familiar with the intricacies of the training ship.

One of these newcomers was John Payton, who was named as Edward Pfleging's replacement. Jose Femenia remarked that Payton didn't play the part of a Chief. "Your typical Chief walks around on the ship in coveralls with a flashlight in his back pockets, gloves and a rag. Payton walked around in a khaki uniform." For the cruise of 1987, Payton ordered marine diesel for the ship, a fuel which they never used. When Femenia explained that the emergency generators on the ship could not use that kind of fuel, Payton dismissed the complaint.

So the ship went to sea with a new Captain, a new Chief Engineer and the wrong kind of fuel. On that cruise, a 2nd Assistant Engineer lost a finger and the ship was for days adrift without power. Femenia, who went on the cruise, recalled that in the middle of the night a cadet woke him up and brought him up to see Captain DeSimone. DeSimone was having a meeting about the problems. Payton blamed the cadets for the troubles with the ship. Tired, Femenia lost his temper and said that the problem was with the new crew of engineering officers since they "didn't know squat about the engine room." The cadets couldn't be at fault since they were the ones being trained. The cruise of 1987 was dubbed "Summer Sea Drift." The ship managed to get through the fiasco, but that cruise was Payton's last.

"A NEGATIVE ATTITUDE"

Nobody could fault Miller for his enthusiasm for his *alma mater*, but despite his best efforts, in 1983, the school entered a long period of decline that would last until the turn of the 21st century. From a high of 1,136 students in 1983, enrollment slipped to 766 by 1999.

Maybe the college had grown too complacent after the highs reached during the Kinney period. Dr. Hartley Spatt, said that there was a "sense that everything was going along fine and we didn't have to do anything."

The evidence suggests that the problem was more complex. The college's depression was caused by demographic, local, political and economic reasons, most of which were outside the control of the school. Each cause fed off the others, creating a vicious cycle of decline. The ensuing soul-searching debate over the college's future dominated the dialogue of the faculty, alumni and administration throughout the period.

There was a downturn in nationwide college enrollment during the 1980s. This trend was mirrored by Maritime College, although because of its smaller size, the numbers were more skewed. There were years in which the college's numbers did not match national figures, such as in 1984 and 1985 when there was a crash in applications that was far lower than the national trend. Still, when Maritime College and national enrollment figures are compared, they correlate.

The Admissions Department was understaffed. This did not prevent Miller from sacking Thomas Cerny, who had been in charge of admissions since the height of the Kinney administration. One internal report stated that college publicity consisted of "a Daily News centerfold when the [training ship] arrives and an occasional front page if there is a food poisoning incident." The college catalog had not been changed for years, and its first section on student life was described as "an invitation to cross the River Styx." The invitation read:

> All students are expected to be well dressed and well groomed while on the college grounds or at college activities. All students are also expected to maintain dormitory rooms in a clean, sanitary and neat condition. No cooking, cooking appliances, or alcoholic beverages are allowed in dormitories. Any questions concerning the rules and regulations of campus life should be addressed to the Commandant of Cadets.

In 1985, the Assistant Director of Admissions, Judy Fine, said that declining enrollment was because the strict regimental policies under Miller were turning off the students from promoting the college. It was reported that the "great majority of students depart from the campus with a determination best described as an escape."

Miller cited the depressed state of the American merchant marine as causing the enrollment problem. This was debatable. The American merchant marine had been in decline all through the post-war period due to changes in technology and government regulation. Any set of figures, be it the tonnage of American ships, or the number of able-bodied seamen, show this. In 1960, the U.S. flag fleet comprised 16.9% (2,926 ships) of the world's fleet. By 1985, this figure was 2.9% and in 2008, there were only 133 American flagged vessels composing .8% of the world's total.

Even so, most graduates found jobs, but most were not at sea, and those who did sail tended to work under foreign flags. The only way that a decline in the American merchant marine could be related to low enrollment was by giving the perception to recruits that it was a dead-end career in which graduates could only work at sea. An internal college report said ". . . the 'Marine Industry' does not have a progressive image with a bright future. Would you send your kid to the Shoe Manufacturing Institute of Technology?"

In February, 1984, just as the country was emerging from a recession, it was reported by the *Porthole* that only 3% of 1983 deck graduates went to sea. This brought on demands for a placement officer. Martin Muniz, the editor of the *Porthole*, asserted that students were transferring out of the school for lack of jobs, and recommended that graduates obtain work on foreign-flagged ships. Stephen B. Luce would not have approved.

What was really aggravating to Muniz was how Miller dismissed the issue. "You are too young to be concerned with such matters," Miller said to Muniz. This comment set off a miniature mutiny as Muniz followed this conversation with an article stating, "I have received 54 letters to the editor condoning the negative aspects of the school. Of which, only six gave constructive criticism and solutions to the problem. Everybody has a negative attitude, including me."

The administration finally gave in and hired 1979 graduate Anthony Palmiotti to be the college's first placement officer. By 1988, the job situation improved, and students obtained more sea-going jobs as retirements opened positions, and graduates signed on as able-bodied seamen.

A "FALSE ECONOMY"

The election of Ronald Reagan began a movement to reduce government spending in social programs and education. The national mood was for smaller government and this extended to the states.

SUNY had been riding high since Nelson Rockefeller pushed through massive investments in the system. It was only in the mid-1970s that the first budget cuts happened. At that time, the college was hit by a $50,000 cut, which was modest when compared to what came in the 1980s.

In 1983, with declining funding from New York State, SUNY was forced to issue massive cuts and increase fees. There were layoffs. The college could not expect much help from Governor Mario Cuomo either, who actively sought to reduce SUNY. He saw little need for Maritime College. Sometimes Cuomo would attend SUNY meetings. When he saw Professor Karen Markoe, who from 1987 to 1991 was president of the statewide University Faculty Senate, he would remark, "Karen's here—we still have a Maritime College." This was true for the state legislature as well. In one instance, a high ranking member of the legislature asked Markoe, "Why does New York needs two maritime schools?" Many in the state government could not distinguish between the federal and state maritime schools.

Miller then made the decision, much like the Board of Governors 69 years earlier, to send the *Empire State V* to Albany on the cruise of 1983 to promote the school. It was reported that many politicians in Albany "had no idea of what the Maritime College was about, and that it was a part of the State University of New York." Cuomo proclaimed June 6, 1983 as "Maritime College Day."

This did not stop more SUNY-wide budget cuts and tuition increases in 1989. Unlike the closure crisis of 1914, the college was no longer an independent entity, and it sank or swam with the rest of SUNY. More faculty and staff were laid off. Hours were cut back on services, and even the campus doctor was limited to two office hours per day resulting in the college making arrangements with Throgs Neck Urgent Care for medical emergencies. Baseball, hockey, men's volleyball and rugby were cancelled for the 1988-1989 season. In 1989, the football program was cancelled indefinitely.

In 1991, Edward Regan, the State Comptroller, recommended that SUNY close the college along with some other campuses. This was reported by *Newsday*, the chief Long Island newspaper. Since that was where most of the school's recruiting took place, it aggravated the enrollment situation.

Along with service cuts, the college's academic programs were reduced. In 1985, the college eliminated the Ocean Engineering major. In 1991, the Mathematics-Computer Science major was terminated along with the Nuclear Science program. In 1996, the Meteorology and Oceanography majors were eliminated.

While New York State was gutting SUNY, the federal government was also whetting its budget cutting knife. Ronald Reagan, who campaigned as a supporter of the merchant marine, nevertheless subjected the federal government to an investigation called the Private Sector Survey on Cost Control, commonly referred to as the Grace Commission. The Commission studied all areas of government spending which included support of merchant marine training. It reported that better technology lessened the demand for merchant sea officers. The Grace Commission suggested cutting aid to all maritime schools and reducing the number of training ships to two—one for Massachusetts and one for California.

To defend the college, Miller employed the arguments that Admiral Durgin had used in the 1950s. Since state maritime schools were cheaper, money should be cut from the USMMA. Miller commented that the USMMA cost the federal government three to four times more than "the state schools while training students for civilian occupations."

He argued that since the students at SUNY chipped in by paying their tuition and board, and the school received money from the state, which operated the college as well as the training ship, that ending federal aid was a "false economy."

"MOTHBALLED MARINERS"

Miller hired a lobbyist and also relied on the help of Mario Biaggi.* Miller had to fight a running battle with Washington. There was antagonism between the White House's Office of Management and Budget (OMB), MARAD and the college. The OMB tried to deny any federal funding to the state maritime schools in the budget years of 1986 through 1988, which was only countered by the state schools aggressively lobbying Washington. MARAD, whose own budget was cut, attempted to have the state academies share training ships. Again this was resisted. Then, in January, 1987, MARAD recommended decommissioning all the state school ships. The state schools fought this through their contacts in Congress. Again, in 1989 MARAD and the OMB proposed a ship-sharing scheme to save money. Miller went to Washington for a hearing and said that the "OMB has a vendetta against the state academies." Miller

---

*In 1988, Mario Biaggi, was embroiled in a political scandal and was forced to resign his seat in Congress. The college lost a valuable ally and suffered more bad press.

argued that to remove federal funding was short-sighted to the long term interests of the country. "If the state academies cease to exist, where will the predominance of licensed officers come from? If mothballed ships are needed for whatever reason, will there be mothballed mariners?"

These efforts were productive enough so that federal budget cuts never materialized.

Newsday reported on the situation, again hurting enrollment. One article reported how removing the training ship would kill the program. A student commented, "It would mean the loss of this ship, and unless we could find another way to get the sea time, we'd lose the whole reason for being here: our licenses." Another student remarked, "You have heard about welfare cuts, but you don't know what it means until it affects you." The school was about to lose its critical mass.

Then, in what would become an ill-timed episode of outreach, Admiral Miller hired Joseph Hazelwood as a watch officer for the 1992 cruise. A graduate of the class of 1968, Hazelwood was the captain of the notorious *Exxon Valdez*. In March, 1989, while Hazelwood was not on the bridge, the ship struck a reef and spilled 11 million gallons of oil into Alaska's ecologically diverse Prince William Sound. Hazelwood was accused of drunkenness and negligence. He was widely vilified for the incident. He was exonerated of the felony charges but had to pay a fine and do community service. In 1990, the Coast Guard suspended his license for nine months. When Alaska's Attorney General was told of Hazelwood's appointment as a watch officer he commented, "Perhaps of all people he [Hazelwood] now may be the very best to relate to the students the hazards of not standing watch on the bridge." As the news spread through the national press, Miller, who brought on Hazelwood in a show of solidarity for an alumnus, said, "I hired him, I guess I'm the one who should take the flak."

By 1993, the budget situation was so bleak and the layoffs so deep, that Admiral Miller commented, "I'm doing three jobs now. I used to have two other people doing public relations and development / fund-raising. I started out here with 249 full-time faculty and staff and I'm down to 178 now."

With rumors that the college was going to close, applications dried up. To aggravate the problem, faculty reported that students entering the college were less prepared than they were before. Between 1981 and 1990, there was a decline in entering students' SAT scores which had declined from a high of 1070 in 1982 to 980 in 1990. According to one report: "The general decline in knowledge and ability has been noted by faculty members from all departments." This resulted in the formation of the institution's first remedial classes in Math and English.

Dr. Hartley Spatt said that the problem was not one of lowered standards on the part of the college but lower graduation standards from high school. "We accepted the same number, but they couldn't hack it." Spatt conducted research of the student body at the time and found that the normal distribution curve of student abilities was skewed. There were large groups of well-prepared students and under-prepared students, but few in between. What this meant was that the under-prepared students would fall behind, and the instructors would work to catch them up. But this would frustrate the well-prepared students who would then drop out of the college. The student body was losing its leaders, and as a result the whole school suffered.

"Commie Bob" Sennish, the rabble-rousing Humanities professor who helped organize the 1969 Moratorium demonstration, also noticed the difference. On the eve of his retirement in 1989, he claimed the students were better educated in 1960 when he started teaching. He said that "for courses in which I now teach six books, I then taught ten. And they had read the stuff." He added that there was a revival of student learning from 1968 to 1978 in relation to the Vietnam War protests. "The kids were really coming alive," Sennish said. But from 1979 to 1989 the nature of the college changed. "The idea of getting ahead and getting a job is more important than actually learning something, as it was in the sixties, or doing something, as it was in the seventies. This place is now pretty blah." Sennish contended that with the "exception of only a few people . . . there isn't really anyone in the administration with any experience or training in the field of higher education."

"I WISH I KNEW"

Despite all these problems, the college clung to life. James DeSimone gave Miller credit. He said the Admiral would have "given up his life for this school" and that he was "a very skilled politician. During the worst of budgets, Maritime always got an add-on from Albany. He knew how to play the game up there and knew how to exert power politically. He was a strong person."

DeSimone stated that even though Miller got "criticized for a lot of different things, he was president at a very pivotal time. . . . I firmly believe, after sitting up in Albany during some of these meetings, that there is not a doubt this place would have been shut down if he hadn't been president."

But the majority of opinion blamed Miller for not providing the vision needed to pull the school out of its depression. One professor noted that "Miller was slow to realize the decline was not just the demographics but forces at work that were making our institution less attractive."

Miller appeared distracted and unsure what to do. He seemed focused on the spit-and-polish image of the school. One senior commented in October, 1985, "I find it quite distressing that Admiral Miller persists in mentioning the unfinished windows of the fort instead of addressing the more pertinent issues affecting the college."

The evidence suggests that Miller did not have a long range plan nor know how to communicate positively with the college. When the Admiral spoke about the problems afflicting the school, he said that the college was comparatively not so bad off. "Every maritime school's got the same problem," Miller said. "In fact, some of the other ones are in a lot worse condition than we are." When asked about how the college would have to change in the face of the transforming maritime industry he responded, "Well I think we have to see what the marine industry does. It's going to continue to go through, I believe, many changes, and not just in this nation but worldwide." When asked what the solutions were, Miller responded, "I wish I knew. I keep working on it. You know I have meetings with people and can't seem to communicate down to the lowest level."

Jose Femenia recalled that Miller said his admissions strategy was the *chili policy*. "You take a lot of chili, throw it up against the wall and some beans will stick."

Femenia himself came into the Admiral's crosshairs. After two decades as Engineering Chair, Femenia found himself removed when Miller instituted a policy of term limits for department chairs. Femenia suspected that the policy was created specifically to remove him. He went on to head the Engineering Department at Kings Point.

"WHY SETTLE FOR JUST A DEGREE?"

Several ideas to resuscitate the college were floated at this time. One introduced a new job-focused slogan: "Why settle for just a degree?" This was criticized for assuming that the general public had knowledge of the competitiveness of Maritime College graduates in the job market. "The slogan deemphasizes the value of our academic programs to a population we must assume is in the process of evaluating degree-granting institutions."

Several people suggested changing the name of the college back to the New York State Maritime Academy because it would sound more prestigious. This was strenuously objected to by the faculty who believed it would signal to "the world, including students and prospective students, that our academic bent has changed."

More serious efforts addressed the curriculum. Dual programs in which a student could earn both engineering and deck licenses, were examined but found to be too long and expensive to appeal to students. The college introduced an associate degree program focused on limited license training for tugboats. To sustain it, the college procured the necessary boats from donations.

Yet the chief solution that was first offered in 1986 by an *ad hoc* committee of students and faculty was to bring in large groups of non-cadet students and make the licensing program optional. This would allow the college to expand into other areas and recruit 'civilian' students, specifically transfer students. It would introduce an 'intern option' throughout the various programs in which a student could forgo the regiment and work for a company or an organization. It was to target upper division transfer students including those students who held associate degrees. While the civilian student would not be qualified to sit for a merchant mariner license, the degree would prove valuable to the maritime industry. Besides, not as many students were sailing anyway.

In support, an anonymous author wrote in the *Porthole*:

> Some people will resist revamping the regimental system, saying that military discipline is necessary for self-improvement whether or not a student goes to sea. I find this reasoning ridiculous. The vast majority of American colleges are non-military, and the business and professional world has absorbed these 'undisciplined' graduates without dissolving into anarchy. It's quite obvious to all that Maritime is in trouble. We've reached an impasse, and all of us—students, alumni and faculty—have a stake in what lies on the other side.

The faculty presented the proposal to enroll non-cadets on a controlled basis to the Admiral. But Miller never liked the idea of non-regimental students. After coming to office, he worked to eliminate the old day student program. He refused the recommendation and insisted that the college would enjoy a resurgence of the merchant marine.

Miller cited a study by Vice Admiral T.J. Hughes, which concluded that while there were currently enough ships to operate a massive military sealift in a time of war, by the 1990s there would be a shortage of licensed officers for such a scenario. At a faculty meeting, Miller said that in the event of a national emergency by 1995 there would be a shortage of 2,900 licensed officers. Miller then wrote on the blackboard: "1995—2,900 jobs!" Few of the faculty believed Miller.

It is puzzling that Miller used this data since the economic conditions that sustain the United States commercial fleets are separate from the needs of a what-if scenario from the Navy. The assumption was that in 1995 the merchant fleet would miraculously build itself up without any stimulus from the federal government to supply jobs for an unknown sealift against an unknown enemy.

Miller showed charts of a "License Officers Manpower Curve" to demonstrate how current officers were aging and assumed that an equal number was needed to replace them. Conrad Youngren commented, "Whether a crafty political calculation or gross delusion (I thought the latter), his insistence on the imminent rebound of the American Merchant Marine made discussion of innovative, long-range planning nigh-on impossible." Miller and the College Council would not change the institution's mission to include non-licensing programs believing that it was "correct and sacrosanct for the foreseeable future."

Desperate, the faculty sent an unauthorized delegation to Albany in 1989 to ask the SUNY Chancellor: "Is the status of the Maritime College as a specialized college within SUNY contingent upon *every* graduate qualifying for a U.S. Coast Guard Merchant Officer's License?" Youngren, Femenia, Humanities Chairman Joel Belson and the Provost, William Porter went.

According to faculty accounts, Miller found out what the delegation was up to and got to Albany before they did. He intercepted the Chancellor. He was not going to have his faculty try to force him to enroll non-regimental students. He then provided to the Chancellor the data from the Hughes study.

When the delegation arrived and plied their question to the Chancellor, it was too late. The Chancellor responded, "Yes—that is what your mission states." After that, the faculty gave up on trying to introduce non-regimental students. There could be no change.

In 1991, Middle States panned the college. In its report, the commission criticized the self-study the school submitted stating that at best it "was disappointing." They indicated there were large information gaps and

> no studying of where the institution had been. . . . In actuality it was not a self-study at all, but a recapitulation of the status quo and hoped for plans for the future. The document was not assigned an editor to smooth the disparate parts into a coherent whole. Studies, and subsequent analysis of the results, to provide a foundation for basing funding statements, future program initiatives, long-range academic and institutional planning, etc., were almost absent. . . . The team believes that the relevance of current and future institutional needs are suspect because Maritime did not truly study itself.

The Middle States review team concluded: "More than a handful of faculty would appreciate consideration of a dialogue regarding providing other educational opportunities." This issue turned the college into a time bomb.

CHAPTER 19

In Step with the Future

"Change is never easy..."
—Rear Admiral David Brown

TO TRAIN OR EDUCATE?

The retirement of President Miller in 1995 was the climax of a long and complex process in which Maritime College, in a gradual spiral, approached a nadir. Despite Miller's best efforts, enrollment had collapsed and rumors swirled of the college's imminent demise. It was the worst predicament the institution faced since the closure crisis of 1893.

The central issue of the day, and indeed one that had been debated many times since the institution was formed, was its direction. The long simmering tension between the academic and the traditional training sides of the college had reached a boiling point as it became evident to many that maintaining a traditional licensing program solely would no longer serve the best long-term interests of the college. One 1961 graduate, Donald Brennan, succinctly encapsulated the issue: "Are we here to train, or are we here to educate?"

THE BUDGET CRISIS

The impetus to the crisis was funding. As enrollment decreased, so did tuition income. What's more, SUNY had been plagued by budget cuts all through the 1980s and 1990s which had filtered down to the college. During that time, the college's administration concentrated its efforts on maintaining the training program, which meant maintaining the ship. As a result, funds that might have been used for academic programs and student life was rerouted.

For example, it was cited in an institutional self-study that salaries were being paid from a dormitory fund which was earmarked to maintain the campus. This in turn led to the decay of student housing. With all the manipulating, tracing the ledgers was a Herculean task.

The college was also amassing deficits: $69,400 in 1994-95, $455,700 in 1995-96, $476,400 in 1996-97, $986,400 in 1997-98 and $500,000 in 1999. The deficits might have gone back further, but the State did not have the records. The college had submitted the same budget requests to SUNY, year after year. In addition, not all tuition dollars were being collected. The self-study stated, "There were no written documents of budget reconciliation on campus. In fact, there were no accurate personnel lists. Hires were not a result of academic or administrative planning."

Donald Brennan, who after graduating served as an intelligence officer in the Navy and eventually became a financial executive for Morgan Stanley, remarked that if the school had been a private business it would have filed for "preemptive bankruptcy as it had become self-liquidating. It was generating huge operating losses even with all the finagling." Like a century earlier, the greatest foe of Maritime College in the late 1990s was its "extraordinary cost per student as it did not simply have sufficient enrollment to support the overhead of the institution."

"A KINDER, GENTLER ADMINISTRATION"

These problems were inherited by Miller's successor, David Brown. A Naval Academy graduate and Vietnam War veteran, he had experience in maritime education as an instructor at the Naval War College and later as superintendent of the Great Lakes Maritime Academy. It was when he left the Navy and joined Great Lakes that he was appointed the rank of Rear Admiral by the U.S. Maritime Service in 1992.

Dr. Karen Markoe referred to this new administration as a "much kinder, gentler administration." A great asset to Brown was his wife, Sheila McCurdy, who inserted herself into campus life by hosting dinners, book clubs and other events. Wonderful for morale, McCurdy was respected by faculty and students alike. Brown met on a regular basis with senior staff and the college community's various constituencies. As part of this, he held "Town Meetings" with the campus community to discuss current issues and engaged the students at regular meetings. But Brown had his hands full. Upon his arrival to the campus, Brown recalled that Miller "apologized for leaving me to identify the last $240,000 in program cuts. . . ."

In 1998, Brown recruited Donald Brennan to become Chair of the College Council. Brennan had a resume that made sense for the college at that time. Aside from his management and financial skills with Morgan Stanley, he was an expert analyst as a former intelligence officer in the U.S. Navy. He was also the Vice Chairman of the Board of Trustees for the Catholic Hospital System of New York and had been appointed to Presidential Commissions by Gerald Ford and Jimmy Carter. Still, Brennan, who was aware of the college's problems, took the position with reservations, stating that he only did so to help save his *alma mater*. "It was dark and damp . . ." Brennan recalled. "The students were like inmates walking around a minimum security prison. . . . People spoke in terms of 'when they get out of here'—like it was a penitentiary. No one talked about graduating. They were 'getting out.'" To Brennan, and many others, the solution was to refocus the college toward academics and significantly increase enrollment by recruiting students of high academic standards who did not desire to be in the licensing program. Yet to do this, the mission of the college needed to change.

RETHINKING SUNY

In 1995, SUNY's Board of Trustees introduced "Rethinking SUNY," an initiative to increase efficiency and reduce costs across the university system. A key part to "Rethinking SUNY" was that each campus was mandated to review its mission.

Brown created a Strategic Planning Committee in order to look at the college's options. But the committee became stymied because it lacked direction, and some faculty did not want to change the school in any way. In the end, the group was asked to form wish lists of what they would like to see happen at the college. In frustration, Professor Conrad Youngren, who was on the committee, sent a letter to Brown: "A letter to Santa, no matter how eloquent, is not strategic planning. We recognize that this railroad doesn't run well. If we think we are solving the problem by taking inventory of burned out bulbs, documenting the need for refrigerant in the air-conditioning system, suggesting that the square wheels on the locomotive have its corners filed down a bit, and fantasizing about having a shiny red caboose like our competitors—only to find out that the tracks now connect a pair of ghost towns—we have missed the point."

In retrospect, Brown admitted that the committee needed "more focused presidential direction," but added that it "represented a beginning, and ... informed the campus community that well-reasoned initiatives and changes to the traditional ... licensing program would be welcomed." According to Brown, this effort resulted in a focused mission review.

THE NEW MISSION

The primary authors of the new mission were Professors Joseph Hoffman and Conrad Youngren. After extensive meetings in which all members of the college community were invited, they crafted a mission that allowed for the academic side of the institution to expand. The license program was described as an "opportunity for its graduates" rather than a requirement. The word "cadet" was eliminated. The regiment became a "structured community which emphasizes responsible citizenship and self-discipline, and which maximizes opportunities for exercising leadership." Educational terminology was used for the first time, such as creating "a learning environment that stimulates intellectual growth, scholarship and creativity."

The College Council approved the mission after making revisions that emphasized education over training and focused on the role of the maritime industry and the international business community. In September, 1998, the revised mission was accepted by SUNY. Non-license programs were authorized by the faculty, and in 1999 curricula outside the regimental system leading to degrees in Marine Environmental Science and International Transportation and Trade were implemented. A Student Life Committee was formed in April, 1999 to develop a plan to integrate the new cohort of students not in the traditional program. Meanwhile, other institutional renewal activities started, which included a Transition Plan, a Long-Range Strategic Plan, a Campus-wide Assessment Plan, a Student Life Plan and an Enrollment Marketing Plan.

THE "GANG OF FOUR"

Brown also had an advisory committee since the college faced considerable problems. There was 1962 graduate Thomas Fox, the president of the Alumni Association, maritime arbitrator, retired Commander in the U.S. Navy Reserve and a licensed master who headed a maritime consulting firm.

There was 1964 graduate John Ingram, a past-president of the alumni association who was senior partner at an admiralty law firm and a member of the Fort Schuyler Foundation. Ingram had sailed as a second and third mate and was a retired Captain in the U.S. Navy Reserve. There was also 1971 graduate and College Council member Thomas Keenan, another past-president of the alumni association and a retired Lieutenant in the U.S. Navy Reserve. He was a senior executive for a major shipping company. The group was headed by College Council Chair Donald Brennan. The people on this group were all prominent alumni who were meant to represent broad sectors of the college's key stakeholders—both at sea and ashore. According to John Ingram they were "four very accomplished graduates who had sailed, served in the Navy and were top professionals in their fields who saw the college as it could be and not just a vocational school to turn out licensed merchant marine officers for a declining U.S. flag merchant marine."

However, to some, much of what the group did seemed secretive in nature and at that time there was a perceived lack of communication. The group soon got the nickname "Gang of Four" after the Chinese cabal of the same name. But Brennan referred to it as Brown's "Kitchen Cabinet." He emphasized that the group was necessary because the problems that the college faced were just too overwhelming for one person. Brennan asserted that this group led the charge to implement the new programs with the intent of resuscitating the institution.

Whether it was a "Gang of Four" or a "Kitchen Cabinet" there was nothing sinister about the group. What this nickname does show is a certain sense of dark Fort Schuyleresque humor. Everybody was concerned for the college's future and wanted the institution to succeed. There were no villains, but there would be martyrs.

According to Brown, "Many options were considered during meetings with this group . . . including eliminating the traditional program completely and changing to a 'maritime business' school with a focus on the business side of shipping and not the training of officers to run the dramatically reduced number of American flag ships."

"RATIONING TOILET PAPER"

It was in this context that the college hired a consulting firm, the Pappas Group, to study the college and create a report that would help them obtain

$4 million in additional state funding. They documented the dramatic decline in real dollars in annual funding, salary disparities, deteriorating campus conditions and other issues.

The report was completed by April, 1999 and submitted by Brown to SUNY. The SUNY auditor then presented the college's budget deficits, and a frank discussion followed. Brown later said, "believe me, our continued operation was very much in question. . . ."

Donald Brennan recalled that at this time SUNY contemplated what to do with the college. SUNY did not want to lose Fort Schuyler as the State University System had little presence in New York City. Several options were considered. The campus could have formed a partnership with Baruch College, focusing on international business. This option was rejected because of jurisdiction agreements between SUNY and CUNY. Next, the college could have turned entirely toward an associates degree-based licensing program. This was dismissed. The most serious option that was entertained was putting the college under the administration of SUNY's large university at Stony Brook. It was reasoned that since Maritime College was smaller than some of Stony Brook's academic departments, Fort Schuyler could be administered by the much larger institution.

But through lobbying by Brown, Brennan and the rest of the "Gang of Four," and with the strong support of John J. O'Connor, a SUNY Vice Chancellor, the college was granted a reprieve. SUNY gave $2 million in transition funds as long as targeted goals for enrollment and spending were met. SUNY assured Brown that he would have control of the ship for at least three years to meet Summer Sea Term commitments for students already in the program. This was all documented in a 2000 Memorandum of Understanding which Brennan likened to a "Magna Carta." This was the deal that gave the college time to allow the new programs to take root.

Meanwhile, Brown was directed by the SUNY Chancellor to investigate alternatives to a dedicated training ship. In retrospect, Brown wished he had emphasized "investigate."

Brennan advised Brown to replace key administrative positions. Brown, realizing the need, shook things up. The chief of the new hires was Dr. Kimberly Cline, who was appointed Vice President for Administration and Chief Operating Officer. She was tasked with resolving the budget issue.

In a painful process of budget cutting, layoffs and hiring freezes, financial solvency was restored. But Cline was maligned for the cuts. The faculty at one

John J. Foody was the long-time head of the Engineering department (1952–1974). He was nicknamed "God."

Meier Degani was the long-time head of the Science Department (1947–1973). A brilliant scientist, he helped establish the college's nuclear program and was, erroneously, believed to have worked on the Manhattan Project.

Alfred F. Olivet (1900–1986), served as Commandant of Cadets from 1946–1965. He was renowned for his fierce temper.

Admiral Durgin (center) with Captain Olivet (right) showing alumnus Henry Stamp (class of 1916) the campus. Circa 1955.

This 1952 cartoon published in the student newspaper, the *Porthole*, reflects the feelings of the college toward the USMMA.

The *Empire State III* was the former *Mercy*, a World War II hospital ship. It received two battle stars for service during operations at Leyte Gulf and Okinawa. It served as the college's training ship from 1956–1960.

The *Empire State IV* was the former *Henry Gibbins*. A World War II era troop transport, it notably shuttled Holocaust survivors to the United States in 1944. It served as the college's training ship from 1959–1973.

Filomena Magavero, librarian, was the first female faculty member at SUNY Maritime College. She worked at the college from 1949 to 1995 but officially named a faculty member in 1962.

When Marjorie Murtagh graduated in 1974, she was the first female graduate of any American maritime school. She was also the first woman to receive a Coast Guard Engineering License. Here she is receiving her certificate from Captain Arthur Gove (right) and Admiral Sheldon Kinney (left) in 1975.

The *Empire State V* was the former *Barrett*. A troop and passenger transport, it received one battle star for Korean War service and three battle stars for Vietnam War service. It served as the college's training ship from 1973–1990.

The *Empire State VI* was the former *Mormactide*. The college converted it to a training ship in 1990.

James Cordara (facing camera) was a 1985 graduate who, as part of the Nassau County Marine Bureau, served as a first responder at the 9/11/2001 disaster.

Students in the licensing program still go through a rigorous semi-military education, 2010.

Fort Schuyler with cadets in formation during homecoming, 2010.

Incoming students entering the licensing program go through a period of indoctrination, 2007.

Cadets going through training drill on how to plug leaks aboard ship, 2010.

Cadets mustering during summer sea term aboard the *Empire State VI*, 2011.

Rear Admiral Wendi B. Carpenter became the first female president of Maritime College on August 31, 2011. SUNY Chancellor Nancy L. Zimpher is seated on right.

Cadets on deck during the 2012 Summer Sea Term.

The SUNY Maritime College Campus in 2011.

Vice Admiral Herbert Fairfax Leary (1885–1957). Superintendent, 1946–1949; President, 1949–1951.

Vice Admiral Calvin T. Durgin (1893–1965). President, 1951–1959.

Vice Admiral Harold Moore, Class of 1924 (1901–1981). President, 1959–1967.

Rear Admiral Edward O'Donnell (1907–1991). President, 1967–1972.

Rear Admiral
Sheldon H. Kinney
(1918–2005).
President, 1972–1982.

Rear Admiral Floyd
H. Miller. President,
1982–1995.

Rear Admiral David C. Brown. President, 1995–2001.

Vice Admiral John Ryan. President, 2002–2005.

Vice Admiral John Craine. President, 2001–2002 (interim); 2005–2011.

Rear Admiral Wendi B. Carpenter. President, 2011–2013.

point voted no confidence in her for creating ". . . a hostile working environment, lowered morale and unsound financial and personnel decisions." This was unfair as Dr. Hartley Spatt pointed out that her "methods were not cruel, but they weren't generous either. If you're a million or a million and a half dollars in the red on a budget that is only $15 or $16 million you got a lot of work to do; and you can't do that by rationing toilet paper."

"AN ALTERNATIVE TO LICENSING"

In August, 1999, Brown laid out the changes in a program titled "In Step with the Future." He stated that the focus of the college would be on the maritime industry's role in international business. This made sense as jobs at sea were fewer, but opportunities in business were greater:

> The college will develop an alternative to licensing which, unlike the current program, will not compete for the students' time during their degree studies. The college also will seek an alternative to the high cost full-time operation of a training ship for the sea time necessary for licensing, including the use of other training ships and commercial vessels.

Brown wrote that the "leadership opportunities provided through the cadet experience will continue but will be delivered in an optional format that does not overshadow the academic program or the campus life experience."

According to Brennan, he, Keenan, Fox, and Ingram met with the Alumni Association's Board of Directors to discuss the future of the school. During this meeting, they emphasized that the new programs were needed for the future of the college. Then Brennan said off-handedly that otherwise "the ship might be gone in three years, the regiment in four." This remark was taken out of context, and according to faculty member Conrad Youngren, "turned out to be a galvanizing event and an albatross around Brown's neck."

"DON'T GIVE UP THE SHIP"

All the changes and rumors of changes had created a strong opposition to "In Step with the Future" which coalesced primarily among some prominent members of the Alumni Association. In their opinion, the proposed changes to the college would strip it of its uniqueness and identity. In the Fall of 1999 banners reading "Don't Give up the Ship" were hung in protest, and resistance centered around the mantra: "The ship *will* be gone in three years, the regiment in four." As the administration assessed the situation, the opposition grew louder and angrier. Accusations flew which included that Brown had not consulted with the alumni. These allegations were unfounded as the "Gang of Four" were all prominent alumni; there were also many faculty, also alumni, who were involved in the process.

Opposition to Brown grew as weeks then months passed—there was seemingly nothing that could be done to diffuse the situation. According to Brown, the opposition would not open any dialogue with him. Still, he fought on by trying to win over those who he believed had received inaccurate information. In his 1999 Homecoming address, he remarked that Maine Maritime Academy had been mixing cadet and non-cadet students for years. "Does anyone here doubt that anything Maine can do, we can do better?" he asked. Brown later wrote, "We could only reach the needed enrollment numbers by having a parallel non-regimental program to complement the traditional program." In his speech, he insisted there were "no plans at present, secret or otherwise, to eliminate the Regiment of Cadets . . . there are no plans to eliminate license instruction at the College. . . . The college would retain its maritime specialization and identity, but with a refocused mission and an enrollment which assures financial viability." It may be argued in hindsight that Brown was *too* courteous, because it became evident that he personally became targeted by the opposition. Thomas Keenan later commented everything was "hard over and locked in."

Thomas Fox, to his credit, tried reason. On September 14, 1999, he circulated a memorandum to the alumni explaining the rationale for the changes. Aside from citing statistical data which revealed declining enrollment, poor retention and the high cost to the State per student, he emphasized how the industry had changed. There were not nearly as many jobs sailing under American-flagged vessels as there had been decades ago. Fox warned, "Alternatives to success will not be tolerated by SUNY and the consequences of failure won't be pleasant. Only with that success will we then be able to truly claim that we are First and Foremost." Yet the division between those who promoted the new programs versus traditionalists was proving unbridgeable. Fox shortly afterward resigned as president of the Alumni Association. Also at about this time, Brennan's term on the College College expired. He stepped down to be replaced by Thomas Keenan.

Brown's opponents grew bolder. No matter what he said, they insisted that the college was doing away with the license program and that SUNY could not be trusted. The situation grew ugly as Brown found himself increasingly isolated.

Charles Balancia, a College Council member, told *Newsday* that Brown "has no following now and a leader cannot lead without followers." Charlie Munsch, the Chair of the Engineering Department at the time said, "The president has essentially turned off every person he has dealt with." In what Brown asserted (probably correctly) were orchestrated moves, the College Council, the Parents Association, the Alumni Board, the Fund Raising Foundation Board and the Faculty all voted no confidence in him.

The faculty vote cited five items in their resolution including alienating the Alumni and Parents Association, poor enrollment and low morale. It culminated with: "he has created mistrust on campus so deep that very few amongst the students, faculty and staff believe anything that the president says," and "any plan brought forward by the president is believed to be just more empty promises." They argued that Brown had failed to promote harmony on campus. Certainly there was little harmony at Fort Schuyler.

Youngren, who tried to delay the no-confidence vote, said that it was not constructive. He commented, "In all of academic wimpdom that's about the wimpiest thing you can do. You walk away and don't try to solve any problems." Thomas Keenan, who opposed the College Council vote, commented that it would "just create another obstacle for us to move forward."

By November of 2000, Brown announced that he would retire at the end of the 2001–2002 academic year. Under increasing pressure, he accepted a sabbatical and left in the fall of 2001 after welcoming the first cohort of nontraditional students.

Despite the drama, the changes had been enacted through SUNY and the new programs implemented. It can be argued that these programs, as well as the commitment from SUNY to support the college, set the stage for one of the most remarkable comebacks in the institution's history. Many faculty gave Brown credit for the changes. The last time Conrad Youngren ever spoke to Brown he told him, "You will become Maritime's Gorbachev."

Even if Brown was a Gorbachev or even a Yeltsin, all these changes cannot be credited to one person. Certainly, the "Gang of Four" and those faculty who supported the changes must be given their due.

It is clear that the crisis of 1999-2000 was, as Donald Brennan put it, an "inflection point" in the institution's history. In retrospect, he said that all the time and effort was worth it. "I felt I had taken the college to where it needed to be. It was heading in the right direction albeit in one deliberate step at a time."

Brown once said, "Change is never easy. This is a very specific program with a lot of tradition and emotion attached. When you propose any change, it's almost immediately threatening." He had learned this lesson the hard way.

But Fort Schuyler had regained its sea legs.

CHAPTER 20

The Ship Sails On

"Some parts of the college must never change, and some must change if we're going to be relevant in the 21st century."
—Vice Admiral John Ryan

THE AVIATORS

After the trauma of the turn of the 21st century crisis, the morale of Maritime College had ebbed. There was a need at that time for strong leaders who could bring order—leaders like Vice Admirals John Ryan and John Craine.

Ryan, who had been selected to succeed Brown was, with his twin brother Norbert, a 1967 Annapolis graduate. Ryan was fortunate to have his identical brother with him at Annapolis. When undergoing the rigors of his plebe year, he and his brother were ordered to do "uniform races" in which the freshmen were ordered to change uniforms in only a couple of minutes, something that was virtually impossible. One of the Ryan brothers would be in one uniform while the other was hidden in the uniform he was to change into. When the races were underway, the plebes charged to the dorms to change. As they were scrambling to put on their uniforms, the other Ryan twin would step out, immaculately dressed. Their classmates would be yelled at for not being as efficient.

Upon graduation, Ryan became an aviator and flew for Patrol Squadron Eight until 1972. He then renewed his connection to the Naval Academy, this time as a candidate guidance officer. He stayed on until 1975, then was promoted to a variety of commands and at one point headed the Fleet Air and Maritime Air Forces in the Mediterranean. Yet his connection to the Naval Academy was strong enough to bring him back in 1998 as its superintendent—despite intense competition from the Marine Corps, which wanted one of their own for the slot.

A consummate professional, Ryan was popular at the Naval Academy. He raised a $254 million capital campaign. The Faculty Senate praised his support of academics and passed a resolution that he serve another four year term—something unheard of. Accordingly, after receiving the appointment to SUNY, he needed to serve out the remainder of his term at the Naval Academy, until 2002

In the interim, SUNY appointed a rival applicant to the presidency, Vice Admiral John Craine. Described by Admiral Vern Clark as "a gentleman," Craine's paternal demeanor and optimism did much to raise the morale of the college. His charismatic wife, Wendy, also did much by involving herself in student and faculty life.

Craine, like Ryan, was a Naval Aviator and flew over 100 missions during and after the Vietnam War in the VF-101 "Grim Reapers" and the VF-103 "Sluggers." He rose through the ranks and, among other duties, commanded a fighter squadron and a naval air station. On reaching flag rank in 1997, he was appointed the commander of Naval Shore Activities of the Atlantic Fleet in which he oversaw 26 Navy bases and air stations. In the last stages of his Navy career, Craine was the Director of Naval Training in the Office of the Chief of Naval Operations.

Craine prepared the way for Ryan by being on hand for the 2002 Middle States accreditation review. This review was especially important after the disaster of the 1991 Middle States visit. The preparation for this visit was done by Professors Youngren and Hoffman who spent two years preparing all the necessary documentation. Upon their visit, the Middle States team saw that the campus was in a state of changeover and felt the friction of the switch between its traditional mission of training graduates for licensing and the new, broader mission to serve the maritime industry. The Middle States Report noted that "not all of the key college stakeholders have yet concurred in the revised institutional mission and initiation of non-traditional programs on campus." This, they said, had resulted in "difficulty in aligning its available resources with institutional goals." They urged the College to address this issue and to fully accept and adapt to the new cohort of non-regimental students. Yet on the whole, the Middle States team was convinced about the future viability of the college, so long as they carried out the plan. To a large degree, the success of the reaccreditation review created greater buy-in to the new non-traditional programs. In fact, the plan that was devised for the reaccreditation visit was for several years upheld as a best practice for institutions in transition.

Ryan took these recommendations to heart when he took command in 2002 and continued the course set out by the prior administration. He recognized that while change was necessary, it was important to be sensitive to the college's traditions. During the change of command ceremony Ryan stated, "What we are talking about is how to balance continuity and change. You've got to get that right. Some parts of the college must never change, and some must change if we're going to be relevant in the 21st century."

Much to Hoffman's surprise, Ryan *actually* enacted and executed the transition plan, which had as its basis the rewritten mission statement. Proposed non-license programs were systematically implemented, and agreements were made with area institutions, such as Nassau County Community College, to recruit students with associate degrees as transfer students. The license programs that required regimental obligations remained in place.

Kudos were given to Ryan's leadership abilities. Youngren commented, "Whatever Ryan's magic was . . . the whole campus bloomed and improved almost overnight." Hartley Spatt compared Admiral Ryan to President Bill Clinton: "He walked into a situation that was improving. He could have been terrible and the improvements would not have stopped happening. As it happened, he walked into the situation, seized the moment and we got a multiplier effect."

The regiment resurged and grew, even with the non-cadets on campus. Commandant of Cadets, Captain Richard Smith, said that the comeback was due to refocusing the college's objectives, changing recruiting tactics, but most importantly, rebuilding pride. Smith gave credit to the reunification of the Master and the Commandant roles, something that had been separated since DeSimone left in 1996 since the college did not have people with the credentials to be both Master and Commandant. The two roles and their relationship to each other were controversial since the level of work to be both Commandant and Master was considerable. Smith said that the reunification was the key to bringing a semblance of order to the regiment. As head of the cadet corps, Smith emphasized accountability and ownership. He strongly believed that linking the two positions made his work and the regiment more effective by leading to greater cadet buy-in since the students would be getting the same message from one person. He commented that Maritime cadets were different from federal cadets and "they connect very easily if they see a reason to."

After Ryan's appointment, enrollment more than doubled. From the low of 766 in 1999, it had reached 1,972 by 2010, a historic high. Of these, over 1,200 were in the regiment, making it the largest merchant marine training corps in the nation and a personal point of pride for Captain Smith. To accommodate the swelling student body, in 2010, training cruises were divided into two sections of 45-days each. As an extra bonus, graduates were finding well-paying jobs; the 2005-2006 annual report claimed virtually 100% job placement with only 37% of the graduates not entering the maritime field either ashore or at sea. Even after the economic recession of 2008, the school still maintained high placement rates, with graduates receiving high paying jobs.

Critics of the curricular changes claimed the growth was "on the backs of lower standards and non-cadets." But this flies in the face of the tremendous growth of the regiment. Youngren gives credit for this to President Brown who saw that if "you grow the population with qualified people, they will see the benefits of the license programs. And they do."

THE ALUMNI ASSOCIATION SEPARATION

But Ryan had his own set of problems, and the greatest difficulty was the estrangement between the Alumni Association and the college. During the Brown administration, many prominent alumni were angry over the "In Step with the Future" plans. There was a feeling among the alumni that SUNY was attempting to exercise more control over the school and transform it into just another college. When Ryan became president, these feelings were still raw.

Then in May, 2003, SUNY published new guidelines for how the various campuses should relate to their fundraising foundations, auxiliary services and alumni associations. SUNY cited instances where some campus organizations were engaged in activities that far transcended their original charge. In addition, to that point no policies had been implemented regarding alumni associations and their activities. The new guidelines tried to bind the campuses closer with their various alumni associations, but also make them subordinate as a supporting organization instead of a charitable one.

The venerable Maritime College Alumni Association, which had an office on the campus, saw the contract as another mode in which SUNY was attempting to change the school for the worse. It might be said that the new guidelines were ill-timed for the college, which had just started to recover from the turn-of-the-century fiasco. The Association wrote in October, 2003, "SUNY tried to convert the campus to an open campus and eliminate the ship, license and regiment in recent years and could, in subsequent years, try again. The Alumni cannot support such a position. The Alumni are not products of a mediocre general studies program—their training and belief systems are widely different." They would not consider yielding any financial sovereignty of their organization to SUNY, especially in light of the financial missteps of the college in the prior decade.

If the guidelines had been published at any other time, it is likely that they would have been accepted by the Alumni Association. But now, they attempted to get grandfathered under the new guidelines so they could be exempt from direct control. This effort failed with the Association claiming that their petition to be grandfathered was rejected three times. In a mailing, the Association's leadership wrote that they believed SUNY's "real objective is control, and we see little evidence that they would be more effective in serving the College and its alumni than we have been. There appears to be no justification for employing a controlling rather than a cooperative framework."

Ryan, as a representative of SUNY, gave the Association an agreement and told them that they had to sign it. The Association balked and put it out to the membership to vote. The polling was described as similar to a push poll, where the information on the ballot favors a vote in a certain direction. In this case, the ballot worded the choice to reject the agreement as "to give up its independence as an unincorporated association, conform its activities to those defined in the SUNY Guidelines, lose effective control of its assets (staff, data, monetary), and be subject henceforth to a high degree of direction and control by the College President, SUNY and the State of New York."

The result was an overwhelming 1,636 to 74 vote not to sign the agreement. Shortly after the vote, on Friday January 31st, SUNY's Central Office sent a fax to the Association notifying them to leave the campus by Monday. The move was coordinated by the Association's Director, Eileen Femenia, who scrambled to gather friends and relatives to relocate their offices temporarily before they reincorporated as the "Fort Schuyler Maritime Alumni Association" since they were no longer allowed to use the name of Maritime College. That spring, the bittersweet 100th anniversary of the Association was celebrated by 650 alumni and guests at Pier 60 in Manhattan.

The ramifications of this break are still being played out. The Alumni Association's leadership has said that their organization is being singled out from other SUNY alumni groups resulting in a division of its membership. In 2011, the Association's president, John Bradley wrote:

> The questions of sustainability and relevance are of concern to me as I consider our current relationship with the college. We have no presence on campus and no contact with the graduating classes. There is no collective input from the association to the administration on the operation and direction of the school. Is this sustainable over the long run? What relevance and input do we have to the future direction and focus of the school within the current arrangement?

In many times in the course of its history, the Alumni Association has taken the lead in helping the school in troubled times. The Association has reached out to the college to come to a resolution. The college has recognized this and the Carpenter administration, in 2013, had begun to seek ways to repair the rent.

Yet despite the split, the college continued to grow. Ryan was so esteemed and politically savvy, that he was named Chancellor of the SUNY in 2005.

Craine, who after stepping down as interim President to head the Neil D. Levin Graduate Institute of International Relations and Commerce then the SUNY Board of Trustees Task Force on Efficiency and Effectiveness, comfortably slipped into place as Ryan's permanent successor. He carried on the plan and used funding obtained by Ryan to continue improving the campus. Burke said that Craine had "really done a great job in terms of keeping us focused . . . planning, executing, planning, executing."

Under Ryan and Craine, the college undertook its first major building projects since the 1970s. The campus was updated with walkways, internet capabilities and other infrastructure. In 2004, a new 4-story dormitory complex was completed, and in 2006 the football program was restored. By 2011, the pier for the training ship was expanded. Yet the crowning achievement to the college's renaissance was the erection of a new academic building whose foundations were laid in 2011. When Craine retired that same year, the dormitories were full and admissions had become more selective.

The growth of the 2000s can also be attributed to a variety of events outside the purview of the college. The September 11th attacks and following events had, according to one professor, "created a sense that a regimental education and military background is in many ways a good thing." And to the students, some of the stories of the September 11th attacks answered the question: *why Maritime?*

FIRST RESPONSE

On the morning of September 11, 2001, Sergeant Jimmy Cordara was in East Rockaway at the Marine Bureau Headquarters of the Nassau County Police. A little after 9:30, a teletype came in from the New York City Police Department. The city needed assistance. Cordara went to the boats.

Jimmy is a bright-eyed and friendly Long Islander. It is impossible not to like his down-to-earth manner and sense of humor. His story tells us a bit about how young men and women find themselves in the maritime field—and how they get drawn into acts of heroism.

Jimmy entered Maritime College in 1981. He picked the school because it was the cool thing to do. "The big kids in my neighborhood went there," Jimmy said. He didn't really know what he was getting into—but he knew he was going to sail to Europe, something his friends in other colleges would never experience. There were also drawbacks. "Who wants to stand watch at 4 o'clock in the morning?" Jimmy asked.

Jimmy quickly learned to fly under the radar. He didn't want trouble and never had a rate. He said with a mischievous glint in his eye that he was "a trooper through and through. I was like an electron. I wanted to follow the path of least resistance."

He graduated in 1985 with a degree in Marine Transportation and immediately sailed from New York to St. Croix on the Apex's *Jacksonville*. Afterward, he found a job on a sludge boat in New York City. Jimmy said this was heaven, even though it left him smelling like sewage. He soon left the boats and found that it was hard to get other sailing jobs. He gave up the sea and joined the Nassau County Police as a patrol officer.

After five years, the police moved Jimmy to the Marine Bureau. There he got to work on disasters. In 1990, he was at the scene of the Avianca Flight 52 crash in Cove Neck, New York, and in 1996 he was on the dive team for the TWA flight 800 disaster. By September 11, 2001 Jimmy had been promoted to sergeant and led about a dozen men on a fleet of four, 45-foot jet-drive, patrol boats. Two were stationed on the north shore and two on the south shore of Long Island.

Jimmy had a nose for trouble. Even before the teletype from the city came in, he heard reports of American Airlines Flight 11 crashing into the North Tower of the World Trade Center. He thought the day was too clear for such an accident. Jimmy ordered his men to fuel the boats, limit patrols and standby.

After United Flight 175 struck the South Tower, Jimmy knew that the situation was serious, especially when the city was asking all neighboring areas for help.

"New York City is the 800-pound gorilla," said Jimmy. "They don't need help for anything. They're an army for crying out loud." The city also specifically called for maritime units, since there was no way to get on and off Manhattan.

Jimmy Cordara's four boats hurried to New York City. The south shore pair went via the Atlantic Ocean while the north shore duo sped down the East River. Water conditions were ideal for marine operations. Jimmy said, "It was a perfect way for us to get supplies in; get firemen and rescue workers in; and get injured out." The boats rendezvoused at the North Cove Marina, just west of the World Trade Center. It was 12:30.

As they arrived, Jimmy saw "freakin' chaos." It was like "entering the gates of hell. There was no color—everything was black and white." Dust and paper covered all. The smell of burning was everywhere.

People immediately rushed to Cordara's boats to evacuate, but instead he tied the vessels up. He marched to the ruins of the World Trade Center. "We were looking for our own. We were looking for cops and firemen that were hurt."

Jimmy and his men immediately headed straight to the ruin that was the former World Trade Center. There, among the mountain of smoking rubble, they saw a hand poking through the debris in agony. It was a firefighter. His helmet had saved him. They pried off the rubble with crowbars, set him on a backboard and hauled him out. They rushed him back to the boats with some other firefighters to evacuate. As the vessel sped through the harbor, Jimmy administered medical care to the firefighter, assuring him that he was going to be all right. But the firefighter took Jimmy's hand and wept, "They're all dead! They're all dead!" The call was taken up by another of the firefighter's crew, who stood behind, tears rolling down dusty cheeks.

Jimmy Cordara never learned the man's name or his command, but he was the first of many that he would evacuate over the following days. Jimmy was part of what was to become the largest sea evacuation in history, even outstripping the Allied evacuation of Dunkirk during World War II.

The Coast Guard sent word for help, and every kind of vessel headed for lower Manhattan. Jimmy even saw rowboats trying to assist. He said, "If it floated, they brought it down." Anybody who could assist was welcome. "I would have taken help from Mickey Mouse."

After he had brought the firefighters to safety, he returned to North Cove to continue search and rescue operations. After the initial chaos, a semblance of order came during the early afternoon. Yet after 5:00 p.m. this changed, as 7 World Trade Center collapsed. As more smoke and dust poured through the streets, panic ensued:

> I would like to tell you that we bravely and calmly retreated to the marina and in an orderly fashion to load passengers. But when Building 7 came down, that was not the case. Speaking for myself, the noise, the choking cloud of dust and the sheer fear made me run like hell.

He arrived back at his boat and started the engine. As it revved to life people came begging to get off the island. He and his men forced them into a single line and loaded them onto the vessel, women and children first. He filled his boat far past its ten-person capacity and took upon himself the responsibility for any accident that might happen.

"The proper way is to get a log and get their names and their date of birth and their address, but it was absolute chaos."

With people fleeing in panic, they took whoever they could fit aboard to evacuate. At one point, Jimmy jammed 35 people aboard. He knew there were not enough life jackets to go around. "How could you say no?" Jimmy asked.

Later, he reflected, "I realize now I disregarded departmental procedure, but I just couldn't bring myself to worry about some stupid paperwork at that time. It was one of the many 'command decisions' that I made that day."

Jimmy is still haunted by the decision. "If our vessel foundered or overturned that day, I would have been responsible for even more loss of life. It didn't, and we were just plain lucky and that's the truth."

It was the beginning of two life-changing weeks for Jimmy Cordara and many other rescue and recovery workers. Jimmy's patrol boats shuttled people to a staging area set up beneath the Colgate Clock in Jersey City, and they returned with rescue workers and supplies. Jimmy liked the Jersey City location since it was closer to the disaster site than the other staging area set up at Liberty Island. He and his men "wanted to get back into the game quickly." Navigation was difficult and dangerous work for the metal-hulled patrol boats due to the pilings that were scattered around the harbor.

Aside from rescue workers, supplies and equipment, they brought body bags. But there were few remains of the victims. Jimmy, who had seen bodies at other disasters, found this remarkable. "I didn't see any bodies at 9/11."

When asked about how many people he transported in the two weeks he was there, Jimmy responded that he had "no idea." He hardly slept during his time as a 9/11 rescue and recovery worker.

"When you got exhausted, you went down below, took a catnap and somebody else grabbed the wheel and kept going." He estimated that in the first two weeks, he got 36 hours sleep.

As they worked "the best of New York came out." Civilians brought Jimmy and his men food and water. What most struck him was the weeping among all the people he saw "on the ground on their hands and knees" in clusters of six or seven. "Just the tears," he recalled.

Jimmy encountered many of his fellow graduates. These reunions were brief, such as when he met fellow 1985 graduate, Joe Dugan. Jimmy recalled that Dugan, who became a New York Harbor Pilot, did not hug or shake hands, but asked, "Jimmy, you okay?" Jimmy replied, "Joe, you look like shit." Dugan replied, "So do you."

Jimmy saw many other faces from Maritime College. He was introduced to graduates from other years and sometimes ate with them. The whole time period was such a blur that he could not remember the names, but he remarked that seeing his fellow "Domers" at the scene strengthened him. He asserted, "I knew we were going to be okay. I knew that we were fine, because these guys would come get me. I sailed with these guys, I crossed the Atlantic with these guys and I knew what they were capable of. It was a good feeling, I don't know how else to put it."

After September 11th, Jimmy stayed with the Marine Bureau. But in 2009, his wife was diagnosed with terminal cancer. Doctors could not determine how she got it, so it was diagnosed as CUPS (cancer with an unknown primary source). She died after a nine-month battle.

Jimmy attributed her illness to the September 11th attacks. When he finally did get home during that time, she would clean his clothes and change his uniform. He suspects that she took in some of the toxic dust that ruined the health of so many rescue workers. Aside from his wife, Jimmy has seen several of his fellow rescue workers pass away.

Jimmy's own health was compromised. As of 2011, his lung capacity was 54% and was under observation by the World Trade Center Medical Monitoring Program.

"It is a good thing. Good program," he said.

Jimmy is considering filing for disability and thinks that there is not much that can be done to help him as he faces a slow decline. Yet he has no regrets and would not have done anything differently. He extolled the bravery of his fellow rescue workers who gave no thought to their own long term health or immediate safety but went in as quickly as possible to get the job done.

"None of these people had the proper safety gear and ran in anyway," said Jimmy. "It is about time the government steps up and takes care of these people."

After his wife passed away, he requested a desk job with the Nassau County Police and took over the care of his children. He used his maritime training to supplement his parenting skills, such as introducing "field days" to his children, like the ones he had had as a cadet.* "That's what helped us get through it," he said.

Jimmy gave credit to his experience at Maritime College for helping him through rough times. He said, "I was very proud of what I did, and I think the only reason why I was there at that time started here at Maritime." He said it provided him "fortitude" and without it, he would have been "a lost soul." It gave him direction, challenged him and pushed him in the right direction. It made him realize that he "could get through anything."

Jimmy Cordara's story was just one of the many tales of bravery and self-lessness that occurred on September 11, 2001. He and the fellow graduates who made sacrifices to save others deserve the recognition that all the other famous alumni of the school have earned. Paul Grening, Ross Marvin and Jimmy Cordara are all products of the same tradition.

THE ESSENCE

Not all Maritime students go to sea these days, but the heart and soul of the college has been its licensing program. In a way, this is one of the college's

---

*A "field day" is a period of frenetic cleaning.

greatest strengths. Captain Richard Smith emphasized the fact that the college covered a niche industry that makes Maritime stand out from other schools. Dr. Richard Burke said, "If we didn't have the license programs we're just another college."

Captain Ernest Fink, the head of the Professional Education and Training Department, is quick to point out that changes in regulations on merchant marine licensing create its own problems. The need to balance licensing regulatory requirements with the academic needs of the college within a reasonable space of time is a major concern. Science Department Chair, Dr. Kathy Olszewski, said this was maddening to the faculty since they are always "forced to drop what they're doing and switch around everything to accommodate the new rules." As a result of all the requirements, the curriculum is heavy. It is a standing joke on campus that students are really entering a 5-year program.

Also, the licensing programs are tied to the training ship. In 2013, the *Empire State VI* reached its 52nd birthday. Of its 52 years, over 24 have been spent as a training vessel for Maritime College, making it the second longest serving schoolship in the institution's history. Despite this venerable statistic and the efforts of the college to maintain the aged vessel, it is in need of a modern replacement.

But finding a replacement is difficult. The American-flagged fleet is less than a shadow of its former self. The once vigorous reserve fleets controlled by MARAD are no more and, in effect, the purpose of the school's foundation—American sailors on American ships—is no longer completely true. There is little indication on the part of the federal government to help build up American shipping and shipbuilding. In a bellwether of national involvement in maritime education, recent criticism has been launched at the USMMA citing that the government is wasting its money by sending students to a service academy that trains them for a private function. It is an old argument.

The State has its own problems. New York State has repeatedly cut the budget to its university system. Maritime is a small school and per capita, the cost of education there is higher than other SUNY schools because of the special nature of the program. Enrollment in the licensing programs is not likely to increase because of the lack of space on campus to build new housing and facilities. Burke said that unless the school can obtain more property "we are pretty much as big as we'll ever get." He said that to be small is a problem in SUNY since their financial model "punishes small campuses." He hoped the school could obtain more property from the U.S. Naval Training Center or from the residential development at Silver Beach that abuts the campus. In the meanwhile, the trend has been to put more non-license programs online. Graduate programs for Facilities Management Engineering and Maritime and Naval Studies are being prepared.

To answer the college's problems, some say the school must forge closer bonds with the maritime industry. Smith said that the college has to "prove the point of what we are doing for these industries to get that money in here because at the end of the day the cost of fuel isn't going down and the cost of the cruise is going up." Olszewski said, "It's more important that the college is able to bring in its own money. They have sort of segregated the alumni away—we are not getting money worth speaking of from our alumni. There is no real endowment worth speaking about so these things have to get built up. They have to figure out how to get money in if the state isn't giving the money it once was."

The important thing, Spatt said, is to be sure that "SUNY recognizes that the kind of educating we do here is going to be more expensive than the kind of educating they do [at other colleges]. . . . SUNY and the federal government occasionally go through these cost-benefit spasms and that's dangerous for us. . . . What we do is valuable. It's valuable for the country, it's valuable for the industry, it's valuable for the students that come through here because they have both extremely advanced skills and a wide ranging, solid foundation for whatever they choose to do."

In 2011, SUNY selected Rear Admiral Wendi B. Carpenter, another career Navy pilot, to succeed President Craine. After obtaining a bachelor's degree in psychology at the University of Georgia, Carpenter went on to Officer Candidacy School for Aviation where she graduated in 1978. As an aviator, Carpenter served as a mission commander, aircraft commander and instructor pilot. In her Naval career, Carpenter held five commands and became the first female aviator to obtain flag rank. Carpenter has been a first at many things including being the first female president of Maritime College. However, her tenure was short, and she resigned in the fall of 2013 for personal reasons.

SHIPMATES

Much has changed in the institution, America and the world since those 26 boys marched up the gangplank of the *St. Mary's* in 1875. No longer do the students do cutlass drills or fire the great guns. Instead, they learn about electronic navigation systems, modern hydrodynamics and global treaties on trade. But most of them, like their predecessors, still earn licenses to rove the seas. The great continuity of the institution has been its cruises—and it is there that students go through the experience of becoming shipmates.

Dr. John J. Foody discussed years ago the purpose of the annual voyage, "It's not a cruise. When you hear the word cruise you immediately think of a luxurious journey with sun bathing, swimming pools, tennis courts . . . etc., this it isn't. Around here we like to think of it as an educational training period as sea." Dr. Meir Degani once remarked of the change he saw in students after their first cruise. "When he comes in as a freshman it is usually the first time he is away from home. He is scared and has lots of butterflies. Then he goes on a cruise; he visits several countries in Europe; his thoughts have changed. Never did I see that much difference as between these two periods."

And so it is. As the end of April nears and finals finish, the college lurches into "pre-cruise" mode. The college spends weeks preparing the ship for the voyage. Cadets stay aboard the ship and are put to work. The itinerary of the annual cruises is dynamic and subject to ever changing conditions. It has been said that the school does not know where the ship is going until it leaves the pier. The unexpected should often be expected on the cruise, which it what it turns it into a valuable learning experience.

In 2003, due to a miscalculation by a mate, the ship scraped a sandy shoal at the bottom of "the Race," where Long Island Sound meets the Atlantic Ocean. In this case, the Captain made the best of it and had naval architecture students calculate the "squat" of the vessel, a phenomenon where the ship sinks deeper by the stern when passing through shallow or restricted waters. Dr. Richard Burke, who was on the cruise, wrote, "Some mates said that they hadn't allowed for the estimated 2½ feet of squat. This led me to observe to all listeners (and they fled promptly) 'They didn't do squat!'" Puns are common on the training ship.

The value of a cadet's first voyage is for the experience itself. Typically, Mugs on their first cruise are given maintenance duties. Those working on a deck license chip and paint. Engineering students work on pumps and valves. For these aspiring mariners, their inaugural cruise is often the first time they are exposed to practical work aboard ship. Burke wrote:

> Cadets are not the most efficient of workers. Many are using tools for the first time, and they look clumsy as they try to do simple jobs.... I watched three cadets sharing a paint brush the other day.... Two male cadets were up on a lifeboat davit where they had been chipping, and rather than unhooking and coming down to get buckets of primer and brushes, they persuaded the female cadet on deck to pass up the brush. So she would load the brush with paint, climb up high enough to hand it to one guy while the other waited. When the brush was dry, it was handed down to her, she reloaded the brush with paint, and then she climbed up to hand it to the other fellow. This process was repeated a number of times. At that rate, Noah's Ark would have been late getting out of drydock.

One thing that these tyro seafarers know how to do well is get dirty. Most of the ship's community wears coveralls while at sea. Burke noted:

> Some of them look as if they roll in dirt before they start working. You can imagine some short, nineteen year old with a baby face, wearing a dirty boiler suit several sizes too big, and especially too long in the legs, wearing a massive tool belt packed with wrenches and screwdrivers, big boots and a silly lightweight hard hat called a "bump cover" that makes his head look too small. None of them will want to show this photograph to their children in fifteen years or so.

The training voyages do something to a person. The feeling of isolation is complete, and people become engrossed in their daily routine which repeats themselves in the two weeks the ship takes to cross the Atlantic. It is easy to see why students in the old schoolships deserted when they got to a foreign port.

As in former days, the upperclassmen monitor and mentor the underclassmen but without (for the most part) hazing. As students learn their jobs, daily routine takes over. Students follow a "plan of the day" which includes regular musters (to account for all hands on the ship) and duties assigned. Notably, while on cruise, there are protracted periods of time without days off for the cadets. As the cruise continues, students are assessed with "Qualifying Exams," normally abbreviated to "Qs." These are oral tests to measure competency in specific areas. Burke noted that these exams took 60 to 90 minutes for each student to complete.

Humor is never far from the ship's community and even near-tragedy is met with gallows-wit. Burke wrote of how on the cruise of 2009, a 14-inch adjustable wrench fell out of the pocket of a cadet who was working high on a boiler and struck First Engineer, Bill McCaney, on the head, ten feet below. Fortunately the First Engineer

> was not badly injured, and after a trip to sickbay to bandage up his bleeding scalp . . . he returned to the engine room to find the chalked outline on the deck plates of a man's body with the chalked outline of an adjustable wrench nearby. When Bill went to his room that night, he found a note on his pillow warning him that 'Tonight you sleep with the wrenches.'

Modern entertainment on the training ships is elusive. Sea stories are one of the main forms of amusement, with the tale growing more preposterous at each telling. Good conversation is cherished. In May, 2006, Burke wrote:

> Last night the sunset and sky were very pretty. It was one of those evenings that everyone remembers when thinking about being at sea. I stood out on deck and chatted with the Chief Engineer, the Chief Mate, the First and a couple of the engineering watch officers. Without the TV blaring, errands to run, the phone ringing and all of the other interruptions and annoyances of modern life, one can actually practice the dying art of conversation, although it is hard to imagine that the sea story is the last vestige of conversational art.

Sometimes, the Captain will authorize parties and barbecues. Also for fun, when the ship crosses a significant degree of latitude they hold line crossing ceremonies. In these ceremonies, a ship officer dresses up as "King Neptune" and makes those who never had crossed the line of latitude go through an obstacle course of fun humiliation. In 2009, the training ship crossed the Arctic Circle and a ceremony of the Order of the Blue Nose was conducted:

> King Neptune's arrival aboard *Empire State*, accompanied by a retinue of devious and malicious attendants, was hilarious and fun. Each supplicant had to submit to being smeared with grease, crawling through obstacles while being soaked by buckets-full of seawater, then sprayed with fire hoses, compelled to drink undelicious beverages and, as a final indignity, having their noses decorated with bright blue chalk. And it was cold while all of this was going on!

In many ways, the training cruises do not reflect contemporary sailing. People on merchant vessels are lucky to get liberty in a port, and life is much more regulated. Merchant ships have much smaller crews. That being said, the college's training teaches what it means to be a shipmate. Burke wrote that, in the past, a shipmate was "someone who has tacitly taken the pledge to be companionable and helpful, to tell a good story when possible and to do his own job. . . . Relationships on a ship were far more intense than relationships between neighbors ashore, and those relationships were highly valued." Burke reflected on the changing nature of the modern maritime industry by writing that he felt "like I am seeing a whole way of life sail off into the mist."

Still, this does not undervalue what Maritime College does. This unique form of education teaches students how to work as a team, build enduring relationships and lead. It was the same way for the boys of the *St. Mary's*, and it is the same for the young women and men of the *Empire State*.

APPENDIX A

Names and Places

Names of the Institution

Years	Name
1873–1913	New York Nautical School
1913–1929	New York State Nautical School
1929–1941	New York State Merchant Marine Academy
1941–1949	New York State Maritime Academy
1949–	State University of New York Maritime College

Cruise Destinations (1874 to 2013)—A list of known destinations during the yearly cruises of the training ships. Destinations are given in chronological order of arrival.

Year	Destinations
1875	Long Island Sound
1876	Hempstead Harbor; New London, CT; Horta, Fayal; Glen Cove, NY; Newport, RI; Philadelphia, PA
1877	New London, CT; Lisbon, Portugal; Funchal, Madeira; New London, CT; Glen Cove, NY
1878	New London, CT; Lisbon, Portugal; Funchal, Madeira; New London, CT; Glen Cove, NY; Newport; RI
1879	Lisbon, Portugal; Funchal, Madeira; New London, CT
1880	Lisbon, Portugal; Cadiz, Spain; Funchal, Madeira; "several ports" in Long Island Sound, Block Island Sound and Narragansett Bay
1881	"ports on the coast of Spain and Portugal"
1882	Long Island Sound; New London, CT; Lisbon, Portugal; Madeira; New London, CT
1883	Glen Cove, NY; New London, CT; Lisbon, Portugal; Funchal, Madeira; New London, CT
1884	Gibraltar; Tangier; Teneriffe; Canary Islands

Year	Destinations
1885	Glen Cove, NY; New London, CT; Azores; Madeira; Canary Islands; New London, CT
1886	New London, CT; Lisbon, Portugal; Funchal, Madeira; New London, CT
1887	New London, CT; Fayal, Azores; Cadiz, Spain; Gibraltar; Tangier, Morocco; Madeira; New London, CT; Glen Cove, NY; Vineyard Haven; Gloucester, MA; Marblehead, MA
1888	Newport, RI; Southampton, England; Lisbon, Portugal; Madeira; Teneriffe; New London, CT; Glen Cove, NY; Vineyard Haven; Newport, RI
1889	Glen Cove, NY; New London, CT; Fayal, Azores; Cadiz, Spain; Funchal, Madeira; New London, CT; Glen Cove, NY; Long Island Sound, Gardner's Bay; Vineyard Haven; Pollock Rip; Cape Cod; Marblehead; Provincetown, MA; New London, CT
1890	New London, CT; Gibraltar; Funchal, Madeira; Queenstown (Cobh, Ireland)
1891	Glen Cove, NY; New London, CT; Azores; Queenstown, (Cobh, Ireland), Southhampton, England, Cherbourg, France
1892	New London, CT; Southampton, England; Cowes, England; Cherbourg, France; Lisbon, Portugal; Gibraltar; Tangier, Morocco; Madeira; New London, CT; Glen Cove, NY
1893	No cruise—the ship was in for repairs
1894	Glen Cove, NY; New London, CT; Fayal, Azores; Gibraltar; Madeira; New London, CT
1895	Glen Cove, NY; New London, CT; Ponta Delgada, St. Michael's; Lisbon, Portugal; Funchal, Madeira; New London, CT
1896	Glen Cove, NY; Queenstown (Cobh, Ireland); Southampton, England; Havre, France; Lisbon, Portugal; Funchal, Madeira; New London, CT; Glen Cove, NY
1897	Glen Cove, NY; New London, CT; Fayal, Azores; Horta; Lisbon, Portugal; Gibraltar; Tangiers, Morocco; Funchal, Madeira; Glen Cove, NY
1898	Oyster Bay, NY; New London, CT; Newport, RI; Glen Cove, NY
1899	Glen Cove, NY; Bridgeport, CT; New London, CT; Gardiners Bay; Lisbon, Portugal; Gibraltar; Tangier, Madeira; Glen Cove, NY
1900	Glen Cove, NY; Bridgeport, CT; New London, CT; Lisbon, Portugal; Gibraltar; Funchal, Madeira; Glen Cove, NY
1901	Glen Cove, NY; New London, CT; Lisbon, Portugal; Gibraltar; Funchal, Madeira; Smithtown Bay, NY; Glen Cove, NY
1902	Glen Cove, NY; New London, CT; Southampton, England; Havre, France; Madeira

Appendix A: Names and Places 299

Year	Destinations
1903	Glen Cove, NY; New London, CT; Queenstown (Cobh), Ireland; Cherbourg, France; Funchal, Madeira; New London, CT; Glen Cove, NY
1904	Glen Cove, NY; New London, CT; Southampton, England; Lisbon, Portugal; Funchal, Madeira; Fishers Island;
1905	Glen Cove, NY; New London, CT; Gardiners Bay; Queenstown (Cobh), Ireland; Cherbourg, France; Madeira, Spain
1906	Glen Cove, NY; New London, CT; Lisbon, Portugal; Cadiz, Spain; Gibraltar; Campamento; Madeira, Spain; New London, CT; Glen Cove, NY
1907	Glen Cove, NY; New London, CT; Plymouth, England; Funchal, Madeira
1908	Glen Cove, NY; Northport Bay; New London, CT; Plymouth, England;Cherbourg, France; Falmouth, England; Jeremias Anchorage, Morocco; Gibraltar; Funchal, Madeira; Gardiner's Bay; Oyster Bay
1909	Greenport, NY; Oyster Bay, NY; Glen Cove, NY; New London, CT; Gardiners Bay; Falmouth, England; Helsinger, Denmark; Copenhagen, Denmark; Amsterdam, Netherlands; Gravesend, England; Plymouth, England; Horta, Fayal; Hamilton, Bermuda; Greenport, NY; New London, CT; Glen Cove, NY; New York, NY; Newburgh, NY; Poughkeepsie, NY; Kingston, NY; Poughkeepsie, NY
1910	Glen Cove, NY; Huntington Bay; New London, CT; Gardiner's Bay; Belfast, Ireland; Greenock, Scotland; Campbeltown, Scotland; Kyle Loch Alsh (Kyle of Lockalsh), Scotland; Wick, Scotland; Helsingor, Denmark; Copenhagen, Denmark; Stockholm, Sweden; Dalaro, Sweden; Presen, Fehmarn Island; Kiel Canal; Southampton, England; Plymouth, England; Falmouth, England; Funchal, Madeira; Hamilton, Bermuda; Gardiners Bay; New London, CT; Glen Cove, NY
1911	Glen Cove, NY; Smithtown Bay; New London, CT; Vineyard Haven; Nantucket Sound; Provincetown, MA; Boston, MA; Portland, ME; Halifax, Nova Scotia; Hamilton, Bermuda; Fort Monroe, VA; Annapolis, MD; Norfolk, VA; New London, CT; Newport, RI; Buzzards Bay; New Bedford, MA; New London, CT; Gardiners Bay; New London, CT; New Haven, CT; New London, CT; Smithtown Bay
1912	Glen Cove, NY; New London, CT; Plymouth, England; Stockholm, Sweden; Copenhagen, Denmark; Christiana, Norway; Plymouth, England; Funchal, Madeira; Hamilton, Bermuda; New London, CT; Glen Cove, NY
1913	Glen Cove, NY; New London, CT; Gardiners Bay; Newport and Narragansett Bay; Hamilton, Bermuda; Hampton Roads, VA; Chesapeake Bay, VA; Annapolis, MD; Chesapeake Bay; Norfolk, VA; New London, CT; Newport, RI; Narragansett Bay (cruising); Provincetown, MA; Boston, MA; Portland, ME; Halifax, Nova Scotia; Provincetown, MA; Newport and Narragansett Bay; New London, CT; New Haven, CT; Glen Cove, NY

Year	Destinations
1914	Athens, NY; Albany, NY; Kingston, NY; Poughkeepsie, NY; Newburgh, NY; Algiers, Algeria; Naples, Italy; Leghorn, Italy; Marseilles, France; Genoa, Italy; Funchal, Madeira; Newport, RI; Cape Cod Canal; Glen Cove, NY
1915	St. Thomas, Virgin Islands; Cristobal, Canal Zone; Balboa, Canal Zone; Hilo, HI; Honolulu, HI; San Francisco, CA; San Diego, CA; Balboa, Canal Zone; Cristobal, Canal Zone
1916	Glen Cove, NY; New London, CT; Horta, Fayal, Azores; Hamilton, Bermuda
1917	Glen Cove, NY; New London, CT; Greenport, NY; Green's Ledge, NY; Glen Cove, NY; New York, NY; Yonkers, NY; Peekskill, NY; Poughkeepsie, NY; New York, NY; Bedloes Island, NY; Glen Cove, NY; Northport, NY; New Haven, CT; New London, CT; Gardiners Bay; Greenport, NY; Shelter Island Sound; Greenport, NY; Newport, RI; Block Island; New Haven, CT; Glen Cove, NY; New York, NY; Brooklyn Navy Yard; New York, NY; Poughkeepsie, NY; Kingston, NY; Newburgh, NY; Yonkers, NY
1918	Glen Cove, NY; Savin Rock, New Haven, CT; Greenport, NY; New London, CT; Savin Rock, CT; Greenport, NY; Nyack Bay; Greenport, NY; New London, CT; Greenport, NY; Glen Cove, NY; New York, NY; Brooklyn Navy Yard; Tietzen & Lang Shipyard; Brooklyn Navy Yard; Glen Cove; Savin Rock; Greenport; Glen Cove; Savin Rock; Glen Covel; Greenport; Glen Cove; Savin Rock; Greenport; Glen Cove; Smithtown Bay; Glen Cove; New York; Glen Cove; Savin Rock; Bridgeport; Glen Cove; Huntington Bay; Glen Cove; Orient Point; Glen Cove; Savin Rock; Glen Cove; Brooklyn Navy Yard
Winter Cruise 1918–1919	Warrington, FL; Pensacola, FL; Key West, FL; Havana, Cuba; San Juan, Puerto Rico; Fredericksted, St. Croix; St. Thomas;
1919	Glen Cove, NY; New London, CT; Quebec, Canada; Buffalo, NY; Montreal, Canada; Bermuda; Philadelphia, PA
1920	Nantucket, MA; Portsmouth, England; Antwerp, Belgium; Lisbon, Portugal; Funchal, Madeira; Bermuda
1921	Ponta Delgada, Azores; Cadiz, Spain; Naples, Italy; Algiers, Algeria; Gibraltar; Funchal, Madeira; Hamilton, Bermuda
1922	Gibraltar; Naples, Italy; Piraeus and Rhodes, Greece; Alexandria, Egypt; Valetta, Malta; Bone, Algeria; Algiers, Algieria; Funchal, Madeira; St. George, Bermuda
1923	Glen Cove, NY; New London, CT; Santa Cruz, Teneriffe, Canary Islands; New London, CT; Glen Cove, NY
1924	Glen Cove, NY; Brooklyn Navy Yard; Glen Cove, NY; New Rochelle, NY; Glen Cove, NY; Gardiners Bay; New London, CT; Gravesend, England; Antwerp, Belgium; Cadiz, Spain; Palos, Spain; Funchal, Madeira; Santa Cruz, Teneriffe, Canary Islands; Bermuda; New York, NY; Yonkers, NY; Newburgh, NY; Poughkeepsie, NY; Kingston, NY; Newburgh, NY

Appendix A: Names and Places

Year	Destinations
1925	Long Island Sound; Glen Cove, NY; Greenport and Smithtown Bay, NY; New London, CT; Three Mile Harbor; Newport, RI; Lisbon, Portugal; Gibraltar; Funchal, Madeira; Santa Cruz, Canary Islands
1926	Yonkers, NY; Jones Point; Newburgh, NY; Poughkeepsie, NY; Ponta Delgada, Azores; Funchal, Madeira; Las Palmas, Canary Islands; Bermuda
1927	Newport, RI; Plymouth, England; Cherbourg, France; Cawsand Bay and Las Palmas, Canary Islands; Bermuda
1928	Newport, RI; Gibraltar; Marseilles, France; Nice, France; Naples, Italy; Algiers, Algeria; Las Palmas, Canary Islands
1929	Glen Cove, NY; Plymouth, England; London, England; Hamburg, Germany; Le Havre, France; Ponta Delgada, Azores; St. Georges, Bermuda
1930	Algeciras, Spain; Gibraltar; Villefranche, France; Leghorn, Italy; Algiers, Algeria; Gibraltar; Ponta Delgada, Azores; St. Georges, Bermuda; Murray, Bermuda
1931	Cristobal, Canal Zone; Balboa, Canal Zone; Manzanillo, Mexico; San Diego, CA; Bremerton, WA; Port Townsend, WA; Mare Island; San Pedro, CA; Balboa, Canal Zone; Cristobal, Canal Zone; Hampton Roads, VA
1932	Albany, NY; Washington, DC; Baltimore, MD; Norfolk, VA; Jacksonville, FL; Miami, FL; Tampa, FL; New Orleans, LA; Galveston, TX; Miami, FL; Gravesend, England; Le Havre, France
1933	Tompkinsville, Staten Island, NY; Hamilton, Bermuda; Plymouth, England; Le Havre, France; Gibraltar
1934	New London, CT; Hamilton, Bermuda; Leith, Scotland; Antwerp, Belgium; Plymouth, England
1935	Hamilton, Bermuda; Cork, Ireland; London, England; Copenhagen, Denmark; Le Havre, France; Plymouth, England; Gibraltar
1936	Hamilton, Bermuda; Washington, DC; Curacao, Dutch West Indies; Coco Solo, Canal Zone; Balboa, Canal Zone; Callao, Peru; Balboa, Canal Zone; Havana, Cuba
1937	Hamilton, Bermuda; Culebra, Puerto Rico; St. Thomas, Virgin Islands; Amsterdam, Netherlands, Dover, England
1938	Hamilton, Bermuda; Washington, DC; Newport News, VA; London, England; Rotterdam, Netherlands; Le Havre, France
1939	Provincetown, MA; Boston, MA; Hamilton, Bermuda; Fort Schuyler, NY; Smithtown Bay, NY; Fort Schuyler, NY; Plymouth, England; Cherbourg, France
1940	Provincetown, MA; Boston, MA; Yorktown, VA; Hampton Roads, VA; New London, CT; San Juan, Puerto Rico; Coco Solo, Canal Zone; Havana, Cuba; Pensacola, FL

Year	Destinations
1941	New London, CT; Hamilton, Bermuda; Curacao, Dutch West Indies; Guantanamo Bay, Cuba; New Orleans, LA; Charleston, SC; Portland, ME; Norfolk, VA
1942	Philadelphia, PA; Claiborne, MD; Newport News, VA; Washington, DC; Baltimore, MD; Norfolk, VA
1943–1945	Long Island Sound
1946	New London, CT; Hamilton, Bermuda; Coco Solo, Canal Zone; Callao, Peru; Balboa, Canal Zone; Havana, Cuba; St. Petersburg, FL; Miami, FL
1947	Bermuda; Lisbon, Portugal; Gibraltar; Villefranche; Trinidad; Miami, FL
1948	Trinidad; Madeira; Algiers, Algeria; Genoa, Italy; Nice, France; Gibraltar
1949	Gardiner's Bay; Cork, Ireland; Portsmouth, England; Amsterdam, Netherlands; Antwerp, Belgium; Rouen, France; Provincetown, MA
1950	Fort Pond Bay, NY; Lisbon, Portugal; Naples, Italy; Haifa, Israel; Villefranche, France; Barcelona, Spain; Bermuda
1951	Miami, FL; Bilbao, Spain; Rotterdam, Netherlands; Edinburgh, Scotland; Cherbourg, France
1952	Fort Pond Bay, NY; Hamilton, Bermuda; Gibraltar; Balearic Islands; Venice, Italy; Piraeus, Greece; Nice, France; Valencia, Spain
1953	Southampton, England; Copenhagen, Denmark; Hamburg, Germany; Amsterdam, Netherlands; Bordeaux, France; San Sebastian, Spain
1954	Bermuda; Naples, Italy; Antwerp, Belgium; Rotterdam, Netherlands; Santander, Spain; Washington, DC
1955	Villefranche, France; Seville, Spain; Oslo, Norway; Kiel, Germany; Cascais, Portugal; Lisbon, Portugal
1956	Bermuda; Le Havre, France; Goteborg (Gothenburg), Sweden; Copenhagen, Denmark; London, England; Cadiz, Spain
1957	Albany, NY; Dublin, Ireland; Amsterdam, Netherlands; Bilbao, Spain; Genoa, Italy; Villefranche, France
1958	Bermuda; Belfast, Northern Ireland; Copenhagen, Denmark; Antwerp, Belgium; Lisbon, Portugal
1959	Plymouth, England; Oslo, Norway; Santander, Spain; Marseilles, France; Funchal, Madeira
1960	Bermuda; Dublin, Ireland; Amsterdam, Netherlands; Naples, Italy; Barcelona, Spain
1961	Southampton, England; Copenhagen, Denmark; Lisbon, Portugal; Villefranche, France; Ceuta, Spain

Appendix A: Names and Places

Year	Destinations
1962	Malaga, Spain; Genoa, Italy; Rotterdam, Netherlands; Oslo, Norway
1963	Albany, NY; Dublin, Ireland; Bremen, Germany; Antwerp, Belgium; Naples, Italy; Palma de Majorca
1964	Portsmouth, England; Copenhagen, Denmark; Amsterdam, Netherlands; Villefranche, France; Barcelona, Spain
1965	Valencia, Spain; Leghorn, Italy; Le Havre, France; Oslo, Norway; Belfast, Northern Ireland
1966	Ceuta, Spain; Palma de Majorca; Lisbon, Portugal; Hamburg, Germany; Goteborg (Gothenburg), Sweden; Antwerp, Belgium
1967	Miami, FL; San Juan, Puerto Rico; Montreal, Quebec; New York, NY; Amsterdam, Netherlands; Copenhagen, Denmark
1968	Genoa, Italy; Barcelona, Spain; Bergen, Norway; Dublin, Ireland
1969	Cruise A: Alicante, Spain; Marseilles, France; Cruise B: Tilbury, England
1970	Cruise A: Rotterdam, Netherlands; Cardiff, Wales; Cruise B: Copenhagen, Denmark; Rouen, France
1971	Cruise A: Civitavecchia, Italy; Valletta, Malta; Cruise B: Bremen, Germany; Cork, Ireland
1972	Cruise A: Genoa, Italy; Palma de Majorca; Cruise B: Edinburgh, Scotland; Antwerp, Belgium
1973	Cruise A: Funchal, Madeira; Barcelona, Spain; Cruise B: Copenhagen, Denmark; Amsterdam, Netherlands
1974	Cruise A: San Juan, Puerto Rico; New Orleans, LA; Cruise B: Miami, FL; Quebec, Canada
1975	Malaga, Spain; Glasgow, Scotland
1976	New Orleans, LA; Norfolk, VA; Boston, MA
1977	Southampton, England; Copenhagen, Denmark
1978	Naples, Italy; Palma de Majorca
1979	Las Palmas, Canary Islands; Lisbon, Portugal
1980	Ft. Lauderdale, FL; Montreal, Canada
1981	Malaga, Spain; London, England
1982	Lisbon, Portugal; Le Havre, France
1983	Albany, NY; Rotterdam, Netherlands
1984	Palma de Majorca; Southampton, England; Copenhagen, Denmark
1985	Alicante, Spain; Genoa, Italy; Hamburg, Germany

Year	Destinations
1986	Ft. Lauderdale, FL; Montreal, Canada; OPSAIL '86, NY; Albany, NY
1987	Dublin, Ireland; Stockholm, Sweden; Edinburgh, Scotland
1988	San Juan, Puerto Rico; Portsmouth, England; Bremen, Germany
1989	Miami, FL, Albany, NY; Palma de Majorca, Spain
1990	Tenerife, Canary Islands; Gaeta, Italy; Genoa, Italy
1991	Bergen, Norway; Amsterdam, Netherlands; Bermuda
1992	Gibraltar; New Orleans, LA; Curacao
1993	Plymouth, England; Piraeus, Greece; Palma de Majorca, Spain
1994	Galveston, TX; San Juan, Puerto Rico; Dublin, Ireland
1995	Norfolk, VA; Naples, Italy; Toulon, France
1996	Piraeous, Greece; Teneriffe, Canary Islands; Copenhagen, Denmark; Stavanger, Norway
1997	St. Georges, Bermuda; Philadelphia, PA; Lisbon, Portugal; Portsmouth, England
1998	Albany, NY; Malaga, Spain; Hamburg, Germany; Dublin, Ireland
1999	Charleston, SC; Bridgetown, Barbados; Naples, Italy; Cardiff, Wales
2000	Rota, Spain; London, England; OpSail 2000, NY; Norfolk, VA
2001	Philadelphia, PA; Las Palmas, Canary Islands; Copenhagen, Denmark; Edinburgh, Scotland; Sandy Hook, Anchorage, NJ
2002	Dry Tortugas, FL; New Orleans, LA; Dublin, Ireland; Bergen, Norway; Freeport, Bahamas
2003	Norfolk, VA; Gaeta, Italy; Palma de Majorca; Tallinn, Estonia; Hamilton, Bermuda
2004	Piraeus, Greece; Kiel, Germany; Barcelona, Spain; Nassau, Bahamas
2005	Palma de Majorca; Antwerp, Belgium; Istanbul, Turkey; Lisbon, Portugal
2006	Piraeus, Greece; Constanta, Romania; Dubrovnik, Croatia; Dublin, Ireland
2007	Charleston, SC; Rome, Italy; Tallin, Estonia; Copenhagen, Denmark
2008	Nassau, Bahamas; Majorca, Spain; Toulon, France; Liverpool, England
2009	Azores; Gibraltar; Reykjavik, Iceland; Belfast, Ireland
2010	Cruise A: Malaga, Spain; Andros Island, Greece; Piraeus, Greece; Dublin, Ireland; Cruise B: Valetta, Malta; Brest, France
2011	Cruise A: Aalborg, Denmark; Riga, Latvia; Gdynia, Poland; Cobh, Ireland; Cruise B: Rijeka, Croatia; Palma de Majorca, Spain
2012	Cruise A: San Miguel, Azores; Reykjavik, Iceland; Norfolk, VA; Cruise B: Gibraltar; Liverpool, England
2013	Cruise A: New Orleans, LA; St. John's, Newfoundland; Dublin, Ireland; Cruise B: Trieste, Italy; Valetta, Malta

APPENDIX B

People

(Ranks and Affiliations Noted When Known)

Superintendents of the New York Nautical School, the New York State Nautical School, the New York State Merchant Marine Academy and the New York State Maritime Academy

Name	Dates of Administration
Robert Lees Phythian, CDR (USN)	1874-1879
Henry Erben, Jr., CAPT (USN)[1]	1879-1882
Edwin Malcolm Shepard, CDR (USN)	1883-1886
Arent Schuyler Crowninshield, CDR (USN)	1887-1890
John McGowan, Jr., CDR (USN)	1891-1894
Wells Laflin Field, LCDR (USN)	1894-1897
William Herren Reeder, LCDR (USN)	1897-1901[2]
Howard Patterson, LT (New York Naval Militia) (acting)	1898
Albion Varet Wadhams, CDR (USN)	1901-1902
Gustavus Charles Hanus, CDR (USN ret)	1902-1908
Lay Hampton Everhart, LCDR (USN ret)	1908-1911
Harry Mason Dombaugh, LCDR (USN ret)	1911-1912
Edwin Hord Tillman, CDR (USN, ret)	1912-1914
James R. Driggs, Class of 1882, LCDR (USNR)	1914
Frederick Shepard McMurray, Class of 1896, LCDR (USNR)	1914-1917
Felix Riesenberg, Class of 1897, LCDR (USNR)	1917-1919
Thomas W. Sheridan, Class of 1906, LCDR (USNR)	1919
John Stansbury Baylis, Class of 1903, LCDR (USCG)	1919-1923
Felix Riesenberg, Class of 1897, LCDR (USNR)	1923-1924

Superintendents of the New York Nautical School, the New York State Nautical School, the New York State Merchant Marine Academy and the New York State Maritime Academy (*continued*)

Name	Dates of Administration
Edward V.W. Keen, Class of 1900, CDR (USNR)	1925–1927
James Harvey Tomb, CAPT (USN ret)	1927–1942
Thomas Tingey Craven, VADM (USN ret)	1942–1945
Herbert Fairfax Leary, VADM (USN ret)	1946–1949

Presidents of SUNY Maritime College—1949 to 2013

Name	Dates
Herbert Fairfax Leary, VADM (USN ret)	1949–1951
Calvin Thornton Durgin, VADM (USN ret)	1951–1959
Harold C. Moore, Class of 1922, VADM (USCG ret)	1959–1967
Edward J. O'Donnell, RADM (USN ret)	1967–1972
Sheldon Hoard Kinney, RADM (USN ret)	1972–1982
Floyd H. Miller, Class of 1953, RADM (USN ret)	1982–1995
David C. Brown, RADM (USMS), CAPT (USN ret)	1995–2001
John W. Craine, Jr., VADM (USN ret) (interim)	2001–2002
John R. Ryan, VADM (USN ret)	2002–2005
John W. Craine, Jr., VADM (USN ret)	2005–2011
Wendi B. Carpenter, RADM (USN ret)	2011–2013
Michael A. Cappeto (interim)	2013–

Chairs of the Nautical School Executive Committee, New York City Board of Education

Name	Dates
David Wetmore	1874–1887
Isaac Bell	1887
Henry L. Sprague	1888–1889
Frederick W. Devoe	1889–1890
Robert Maclay	1890–1892
John S. Crosby	1892–1893

Chairs of the Nautical School Executive Committee, New York City Board of Education (*continued*)

Name	Dates
Hugh Kelly (acting)	1893
Miles M. O'Brien	1893–1895
Charles Bulkley Hubbell	1895–1896
Hugh Kelly	1896–1897
Auguste P. Montant	1897–1898
John G. Agar	1898–1899
John Griffin	1899–1900
Alfred H. Morris	1900–1901
Arthur S. Somers	1901–1902
James Weir, Jr.	1902–1903
William H. Maxwell	1903–1904
Richard B. Aldcroftt, Jr.	1905–1912
Michael J. Sullivan	1912–1913
John R. Thompson	1913

Chairs of the Board of Governors of the New York State Nautical School

Name	Dates
Jacob W. Miller	1914–1917
John C. Hatzel, Class of 1877	1917–1918
Marcus H. Tracy	1918–1922
Reginald Fay, Class of 1886	1922–1926

Chairs of the Board of Visitors of the New York State Nautical School, the New York State Merchant Marine Academy, the New York State Maritime Academy and SUNY Maritime College

Name	Dates
Reginald Fay, Class of 1886	1926–1929
Nathaniel L. Cullin	1929–1931
Milan L. Pittman, Class of 1907	1931–1942
Arthur Monroe Tode, Class of 1912, LCDR (USNR)	1942–1955

Chairs of SUNY Maritime College Council

Name	Dates
Carl Vander Clute, Class of 1921	1955-1960
George M. Wauchope, Class of 1923, VADM, (USNR ret)	1961-1970
William E. Ryan, Class of 1945	1970-1981
Raymond Hayden, Class of 1960	1981-1998
Donald P. Brennan, Class of 1961, LCDR (USN)	1998-2000
Thomas Keenan, Class of 1971, LT, (USNR ret)	2000-2009
Timothea S. Larr	2010-

Assistant Superintendents/Commanding Officers/Vice Presidents for Student Affairs/Commandants

Name	Dates
Lucien B. Green, Class of 1911, LCDR (USN, USMC)	1932-1933
George W.R. Hughes, Class of 1916, LCDR (USNR)	1933-1941
Charles Daniel Schutz, Class of 1915, LCDR (USNR)	1941-1943
Edward R. Glosten, Class of 1908, CDR (USNR)	1943-1944
Edmund H. Danesi, Class of 1922, CDR (USNR)	1944-1946
Alfred Francis Olivet, Class of 1921, CAPT (USNR)	1946-1962
Arthur J. Spring	1962-1971
William P. Toran, CAPT (USN ret)	1971-1974
Gary Russell, LCDR (USCG ret)	1974-1977
Frank W. English, Jr., CDR, Class of 1946 (USN ret)	1977-1978
Richard W. Trimble, CDR (USN ret)	1978-1979
George C. Previll, CAPT (USMS)	1980-1983
Richard O. Gooden, CAPT (USN ret)	1983-1987
James DeSimone, Class of 1973, LCDR (USNR)	1987-1996
Robert J. Weaver, Class of 1969, CAPT (USCG, ret)	1997-2001
Richard S. Smith, Class of 1981	2001-

Masters of the Training Ship of the New York State Maritime Academy and SUNY Maritime College

Name	Dates
Alfred M. Moore, CAPT (USMS)	1942-1945[3]

Masters of the Training Ship of the New York State Maritime Academy and SUNY Maritime College (*continued*)

Name	Dates
Edmund H. Danesi, Class of 1922, CDR (USNR)	1945–1946
Alfred Francis Olivet, Class of 1921, CAPT (USNR)	1946–1963
Robert A. Philips	1964–1971
Gerard J. Nolan, Class of 1956	1972–1977
Frank W. English, Jr., CDR, Class of 1946 (USN ret)	1977–1978
Robert P. Thompson, Class of 1964	1978
Richard W. Trimble	1978–1979
George C. Previll, CAPT (USMS)	1980–1983
Douglas A. Hard	1983
Richard O. Gooden, CAPT, (USN ret)	1983–1987
James DeSimone, Class of 1973, LCDR, USNR	1987–1996
Peter Scott James, Class of 1979	1996–1998
Joseph Ahlstrom, Class of 1982, CDR (USNR)	1998–2000; 2012 (temporary from May 10 to May 17)
Richard S. Smith, Class of 1981	2001–

Executive Officers/Chief Mates of the Training Ships

Name	Dates
George H. Wadleigh, LCDR (USN)	1875–1876
George W. DeLong, LT (USN)	1876–1878
John J. Hunker, LT (USN)	1878–1880
G.A. Norris, LT (USN)	1881–1883
R.M. Berry, LT (USN)	1883–1885
Wells Laflin Field, LT (USN)	1886–1889
V.L. Cottman, LT (USN)	1889
William M. Wood, LT (USN)	1889
C.C. Cornwell, LT (USN)	1889–1893
W.J. Barnette, LT (USN)	1893–1894
J.R. Selfridge, LT (USN)	1894
D.D.V. Stuart, LT (USN)	1894–1895
Hal M. Hodges, LT (USN)	1895–1897

Executive Officers/Chief Mates of the Training Ships (*continued*)

Name	Dates
C.M. Knepper, LT (USN)	1898-1899[4]
Henry Campling	1898[5]
William Dreilick, ENS (USNR)	1898[6]
George R. Evans, LT (USN)	1899-1900
Lay Hampton Everhart, LT (USN)	1900-1902
W. A. Moffett	1902
Christopher Marsden	1902-1908
R.J. Hartung, ENS (USN ret)	1908-1910
Felix Englebert Gross	1910-1911
Charles E. Morgan	1911-1912
Berthold Ackerman, LT (USNR)	1912-1915
Charles E. Littlefield	1915-1917
Charles E. Morgan	1917-1918
Gershom Bradford	1918-1919
Charles Daniel Schutz, Class of 1915, CDR (USNR)	1919-1920
Henry W. Stock, Class of 1917	1920-1923
John H. Boesch, Class of 1906	1923-1925
Charles Daniel Schutz, Class of 1915, CDR (USNR)	1925-1941
Henry W. Stock, Class of 1917	1943
Guy J. DeSimone, Class of 1936, LCDR, (USNR)	1944-1945
James M. Maley, Class of 1931, LCDR (USNR)	1946-1961
Harry Archer Clark, Class of 1938, CDR (USN ret)	1961-1966
Gerald J. Nolan, Class of 1956	1966-1972
Eugene McAvoy, Class of 1965	1973-1976
John Hagedorn, Class 1967	1976-1979
Peter Barnett	1980
Richard Sandifer, CDR (USMS)[7]	1981
William Imkin, Class of 1975, CDR (USMS)	1981
William Lindman, Class of 1973	1982-1984
Arthur H. Sulzer, Jr., Class of 1974	1984-1989
Richard Russell	1989
Peter Scott James, Class of 1979	1990-1996

Appendix B: People

Executive Officers/Chief Mates of the Training Ships (*continued*)

Name	Dates
Elizabeth A. Christman, Class of 1987	1997
Christopher Zola, Class of 1993	1998–2003
Matthew J. Mahanna, Class of 1994[8]	2003–
Peter G. Vecchio, Class of 1992[9]	2010–

Chief Engineers of the Training Ships

Name	Dates
C.P. Eaton, CDR (USN ret)	1907–1908
C.H. Matthews, CDR (USN ret)	1908–1914
Ingvold Tonning	1914
C.H. Matthews, CDR (USN ret)	1914–1919
Arthur Monroe Tode, Class of 1912, LCDR (USNR)	1919–1923
Cyrus E. Davison	1923–1926
Joseph D. Kelly	1926[10]
C.P. Burt, LCDR (USN ret)	1926–1927
Walter G. Gronbeck, Class of 1912, LT (USNR)	1927–1942
Hugh Peckford "Bud" Rainey, Class of 1942	1946
Andrew P. Hirth, Class of 1936, LT (USNR)	1946–1954
Richard Kirchoff, Class of 1945	1954–1956
Hugh Peckford "Bud" Rainey, Class of 1942	1957–1959
Edward F. Pfleging	1959–1987
John Dewey Payton (USN)	1987
Steven J. Miller, Class of 1976	1988–1998
Ronald E. Jackson, Class of 1970	1998–2001
Edward Kessler, Class of 1981	2001
Matthew O'Donnell	2001–2008
Thomas Dowd (USN, USCGR)	2008–2012
Eugene Ennesser	2012–

Vice Presidents of Academic Affairs/Provosts

Name	Dates
Ralph E. Page	1946–1947

Vice Presidents of Academic Affairs/Provosts (*continued*)

Name	Dates
Albert Ogden Porter	1947–1961
Albert A. Lawrence	1962–1966
Meir H. Degani (acting)	1967
Daniel J. Duffy	1968–1973
William H. Sembler (acting)	1973–1974
William R. Porter	1974–1994
Howard L. English, Jr.	1994–1999
John Hampton	1999–2000
Phillip Smukler	2000–2002
Jeffrey A. Weiss, Class of 1978 (interim)	2002
Robert Kraushaar (interim)	2002–2003
William R. Gehring	2003–2006
Joseph Hoffman, Class of 1975	2006–2012
Michael A. Cappeto	2012–2013
Gilbert Traub (interim)	2013–2014
Timothy Lynch	2013–

Heads of the Athletic Department

Name	Dates
W. Roger Reinhart LCDR (j/g) USN	1945–1983
James Migli	1983–2002
Donald Fay	2002–2003
William Martinov	2003–2007
Russell Ketcham	2007–2008
Dick Hack	2008–2012
Heather MacCulloch	2012–

Heads of the Deck Department

Name	Dates
Emery K. Bicknell LT (USNR)	1941–1944
Guy J. DeSimone Class of 1936, LCDR, (USNR) (Acting)	1944–1945

Heads of the Deck Department (*continued*)

Name	Dates
James M. Maley, Class of 1931, CDR (Acting)	1945–1946
Stuart A. Maher, CDR (USN, ret)	1946–1958
Guy J. DeSimone, Class of 1936, LCDR (USNR)	1958–1959[11]

Heads of the Department of Economics and Transportation*

Name	Dates
Guy J. DeSimone, Class of 1936, LCDR (USNR)	1959–1960
Herbert Millington	1960–64

Heads of the Engineering Department

Name	Dates
Walter G. Gronbeck, Class of 1912, LT (USNR)	1942–1946
Jeremy B. Blood	1946–1952
John J. Foody	1952–1974
Jose Femenia, Class of 1964	1974–1995
Charles Munsch, Class of 1973	1995–2001
Richard J. Burke, Class of 1972	2002–2012
Carl Delo (interim)	2012
Peter Domalavage	2012–2013
Richard J. Burke, Class of 1972	2013 (interim)

Heads of the Humanities Department

Name	Dates
George M. Gregory	1946–1959
A. Sanford Limouze	1959–1962
Oscar B. Goodman	1962–1970
W. Dwight Todd	1970–1975
Joel J. Belson	1975–1992
Karen Markoe	1992–

*Renamed to Economics Department in 1961, this department was split from the Marine Transportation department in 1959 and then merged back into it in 1964.

Heads of the Graduate School of International Transportation Management/Global Business and Transportation Department*

Name	Dates
Jeffrey A. Weiss, Class of 1978	2000-2002
Mark Chadwin	2002-2005
Larry Howard	2005-2012
James Drogan	2012-

College Librarians

Name	Dates
Terence Joseph Hoverter	1945-1960
Joseph N. Whitten	1961-1970
Richard H. Corson	1971-2001
Constantia Constantinou	2001-2013
Shafeek Fazal	2013-

Heads of the Department of Marine Transportation**

Name	Dates
James M. Maley, Class of 1931 (CDR)	1959-1960
Guy J. DeSimone, Class of 1936 (LCDR, USNR)	1960-1972
Lester Archibald Dutcher, Class of 1949	1973-1979
Austin L. Dooley, Class of 1968	1979-1981
Dee N. Fitch	1981-1991
Jeffrey W. Monroe, Graduate Class of 1992, CAPT (USMS)	1991-1992
Robert P. Lucas, Class of 1957, CAPT (USN ret)	1992-1993
Richard S. Smith, Class of 1981	1994-1996
Dennis Frederick, Class of 1969 (acting)	Fall, 1996
Phillip Smukler	1996-1998
Dennis Frederick, Class of 1969	1998-2002
Richard S. Smith, Class of 1981	2002-2003
Joseph Ahlstrom, Class of 1982, CAPT (USNR)	2003-2005
Anthony Palmiotti, Class of 1979	2005-2013
Walter Nadolny, Class of 1978	2013-

*Prior to 2000, the Marine Transportation Department headed the Graduate Program.
**Called the Department of Marine Science until 1963.

Appendix B: People

Heads of the Department of Naval Science (later NROTC)

Name	Dates
Beale M. Gordon (LCDR, USNR)	1942-1946
Leo C. Keating (CDR, USNR)	1946-1948
John H. Van Gelder (LCDR, USN)	1948-1953
Bayer (LCDR, USN)	1953-1956
John C. Spencer (CDR, USN)	1956-1957
Ralph S. Stevens, Jr. (CDR, USN)	1957-1959
John L. Butler (CDR, USN)	1959-1962
G.W. Agee (CDR, USN)	1962-1963
James L. Harrison (CDR, USN)	1963-1965
Richard Chesebrough (LCDR, USN)	1966-1972
Robert E. Malaney (CDR, USN)	1973-1975
Dee N. Fitch (CDR, USN)	1975-1978
Kellie S. Byerly (CDR, USN)	1978-1980
Arthur J. Tuttle (CDR, USN)	1980-1985
Richard W. Hyde, Jr. (CDR, USN)	1985-1987
David C. Rollins (CDR, USN)	1988-1989
Andrew J. Laska (CDR, USN)	1989-1990
Donald B. Disney, Jr. (CDR, USN)	1990-1994
Robert J. O'Neil (CDR, USN)	1994-1999
Carlton Baldwin (CDR, USN)	1999-2000
Allen Stubblefield (CDR, USN)	2000-2003
Howard Stone (CAPT, USN)	2003-2007
James Driscoll (CAPT, USN)	2008-2011
Matthew E. Loughlin (CAPT, USN)	2011-

Heads of the Science Department

Name	Dates
Meir H. Degani	1947-1973
Joseph D. Longobardi	1973-1984
Fred C. Hess	1984-1986
Bruce R. Boller	1986-1990

Heads of the Science Department (*continued*)

Name	Dates
Paul Levy	1990–2002
Joseph Hoffman, Class of 1975	2002–2006
Kathy Olszewski	2006–

Heads of the Professional Education and Training Department

Name	Dates
Ernest Fink, Class of 1975 (CAPT, USCG)	2007–

Presidents of the Alumni Association

Name	Dates
Edward H. Cole, Class of 1878	1903–06
John C. Hatzel, Class of 1877	1906–08
Reginald Fay, Class of 1886	1908–10
Charles Filly, Class of 1880	1910–12
Felix Riesenberg, Class of 1897	1912–14
John C. Redel, Class of 1889	1914–16
Charles Williamson, Class of 1876	1916–19
John C. Hatzel, Class of 1877	1919–22
William J. Rague, Jr., Class of 1914	1922–24
Milan L. Pittman, Class of 1907	1924–26
Lawrence C. Howard, Class of 1911	1926–27
Thomas W. Sheridan, Class of 1906	1927–29
Arthur M. Tode, Class of 1912	1929–30
Thomas W. Sheridan, Class of 1906	1930–31
Carl F. Vander Clute, Class of 1921	1931–32
John S. Baylis, Class of 1903	1932–33
Lewis L. Smith, Class of 1906	1933–34
Jay H. Halsey, Class of 1903	1934–35
Vincent J. Riker, Class of 1906	1935–36
Walter G. Gronbeck, Class of 1912	1936–40
Carl A. Maass, Class of 1911	1940–41
Edward R. Glosten, Class of 1908	1941–43

Presidents of the Alumni Association (*continued*)

Name	Dates
Louis Weickum, Class of 1903	1943-44
Arthur L. Centoz, Class of 1922	1945-50
John W. Anderson, Class of 1915	1951-52
Alfred F. Olivet, Class of 1921	1952-55
William R. Lawrence, Class of 1917	1955-56
William E. Ryan, Class of 1945	1957-58
George Mortensen, Class of 1938	1959
Gordon M. Lee, Class of 1922	1960-61
John C. Haeussler, Class of 1945	1962
Forrest H. Smith, Class of 1921	1963-64
Robert C. Moore, Class of 1936	1965-66
Abraham Rosenburg, Class of 1924	1967-68
James M. Maley, Class of 1931	1969
Brian A. McAllister, Class of 1956	1969
C.P. Georgiopoulos, Class of 1958	1970-71
Raymond P. Hayden, Class of 1960	1972-73
Howard L. Humphries, Class of 1938	1974-75
John G. Ingram, Class of 1964	1976-77
John M. O'Neill, Class of 1964	1978-79
John Antonetz, Class of 1941	1980-82
Richard J. Baumler, Class of 1952	1983
Stanley F. Junemann , Class of 1944	1984-86
Austin L. Dooley, Class of 1968	1987-89
Thomas F. Keenan, Class of 1971	1990-94
James J. McNamara, Class of 1964	1995-96
Thomas F. Fox, Class of 1962	1997-99
Stephen J. Carbery, Class of 1980	1999-01
Theodore T. Mason, Class of 1957	2002-03
Francis X. Gallo, Class of 1964	2004-2005
Steve Gulotta, Class of 1980	2006-2008
Dick Bracken, Class of 1956	2008-2010
John Bradley, Class of 1983	2010-2013
Charlie Munsch, Class of 1973	2013-

NOTES

1. Commander until November 1, 1879, then Captain.
2. Reeder was detached for duty for the Spanish-American War on April 22, 1898 and returned to duty on November 1, 1898.
3. The training ship was commanded by the Superintendent of the school through May, 1941. In June, 1941 the *Empire State I* was taken over by the Maritime Commission for the training of unlicensed personnel by the Coast Guard. The ship was returned by the Coast Guard to Fort Schuyler in 1942, renamed the *American Pilot* and shared as a training ship by New York, Massachusetts and Maine for the duration of the war. Between June, 1942 and 1945 the *American Pilot*, crewed by the U.S. Maritime Service, was commanded by Captain Alfred M. Moore, USMS.
4. Knepper was detached for service in the Spanish-American War on April 13, 1898 and reappointed to the school on November 1, 1898.
5. Campling was a temporary appointment. He fell sick two days after reporting for duty on July 1, 1898, and "he was more or less prostrated during all the month that he remained on board." He resigned on August 5. 1898 Annual Report.
6. Dreilick was an "Acting Executive Officer" during the cruise of 1898 after Campling's resignation.
7. Sandifer left before making a cruise. Imkin temporarily took the role for the cruise of 1981.
8. 2010–2012 Mahanna "A" (2011); "B" (2012); "A" (2013).
9. 2010–2012 Vecchio "B" (2011); "A" (2012); "B" (2013).
10. Served from January 11 to June 10 of 1926.
11. In 1959 the deck department was split into the Department of Economics and Transportation and the Department of Marine Science.

APPENDIX C

Vessels

Specifications of the Primary Training Ships used by SUNY Maritime College and Preceding Organizations

Name	St. Mary's
Class	Sloop-of-War
Displacement	958 tons
Dimensions	149'3" length; 37'4" beam; 18' draft; 195 complement
Armament	16 32-pounders; 6 8-inch guns
Shipbuilder	Charles B. Brodie
Place of Construction	Washington Navy Yard
Laid Down	1843
Delivered	1844
First Commander	John L. Saunders, CDR (USN)
Propulsion	Sail; Square-Rig
Service Record	1844–1875 (USN); 1875–1908 Training Ship for the New York Nautical School
Final Disposition	Sold to Thomas Butler and Co., Boston and scrapped in 1908
Notes	There has been some dispute in the correct spelling of this ship as "Marys" or "Mary's." The majority of primary documents (including Navy documents) use the spelling with the apostrophe and is certainly the correct style for the spelling of the ship's name.

Name	*Newport*
Designations	PG-12; Gunboat no. 12; IX-9
Class	Patrol Gunboat

(*continued*)

Dimensions	1,153 tons; 204'5" length; 36' beam; 12'9" draft; 156 complement
Armament	1 4", 2 3", 2 6-pdr. (1905: six 4" rapid fire mounts; four 6 pound rapid fire mounts; two 1 pound rapid fire mounts; one .30 caliber Colt machine gun)
Shipbuilder	Bath Iron Works, Bath, ME
Place of Construction	Bath Iron Works, Bath, ME
Laid Down	March, 1896
Launched	December 5, 1896
Commissioned	October 7, 1897
Sponsor	Miss Frances La Farge
First Commander	B.F. Tilley, CDR (USN)
Propulsion	Barkentine rig steam-sail hybrid with 2 single-ended cylindrical boilers; one 1,009 horsepower vertical triple expansion steam engine; 12.8 knots
Service Record	December, 1897 to August, 1898 service in USN. Decommissioned September 7, 1898. Recommissioned May 1, 1900. Served as training ship at the USNA and Naval Training station, Newport, RI. Decommissioned December 1, 1902. Recommissioned May 18, 1903 and active in USN. Decommissioned November 17, 1906. June 2, 1907 to October 27, 1907 loaned to the Massachusetts Naval Militia. October 27, 1907 to 1931 training ship for the New York Nautical School. Struck from Navy list on October 12, 1931.
Final Disposition	Given to city of Aberdeen, WA May 14, 1934 to train Naval reserves. Scrapped at Grays Bay, WA 1939.

Name	SS *Shaume* (1919–1921); *Procyon* (1921–1931); *Empire State* (1931–1941); *American Pilot* (1941–1946); *Bay State II* (1956–1948)
Designations	AG-11; IX-38
Class	Antares Class Miscellaneous Auxiliary; Flagship of Fleet Base Force; Shipping Board Vessel; Troop and Cargo Carrier
Dimensions	4,060 tons; 380' length; 54'2" beam; 9'8" draft; 218 complement
Armament	None, although five gun platforms were installed to take 5" 50 caliber guns
Shipbuilder	American International Ship Building Corporation
Place of Construction	Hog Island, PA

(continued)

Appendix C: Vessels

Laid Down	1919
Commissioned	November 30, 1921
First Commander	Bertram David, LT (USN)
Propulsion	3 oil-burning boilers; 1 Curtis-type prime mover; 2,500 horsepower steam engines; 11.5 knots
Service Record	1921–1931 (USN); 1931–1941 service as a training ship for the NYSMMA; NYSMA; 1941–1945 run by the Maritime Commission; 1946–1948 Massachusetts Maritime Academy
Final Disposition	Sold for scrapping March 3, 1948 to American Shipwreckers, Inc. Scrapped in Wilmington, DE

Name	*Seneca* (1908–1941); *Keystone State* (1941–1950)
Class	Coast Guard Cutter
Dimensions	1,106 gross tons; 710 net tons; 192.5' length; 34' beam; 25'9" draft; 9 officers, 65 enlisted (1908) complement
Armament	4 × 6-pounders (1908)
Shipbuilder	Newport News Shipbuilding and Drydock Company, Newport News, VA
Year Built	1908
Propulsion	Triple-expansion steam engine, two boilers; 11.2 knots maximum (1930)
Service Record	1908–1936 (USCG); 1936–1941 (sold to Boston Iron and Metal, then sold to Texas Refrigeration Steamship Lines then rebought by Boston Iron and Metal); 1941–1948 (bought by USCG and turned over to state of Pennsylvania used as a shared training ship by Maritime Commission)
Final Disposition	Sold for scrap in 1950
Notes	Served as a shared training ship for NYSMA from July 1, 1942 to August 7, 1942.

Name	*Alleghany* (1923–1942); *American Seafarer* (1942–1949)
Class	Coastal Passenger Cargo Ship
Dimensions	3,261 tons (net); 5486 tons (gross); 350.7' length; 46' beam; 19'1" draft (loaded)
Shipbuilder	Federal Shipbuilding Company, Kearny, NJ

(*continued*)

Year Built	1923
Propulsion	4 Cylinder Triple Expansion steam engines; 2,700 Indicated HP
Service Record	1923-1941 (private service—Merchants and Miners Transportation Company); 1941-1946 (War Shipping Administration as a training ship); 1946-1949 (in reserve, Suisan Bay, CA)
Final Disposition	Sold for scrapping, January, 1949
Notes	Served as a shared training ship for NYSMA from August 8, 1942 until December 12, 1942.

Name	*Hydrus* (1944-1946); *Empire State II* (1946-1964)
Designations	AKA-28
Class	Artemis Class Attack Cargo Ship
Dimensions	4,087 tons (light) ; 426' length; 58' beam; 16'6" (loaded) draft; 303 complement
Armament	1 single mounted 5" 38 caliber dual purpose gun mount; 4 twin 40 mm AA gun mounts; 10 single 20 mm AA gun mounts
Shipbuilder	Walsh-Kaiser Company
Place of Construction	Providence, RI
Launched	October 28, 1944
Commissioned	December 9, 1944
Sponsor	Mrs. Alexander Hylek
First Commander	R.J. Wissinger, LCDR (USN)
Propulsion	Twin screws, 3,300 horsepower; max 2,210 AC; 2 Westinghouse Turbo electric engines; 2 Wickes boilers; 2-Drum D-type Superheaters; 44,000 lb/hour each 450 psi at 750 degrees Fahrenheit; 2 desuperheaters; 2 economizers; Mechnical ventilation, 213,135 CFM; Ship's Service Generators; 2 turbo-drive 100 Kw 120V/240V DC; 1 turbo-drive 150 Kw 450V AC; 2 turbo-drive 250 Kw 450 v AC; twin propellers, 6,000shp; 17 knots.
Service Record	1944-1946 (USN) Received one battle star; 1946-1956 (NYSMA;SUNYMC); 1956-1964 (National Defense Reserve Fleet)
Final Disposition	Sold in April, 1964 to Union Minerals & Alloys Corp. of New York. Scrapped.

Appendix C: Vessels

Name	Mercy (1943–1956); Empire State III (1956–1973)
Designations	AH-8
Class	Comfort Class Hospital Ship
Dimensions	11,250 tons (lim.); 416' length; 60'2" beam; 24'6" (lim.) draft; 516 complement
Shipbuilder	Consolidated Steel Corporation
Place of Construction	Wilmington Yard, Wilmington, CA
Laid Down	February 4, 1943
Launched	March 25, 1943
Commissioned	August 7, 1944
Sponsor	Doris M. Yetter, LT(jg) (USN)
First Commander	Thomas A. Esling, CAPT (USNR)
Propulsion	1 JH geared steam turbine; three Babcock and Wilcox header-type boilers, 450 psi 750 degrees Fahrenheit; double JH Main Reduction Gear; 3 turbo-drive 300Kw 120v/240v DC Ship's Service Generators; single propeller, 4,000 shp; 15.3 knots
Service Record	1944–1946 (USN), two battle stars for supporting landing operations at Leyte Gulf and Okinawa; 1946–1950 (US Army); 1950–1956 (Maritime Commission); 1956–1960 (SUNYMC); 1960–1970 (National Defense Reserve Fleet, Hudson River Group)
Final Disposition	Sold November 23, 1970 to Aguilar y Peris, SL, Valencia, Spain for scrapping.

Name	Biloxi (1941–1943) ; Henry Gibbins (1943–1959); Empire State IV (1959–1973); Bay State III (1973–1983)
Designations	T-AP 183
Class	Troop Transport; Military Sea Transport Service
Dimensions	10,556 tons; 489' length; 70' beam; 26' draft; Can accommodate up to 1,976 troops. Regular complement unknown.
Shipbuilder	Ingalls Shipbuilding Corporation
Place of Construction	Pascagoula, MS
Laid Down	August 23, 1941
Launched	November 11, 1942
Commissioned	February 27, 1943

(continued)

Sponsor	Mrs. H.I. Ingalls, jr.
Propulsion	Turbine engines, single shaft, 8,500 shp; 16.5 knots
Service Record	1942–1950 (US Army Transportation Corps); 1950–1959 (MSTS); 1959–1973 (SUNYMC); 1973–1978 (Massachusetts Maritime Academy)
Final Disposition	Condemned in 1978 by Coast Guard due to hull damage; Scrapped in 1983 after an engine room fire.
Notes	In June, 1944 as the *Henry Gibbins*, President Franklin Roosevelt commissioned the ship to transport Jewish concentration camp survivors to the United States.

Name	*President Jackson* (1949–1952); *Barrett* (1952–1973); *Empire State V* (1973–2007)
Designations	T-AP-196
Class	Barrett Class Passenger Transport
Dimensions	11,255 tons (lt); 533'9.75" length; 73'3" beam; 27'1" draft; 219 complement (2,000 troop accommodation)
Shipbuilder	New York Shipbuilding Company
Place of Construction	Camden, NJ
Laid Down	June 1, 1949
Launched	June 27, 1950
Propulsion	2 Babcock and Wilcox sectional head water tube boilers; Steam turbine (General Electric), single shaft, 13,750 hp
Service Record	1952–1973 (MSTS), one battle star for Korean War service, three battle stars for Vietnam War service; 1973–1990 (SUNYMC); 1990–2007 (Maritime Administration, James River National Defense Reserve Fleet)
Final Disposition	Sold June 13, 2007 to Bay Bridge Enterprises, Chesapeake, VA for scrapping ($851, 194)

Name	*Oregon* (1961–1970s); *Mormactide* (1970s-1988); *Empire State VI* (1988–)
Designations	T-AP-1001
Type	Mariner Class Passenger/Cargo Vessel

(continued)

Appendix C: Vessels

Dimensions	11,615 tons (lt); 17,240 tons (fl); 565' length; 76' beam; 32' (max) draft
Shipbuilder	Newport News Shipbuilding and Drydock
Place of Construction	Newport News, VA
Laid Down	March 1, 1961
Launched	September 16, 1961
Propulsion	Steam turbine; single propeller (4 blade 22'); High Speed, Cross Compound, Double Reduction Geared Turbine; shaft hp, 17,500; 22 knots
Service Record	Delivered to the States Steamship Company in April, 1963 as the S.S. *Oregon*. She sailed for Moore-McCormack Lines and United States Lines as the *Mormactide*. She was then laid up into the James River Fleet. Rebuilt in 1988 and given to SUNYMC.

Selected Auxiliary Ships (arranged alphabetically by earliest known name)

Name	*Captain J.H. Tomb*
Type	Tugboat
Service Record	1986–unknown disposition (SUNYMC)

Name	*Esso Maine; Justine McAllister; Privateer*
Designations	ESSO Tug no 10
Type	Tugboat
Specs	96.3' length; 25.2' beam; 1,800 HP; ; 1 scr, d-e, 1 el-mot .1020shp, diesel 2tew 12cyl GM Cleveland, 1200bhp, sp 12kn
Shipbuilder	Gulfport Shipbuilding Company
Year Built	1951
Propulsion	1,800 HP
Service Record	1951-1968 (ESSO—Humble Oil & Refining Company); 1968-2004 (McAllister Brothers, Inc); 2004-2006 (SUNYMC); final disposition—Sold for Scrap

Name/Designation	George H. Barnes; Guilford D. Pendleton (sometimes spelled Gilford); Annex
Type	Schooner
Specs	1,456 net tons; 1,611 gross tons; 205.8' length; 41.5' beam; 24.5' depth; 19.6' draft (loaded)
Shipbuilder	Baxter Shipyards, Inc., Jacksonville, FL
Building Date	1918
Comments	This ship was obtained in 1928 as a hulk, and converted to classrooms and dormitories by the Morse Dry Dock and Repair Company for $9,210. It was used by NYSMMA until 1938 (approx.). Final disposition unknown but seen as a crushed hulk lying at Noank, CT in 1965.

Name	McAnn (1943) Balfour (1943–1946)
Designations	DE 73
Type	Destroyer Escort
Specs	(DE 73: displacement 1,300 tons; length 306'; beam 36'9"; draft 10'9"; speed 24 knots; complement 200; armament 3 3-inch, 8 20mm., 1 depth charge projector (hedge hog.), 2 depth charge tracks, 4 depth charge projectors; class Buckley)
Shipbuilder	Bethlehem Hingham Shipyard, Hingham, MA
Laid Down	April 19, 1943
Launched	July 10, 1943
Service Record	During World War II, Balfour earned "battle honors" for service in the Atlantic, off Normandy, and in the English Channel. On June 25, 1944, Balfour teamed with HMS Affleck (K.462) in destroying U 1191, and she scored a solo "kill" less than a month later, when she sank U 672 on 18 July.
Disposition	Sold to NYSMA on October 25, 1945 for $1. The ship was used for instruction and stripped for parts by the academy. Final disposition unknown.

Name	Mahoning; General Philip Schuyler
Designations	WYT-91
Type	Yard Tug

(continued)

Appendix C: Vessels 327

Specs	328 tons; 110' length; 26'5" beam; 11'5" draft (full load); 10 knots cruising speed; up to 45 passengers
Shipbuilder	Gulfport Boiler Works, Port Arthur, TX
Launched	August 7, 1939
Propulsion	1000 HP
Service Record	1939–1941 (USCG); 1941–1946 (USN); 1946–1984 (USCG); 1986–2001 (SUNYMC); Sold for scrap in 2001.

Name/Designation	*Meridian* (1936–1941); *Blue Water* (1941–1946); *Shoal Water* (1946–1957); *Genie* (1957–1960); *Lord Jim* (1960–)
Type	Alden/Lawley Schooner
Specs	(at time of possession by SUNYMC) 36 net tons; 72' length; 8'6" draft; 16'4" beam; 2,500 square feet of canvas; complement—12; GM diesel auxiliary engines.
Shipbuilder	John Alden (Designer); George Lawley & Sons Shipyard
Launch Date	1936
Comments	*Lord Jim* has had a long history that included World War II duty as a submarine patrol boat and racing. She was donated to SUNYMC in 1953 as the *Shoal Water*, but due to lack of funds to maintain the ship, she was returned to her owners in 1957.

Name	*Raritan*
Designations	WYT93
Type	Yard Tug
Specs	328 tons; 110' length; 27' beam; 11.2 knots speed
Shipbuilder	Defoe Boat Works, Bay City, MI
Launched	March 23, 1939
Service Record	1939–1941 (USCG); 1941–1946 (USN); 1946–1988 (USCG); 1988–2001 (SUNYMC); Sold for scrap in 2001.

Name/Designation	*Resistance* (commissioned May, 1968)
Type	Sailing yacht; ChrisCraft's Comanche class

(continued)

Specs	42' length; 10'10" beam; 6'6" draft; load displacement 19,000 lbs; sale area 740 square feet. Teak planked patterned non-skid fiberglass deck; mainmast (aluminum) 50' above deck. Auxilary 15-horsepower Volvo Ponta Diesel engine
Comments	Named after the first vessel of the Continental Navy to fly the Stars and Stripes. Purchased by SUNYMC for $50,000; disposition unknown.

Name/Designation	SC-678
Type	SC-497 Class Submarine Chaser
Specs	148 tons; 110' length; 17' beam; 6'6" draft; 15.6–21 knots speed; 28 complement; armament 1 40 mm gun mount; 2 .50 caliber machine guns; 2 dcp "Y Gun" 2 dct
Shipbuilder	Thomas Knutson Shipbuilding Corporation, Halesite, NY
Laid Down	March 10, 1942
Launched	August 17, 1942
Commissioned	November 9, 1942
Propulsion	2 800 bhp General Motors 8-268A diesel engines, Snow and Knobstedt single reduction gear; two shafts
Service Record	1942–1946 (USN); 1946–1948 (NYSMA); returned to Navy and disposed of April 9, 1948; fate unknown

Name/Designation	SC-1057 (1943–1948); *Palace II* (1948–1990); *Bonner Lee* (1990–2003)
Type	SC-497 Class Submarine Chaser
Specs	95 tons; 110'10" length; 17' beam; 6'6" draft; 21 knots speed; 28 complement; 1 40 mm gun mount; one/two twin mount .50 caliber machine guns; two/three depth charge projector "K Guns"; 14 depth charges with six single release chocks and two sets Mk 20 Mousetrap rails with four 7.2 projectiles
Shipbuilder	Gulf Marine Ways, Inc., Galveston, TX
Laid Down	May 7, 1942
Launched	November 11, 1942

(*continued*)

Appendix C: Vessels

Commissioned	May 19, 1943
Propulsion	2 800 bhp General Motors 8-268A diesel engines, Snow and Knobstedt single reduction gear; two shafts
Service Record	1943–1946 (USN); 1946–1948 (NYSMA); 1948–2003 (sold to private interests and eventually declared derelict and dumped in a landfill, Citrus County, FL.)
Comments	June 6, 1945—rescued all 66 survivors of the freighter SS *Ayuruoca*

Name	*Stalwart*; SUNY Maritime
Designations	T-AGOS-1
Type	Stalwart Class Ocean Surveillance Ship
Specs	1,565 tons (lt.); 224 length; 43' beam; 15' draft; 11 knots speed; 18 civilian, 15 navy complement;
Shipbuilder	Tacoma Boat Building Company, Tacoma, WA
Laid Down	November 3, 1982
Launched	July 11, 1983
Propulsion	Diesel-electric, two shafts; 1,600 hp
Service Record	1984–2004 (USN); 2004–2011 (SUNYMC); Sold 2011

Name	*Waubansee* (1944–1983); *Domer* (1983)
Designations	YTB-366
Type	*Sassaba* class tugboat
Specs	345 tons; 100' length; 25' beam; 9'5" draft; 12 knots speed; 14 complement
Shipbuilder	Consolidated Shipbuilder, Morris Heights, NY
Laid Down	April 24, 1944
Launched	June 10, 1944
Service Record	1944–1983 (USN); 1983 (SUNYMC—never put into service); Final disposition unknown.

Name	YW98
Type	Water tanker
Service Record	Acquired by SUNYMC in 1991; disposition unknown

Selected Bibliography

The main sources for the bulk of this book were: 1) archival documents, 2) historic newspapers and 3) extensive interviews conducted with alumni and faculty. The primary documents and manuscript collections housed in the Stephen B. Luce Library Archive were of especial importance to the creation of this work.

Scholarly journal articles, books and governmental materials supplemented these sources. Listed below are the main sources which can be cross-referenced in the notes section.

ARCHIVAL COLLECTIONS (Full Citations Listed in "Notes" Section)
Stephen B. Luce Library Archives, SUNY Maritime College, Bronx NY:
  John S. Baylis Papers
  Calvin T. Durgin Papers
  Institutional Records
  Frederick S. McMurray Papers
  Arthur M. Tode Papers
  James H. Tomb Papers
  Louis Weickum Papers
  Papers of the Marine Society of the City of New York
  Sailors' Snug Harbor Collection
  Stephen B. Luce Papers (microfilm copy from the Library of Congress)
DeKalb History Center, Decatur, GA:
  Papers of George M. Everhart
Fort Schuyler Maritime Alumni Association:
  Documents and news items maintained electronically by the Association
Texas Tech University Archives, Lubbock, TX:
  Howard Hampton Papers

BOOKS/JOURNAL ARTICLES/GOVERNMENT DOCUMENTS/
ACADEMIC WORKS (Abbreviated Citations Listed in the "Notes" Section)
Abbot, Willis John. *The Naval History of the United States.* New York: Dodd, Mead and Company, 1896.
Alden, Carroll Storrs and Ralph Earle. *Makers of Naval Tradition.* New York: Gin and Company, 1942.

Anderson, Charles Robert. "The Genesis of Billy Budd." *American Literature*. 12:3. (1940): 329–346.
Bauer, K. Jack. *A Maritime History of the United States: The Role of America's Seas and Waterways*. Columbia, SC: University of South Carolina Press, 1988.
Bauer, K. Jack and Stephen S. Roberts. *Register of Ships of the U.S. Navy, 1775–1990: Major Combatants*. New York: Greenwood Press, 1991.
Bolton, Robert Jr. *History of the County of Westchester*. New York: Alexander S. Gould, 1848.
Boston. *Twelfth Annual Report of the Board of State Charities of Massachusetts*, Boston: Wright and Potter State Printers, 1876.
Boswell, James. *The Life of Samuel Johnson*. London: Jones & Co., 1827.
Brady, William N. *The Kedge-Anchor; or Young Sailors' Assistant*. New York: Van Nostrand Company, 1891.
Brouwer, Norman J. *Centennial History of the SUNY. Maritime College at Fort Schuyler 1874–1974: a Thesis Submitted to the Faculty of State University of New York College at Oneonta at its Cooperstown Graduate Programs in Partial Fulfillment of Requirements for the Degree of Master of Arts*. New York: SUNY Maritime College, 1977.
Bureau of Navigation. Department of Commerce. *Fifty-Second Annual List of Merchant Vessels of the United States*, Washington: Government Printing Office, 1920.
Burke, Richard. *Sealogs: Postcards from the T.S. Empire State VI*. SUNY Maritime College: October 24, 2011.
Calkins, Captain Carlos Gilman. "American Admirals in the British Navy." (September, 1909): 685–699.
Caro, Robert A. *The Power Broker*. New York: Vintage, 1975.
Cheater, Colby M. "Diplomacy of the Quarter Deck." *The American Journal of International Law*. 8:3, 443–476
Class of '71: United States Naval Academy. New York: Grafton Press, 1902.
Coker, Michael D. *The Battle of Port Royal*. Charleston, SC: The History Press, 2009.
Conrad, James Lee. *Rebel Reefers: The Organization and Midshipmen of the Confederate States Naval Academy*. Cambridge: Da Capo Press, 2003.
Cook, Harry T. *The Borough of the Bronx: 1639–1913*. New York, 1913.
Cruikshank, Jeffrey L. and Chloe G. Kline. *In Peace and War: a History of the U.S. Merchant Marine Academy at Kings Point*. Hoboken, NJ: John Wiley and Sons, 2008.
Dana, Richard Henry. *Two Years Before the Mast*. Cambridge: University Press, 1868.
Dictionary of American Naval Fighting Ships. Ed. James L. Mooney. Washington: US Naval History Division, Department of the Navy, 1991.
Draper, Henry. *Cruise of the School-ship "Mercury" in Tropical Atlantic Ocean*. New York: New York. Department of Public Charities and Corrections. The New York Printing Company, 1871.
Emmons, George F. *Statistical History of the Navy of the United States*. Washington: Gideon & Company, 1853.
Filbert, Brent G. and Alan G. Kaufman. *Naval Law: Justice and Procedure in the Sea Services*, Annapolis: U.S. Naval Institute Press, 1997.
Fitzpatrick, Jane Brodsky. *Mrs. Magavero: A History Based on the Life of an Academic Librarian*. Duluth, MN: Library Juice Press, 2007.

Flower, Roswell P. *Public Papers of Roswell Flower, Governor*. Albany, NY: 1893.
Forbes, Robert B. *Personal Reminiscences*. Boston: Little, Brown, and Company, 1882.
Forbes, Robert B. *An Appeal to Merchants and Shipowners on the Subject of Seamen*. Boston: Sleeper & Rogers, 1854.
Gleaves, Albert Gleaves. *Life and letters of Rear Admiral Stephen B. Luce: U.S. Navy, Founder of the Naval War College*. New York: G.P. Putnam's Sons, 1925.
Goin, Thomas. *Remarks on the Home Squadron and Naval School*. New York: J.P. Wright, 1840.
Goodrich, Caspar F. *In Memoriam: Stephen Bleecker Luce, Rear Admiral United States Navy. A Tribute*. New York: The Naval History Society, 1919.
Hamersly, Lewis R. *The Records of Living Officers of the U.S. Navy and Marine Corps*. Philadelphia: J.B. Lippincott & Co., 1902.
Hess, Fred. *Fort Schuyler and Me*. City Island, NY: 1996.
Historical Statistics of the United States from Colonial Times to 1970. Washington: Bureau of the Census, 1976.
Homer. *The Odyssey*. Translated by E.V. Rieu. New York: Penguin, 2003.
Hopkins, Fred. "America's First Floating School." In *Ships, Seafaring, and Society*, edited by Timothy J. Runyan. 239-246. Detroit: Wayne State University Press, 1987.
Kobalenko, Jerry. *The Horizontal Everest: Extreme Journeys on Ellesmere Island*. BPS Books: 2010.
Luce, Stephen B. "The Manning of Our Navy and Mercantile Marine." *The Record of the United States Naval Institute* 1:1. (1874): 17-37.
Luce, Stephen B. "Training Ships: Educating Boys for Seamen." *Army and Navy Journal* (December 19, 1863).
Luce, Stephen B. *Text-Book of Seamanship*, edited by Aaron Ward. New York: D. Van Nostrand, 1884.
Luce, Stephen B. *The Writings of Stephen B. Luce*, edited by John D. Hayes and John B. Hattendorf. Rhode Island: Naval War College, 1975.
Lynch, Dr. Daniel. *Captain Alfred F. Olivet and Me*. 2013.
Moore, Capt. Arthur R. *A Careless Word . . . A Needless Sinking*. Kings Point, NY: American Merchant Marine Museum, 1998.
Neison, F.G.P. "Mortality of Master Mariners." *Journal of the Statistical Society of London*. 13:3. (August, 1850): 193-209.
Newman, Simon P. "Reading the Bodies of Early American Seafarers." *The William and Mary Quarterly*, 3rd series 55:1. (January, 1998): 59-82.
New York. Board of Education of the City and County of New York. *Regulations for Admittance, Government & Instruction of Boys Aboard the New York Nautical School Ship "St. Marys"*. New York: Press of Cushing and Bardua, 1876, 1-6.
New York. N.Y. Legislature. *An Act to Authorize the Board of Education for the City and County of New York to Establish a Nautical School*. April 24, 1873.
New York. Laws of New York, 1913. Chap. 322.
New York. N.Y. Legislature. *An Act to Amend the State Departments Act by Providing for an Education Department and Assigning to it Certain Functions of the State Government*, 149th Session. Chap. 322, April, 22, 1926.

New York. N.Y. Legislature. *An Act to Amend the Education Law, in Relationship to the Change in Name of the NY State Nautical School and Qualifications for the Admission Thereto,* 152nd sess., chap. 6, February 8, 1929.

New York. *Trends in Enrollment and Degrees Granted: 1948–1999.* Albany: State University of New York, 2000

New York Red Book, Albany: J.B. Lyon Company,1913

Peary, Robert E. *The North Pole.* New York: Frederick A. Stokes Company, 1910.

President's Private Sector Survey on Cost Control (U.S.) *Report on the Department of Transportation. Washington, D.C.: F, U.S. G.P.O.,* 1983. http://catalog.hathitrust.org/Record/001827758

Proceedings of the Court of Inquiry appointed to inquire into the intended mutiny on board the United States Brig of War Somers, on the high seas; held on board the United States Ship North Carolina lying at the Navy Yard, New-York; with a full account of the execution of Spencer, Cromwell and Small, on board said vessel. New York: Greeley & McElrath, 1843.

Remarks on the Scarcity of American Seamen and the Remedy; the Naval Apprenticeship System by a Gentlemen Connected with the New York Press. New York: Herald Office, 1845.

Rice, Pamela. "Section F: a Legislative Attack on Educational Discrimination." *The Journal of Negro Education* 23:1. (Winter, 1954): 99–106.

Riesenberg, Felix. *Living Again: An Autobiography.* Garden City: Doubleday, Doran & Company, 1937.

Riesenberg, Felix. *Log of the Sea.* New York: Harcourt Brace, 1933.

Riesenberg Jr., Felix. *Yankee Skippers to the Rescue: A Record of Gallant Rescues on the North Atlantic by American Seamen.* New York: Dodd, Mead & Company, 1940.

Rives, John C. *Appendix to the Congressional Globe Containing Speeches, Important State Papers, Laws, Etc., of the First Session Thirty-Fifth Congress.* Washington: Office of John C. Rives, 1858.

Roland, Alex Roland, W. Jeffrey Bolster, and Alexander Keyssar. *The Way of the Ship: America's Maritime History Reenvisioned.* Hoboken: John Wiley & Sons, 2008.

Richmond, Ikk and Mayo-Smith, *Science of Statistics Part II: Statistics and Economics.* London: Macmillan & Co, 1899.

Robinson, Willard B. Robinson, *American Forts: Architectural Form and Function.* Chicago: University of Illinois Press, 1977.

Roscoe, Theodore. *United States Destroyer Operations in World War II.* Annapolis: Naval Institute Press, 1953.

Span, Christopher M. "Educational and Social Reforms for African American Juvenile Delinquents in 19th Century New York City and Philadelphia." *The Journal of Negro Education* 71:3 (Summer, 2002): 108–117.

Speelman, Jennifer Lyn. *Nautical Schools and the Development of United States Maritime Professionals, 1874–1941.* Temple University: 2001.

Speelman, Jennifer L. "The United States Navy and the Genesis of Maritime Education." *Transactions of the American Philosophical Society.* 97.4 (2007): 65–85.

Steamboat Inspection Service, Bureau of Marine Inspection and Navigation. *Ocean and Coastwise General Rules and Regulations.* Washington: Government Printing Office, 1916.

Sutter, Luke Sutter. *The New York Years: Collected Vignettes of Luke Sutter.* Martinsburg, WV: Mountain State Publishing: 2004.
Tomb, James Harvey. "The Education of Merchant Marine Officers." *United States Naval Institute Proceedings* 58:355 (1932): 1277-1284.
Trask, Gustavus D.S. *A Memoir of the Marine Society of New York.* New York: 1877.
Underhill, Harold A. *Sail Training and Cadet Ships.* Glasgow: Brown, Son & Ferguson, 1956.
U.S. Coast Guard. *Summary of Merchant Marine Personnel Casualties, World War II.* Washington: U.S. Government Printing Office, 1950.
U.S. Congress. *An Act to Encourage the Establishment of Public Marine Schools.* June 2, 1874.
U.S. Congress. *An Act for the Establishment of Marine Schools and for Other Purposes.* 61st Congress, 3rd session, 36 stat 1353, March 4, 1911.
U.S. Congress. *An Act Making Appropriations for the Naval Service for the Fiscal Year Ending June 30, 1917.* H.R. 15947, 64th Congress, August 29, 1916.
U.S. Congress. *Hearings before the Committee on Naval Affairs of the House of Representatives on Sundry Legislation Affecting the Naval Establishement. Marine Schools* 67th Cong., 1st sess. Washington: GPO, 1922.
U.S. Congress. *Statement of Vice Admiral T.J. Hughes, Jr. (USN) Before the Merchant Marine Committee of the House Merchant Marine and Fisheries Committee on Maritime Bills,* May 1, 1986.
U.S. Department of Transportation. *National Transportation Statistics.* http://www.bts.gov/publications/national_transportation_statistics/
Villella, Edward. *Prodigal Son: Dancing for Balanchine in a World of Pain and Magic.* New York: Simon & Schuster, 1992.
Whitman, Charles Seymour. *Public Papers of Charles Seymour Whitman.* Albany: J.B. Lyon Company, Printers, 1916.

INTERVIEWS AND CORRESPONDENCE

Robert Barr (Class of 1947)
Robert Berner (Class of 1965)
Donald P. Brennan (Class of 1961)
David C. Brown, RADM (USMS)
Richard Burke (Class of 1972)
William Caldwell (Class of 1958)
Thomas R. Clark (Class of 1961)
James Cordara (Class of 1985)
David Cory (Class of 1950)
Colette Crowther (Class of 1978)
Frank Cuccio (Class of 1982)
George Marshall
James DeSimone (Class of 1973)
Phylipp Dilloway (Class of October, 1946)

Robert Fay (Class of 1980)
Jose Femenia (Class of 1964)
Thomas F. Fox (Class of 1962)
Joseph Hoffman (Class of 1975)
John G. Ingram (Class of 1964)
Richard Kadison (Class of 1945)
Thomas F. Keenan (Class of 1971)
Sean Kirby (Class of 1982)
Daniel Lynch (Class of 1958)
Karen Magliocca-Rocheteau (Class of 1978)
Karen Markoe
Charlie Munsch (Class of 1973)
Arthur Murray (Class of 1945)
Marjorie Murtagh-Cooke (Class of 1974)
Kathy Olzewski
Harold Parnham (Class of 1948)
Richard Smith (Class of 1981)
Hartley Spatt
Jeffrey Spillane (Class of 2002)
Charles Strommer (Class of October, 1946)
Robert P. Thompson (Class of 1964)
Edward Villella (Class of 1957)
Leonard Weiss (Class of October, 1946)
Donald White (Class of October, 1946)
Conrad Youngren (Class of 1967)

NEWSPAPERS/MAGAZINES/YEARBOOKS/PROCEEDINGS
(Full Citation of Articles Provided in the "Notes" Section)

The Afro-American
Albany Journal
The Baltimore Afro-American
Boson's Pipe (held at the Stephen B. Luce Library)
Boston Recorder
Brooklyn Eagle
Bulletin of the Alumni Association
Christian Observer
Cornell Alumni News
Daily Standard Union
The Day
Eight Bells (held at the Stephen B. Luce Library)
The Evening Mail
Fort Schuyler Mariner
Hampton's Magazine

Selected Bibliography 337

Hawaii Herald
Marine Journal
Maritime Exchange Bulletin
Maritime Navigator (held at the Stephen B. Luce Library)
Marine News
Maritime Screw (held at the Stephen B. Luce Library)
Maritime Voice (held at the Stephen B. Luce Library)
Military Affairs
New Orleans States
New York Daily News
New York Evening Post
New York Globe
New York Herald
New York Press
New York Sun
New York Times
New York World
New York World-Telegram
Newsday
News from Fort Schuyler (electronically held by the Fort Schuyler Alumni Association)
Niles Weekly Register
The Nautical Gazette
The Pacific Commercial Advisor
Periscope: the Underwater Porthole (held at the Stephen B. Luce Library)
Popular Mechanics
Porthole (held at the Stephen B. Luce Library)
Proceedings of the American Merchant Marine Conference
Reports of the New York Chamber of Commerce
San Diego Union
San Francisco Call
Sea History
State Maritime Academies Conference (held at the Stephen B. Luce Library)
Sunday Tribune—Providence
Time Magazine
Transactions of the Society of Naval Architects and Marine Engineers
Trumpet and Universalist Magazine
Washington Post

Notes

Notes for pages 1–5

ABBREVIATIONS IN NOTES
AMTP—Arthur M. Tode Papers, Stephen B. Luce Library Archives.
AR—The Annual Reports of the institution. Stephen B. Luce Library Archives.
BE—*Brooklyn Daily Eagle*
CTDP—Calvin T. Durgin Papers, Stephen B. Luce Library Archives.
FSMP—Frederick S. McMurray Papers, Stephen B. Luce Library Archives.
LWP—Louis Weickum Papers, Stephen B. Luce Library Archives.
Minutes—Minutes of the Board of Governors/Board of Visitors/College Council. Stephen B. Luce Library Archives.
MJ—*Marine Journal*
NFFS—*News from Fort Schuyler*. Fort Schuyler Maritime Alumni Association.
NYDN—*New York Daily News*
NYEP—*New York Evening Post*
NYH—*New York Herald*
NYT—*New York Times*
NYWT—*New York World-Telegram*
PH—*The Porthole*. Stephen B. Luce Library Archives.
SBLLA—Stephen B. Luce Library Archives, SUNY Maritime College, Bronx, NY.
Sun—*New York Sun*

CHAPTER 1: AMERICAN SAILORS FOR AMERICAN SHIPS
Richard Dana's Story: Dana.
1850 study: Neison, 193–209.
Revilement of Sailors: Newman, 59–82.
"indigent and distressed shipmasters": *Charter of the Marine Society of New York*. Papers of the Marine Society. SBLLA.
"retired decrepit and worn-out sailors": *Will of Robert Randall*, Sailors' Snug Harbor Collection. SBLLA.
Marine Society Proposal: Trask, 9.
Coffin and the *Clio*: *Niles Weekly Register*, volume 37, 1829–30, p 85.
Closure of the Clio: Calkins, 697–699.
"wild and idle boys": Goin, 2–3.
"feel much more proud and sanguine": *Remarks on the Scarcity of American Seamen*, 9.

Ages in the Apprenticeship program: Abbot, 817.
2,000 boys: Stephen B. Luce, *The Writings of Stephen B. Luce*, 173.
Genealogy of Stephen B. Luce: Luce, *The Writings of Stephen B. Luce*, 9.
Early apprenticeship system: Gleaves, 8.
"thoroughly taught to clean priming wires . . .": Stephen B. Luce, "Nautical Schools in the U.S.: a Historical Sketch." *The Nautical Gazette* 4, no. 86 (15 February 1873): 266. (quoted from Speelman).
On Philip Spencer: "Philip Spencer," *Christian Observer*, January 27, 1843. "Young Spencer, the Mutineer," *Trumpet and Universalist Magazine*, February 4, 1843. "Philip Spencer," *Boston Recorder*, February 16, 1843.
Luce's thoughts on Spencer: Gleaves, 11
On the *Somer's* Mutiny: John R. Spears, "The Mutiny on the 'Somers.' *Frank Leslie's Popular Monthly*, (v. 52), 371–375; Filbert; Charles Robert Anderson, "The Genesis of Billy Budd." *American Literature*, (Nov. 1940): 329–346.
Establishment of the U.S. Naval Academy: Conrad; Speelman.
Battle of Port Royal: Coker.
Service Record of Stephen B. Luce: Hamersly, 107–108.
"the meanest scow": Luce, *The Writings of Stephen B. Luce*, 7–8.
"Every ship in the service . . .": Luce, *The Writings of Stephen B. Luce*, 7.
". . . twelve to fifteen million pounds of opium . . .": Forbes, 144.
The appeal of Robert B. Forbes to establish schoolships: Forbes. *An Appeal to Merchants and Shipowners on the Subject of Seamen*, 9.
On the schoolship *Ontario*: Hopkins, 239–246.
19th Century Decline of the Merchant Marine: Cruikshank, 31. Roland.
***The Evening Star* disaster:** Speelman, *Nautical Schools and the Development of United States Maritime Professionals*, 1–2.
19th Century prison reform movment: Christopher M. Span, "Educational and Social Reforms for African American Juvenile Delinquents in 19th Century New York City and Philadelphia." *The Journal of Negro Education*, Vol. 71, No. 3. Juvenile Justice: Children of Color in the United States *The Journal of Negro Education*. (Summer, 2002), 108–117
"slight misdemeanors and vagrancy": Draper, 3.
"A Correctional Institution robbed . . .": Arabs at Sea: The Voyage of the School-Ship Mercury." *NYT* (January 1, 1873): 8.
"many smart boys . . .": Stephen B. Luce, "Nautical Schools in the U.S.: a Historical Sketch." *The Nautical Gazette* 4, no. 86 (15 February 1873): 266. Quoted from Speelman, 27.
Closure of the *Massachusetts*: Boston, xci.
Closure of the *Mercury*: "The City Charities," *NYT*, January 1, 1876.
"Compared to the army": Luce, *The Writings of Stephen B. Luce*, 7–8.
"Turk's heads . . .": Brady, 28.
Luce's attitudes toward the British nautical training system: Stephen B. Luce, "Training Ships: Educating Boys for Seamen," *Army and Navy Journal* 1, no. 17 (19 December 1863): 260. Also see Stephen B. Luce, "The Manning of Our Navy and

Mercantile Marine," *The Record of the United States Naval Institute.* (Vol. 1, no. 1. 1874): 26.
"Nautical College" "Our ships go to sea . . .": Gleaves, 135–137.
"In an era of growing immigration . . .": Speelman, *Nautical Schools,* 10.
Luce's attitudes toward a foreign takeover of the Navy: S.B. Luce, "Letter to the Secretary of the Navy." November 12, 1872. Stephen B. Luce Papers. SBLLA.
Luce and the Morrill Act: Gleaves, 137–138.
The creation of the New York Nautical School: New York. *Regulations for Admittance, Government & Instruction of Boys Aboard the New York Nautical School Ship "St. Marys,"* 1–6.
Luce's proposals for the federal law: Brouwer, *Centennial History,* 16–17.
The final 1874 Legislation: New York, *Regulations for Admittance, Government & Instruction of Boys Aboard the New York Nautical School Ship "St. Marys".* 8.
Luce and the acquisition of the *St. Mary's*: Norman J Brouwer, "Stephen B. Luce and the Federal Act of 1874." *Sea History,* (Spring, 1991): 12–13.

CHAPTER 2: A SQUARE-RIGGED SCHOOL

Ages of the first class of the *St. Mary's*: *Admission Book for the New York Nautical School,* 1875. SBLLA.
Record of Robert Phythian: Hamersly, 197.
"knowledge of a school teacher . . .": Charles Williamson, *Draft of a History of the New York Nautical School.* Unpublished and undated. SBLLA.
"soft berth": "The Softest Naval Berth," *BE,* December 28, 1886.
"box the compass, etc": "Report of the Superintendent of the Nautical School," 34th Annual Report of the Board of Education of the City and County of New York, p. 402.
curriculum of the early school: AR, 1898, 38–39.
Albert Ruffin's story: *Letter to Richard Aldcroftt, Jr. from G.C. Hanus,* May 2, 1907. Letter Press Book. *Conduct and Admissions Books.* SBLLA. *Letter to Richard Aldcroftt, Jr. from G.C. Hanus,* May 2, 1907. Letter Press Book. SBLLA. *Letter to J.A. Ruffin from G.C. Hanus,* May 9, 1907. Letter Press Book. SBLLA. *Letter to Richard Aldcroftt, Jr. from G. C. Hanus,* May 2, 1907 Letter Press Book. SBLLA. "Raced with Death to Save Sick Cadet," *NYT,* May 3, 1907. "Raced with Death to Save Sick Cadet," *NYT,* May 3, 1907. "St. Mary's Cadet in Race with Death," *BE,* May 2, 1907. *Letter to J.A. Ruffin from G.C. Hanus,* May 4, 1907. Letter Press Book. SBLLA. *Letter to J.A. Ruffin from G.C. Hanus,* May 16, 1907. Letter Press Book. SBLLA. *Letter to J.A. Ruffin from G.C. Hanus,* May 17, 1907. Letter Press Book. SBLLA.
"I should never have taken you . . .": Homer, 98.
"no man will be a sailor . . .": Boswell, 95.
". . . we have hard times ashore . . .": Frederick S. McMurray, *Correspondence with mother,* November 18, 1894. FSMP.
"The Nautical School is doing grand work . . .": "Letters to the Editor," *NYT,* February 17, 1878.

"not offenders to be reclaimed . . .": AR, 1876, 256.
Introduction of advanced coursework: AR, 1898, 38-39.

CHAPTER 3: "A BARNACLE IN THE SCHOOL SYSTEM"

Ross Marvin as quartermaster: "Picked Men Sailed on the Roosevelt," *NYT*, September 9, 1909.
"six men in one": "Death of Ross Marvin," *Cornell Alumni News*, September 29, 1909.
"troublesome and awkward": "Marvin, Who Lost His Life with Peary," *NYT*, September 9, 1909.
Role of Marvin on Peary expedition: "In the North with Peary," *Cornell Alumni News*, January 23, 1907.
"grasped more fully": Peary, 187.
Marvin's comments about the Cornell football team: "Death of Ross Marvin," *Cornell Alumni News*, September 29, 1909.
"the most valuable man in the party": Peary, 187.
"black and melancholy": Robert E. Peary. "The Discovery of the North Pole," *Hampton's Magazine*, (v. 26, 1920), 773.
"support the driver"; the Peary system; Marvin sent south: Peary, 207-254.
"killing all joy": "The Fate of Ross Marvin," *NYT*, September 26, 1926.
Memorial cairn: Peary, 318-321.
"was like a sane man": "Heroes: Revelation," *Time*, October 4, 1926.
"wonderful at getting along": "The Fate of Ross Marvin," *NYT*, September 26, 1926.
"knows that he need . . .": "Eskimo who Killed Ross Marvin," *NYT*, September 30, 1926.
The school banner and astronaut: "North Pole," *NFFS*, March 10, 2008.
Wood's case: "Beaten on the St. Mary's," *NYT*, August 11, 1889. "To be Investigated, Charges Against Executive Officer Wood of the St. Mary's" *NYT, August 23, 1889.* "Army and Navy News," *NYT*, September 29, 1889.
"mistake the public labors . . .": "Wanted, A New Schoolship," *Sun*, December 30, 1906.
". . . in no sense a reformatory": *1911 Admission application*, New York Nautical School. SBLLA
Phythian's comments about foreigners working on the *St. Mary's*: 1875, AR, 403.
". . . had Lot's wife lashed to the mast . . .": "Training Ship *Newport* visited Yesterday by Acting Governor," *The Royal Gazette*, September 16, 1919. From a clipping SBLLA.
". . . would make the reefing . . .": Riesenberg, *Living Again*, 53.
". . . he seemed a demigod": Frederick McMurray, "Boatswain William Dreilick, A Sailorman," FSMP, 1952, SBLLA.
". . . this is too god damn scientific . . .": Lewis L. Smith, *Address Delivered by Lewis L. Smith at the 52nd Annual Dinner of the Alumni Association*, April 6, 1956, SBLLA.
"vell dere were . . ."; Dreilick's grave: Frederick McMurray, "Boatswain William Dreilick, A Sailorman," FSMP, 1952, SBLLA

Enrollment on the schoolship: ARs, (various years), SBLLA
Statistics on merchant shipping: Richmond, 749.
Costs per pupil: AR, 1895, 31. SBLLA.
"A less expensive organization": "Report of the Committee on Salaries and Economy," NYT, January 31, 1878.
"a handful of boys": "The Council of Reform," NYT, February 4, 1878.
"mere pet of some few people": "Cutting Down Estimates," NYT, December 15, 1886.
"many a farmer's boy . . .": "Scope of the Marine School," NYT, December 28, 1890.
Jacob Riis's story: "Boys Desert the St. Mary's," NYT, August 13, 1899.
Influence of the Chamber of Commerce: *Report of the Chamber of Commerce,* (New York: Press of the Chamber of Commerce,1890), 750.
"why several of our wealthy": AR, 1888, 287–288.
"you cannot make a seamen out of boys . . .": *Thirty-Third Annual Report of the Corporation of the New York Chamber of Commerce,* (New York: Press of the Chamber of Commerce, 1891), 67.
$10,000 demand: "The St. Mary's Graduates," NYT, October 22, 1891.
"barnacle in the school system": "Money for the Schools," NYT, December 24, 1891.
McGowan's warning: 1892 AR, 260. SBLLA.
"sixteen children . . .": "It Should be Discontinued," NYT, May 26, 1893.
"consider the support or maintenance": "Thousands will sign petition," NYH. July 7, 1893.
Megie's statements: "Thinks the St. Mary's Useless," NYH, July 13, 1893.
Statistics on Schoolship graduates: *Record of Graduates,* SBLLA.
Megie's dismissal: "Naval Officers Sentenced," NYT, August 1, 1894.
Efforts of friends of the Nautical School: "Trouble Brewing Over *St. Mary's*," NYH, June 29, 1893.
Petition: "Thousands will sign petition," NYH. July 7, 1893.
Suspension of activity on the schoolship: "Forced to Tie Up the *St. Marys*," NYH, July 13, 1893.
"continuous drain . . .": Flower, 135–136.

CHAPTER 4: A NEW ERA

On Wells Field: Riesenberg, *Living Again,* 56.
"unworthy graduates": AR, 1894, 289. SBLLA.
Conditions of the *St. Mary's* in 1894: AR, 1894, SBLLA.
Refinancing of the *St. Mary's*: AR, 1895, 30. SBLLA.
"commencement of a new era": AR, 1896, 213. SBLLA.
"the least desirable members of the class": AR, 1896, 214–15. SBLLA.
William Reeder and Edwin Jacob: AR, 1898. SBLLA.
"What do you understand by the mariner's compass?": AR, 1898. SBLLA.
"A complete Revolution": Visit of Stephen B. Luce: AR, 1898. SBLLA.
King of Portugal: AR, 1900. SBLLA.
". . . the Southampton Ladies Guild . . .": AR, 1901, 338. SBLLA.

Naval career of G.C. Hanus: *Class of '71*. See entry on Gustavus Hanus.
"We dragged our anchor . . .": Frederick S. McMurray, Correspondence with mother, September 18, 1903. FSMP.
". . . courteous and genial . . .": From a draft of an unpublished and undated booklet created by the class of 1889, 12. SBLLA.
"all boys in New York . . .": AR, 1904, 454. SBLLA
Creation of the alumni association; Hatzel's Donation: Frederick S. McMurray "The Lure of the Sea." Undated, FSMP.
"so old that she may become unseaworthy . . ."; "the graduates of the *St. Mary's* are well trained . . .": "St. Mary's Skipper Aroused," *NYT*. October 7, 1906.
"sailing ship with auxiliary steam": AR, 1906, 513. SBLLA
Appeal to Theodore Roosevelt: *Sun*, New York, January 20, 1907.
the rejection by Roosevelt to supply the *Hartford*: *The Daily Standard Union*, February 14, 1907.
"would simply mean maximum . . ."; ". . . the best of all the small vessels . . ."; repairs needed by the *St. Mary's*: G.C. Hanus, *Correspondence to Richard B. Aldcroftt, Jr,*. November 26, 1906. Letter Press Book, SBLLA. G.C. Hanus, *Correspondence to Richard B. Aldcroftt, Jr.*, April 8, 1907. Letter Press Book, SBLLA.
Building a custom ship: AR, 1907, 260. SBLLA.
". . . learned the government doesn't want her . . ."; "with the crew . . .": G.C. Hanus, *Correspondence to Richard B. Aldcroftt, Jr.*, April 16, 1907. Letter Press Book, SBLLA.
"it is interesting to note . . .": 1907 AR, 260. SBLLA.
Failure to convert the ship to a museum; plan to convert the *St. Mary's* to a clubhouse: "Fate of Old Schoolship," *NYEP*, April 16, 1908.
The sale and breaking of the *St. Mary's*: "Schoolship Alumni Dine," *NYT*, February 14, 1909. "Cat Won't Leave Old Ship," *NYT*, October 18, 1908. "St. Mary's off to Pyre," *NYEP*, October 8, 1908.
"Our boat was beached . . .": "Schoolship Alumni Dine," *NYT*, February 14, 1909.— An excerpt of the full poem was published in the *NYT*. The full version, shown here, was extracted from Alumni Bulletins in the SBLLA (clippings) dated from 1911 and onward.

CHAPTER 5: THE WAY OF THE SCHOOLSHIP

Note: The actual Halladay Van Horn was from New York. He ended up deserting the schoolship after three months of attendance.

Van Horn's fight with Dahl: Riesenberg, *Living Again*.
List of items for schoolship boys: W.H. Jaques ed., *New York Nautical School Ship "St. Marys"* (New York: Press of Cushing and Bardua, 1876), 21. SBLLA.—This list remained more or less the same for the duration of the New York Nautical School. The location of the school is found in the Annual Reports. The mention of Bellvue is prominent in Riesenberg's *Living Again*. SBLLA.

Organization into Tops: The organization of the school into Tops is found in several sources, including Jaques. Other important sources are from the McMurray Papers and anonymous reminisces of *St. Mary's* Graduates. See *Old Mugs and New Mugs*. SBLLA.

Ivan the Terrible: The nickname "Ivan the Terrible" was provided by McMurray. FSMP. Riesenberg, in his *Log of the Sea*, writes that Hodges's nickname was "Billy Buttons." Regardless, both McMurray and Riesenberg agree on the character of the executive officer.

Organization of students: This system of organization would change after the acquisition of the *Newport*. Students after that time would be organized as engineering or deck, although they would still be in small crews.

Cats of the schoolship: See the letters of Frederick McMurray. FSMP.

Goat story: See Donald White, *Correspondence with Parents*, June 26, 1946. The goat was actually doing its business under the hammock of Alfred Olivet. SBLLA.

Rattle of the St. Mary's: The *St. Mary's* indeed used a rattle instead of a drum or bugler. It was a very old fashioned ship. See McMurray, "Schoolship Life in the Old *St. Mary's*." FSMP as well as various clippings in the scrapbooks of the SBLLA.

Seams: Seams were the old-fashioned term for demerits. The term went out of style circa 1900. See the *Conduct Books of the New York Nautical School*. SBLLA.

Boatswain: The boatswain is obviously modeled on William Dreilick. For the quotation concerning Cape Horn, see Riesenberg's, *Log of the Sea*. Also see "Boatswain William Dreilick." FSMP.

Fred's description of Pete: For this vivid description, see "Schoolship Life in the Old *St. Mary's*." FSMP.

Food of the schoolships: All sources from the schoolship period speak about how awful the food aboard was. See Riesenberg, McMurray, "Old Mug's and New Mugs," various clippings from newspapers, etc. This section provides a composite view of the sources.

Schedule: See Jaques for the schedule of the early New York Nautical School. SBLLA.

On the boatswain: Both Riesenberg, McMurray and other sources devote many pages of material describing the abilities of Dreilick. SBLLA.

Knot-tying story: This incident is taken from Riesenberg, *Living Again*.

Miss Stone: *Address Delivered by Lewis L. Smith at the 52nd Annual Dinner of the Alumni Association*, April 6, 1956. SBLLA. Singing lessons were introduced by G.C. Hanus, with similar results.

"Have your head bumped against a wall . . .": This type of incident is described in the LWP. SBLLA.

Nosey Bluff: *Reminisces of Charles Williamson*. SBLLA.

"Going over the rigging": The hazing is vividly described in Edward "Nick" Carter's *Tall Ship Tales*. SBLLA.

"Tough-handed brats": This quote is taken from Riesenberg, *Log of the Sea*.

The blanket and hammock incident: untitled piece by Louis Weickum. LWP.

Pranks in the head: Carter.

On rates: Information on rates is provided by Carter, "Tall Ship Tales." By the 1920's, the highest ranking cadet was the Cadet Executive Officer. SBLLA.
Food as contraband story; bible story: adapted from Riesenberg, *Log of the Sea*.
Flashback story for cruise: There are several sources for this section. See LWP *Cruise of 1903*, Riesenberg's *Living Again*, McMurray letters, "Centoz '22 Recalls Mast Aboard Newport," *Port Hole*. March 21, 1951, Carter. SBLLA.
Contraband in piano: "Recollections of the *St. Mary's*." SBLLA. I suspect that this is McMurray, Williamson, or Weickum.
Swimming on bench: In news clippings. SBLLA.
Mutiny story: This is an expanded version of the story found in Riesenberg, *Log of the Sea*.
Van Horn's victory: See Riesenberg, *Living Again*.

CHAPTER 6: "THE ONLY PEBBLE ON THE BEACH"

Career of Lay Everhart: "The Bynum Branch of the Hampton Family," Howard Hampton Papers, Texas Tech University, Lubbock, TX. Papers of George M. Everhart, DeKalb History Center, Decatur, GA.
Everhart promising to serve three years and taking command: "Commander Quits City Schoolship," NYT, March 29, 1911. "A Teacher Fined for Beating Pupil," NYT, April 9, 1908. "Dr. O'Brien explains row on Newport," BE, May 21, 1909
Franklin Tighe's behavior record: Lay H. Everhart, *Letter from Lay H. Everhart to the United States Consul*, June 20, 1908, SBLLA.
Tighe's desertion and plans: A.D. Dorry, *Letter from A.D. Dorry to Lay H. Everhart*, July 9, 1908, SBLLA.
"Feeling sure . . .": Edward W. Matthews, *Letter from Edward W. Matthews to Lay H. Everhart*, July 6, 1908, SBLLA.
Everhart's response to Matthews: Lay H. Everhart, *Letter from Lay H. Everhart to Edward W. Matthews*, August 6, 1908. SBLLA.
". . . the only pebble on the beach . . .": Keran O'Brien, *Letter from Keran O'Brien to Lay H. Everhart*, July 9th, 1908. July 9, 1908. SBLLA.
". . . a clean slate.": Lay H. Everhart, *Letter from Lay H. Everhart to A. Emerson Palmer*, August 3, 1908. SBLLA.
"police force present . . .": Keran O'Brien, Letter from Keran O'Brien, MD, to L.H. Everhart, August 1, 1908. SBLLA.
Return of Tighe to the Schoolship: Lay H. Everhart, *Letter from Lay H. Everhart to A. Emerson Palmer*, August 3, 1908. SBLLA.
"drunk and disorderly . . .": Lay H. Everhart, *Letter from Lay H. Everhart to Robert A. Tighe*, September 2, 1908, SBLLA.
". . . for such a brutal statement.": Robert A. Tighe, *Letter from Robert A. Tighe to Lay H. Everhart*, September 4, 1908, SBLLA.
Tighe's transportation costs: Lay H. Everhart, *Letter from Lay H. Everhart to Robert A. Tighe*, September 8, 1908, SBLLA.
Everhart in the right to expel Tighe: Egerton L. Winthrop Jr, *Letter from Egerton L. Winthrop, Jr. to Lay H. Everhart*. October 29, 1908. SBLLA

Everhart's proposals for the merchant marine: "Fleet of Ships for Training the Nation's Boys," *NYT*, March 27, 1910.
"unsafe to sail": "Affairs Intolerable Aboard the Newport", *NYH*, undated clipping, SBLLA.
"make trouble for the school": Lay H. Everhart, *Letter to Egerton L. Winthrop*, October 24, 1908. SBLLA.
Relation of Christopher Marsden to Roland Marsden: Correspondence with Captain George Marshall, grandson of Christopher Marsden. March, 2010.
A new set of officers: Brouwer, 56.
Investigation by the Marine Society and support of Littlefield and Marsden: "Schooship Men Everhart's Choice" *NYH*, November 29, 1908. "Raps Schoolship's Officials," *New York Press*, 1909.
"the captain of the schoolship *Newport*": "Trouble on the Schoolship Newport," *MJ*, March 18, 1909.
Everhart's problems with Keran O'Brien: "Everhart wins in Schoolship Clash," *NYH*, May 21, 1909, 5. "Angry Surgeon Quits Schoolship Halting Voyage," *NYH*, May 20, 1909. "Dr. O'Brien explains row on Newport," *BE*, May 21, 1909. "Lay All the Blame for Trouble on Dr. O'Brien," *The Day*, May 21, 1909. "Dr. O'Brien explains row on Newport," *BE*, May 21, 1909.
"there was much less sickness . . .": 1909 AR, 263. SBLLA
"several captains of our coastwise . . .": "A Brief Bit of Local History," *MJ*, February 7, 1914.
Excessive boxing matches: Untitled, *Sun*, March 28, 1911.
"We feel that we are losing . . .": "Commander Quits City Schoolship," *NYT*, March 29, 1911.
Libel suit: "*Newport*'s ex-skipper sues," *Sun*, October 10, 1911. *NYH*, December 14, 1911, 16.
1910 funding cut: 1910 AR, 289.
1911 legislation: U.S. Congress, *An Act for the Establishment of Marine Schools and for Other Purposes*. 61st Congress, 3rd session, 36 stat 1353, March 4, 1911.
Pigeon-holed: "Jibboom Observations," *The Day*, April 29, 1912.
Dombaugh as superintendent: 1911 AR. SBLLA. "Boys Mutiny on Schoolship," *Sun*, December 21, 1911.
Appointment of Sullivan: "Education Notes." *NYT*, October 30, 1912.
"report it was very doubtful . . .": *New York Chamber of Commerce Proceedings*, 1914, 18.
Background on Jacob Miller: *Transactions of the Society of Naval Architects and Marine Engineers*, v. 26. "Com. J.W. Miller Dies of Pneumonia," *NYT*, March 9, 1918.
"seemed friendly . . .": *New York Chamber of Commerce Proceedings*, 1914, 18.
Sullivan and Wile's move to disband the school: Untitled 1912 newsclippings— SBLLA. "It Costs City $14,550 to Make One Mariner," undated clipping—SBLLA.
"I have been at times . . ."; "**. . . that the pupils from this school . . .":** AR, 1912, 274. SBLLA.
"maritime fraternity": "Would Save Schoolship," *NYEP*, January, 23, 1913.
Movement to transfer school to state: *New York Chamber of Commerce Proceedings*, 1914, 19. "Want Nautical School Kept and Reorganized," *New York Globe*, January 15, 1913; "Urges Importance of Nautical School," *BE*, January 15, 1913.

Opinions of the press: "A State Nautical School," *NYH*, March 22, 1913. "A Brief Bit of Local History," *MJ*, February 7, 1914.

Blauvelt and McKee: *New York Red Book*, 86-87.

"the time is at hand": "Governor Sulzer Likes 'Port' and 'Starboard,'" *New York World*, undated clipping from Stephen B. Luce Library Archives.

Legislation transferring school to the State: New York. Laws of New York, 1913. Chap. 322.

"It will be our aim . . .": "On Board the Newport,"*MJ*, November 8, 1913.

"We are giving a child to a foster parent . . .": "Nautical School and the Newport Taken by State," *NYH*, November 2, 1913.

CHAPTER 7: "WE ARE ALL DIRTY IN CONSEQUENCE"

Information on the Board of Governors: New York. Laws of New York, 1913. Chap. 322. Full Roster of the Board of Governors can be found in the *Minutes*, 1913; AR, 1914. SBLLA.

Miller's speech and the early plans of the NY State Nautical School: *Minutes*, August 5, 1913. SBLLA

Background of James Driggs: "Schoolship Graduates that have Made Good as Merchant Mariners and as Business Men Ashore," *MJ*, February 9, 1914.–Clipping, SBLLA

"This is a red-letter day . . .": "An Event of Interest," *MJ*, November 1, 1913.–Clipping, SBLLA.

The *Hartford*; federal appropriation: 1914 AR, 12-14. SBLLA.

The *Newport*'s Hudson Valley Tour: "The Newport Arrived in this City To-day," *Albany Journal*, May 14, 1914. State Sailors Get Library in Albany," *Knickerbocker Press*, May 16, 1914. 1914 AR, 18. SBLLA;

The Cruise of 1914: "Old Warship Brings Rhode Islanders from France," *The Sunday Tribune–Providence*, September 6, 1914. "Brought Home on Gunboat," *NYT*, September 6, 1914.

The Refugees: "Will not Make Report on Nautical Ship Matter," clipping from September 12, 1914–SBLLA; 1914 AR, 20.

"quit the sea altogether": Letter from Frederick S. McMurray to his Mother, March 27, 1914. SBLLA.

Desertion of cadets: Minutes 1914-1915. SBLLA

Frederick McMurray's youth, desire to go to sea and admission into the NYNS: Frederick S. McMurray, "Learning the Ropes." FSMP. "The Nautical Schoolship 'St. Mary's' FSMP.

McMurray's adventures in Ponta Delgada: Frederick McMurray, "Boatswain William Dreilick, A Sailorman," FSMP, 1952, SBLLA.

McMurray as an Instructor on the *St. Mary's*: Frederick S. McMurray, Correspondence with mother, February 27, 1903. FSMP

McMurray's career: "F.S. M'Murray, 79, Ship Master, Dies," *NYT*, September 27, 1958.

Panama Canal: AR, 1915, 13. SBLLA.
The voyage to Hawaii: "Boys in Big Storm Trim Ship Like Tars," *NYT*, August 1, 1915.
"The day the San Mateo...": "New York State Nautical Cadets Bring Training Ship to Port," *The Pacific Commercial Advisor*, July 8, 1915.
Visiting Hawaii; McMurray's comments: "Training Ship Newport Pays Surprise Visit," *Hawaii Herald*, July 2, 1915. Frederick S. McMurray, Correspondence with mother, July 3, 1915. FSMP. AR, 1915, 29. SBLLA.
"The wind calls...": "California Must have Nautical Training School," *The San Francisco Call*, January 31, 1915. Clipping, SBLLA.
"When one considers...": "A Suggestion Worth Considering," *The San Diego Union*, undated. Clipping, SBLLA.
"better off without them...": Letter from Frederick S. McMurray to his Mother, July 3, 1915. FSMP.
The Panama Canal Landslide: AR, 1915, 18-20.
McMurray's proposal to send a class of new recruits to Balboa; "the Board has evidently...": Frederick S. McMurray, Correspondence with mother. October 13, 1915. FSMP.
"They are constantly at some work or other...": Frederick S. McMurray, Correspondence with mother. October 15, 1915. FSMP.
"We could practice one day": "New York Cadets End Eight Month Sail in Ship-Shape," *New York World*, January 3, 1916.
"We have no cold storage system": AR, 1915, 29. SBLLA.
Reopening of Canal: New York Cadets End Eight Month Sail in Ship-Shape," *New York World*, January 3, 1916. SBLLA. AR, 1915, 29.
"In view of other and more pressing...": "Whitman Urges State to Save," *NYT*, January 6, 1916.
"when the prospects...": "Alumni Fight in Nautical School," *New York Globe*, February 17, 1916.
Supplying small arms: AR, 1916, 9. SBLLA.
Protests against closure: "Albany Shadow Over the State Nautical School," *New York World*, February 13, 1916. "Want Nautical School Retained," *New York Globe*, February 21, 1916. Minutes, 1913 to 1919, 249-253. SBLLA. "Many Plead to Whitman for the Nautical School," *New York World*, February 14, 1916.
"The Japanese laughed at us...": "Attack Governor for Turning Back on the Newport," *NYH*, February 20, 1916.
Victory in abolition crisis for Nautical School; Whitman's comments: "Fight for N.Y. Naval School Believed Won," *Sun*, March 1, 1916. Whitman, 721.
Age regulation changes: Steamboat Inspection Service, 132.
Appropriation payments: U.S., Congress, *An Act Making Appropriations for the Naval Service for the Fistcal Year Ending June 30, 1917.* H.R. 15947, 64th Congress, August 29, 1916.
Efforts by Board of Governors to institute further changes: AR, 1916, 6. SBLLA.
Cruise of 1916: AR, 1917, 10-11. SBLLA.
"the additional necessity of men...": AR, 1917, 12-13. SBLLA.

Depression and resignation of Frederick McMurray: Frederick S. McMurray, Correspondence with mother, May 11, 1917; May 23, 1917; June 1, 1917. FSMP; *Minutes*, September 22, 1916. SBLLA. 1917 AR, 12–13. SBLLA.

CHAPTER 8: THE AGE OF RIESENBERG

Biographical Information on Felix Riesenberg: Riesenberg, *Living Again*.
"salty and race . . . a delight to many readers": "This Captain Likes the Sea," *NYT*, March 28, 1937.
$1,000 for his invention of the fountain pen sac: "This Captain Likes the Sea," *NYT*, March 28, 1937.
Move to the 129th Street pier; deal with Columbia University: AR, 1917, 7. SBLLA.
The iceberg incident: "Iceberg Wrecks Piers and Plays Havoc in Harbor," *NYH*. March 7, 1918.'; "The Great Iceberg," undated newspaper clipping from the SBLLA. Riesenberg, *Living Again*. 242.
On Lewis M. Weber: "Schoolship Cook Regales Cadets with French Pastry," *The Evening Mail*, March 8, 1918; "Schoolship's Galley King Lost to Heartless Army," *The Evening Mail*, March 16, 1918.
Riesenberg's resignation and Decision to go to **National** Marine: *Minutes*, March 11, 1919. SBLLA. Riesenberg, *Living Again*, 255.
On the skills of Sheridan: J. Kopec, *Cruise of 1915*. SBLLA.
"There is nothing in the world . . ."; boxing abilities: "Capt. Thomas Sheridan Dies," *NYT*, June 28, 1964.
Eilman case: *Minutes*, May 1, 1917. SBLLA.
Sheridan's proposals and acceptance; cruise to the Great Lakes: *Minutes*, May 13, 1919. SBLLA. AR, 1919, AR, 10–12. SBLLA.
Corporal punishment case: *Minutes*, October 22, 1919. SBLLA.
"capable young officer": AR, 1919, 16. SBLLA.
Paul Grening and the rescue of the *Ignazio Florio*: "Cheers Greet Liner and 28 She Rescued," *NYT*. October 28, 1925. Peter Vischer, "How an Invisible Lifeline Rescues Men from the Sea," *Popular Mechanics*, January, 1926. Boyden Sparkes, "The Voices of Ships," *Popular Mechanics*. February, 1926. "Sea has no Secrets for Harding Captain," *NYEP*. October 28, 1925. "America's New Sea Hero," *NYT*. November 1, 1925. "Sea has no Secrets for Harding Captain," *NYEP*. October 28, 1925. Riesenberg Jr.
Cruise of 1920; Tode's touring of engineering facilities: AR, 1920. SBLLA.
End of the two-cruise per year experiment: AR, 1920, 5. SBLLA.
Abolition crisis of 1921: "Old Salts Rally to Save Sea School," *New York Times* February 24, 1921. "Sailors Try to Save Sea School," *NYEP*, February 24, 1921.
Baylis before the Congress arguing for support of the Nautical schools: United States. Cong. House of Representatives. Hearings before the Committee on Naval Affairs of the House of Representatives on Sundry Legislation Affecting the Naval Establishement. Marine Schools 67th Cong., 1st sess. Washington: GPO, 1922.
"obtain a suitable site ashore": AR, 1919, 22–23. SBLLA

"dignified place": *Letter to Arthur M. Tode from John S. Baylis*, December 1, 1923. AMTP.
"This location is particularly desirable...": AR, 1922, 8. SBLLA.
Baylis claiming credit for transferring the school to the Education Department: *Letter to Arthur M. Tode from John S. Baylis*, December 1, 1923. AMTP.
May, 1923 law: "Smith Wants Curb Put on Rent Laws," *NYT.* May 23, 1923.
1917 Inspection of the *Newport*: Board of Inspection and Survey, "Newport–Report of Inspection held January 12, 1917," January 15, 1917. AMTP. Board of Inspection and Survey. "Newport–Report of Material Inspection," March 17, 1917. AMTP.
"The paid crew on board the *Newport*"; "Due to lack of funds...": *Letter to the Alumni Association from Arthur M. Tode*, December 8, 1923. AMTP.
"good points" of Baylis administration: *Letter to Arthur M. Tode from John S. Baylis*, December 1, 1923. AMTP.
Board of Governor's intention to hire Boesch: Minutes, May 3, 1923. SBLLA.
"tired of the shore": Riesenberg, *Living Again*, 255.
"The old girl...": Riesenberg, *Living Again*, 256–257.
"quite a few on board who needed to be fired.": Riesenberg, *Living Again*, 257.
1923 Inspection of the *Newport*: Board of Inspection and Survey. "Newport–Report of Material Inspection," June 26, 1923. AMTP.
"that unless there was improvement...": "In the Matter of the New York State Nautical School U.S.S. 'Newport'" Office of the Board of Governors. AMTP.
"If the *Newport* had been any other ship...": *Living Again*, 257.
"Two-year cadets...": *Living Again*, 258.
"A concerted movement...": "In the Matter of the New York State Nautical School U.S.S. 'Newport,'"AMTP.
"ablest shipmates": Riesenberg, *Living Again*, 260.
Riesenberg's request to remove the propeller and make the cruise under sail: Riesenberg, *Living Again*, 260.
"If they return I'll be happy.": "State Training Vessel Likely to Sink, Expert Says." *NYDN*, July 28, 1923.
Riesenberg's suspicions of Tode: "In the Matter of the New York State Nautical School U.S.S. 'Newport,'" AMTP.
Riesenberg announcing he would bring his sons: Riesenberg, *Living Again*, 260.
"I'll bring her home clean": Riesenberg, *Living Again*, 260.
Preparing for the 1923 cruise and departure: Riesenberg, *Living Again*, 261. AR, 11.
Riesenberg's sons' behavior: A.A. Bombe, *1923 Cruise of the Newport*. SBLLA.
Narrative of the cruise of 1923: Riesenberg, *Living Again*, 263–273.
"the *Newport* has been thoroughly overhauled...": AR, 1925, 5. SBLLA.
Tode's document including the hearings; the Clothing Fund: "In the Matter of the New York State Nautical School U.S.S. 'Newport.'" AMTP.
Tode's correspondence with James Sullivan: *Letter to Arthur M. Tode from James Sullivan*, March 26, 1924. AMTP. *Letter to Dr. James Sullivan from Arthur M. Tode*, April 8, 1924. AMTP. *Letter to Arthur M. Tode from James Sullivan*, April 12, 1924. AMTP.
Tode's career after the hearings: "Arthur M. Tode is Dead at 72; Supporter of the Merchant Marine." *NYT.* October 14, 1966.

Career of John S. Baylis: "John S. Baylis, 86, Commodore, Dies." *NYT.* November 25, 1971. "Blame for S-4 Loss Put upon both Ships by Naval Court," *NYT*, February 22, 1928.
Herbert Bridgman: "Herbert Bridgman Dies at Sea," *NYT*, September 27, 1924.
"had enough trouble with Tode . . .": Robert G. Herbert, "To correct and replace pages 80 through 84 of Centennial History of the SUNY Maritime College at Fort Schuyler, a Thesis by Norman J. Brouwer," 1977. SBLLA. Herbert was a cadet aboard the cruise of 1923.
Creation of the Board of Visitors: N.Y. Legislature, *An Act to Amend the State Departments Act by Providing for an Education Department and Assigning to it Certain Functions of the State Government*, 149th Session., Chap. 322, April, 22, 1926.
Administrative reforms: *Minutes*, May 21, 1925. SBLLA.
U.S. Navy's insistence on a Naval or Coast Guard Officer to head the school: *Minutes*, February 19, 1925. SBLLA.
Recommendation of Thomas Sheridan: *Minutes*, November 10, 1927. SBLLA.
Keen's joining the Board of Visitors: *Minutes*, May 6, 1927. SBLLA.
"That this Board . . .": *Minutes*, May 19, 1927. SBLLA.

CHAPTER 9: COMING ASHORE

Naval Career of James Tomb: "Capt. Tomb Dies; Led War Seamen." *NYT*, September 24, 1946.
"He's a sea dog of the doggiest type. . . .": *The New Orleans States*, July 8, 1932. From a news clipping, SBLLA.
"Several of us were detailed . . .": Edward F. Carter, *Tall Ship Tales*, SBLLA, 20.
"American merchant marine literature . . .": 1930 AR, 14. SBLLA.
"eliminate the reformatory idea . . .": 1928 AR, 8. SBLLA.
Change of name to the New York State Merchant Marine Academy: N.Y. Legislature, *An Act to Amend the Education Law, in Relationship to the Change in Name of the NY State Nautical School and Qualifications for the Admission Thereto*, 152nd sess., chap. 6, February 8, 1929.
"We haven't time for sails anymore . . .": "Famous Sailing Vessel on her Death March," *San Diego Sun*, June 13, 1931. From a news clipping. SBLLA.
Acquisition of the *Procyon*: AR, 1931, 8. SBLLA.
Legalization of the admission of out-of-state students: AR, 1931, 8.
About the *Procyon*: *Dictonary of American Naval Fighting Ships*. See entry on the Procyon. Also see ARs.
"much impressed . . .": James H. Tomb, *The Saga of Fort Schuyler*, 1943, 1.
Relocation to the Brooklyn Navy Yard: AR, 1929, 8. SBLLA.
Guilford D. Pendleton: Bureau of Navigation, *Fifty-Second Annual List of Merchant Vessels of the United States*, Government Printing Office, Washington, 1920, 120. The *Pendleton* is also entered into the merchant vessel lists of the American Bureau of Shipping.
Change of name to the *Annex*: AR, 1930 AR, 9. SBLLA.

"Godsend but inadequate . . .": *The Saga of Fort Schuyler*, 1. SBLLA.
"Modern life at sea . . .": AR, 1933, SBLLA.
Third System of Coastal Defense: Robinson,, 85.
Tactical value of Fort Schuyler: Records of War Dept. MFI pg. 1. SBLLA. Taken from note cards transcribed by Terrance Hoverter, circa 1951. *Register of Debates in Congress Comprising the Leading Debates and Incidents of the First Session of the Nineteenth Congress*. Washington: Gales & Seaton, 1826. 794-795.
Purchase of Fort Schuyler: "Relative to the Purchase of Throg's Point, on Long Island, for a Fortification." *Military Affairs*, V. 3, 1823-1828, 224-227.
Construction of Fort Schuyler: Fort Schuyler. HABS NY 3—Bronx. No. 4-30. *Historic American Buildings Survey*. Digitized by the Library of Congress.
The decline of Fort Schuyler: Cook. "Squad and Mules Hold Fort Schuyler," *NYT*. July 3, 1911.
"most beautiful three mile walk": "Throgs Neck Offers a Delightful One-Day Outing," *NYT*. August 31, 1913.
Fort Schuyler used as a movie set: Charles Ferreira, Undated Manuscript, 13. SBLLA. Ferreira was the last lighthouse keeper of the Throgs Neck Light and became an authority in local history. Before his death he was interviewed extensively by President Calvin Durgin.
Tomb learning about the availability of the Fort: *The Saga of Fort Schuyler*, 2. SBLLA.
"ideal site": *Minutes*, October 18, 1928. SBLLA.
Examination of other sites: *The Saga of Fort Schuyler*, 2.
"the army to close the base": Caro, 305.
Roosevelt's 1929 letter: *Correspondence from Franklin D. Roosevelt to James W. Good*, April 2, 1929. Papers of the Marine Society of the City of New York.
Parks Association's desire to take the Fort: "Seeks Public Park at Fort Schuyler," *NYT*, December 24, 1931.
Deal offered by the War Department; "By having the Academy there . . .": "War Dept. Ready to Yield Ft. Schuyler for Park, But Seeks Academy Space," *NYH*, June 5, 1932.
"Depriving residents . . .": "Bronx Chamber and Board of Trade Renew Clash on Use of Ft. Schuyler," *NYT*, June 7, 1932.
"being offered the best . . .": "Dolan Considers War Dept. Offer of Ft. Schuyler for Park and Academy," *NYT*, June 9, 1932.
"a few well-meaning . . .": "Urges Park be Made of Fort Schuyler." *NYT*, June 24, 1932.
"city fathers of past generations . . .": "War Dept. Ready to Yield Ft. Schuyler for Park, But Seeks Academy Space," *NYH*. June 5, 1932.
"The campaign was not fair . . ."; Mand's letter: *The Saga of Fort Schuyler*, 3. SBLLA.
Roosevelt's letter responding to Mand: Winston Murril, "Bronx Citizens Up in Arms Over Roosevelt Support of Transfer of Throggs Neck Land, Wanted for Park, to Marine Academy," *NYWT*, August 8, 1932.
Roosevelt ordering all correspondence go through him: *The Saga of Fort Schuyler*, 3. SBLLA.

Roosevelt switching stances: "Putting Marine Base in Park would be Public Outrage, G.F. Mand Tells Governor," *NYWT*, August 14, 1932.

"the value of our merchant marine": "Twenty Acres of Fort Schuyler for the New York State Merchant Marine Academy," *Maritime Exchange Bulletin*, July, 1932.

"It is not clear to us...": "Mand Spurns Plea by Maritime Exchange for Naval Academy Base at Ft. Schuyler," *Bronx Home News*, July 7, 1932.

"The Merchant Marine Academy has an enrollment...": "Opposes Dividing Ft. Schuyler Site," *NYT*, July 8, 1932.

"number of licensed merchant marine..."; suggestion to use Clason's Point: "Straus Appeals to Secretary of War for Adequate Park at Fort Schuyler," *Bronx News*. July 18, 1932.

"the State would not assume...": *The Saga of Fort Schuyler*, 4. SBLLA.

"It can hardly be disputed...": "A Fort Schuyler Park," *NYT*, December 21, 1932.

"Something similar to Jones Beach...": "Make Fort Schuyler a Park," *NYDN*, July 25, 1932.

"Fort Schuyler is the best possible...": "Governor Roosevelt and Fort Schuyler," *Bronx Home News*, July 22, 1932.

"I think that those who favor...": "Throggs Base is Disapproved by Naval Tutor," *NYWT*, August 12, 1932.

Editorial against NYSMMA: "Little Argument Left," *NYWT*, August 13, 1932.

Public opinion, Summer of 1932: *The Saga of Fort Schuyler*, 6. SBLLA.

"was looking a gift horse..."; "It is planned...": "Fort Schuyler Row Draws Warning," *NYWT*. August 19, 1932.

"dispute the value of...": Tomb, 1283.

Delegation of park proponents: *The Saga of Fort Schuyler*, 5. SBLLA.

Hurley informing McKee about lease: "City Loses Fight for Fort Schuyler," *NYT*, December 16, 1932.

Tomb's failure to meet with Lehman: *The Saga of Fort Schuyler*, 6.

"The signing by Gov. Roosevelt...": "Ft. Schuyler Park Forces Confident Despite Roosevelt Lease Signature," *Bronx Home News*, January 14, 1933.

Voiding of Roosevelt lease: *The Saga of Fort Schuyler*, 6.

"arrogant when administering discipline...": Minutes, September 19, 1933.

The rescue of the *Gumersindo*: "Rescue of the Drifter 'GUMERSINDO,'" August 5, 1933. SBLLA.

Frank Bell's comments: *Bulletin of the Alumni Association, New York State Maritime College*, July, 1973. SBLLA.

"definitely opposed to any move...": "Throggs Neck Civics Fight Park Plan," *Harlem-Bronx Journal*, January 28, 1933.

"Property owners in the immediate...": "O'Brien at Albany Pleads for Park," *NYT*, April 28, 1933.

New law to let NYSMMA operate ashore: *The Saga of Fort Schuyler*, 7. SBLLA.

On Lewis Wilson: "Dr Lewis Wilson, Education Chief," *NYT*, May 6, 1969.

"The bill would not be introduced..."; passing of the legislation: *The Saga of Fort Schuyler*, 6. SBLLA.

Tomb's manner of oration: J.H. Tomb, *Letter from J.H. Tomb to John H. Boesch*, April 5, 1934. SBLLA.
Support of the Throggs Neck Property Owners Association: *The Saga of Fort Schuyler*, 4. SBLLA.
"I am not much of a politician . . .": J.H. Tomb, *Letter from J.H. Tomb to Rear Admiral William T. Tarrant*, January 25, 1934. SBLLA.
R.J. Baker: Tomb, *The Saga of Fort Schuyler*, 8. SBLLA.
"This bill is merely permissive . . .": "Marine Base Bill Signed by Lehman," NYT, May 8, 1933.
"a reasonable solution to the problem": "Lehman Settles Ft. Schuyler Row," NYT, March 14, 1934.
$600: *Minutes*, September 19, 1933. SBLLA.
Lease stipulations: *The Saga of Fort Schuyler*, 8. SBLLA.
Need for a modern pier: *The Saga of Fort Schuyler*, 8. SBLLA.
Cost of new pier: *Minutes*, April 17, 1934. SBLLA. AR, 1934, 17. SBLLA.
Work under TERA: *The Saga of Fort Schuyler*, 9. SBLLA. *Minutes*, March 19, 1935. SBLLA.
Start of construction of new pier: *Minutes*, December 15, 1936. SBLLA.
Slow progress in reconstruction efforts: *The Saga of Fort Schuyler*, 9. SBLLA.
"weak sister supervisors . . .": *Minutes*, March 19, 1935. SBLLA.
Increase in worker output: *Minutes*, March 19, 1935. SBLLA.
$1,752,270 grant: *Minutes*, October 22, 1935. SBLLA.
December, 1935 work: *Minutes*, June 7, 1935. SBLLA.
Completion of pier, etc: "New Home is Begun for Marine School," NYT. December 7, 1935.
"The magnitude of the work . . ."; the *Leviathan*: *The Saga of Fort Schuyler*, 10. SBLLA.
Increase of WPA grant: J.H. Tomb, *Letter from J.H. Tomb to Adm. David F. Sellers*, March 23, 1936; Information also from the 1935–36 Annual Report. SBLLA.
"on 1 August, 1936 . . .": *The Saga of Fort Schuyler*, 10. SBLLA.
"1,004 men in all classifications . . .": *Minutes*, April 28, 1936. SBLLA.
"in spite of my desire . . .": *Minutes*, May 19, 1936. Letter by Franklin D. Roosevelt to Governor Lehman attached. SBLLA.
Slowness of construction due to War Department: *Minutes*, January 21, 1936. SBLLA.
Dynamiting of wall; "there was the deuce to pay . . ."; insulting letter from Moses: *The Saga of Fort Schuyler*, 10–11. SBLLA.
Roosevelt not supporting transfer of ownership: "J.H. Tomb, *Letter from J.H. Tomb to Captain Milan L. Pittman*, 26 March, 1937. SBLLA. **War department concerned with other federal property sites:** J.H. Tomb, *Letter from J.H. Tomb to Lewis A. Wilson*, 6 April, 1937. SBLLA.
"if this is not eliminated . . .": J.H. Tomb, *Letter from J.H. Tomb to Royal S. Copeland and Letter to James M. Fitzpatrick*, 14 June, 1937. SBLLA.
25 year lease: *The Saga of Fort Schuyler*, 10–11.
". . . very powerful politically . . .": J.H. Tomb *Letter from J.H. Tomb to Rear Admiral H.G. Hamlet*, 29 June, 1937. SBLLA.

NYSMMA taking permanent control of park section of Fort Schuyler: *Minutes*, January 20, 1942. SBLLA.

CHAPTER 10: THE FEDERAL PROGRAM

1930 Questionnaire: "Answers to Questionnaire Submitted to Various Organizations by the Third National Merchant Marine Conference Committee on Training Merchant Marine Officers," *Proceedings of the State Maritime Academies Conference*, September 6, 1945. SBLLA.
"Fundamental Principles"; federal subsidy: *Minutes*, January, 1936. SBLLA.
Hoffman and Swinburn Islands: "Ready for New Students," *NYT*, May 29, 1939.
Fort Trumbell: "Merchant Marine School to begin Classes Monday", *The Day*, February 4, 1939.
Federal Corps at Fort Schuyler: *Minutes*, December 6, 1939. SBLLA.
Renaming to NYSMA: *Minutes*, November 18, 1941. SBLLA.
"virtually ignored"; training quotas: "Panel Discussion on State Maritime Academies," *Proceedings of the American Merchant Marine Conference*. 1942–1943, 99. SBLLA.
Establishment of the Academy at Kings Point: Cruishank and Kline; Norman Queen, "State Maritime Academies" *Proceedings of the American Merchant Marine Conference*, 1944, 282. SBLLA.
Growing hostility of state academies to the federal training program: "Panel Discussion on State Maritime Academies," *Proceedings of the American Merchant Marine Conference*, 1942–1943. 102–103. SBLLA.
"first loyalty": *Minutes*, April 1, 1942.
Vision problems: "Capt. Tomb to Quit Marine School Job," *NYT*, October 10, 1943.
"oh it doesn't matter what I'm doing . . .": Cadet-Midshipman Raymond Weil, "An Interview with Captain Tomb," *Polaris*, October, 1944. Quoted from Cruishank, 116. This was a USMMA publication—did Tomb prefer the USMMA over the NYSMA? This question is best answered by saying that Tomb, above all else, was committed to Nautical Education.
Death of Tomb: "Capt. Tomb Dies; Led War Seamen," *NYT*, September 24, 1946.
Recommendation of Schutz: *Minutes*, April 1, 1942. SBLLA.
List of admirals; Tode's response: *Minutes*, April 8, 1942. SBLLA. Letter is attached to minutes..
Career of T.T. Craven: *Bosun's Pipe*, February, 1946, 1. SBLLA..
"later seek a younger man": *Minutes*, April 8, 1942. SBLLA.
Nicknames of Craven; "You feed 'em, I'll work 'em.": Hess, 37.
". . . I do not prefer to be idle . . .": *Minutes*, April 13, 1942.
Development of NYSMA under Craven: *Bosuns Pipe*, February, 1946, 1.
Dilloway's Story: Interview with Phylipp Dilloway..
"None of [the cadets] had ever seen . . .": *Eight Bells*, 1942, 91–94. SBLLA.
"A snail leaving . . .": *Eight Bells*, 1942, 95. SBLLA.
"That does not make for contentment . . .": *Minutes*, November 17, 1942. SBLLA.
"Looseness and lack of coordination . . .": *The War Shipping Administration Division of Training Conference*, January 7, 1943, 11. SBLLA.

Craven on the ship-sharing plan: AR, 1943, 12. SBLLA
Knight's regret: *The War Shipping Administration Division of Training Conference*, January 7, 1943, 13. SBLLA.
Fort Schuyler grounds during the war: *Minutes*, November 5, 1945. SBLLA
90-day wonder school: Interview with Phylipp Dilloway.
"Expedite the prosecution of the war effort": Executive Order no. 9083, February 28, 1942.
"It would be very unfortunate . . ."; "Properly a Federal, not a State function": *Minutes*, June 17, 1942. SBLLA.
"If the federal government is going to pay . . .": *Minutes*, April 8, 1942. SBLLA.
Coast Guard subsidy promises: *Minutes*, June 17, 1942. SBLLA.
Transfer to WSA: "Panel Discussion on State Maritime Academies," *Proceedings of the American Merchant Marine Conference*. 1942–1943, 100. SBLLA.
Federal advertising for training program: "Meeting of State Maritime Academy Officials" *State Maritime Academies Conference*, October 18, 1944 at the Waldorf-Astoria, 45. SBLLA.
Federal subsidy for state cadets: AR, 1942–43, 12. SBLLA.
"all shot to pieces . . .": "Panel Discussion on State Maritime Academies," *Proceedings of the American Merchant Marine Conference*. 1942–1943. 100. SBLLA.
"can't compete with the federal . . .": "Panel Discussion on State Maritime Academies," *Proceedings of the American Merchant Marine Conference*. 1942–1943, 105.
"No intention in peacetime . . .": ""Panel Discussion on State Maritime Academies," *Proceedings of the American Merchant Marine Conference*. 1942–1943, 111.
"tremendous problem": Thomas T. Craven, "Some Problems Affecting the Training Program." *Proceedings American Merchant Marine Conference*. 1944, 285. SBLLA
Summary of WWII program: *Minutes*, 1945, 1. SBLLA. *Minutes, Superintendents Report*, June 30, 1945. SBLLA.

CHAPTER 11: EIGHTEEN MONTHS BEFORE THE MAST
Commissions and ages: "The Way we Were," *PH*, May, 1980.
"overwhelmed with applications": *Minutes*, July 21, 1944. SBLLA
Number of graduates during the World War II period: ARs, 1941 to 1946. SBLLA. (various figures and data drawn from the reports)
"Craven's Haven for Draft Dodgers": Anonymous 1946 graduate interviewed in the Fall, 2011.
World War II Merchant Marine Casualties: U.S. Coast Guard, *Summary of Merchant Marine Personnel Casualties, World War II*. July 1, 1950. Moore.
"Program offered the best long-term . . .": Interview with Charles Strommer. 2011.
Dilloway's story: Interview with Phylipp Dilloway, 2011. SBLLA.
"major hazing": *Interview with Leonard Weiss*, 2011. SBLLA.
"what we would call . . .": Interview with Richard Kadison and Arthur Murray, 2011..
Strommer's father-in-law, Claude E. Jones who was expelled for skinny dipping. See *Conduct Books*, SBLLA.

"If we were going to crack . . .": Interview with Richard Kadison and Arthur Murray.
"Lessened the importance": Interview with Phylipp Dilloway, 2011. SBLLA. Correspondence with Phylipp Dilloway, April 8, 2011.
"This was my opportunity . . .": Interview with Robert Barr.
Military induction: *Boson's Pipe*, May, 1945, 4.
"More or less of a degrading . . .": "Do You Remember?" *PH*, March 2, 1961. This is a reprint from the 1946 yearbook.
George Riser: *Eight Bells*, 1943. SBLLA.
"Model of Sartorial Splendor": Fred Hess, *Fort Schuyler and Me*, 55.
"Now listen to me . . .": NFFS, May 13, 1999. Vol 3, no. 25. http://www.fsmaa.org/NFFS/1999/nf990513.cfm
"If you bunch of lolly-gagging . . .": Sutter, 105–106.
"If you smiled . . .": Interview with Robert Barr.
"There was everything from Naval Orientation . . .": Interview with Phylipp Dilloway.
". . . a spectacular sight . . .": Interview with Richard Kadison and Arthur Murray
"Why are you around so much?": Interview with Phylipp Dilloway.
"We've been exempted from war.": *Bosun's Pipe*, vol 1, number 5, January, 1946.
Places that cadets would take liberty: *Bosun's Pipe*, Summer, 1945. *Bosun's Pipe*, vol 1, number 1, May 1945, 8.
"Liberty at the Square": "Liberty at the Square" *Bosun's Pipe*, September, 1945
"Every afternoon . . .": *Bosun's Pipe*, Summer, 1945.
"In a Qualified Sense . . .": Bosun's Pipe, January, 1946.
Letter from Margaret Scharpf: *Bosun's Pipe*, Summer, 1945, 5.
Clarence Holm's story: *Bosun's Pipe*, December, 1945
Walter Hesse's story: Hesse, Walter H. "Convoy to Murmansk—PQ 15," SBLLA.
War dead: *Bosun's Pipe*, Summer 1945, 3.
Death of Craven: "Admiral Craven dies in Hospital", *NYT*, April 7, 1950.
"Suddenly one summer evening . . .": *Bosun's Pipe*, vol 1, number 5, January, 1946.

CHAPTER 12: THE ANNAPOLIS OF THE MERCHANT MARINE

Tension and problems between the Federal Government and State Academies: "Meeting of State Maritime Academy Officials" *State Maritime Academies Conference*. The Waldorf-Astoria, New York, October 18, 1944. SBLLA. *State Maritime Academies Conference*. Fort Schuyler, NY, September 6, 1945. SBLLA. "Panel on Training Program" *American Merchant Marine Conference*. Waldorf-Astoria, NY, October 19, 1944, 60. SBLLA.
"Why should the federal government have . . .": *Minutes*, January 31, 1945.
"How are we to mobilize our strength . . .": *Minutes*, July 21, 1944.
"embrace the whole field . . .": AR, 1932, 10.
Three year program: AR, 1939–1940, 12.
"Should we not . . .": AR, 1941–42.
Cartoon and McNiece's article: *Bosun's Pipe*, Vol. 1, no. 2, 5.
Developing a college curriculum: *Minutes*, January 28, 1943. *Minutes*, April 26, 1944. *Minutes*, July 21, 1944. SBLLA.

"finest diesel and electric shop . . .": *Minutes*, November 28, 1944. SBLLA.
Transfer of Fort Schuyler deed to New York State: *Minutes*, October 9, 1946. Presidents Report to the Board of Visitors for 31 January 1952 to 27 January 1953, found in *Minutes*, 1953. AR, *1948–1949*, 15. SBLLA. Public Law 85-260, September 2, 1957. Public Law 559, Chapter 884, July 16, 1952; Public Law 81-755, 64 Stat. 591, September 5, 1950.
Turnover of staff after World War II: *Minutes*, November, 5, 1945. SBLLA.
Record of Admiral Leary: "A Half Century of Service," *PH*, May 18, 1951.
Description of the character of Leary; "He strode across the pentagon . . .": Correspondence with Donald White, October 22, 2011. Hess.
"Bull" Halsey: Interview with David Cory.
"veritable treasure house . . .": *Bosun's Pipe*, Volume 1, Number 5, January, 1946, 1.
The *Balfour*: *PH*, December 22, 1949.
Record of the *Hydrus*: *Dictionary of American Naval Fighting Ships*. See entry for "Hydrus."
Conversion of the Hydrus to a training ship: *Minutes*, May 13, 1946. SBLLA.
". . . arranged so that when one . . .": Donald White letter to parents June 3, 1946. SBLLA.
"quietly going nuts . . ." Donald White letter to Parents, August 3, 1946. SBLLA.
Bill Muir: Sutter, 98.
"no cases of drunkenness . . .": Superintendents Report May 14, 1946 to October 9, 1946 in 1946 *Minutes*, 2. SBLLA.
"take a great deal of time and money . . .": *Minutes*, October 9, 1946. SBLLA.
Upgrades to the *Empire State II*: *Minutes*, May 26, 1948. SBLLA.
"certain fundamental academic courses": Superintendents Report May 14, 1946 to October 9, 1946 in 1946 *Minutes*, 3. SBLLA.
"educated gentlemen": *Bosun's Pipe*, February, 1946, 1
"a nucleus composed of graduates": *Minutes*, May 13, 1946.
Return of alumni to earn a college degree: *Superintendent's Report to the Board of Visitors*, November 1, 1945 to May 13, 1946. In *Minutes*, 1946.
Albert Porter: *Minutes*, October 8, 1947. Hess, 48.
Olivet's career: "Captain Olivet Retires," *PH*, May 22, 1965.
Leary and Olivet: Hess, 46. NFFS, vol. 3 no. 7, January 27, 1999. http://www.fsmaa.org/NFFS/1999/nf990127.cfm
The Student Association: *PH*, November 9, 1951.
Origin of name Privateers: *PH*, December 12, 1952.
Matthew Twomey; sports program: "Champ," *PH*, March 10, 1950. *PH*, March 4, 1949; *PH*, March 11, 1971; *Guide to the Plaques of Maritime College*, 52. SBLLA.
Development of clubs and extracurricular activities: Information from various *Bosun Pipes* and *PHs* of the period.
Pershing Rifles: "Pershing Rifles Make Marching Worthwhile," *PH*, October 7, 1955.
Number of clubs: *Eight Bells*, 1956. SBLLA.
"extreme military discipline": *Minutes*, October 8, 1947. SBLLA.
Students standing at attention before class: Sutter, 86.
"Operating under legal terminology . . .": *Minutes*, January 20, 1947. SBLLA.

First graduate, Eugene Starbecker: *Minutes,* October 8, 1947. SBLLA.
Return of equipment: *Minutes,* October 8, 1947. SBLLA.
Cadet average: *Minutes,* Superintendent's Report, October 1946 to January, 1947. SBLLA.
"We are still struggling . . .": *Minutes,* January 5, 1948. SBLLA.
"The past year . . .": *Minutes,* May 26, 1948. SBLLA.
1949 Inspection: *Minutes,* January 14, 1949. SBLLA.
Registration of curriculum with the state: *PH,* March 10, 1950, 1. SBLLA.
"the term academy . . .": *Minutes,* January 14, 1949. SBLLA.
"Events have proved the wisdom . . .": *Minutes,* September 27, 1950.
Rumors of the college becoming a pure engineering school: *PH,* April 27, 1956).
"A very nice gentlemen . . .": Interview with Jose Femenia.
Educational Practices Act: Rice, 99–106.
Carl Burnett and Walter Branford: "Double Eagle Lines First Minority Steamship Company," *The Afro-American,* December 1981. Correspondence with Organization of Black Maritime Cadets, September 19, 2011.
"A true American never judges . . .": "Inquiring Reporter," *PH,* October 5, 1956.
Separate engineering degree: *Minutes,* December 16, 1949. SBLLA.
Middle States Review: *Minutes,* January 27, 1953. SBLLA.
Expansion of course offerings: *PH,* March 10, 1950. SBLLA.
Retirement of Leary: "A Half Century of Service," *PH,* May 18, 1951. SBLLA.

CHAPTER 13: "BUT MEN AND OFFICERS MUST OBEY"

Durgin landing by helicopter: "Admiral Durgin Lands for Lunch," *PH,* May 18, 1951.
Record of Durgin: "Calvin T. During, Retired Admiral," *NYT,* March 26, 1965. "Distinguished Naval Career," *PH,* March 15, 1958. Hess, 40.
"Civilized mind and personality": "Professor's Opinion," *PH,* April 10, 1965.
Durgin's acquaintances and relationships: Drawn from Hess, *Minutes* and personal correspondence.
First exchange student program: "Pakistanian Student Prefers Marine Eng.," *PH,* October 22, 1952 and "Pakistan Ambassador Presents Flag," *PH,* May 3, 1952.
"When I took this job": Letter to R. F. Larmour from C.T. Durgin, February 12, 1952. CTDP.
"At first there was a bit of opposition . . .": Letter by C.T. Durgin to William P. Penney, November 6, 1952. CTDP.
Durgin's attempt to change the Sallyport Saying: *PH,* May 14, 1952.
Hawespiper influence: *Minutes of the Parent's Association,* January 4, 1952. SBLLA.
Subsidy issue: Letter from C.T. Durgin to Vice Admiral Edward L. Cochrane. January 31, 1952. CTDP. "Green Light for Cadet Porters," *PH,* February 17, 1956. Letter from C.T. Durgin to Charles E. Bennett. February 11, 1952. CTDP
On the Parent's Association: "History and Achievements—Of the Parents Association," *PH,* April 26, 1958.—Note, this article lists the founding of the Association as 1950. However, the first mention of the Association in the student newspapers including its founding is in 1952. The date in this article is incorrect. *PH,* March 12, 1952.

Holloway plan proposal: Letter from C.T. Durgin to Charles E. Bennett. February 11, 1952. CTDP.
Durgin's interaction with Albert Thomas: Letter from C.T. Durgin to Ralph A. Leavitt, January 16, 1952. CTDP.
State academies' cost versus the federal academy cost: *Minutes*, January 27, 1953. SBLLA.
"Kings Point is my college . . .": Letter from C.T. Durgin to Ralph A. Leavitt, April 4, 1952. CTDP.
"Largely unqualified political appointee . . .": Cruishank, 157-158.
Meeting with Murray and aftermath: *Minutes*, January 27, 1953. "Clash Impends Over U.S. Proposal to Shut Kings Point Sea Academy," *NYT*, November 22, 1953. *Minutes*, January 27, 1953.
Permanency of Kings Point: Cruishank, 164.
Maritime Academy Act: "Subsidy Increase Announced," *PH*, October 25, 1958. "Maritime Commission Increases Subsidy," *PH*, October 12, 1959.
Operation Ram: "Tru Sport Does Feature on Mascots," *PH*, December 12, 1952. "Morgan Made Official Mascot," *PH*, December 12, 1952. "Tru Sport Staff on Jimmy Powers Television Show," *PH*, January 9, 1953.
Edward Villella's story: Villella, 29-33. Interview with Edward Villella, *NYT*, January 16, 2009.
"One of the cadet battalion officers . . .": Sutter, 94.
Dan Lynch's story: Lynch. SBLLA.
Tode's ouster from the College Council: "A Statement Prepared by Arthur M. Tode," AMTP.
Physical Plant development: *Minutes*, June 9, 1955. "Fort Schuyler Acquires Planetarium," *PH*, October 18, 1956.
"luxury liner": Correspondence with William Caldwell.
Throgs Neck Bridge: *Minutes*, October 17, 1957. SBLLA.
Landfill additions to campus: *Minutes*, June 26, 1956. SBLLA.
"The graduate of the future": *PH*, October 16, 1964.
Nuclear Lab: "SUMC Dedicates Nuclear Lab," *PH*, April, 22, 1960. AND "Nuclear Curriculum," *PH*, October 11, 1960.
Masters in Marine Science: "Graduate Program," *PH*, May 20, 1968.
Expansion of Curriculum: College Catalogs, various. SBLLA; "Expansion and Progress Highlight Administration," *PH*, March 15, 1958.
"New York had been thrown in a tizzy . . .": "Maria Callas Returns to Met in 'Tosca,'" *NYT*, March 20, 1965.
Death of Durgin: Hess. "Calvin T. Durgin, Retired Admiral," *NYT*, March 26, 1965.

CHAPTER 14: THE DOME

Poem at beginning of chapter: Anonymous, circa 1970. SBLLA.
Origin of the term "Dome": *NFFS* October 23, 2001. V. 5, no. 28. http://www.fsmaa.org/NFFS/2001/nf011023.cfm; Correspondence with Conrad Youngren. Bridge Log of the *Empire State IV*, 6/9/1969. SBLLA.

Moore as President Emeritus: "Adm. Moore named Pres. Emeritus," *PH*, October 14, 1967.
Career of O'Donnell: "Admiral O'Donnell New President," *PH*, April 18, 1967. Hess, 42.
"Piss in Your Shoe": Correspondence with Charlie Munsch.
"Heck of a nice guy . . .": Interview with Jose Femenia.
"I realize that the Maritime College . . .": *PH*, March 1, 1969.
Fact-finding committee; "Meet and carry out": *PH*, March 29, 1969.
Indoc practices: Interview with Richard Burke.
"I thought the indoctrination period . . .": Interview with Jose Femenia.
1963 questionnaire: "Academics at Maritime," *PH*, March 25, 1963.
"part-timers who know nothing . . .": "Looking Back," *PH*, March 25, 1963.
"almost nihilistic": "Evaluation of Maritime College," *PH*, March 25, 1963.
"Is there no more room for individualistic . . . ?": Eduard P. VanLoenen, "View from the Windmill," *PH*, November 11, 1967.
"Freedom of the press . . .": "A Meeting of the Admiral, the *Porthole* Editors, and their Faculty Advisor in October 1963." SBLLA.
"it should be noted that many . . .": The Case for Free Gangway," *PH*, February 17, 1968.
"This longing for the weekend . . .": " "The Weekend Syndrome," *PH*, November 23, 1968.
Vandalism: *PH*, November 23, 1968. "Honor," *PH*, February 21, 1970. "Telephones," *PH*, April 25, 1970.
"Oliver Stone look very comfortable": Joseph Hoffman interview and email from June 11, 2012.
Sennish at the SUNY Symposium: *Minutes*, 1969.
"People spend four years of their lives . . .": "Bob Sennish Comes Clean," *PH*, February, 1989.
Faculty protest letter: "Observations," *PH*, November 23, 1968,
"For these students to ask . . .": *PH*, December 1, 1965.
"Students for a victorious peace": "Loyalty Day at Maritime," *PH*, May 20, 1968.
Administration neutrality toward demonstrations: *Minutes*, May 20, 1968.
Vietnam Moratorium: *PH*, November 15, 1969.
"I am sure we are all proud . . .": pro-Vietnam petition: *PH*, November 15, 1969.
"Continued and future activities of divisiveness": *Minutes*, October 28, 1969.
Vietnam War opinion poll: "Vietnam Poll Results," *PH*, March 21, 1970.
Concessions made to students: "Campus Forum," *PH*, March 1, 1969.
1970 Referendum: "Referendum Results," *PH*, February 21, 1970.
Inconvenience of Saturday morning classes: Interview with James DeSimone
Faculty vote to do away with Saturday classes: *Faculty Meeting Minutes* of March 24, 1970, Minutes dated April 9, 1970. SBLLA.
Administration opinion on Saturday classes: *Minutes*, May 15, 1969. *PH*, October 19, 1968.
O'Donnell's refusal to meet with students: DeSimone interview.

"We the students . . .": "Maritime Voice"—undated circa 1970. SBLLA
Sit-in on O'Donnell's front lawn: DeSimone interview. David Hugh Brown, Jr. "What the Hell is Going on Here, Anyway?" 1970 pamphlet. SBLLA.
DeSimone's sign-off on the Moratorium: *Minutes,* 1969.
Goodman's letter: *Minutes, 1970.* Letter of O.B. Goodman to E.J. O'Donnell. May 12, 1970. SBLLA.
"eliminated at present": *Minutes of Faculty Meeting,* May 27, 1970.
Class cut policies: "Class Cuts," *PH,* April 22, 1971. Resolution of the Student Policies Committee, March 25, 1971. SBLLA. "Faculty Passes Class Cut Resolution," *PH,* April 26, 1972.
Uniforms and harassment by war protestors: Femenia Interview.
Beer at the TIV: "Beer," *PH,* December 3, 1971.
Cafeteria style dining: *PH,* December, 1972.
Swimming pool on the training ship: "Pool Added to TSES IV," *PH,* April 26, 1972.
Weakening of regimental structure: "Regimental Review Committee Reports," *PH,* November, 1982.
"In a military academy . . .": *PH,* December 3, 1971.
"There are many reasons . . .": "Editorial," *PH,* October 21, 1971.
Effect of personalities during period: Interview with Richard Burke.
"Many of you may question . . .": *PH,* May 15, 1971.
"It is the only proven way . . .": "The Dean's Place," *PH,* October 12, 1977.
"side benefits": Interview with James DeSimone.

CHAPTER 15: "THE WAY IT IS"

Philomena Magavero's story: Fitzpatrick, 66-75.
Promotion of Magavero: See 1959-1960 College Catalog SBLLA; AR, 1961-1962. SBLLA
"In a way I think . . .": Fitzpatrick, 66-75.
"NYSMA men have always . . .": *Bosun's Pipe,* Summer, 1945, 5
"Seventeen, Hot Rod Queen": "Seventeen, Hot Rod Queen," *PH,* October 5, 1956.
"Although several minor adjustments . . .": "Fort Schuyler Goes Coed?" *PH,* October 8, 1954.
"Imagine the dorms . . .": "Fort Schuyler Goes Co-Ed," *PH,* February 6, 1956.
"Believe it or not . . .": "Cadettes," *PH,* December 16, 1967.
On Helen Bentley: "7,500 Get Degrees at N.Y.U. Commencement," *NYT,* June 6, 1973.
"Why are you here?": Interview with Karen Markoe
"design the drapes": Interview with Marjorie Murtagh-Cooke
Operation Day Student: *PH,* March 1, 1969.
Not Physically Qualified classification: December 1971 Monthly Report. Maritime College Catalog, 1973-74.
Admission of Murtagh: "Maritime College Accepts First Woman," *NYT* June 29, 1972. and interview with Marjorie
Murtagh's experiences as a Maritime Student: Interview with Marjorie Murtagh-Cooke.

Admission of women into other academy licensing programs: *NYT*, February 23, 1974.
Number of female cadets: Correspondence with Karen Magliocca-Rocheteau, July 7, 2013. Correspondence with Colette Crowther, July 21, 2013.
"They were assimilated": Hess, 67.
"almost nothing but harassment": Interview with Richard Burke.
"If you wanted to go out and choose a group . . .": Interview with Joseph Hoffman.
Karen Magliocca's story: Correspondence with Karen Magliocca-Rocheteau, July 7, 2013.
Pranks on female cadets while on cruise: interview with Jose Femenia.
Accusations against female cadets: "Discontent with Females," *PH*, March 3, 1975.
"What no one seems to realize . . .": *PH*, April 12, 1976.
"After living through . . .": *PH*, February 23, 1976.
"No eccentricities . . .": "Female Grooming Regulations," *PH*, December 15, 1975.
"College Women Today": 1976 AR.
"Ladies of the Night": Markoe Interview.
Number of women in regiment: "Cites Major Flaws in Regiment," *PH*, November, 24, 1981.
1981 PH interviews of women cadets: "Women at Maritime Surveyed," *PH*, December 17, 1981.
"Fraternization works several ways . . .": "Fraternization," *PH*, October, 1988.
"I am so sick of the attitude . . .": "Unfair to Females . . ." *PH*, December, 1988.
"I find it rather appalling . . .": *PH*, April, 1983.
"The time at sea is a good . . .": "Recent '79 Grad Makes Good," *PH*, October, 1980.
Linda Malay; Alisa Zimmerman: "Female Cadet First Regimental Commander," *PH*, December, 1988.
Civilize the place: Interview with Richard Burke.
Wendi Carpenter: "Rear Admiral Wendi B. Carpenter, USN (Ret.)," *Marine News*, December, 2011.

CHAPTER 16: "A VERY ELEGANT MAN"

Story of the *Rebound*: "Well Taught, Well Learned," *PH*, November, 1987. Interviews with Frank Cuccio and Sean Kirby.
Biographical Information on Kinney: "Sheldon H. Kinney, 86, Dies; Commanded Ships in 3 Wars," *NYT*, January 11, 2005. Jim Maloney. "Remembering Sheldon Kinney," *Fort Schuyler Mariner*. March, 2005. 21-25.
Kinney and the *Bronstein*: Roscoe, 301. Hess. **"absolute gentleman":** Interview with Sean Kirby.
"a very elegant man": Interview with Karen Markoe.
Lack of enthusiasm to enroll in the college due to the Vietnam War: AR, 1971-1972. Interview with Jose Femenia.
Enrollment figures: See ARs for the period.
Deal with SUNY Purchase: 1973 AR.

100 Iranians on campus: 1974 AR.
Gift of Oil by the Shah: *Monthly Report*, August 6, 1974.
Kinney and Porter's visit to Iran: Monthly and Annual Reports, 1976.
"At first I thought I would like it . . .": "Foreign Students," *PH*, October 21, 1971.
Letters denouncing Iranians: *PH*, February, 1974.
Reaction to letters: *PH*, March, 1974.
"They all had much nicer cars . . .": Interview with Hartley Spatt.
Deportment of Iranians: AR, 1979-1980.
Recovery in enrollment: "From the President's Desk," *PH*, February 6, 1975. Data from *Trends in Enrollment and Degrees Granted: 1948-1999*. State University of New York, Report Number 7-00. November, 2000; http://www.suny.edu/provost/MissionReview/MR2/CAttachTable.htm
Remarks of Jose Femenia: Interview with Jose Femenia.
Growth of academic programs: 1971-1972 Annual Report. College Catalogs.
"The college received five applications . . ."; "excellent and rigorous education": 1979-1980 AR.
Praising the college by word of mouth: Interview with Jose Femenia.
Readmission data: "College Attrition Rate Down," *PH*, October 12, 1977.
Fort Schuyler Foundation: AR, 1979-1980; for the start of the foundation, see the 1977 *Annual and Monthly Reports*. SBLLA.
Activation of NROTC: *NFFS*, October 4, 1999. Vol 3. No. 46. http://www.fsmaa.org/NFFS/1999/nf991004.cfm
Increase to Federal Subsidy: "Subsidy Set Straight," *PH*, September, 1982.
"Offset to tuition differentials": 1977-1978 AR.
Demands for $1 million: "Adm. Kinney testifies," *PH*, February, 1980.
Acquisition and Conversion of *Empire State V*: "What Comes After Four?" *PH*, October, 1973. *Monthly Report*, November 5, 1973.

CHAPTER 17: "AS MILITARY AS MICKEY MOUSE"

Bar Scene; lack of recreational activities: "Local Dives," *PH*, October 4, 1985. "Life(?) at the Dome," *PH*, November 3, 1975.
Number of regulations: Rules and Regulations, 1968 and 1974. SBLLA.
Robert Berner's Story: Interview with Robert Berner.
"rather hard to take": "Inspection—HA!" *PH*, September, 1978.
"Why should we be forced . . . ?": *WEJ–Class of 1975*. *PH*, March 1973.
Streaking: "Maritime Outstreaks Kings Point," *PH*, March, 1974.
On Bill Tuthill: Correspondence with Conrad Youngren.
On Frank English: Correspondence Conrad Youngren.
On Robert Thompson: Interview with Robert Thompson.
"on both American and foreign . . .": "Admiral Takes Five Month Leave," *PH*, December 5, 1977.
Crackdown on the return of Kinney from sabbatical: "Campus Crackdown!" *PH*, September 1978.

"Providing a sound military atmosphere": "Trimble Speaks," *PH*, November, 1978
Appointment of tough regimental commander: "Campus Crackdown!" *PH*, September 1978.
Increase in vandalism and other incidents on campus: "The Year in Review," *PH*, December, 1978. "Dormitory Fires Endanger Students," *PH*, February, 1979.
George Previll's attitudes: "The Captain Logs His Views," *PH*, February, 1980.
Food during the World War II era: This is based on multiple interviews and correspondences with Alumni of the Classes of 1946 and 1947.
"My son tells me . . ."; "strived to give a plentiful . . .": *PH*, November 16, 1951.
Cockroaches in mess deck: *PH*, May 20, 1968.
"chew a little more carefully": *PH*, March 29, 1969.
On Charley Rey : *NFFS*, September 24, 1998–Volume 2, No. 44; *NFFS*, September 3, 1998–Volume 2, No. 39; Correspondence with Conrad Youngren.
"Not too bad . . .": Burke
Other nicknames for the food: Correspondence with Conrad Youngren
1969 Student Council health warning: *PH*, December 15, 1969.
1970 improvement in cleanliness: "Messdeck Inspection," *PH*, April 25, 1970.
"I'm sick and tired of jello . . .": *PH*, April 25, 1970.
Switch to cafeteria style service: "Food Service," *PH*, February 23, 1976.
"Having several choices of meals . . .": *PH*, December, 1972.
Greenish tinge in the meat: *PH*, October, 1973.
World War II era food aboard the training ship: Correspondence with Conrad Youngren, December 21, 1973.
"AD. KINNEY, THE FOOD IS BAD NEWS": *PH*, February 6, 1975.
Boycotts and food fights: *PH*, December, 1979.
"Dear Andy": "Dear Andy," *PH*, September 29, 1975.
Outsourcing to Servomation: *PH*, February 6, 1975. "Concerning the Food Service," *PH*, April 3, 1975.
Privatization of the TIV: "New Mgt. for Tiv," *PH*, October 12, 1977.
Food Poisoning Incidents: "Mystery Disease Hits Maritime," *PH*, March, 1979. "Aftermath of Epidemic," *PH*, April, 1979. "We Want Action!" *PH*, December, 1979. "The Great Epidemic- Part II!" *PH*, December, 1979.
Committee to investigate food services: "Subcommittee Considers Food," *PH*, February, 1980.
"Food fights and threats . . .": "Food Ills," *PH*, February, 1980.
Survey results: *PH*, May, 1980.
Switch to United Interstate: "Food Contract Up for Bid," *PH*, November, 1980.
"Grisly concoctions": "Cdr. Mitchell, Dutch Baked Fish, and Dry Meat," *PH*, February, 1984.
"Unless you're one of those people . . .": "Mean Cuisine," *PH*, October, 1988.
"It seems to be slowly improving . . .": "Food Update," *PH*, February, 1989
Food vendors after United Interstate: Correspondence with Hartley Spatt
1981 Middle States Review: *Middle States Report*, 1981. SBLLA.
Regimental Review Committee: Regimental Review Committee "Final Report of the Committee," October 21, 1982. SBLLA.

CHAPTER 18: FIRST AND FOREMOST

"I felt I could offer something back to the school . . ."; biographical information on Floyd Miller: "R. Ad. Miller Lays Aboard," *PH*, September, 1982.

"We are all sure that some day . . .": 1953 *Eight Bells*

"boiler suit with a brush in hand": "Midnight Oil," *PH*, September, 1983.

"I heard you were whistling at my wife!": Interview with Karen Markoe.

"You've got to be approachable . . .": "On The Water Salt's Life Took Unexpected Tack" *Newsday*, June 20, 1993.

"Hard ass, screamer, etc": Interviews with Conrad Youngren, Jose Femenia, Karen Markoe, et al.

"What bothered me about Floyd Miller . . .": Correspondence with Conrad Youngren, April 10, 2012.

Cadet service program: "Cadet Service Program Implemented," *PH*, November, 1982.

"the citizens of Pompei . . .": *Draft of Report of the Faculty/Student Ad Hoc Committee on Recruitment and Retention*, February 11, 1986, 11. SBLLA.

"The post-inspection gatherings . . .": NFFS, September 10, 1999—http://www.fsmaa.org/NFFS/1999/nf990910.cfm

"The year was 1882 . . .": *PH*, October, 1982.

"Marshall of Domer County": *PH*, November, 1982.

No arguing with Admiral Miller: "Return of the Regiment," *PH*, February, 1983.

"No longer is it cool . . .": "Sharp Decline in Vandalism," *PH*, November, 1982.

"practically nil . . ."; "it is an unsettling": "Editorial," *PH*, November, 1982.

Grafitti on the seawall: Interview with Jose Femenia.

"As a parent, I'd like to voice . . .": *PH*, February, 1983.

". . . has been strongly criticized . . .": "Interview: F.H. Miller," *PH*, October 4, 1985.

Merchant mariner museum: "Ft. Schuyler Museum Planned," *PH*, December 25, 1984. "Marine Museum," *PH*, December 25, 1984. "Museum Program Continues Successful Course," *PH*, February, 1989.

$4.2 million in repairs: "A Letter from the Commandant of Cadets," *PH*, April, 1984.

Miller's lobbying efforts: 1987 Annual and Monthly Reports. Letter to Parents, April 30, 1987.

Rudy Cassini's assistance in obtaining funds for a training ship: Correspondence with Conrad Youngren, April 10, 2012.

The Mormactide: "New Training Ship in the Works," *Bulletin of the Alumni Association*, August, 1987.

Christening of the *Empire State VI*: "TSES VI Christening," *PH*, May, 1990.

"pretty good school for academics . . .": Kenny Cox, Comprehensive Math and Science Program (CMSP), *visit evaluation*, November 3, 1982. SBLLA.

"sensitize students and employees . . .": "Affirmative Action Committee is Established at Maritime," *PH*, April, 1984.

"no valid reason": "Captain Previll Resigns," *PH*, February, 1983.

Douglas Hard: "M.C. Salutes M.C." *PH*, September, 1983.

Richard Gooden: "New Captain Takes Command," *PH*, September, 1983.

Hiring of James DeSimone: "Commandant/Master has Been Chosen," *PH*, April, 1987. Interview with James DeSimone; Diane L. Zapach, "Alumni Profile: Captain James D. DeSimone '73" *Maritime Navigator*, Summer, 2005, 4.

Chief Pfleging: Correspondence with Conrad Youngren; Interview with Jose Femenia.
"Your typical Chief . . .": Interview with Jose Femenia
". . . sense everything is going along fine . . .": Interview with Hartley Spatt
Downturn in enrollment: 1988 AR, 5.
"a Daily News Centerfold . . ."; ". . . an invitation to cross the River Styx": *Draft of Report of the Faculty/Student Ad Hoc Committee on Recruitment and Retention*, February 11, 1986. SBLLA.
"All students are expected to be . . .": *College Catalog, 1982–1983*. SBLLA
Turnoff of students to the campus: "Enrollment not so Fine," *PH*, October, 1985.
"great majority of students depart . . .": *Draft of Report of the Faculty/Student Ad Hoc Committee on Recruitment and Retention*, February 11, 1986, 11. SBLLA.
Shrinking of the American Merchant Marine: U.S. Department of Transportation.
"the Maritime Industry does not have a progressive . . .": *Draft of Report of the Faculty/Student Ad Hoc Committee on Recruitment and Retention*, February 11, 1986, 2. SBLLA.
1984 employment problem: "The Need for a Placement Officer," *PH*, February, 1984.
Turn to foreign-flag vessels: "Foreign Shipping: A Lot of Opportunities," *PH*, February, 1984.
"You are too young . . .": "The Need for a Placement Officer," *PH*, February, 1984.
"I have received 54 . . .": *PH*, April, 1984.
Hiring of Palmiotti; improving job situation: "Hearing on Merchant Marine in Defense," *PH*, October 17, 1988. "Maritime Academies' Graduates in Demand," *Journal of Commerce*, August 30, 1988, 1.
$50,000 Budget Cut: *PH*, December 15, 1975.
1983 layoffs: *PH*, March, 1983.
"Karen's here . . .": Interview with Karen Markoe.
"Had no idea . . .": "Editorial," *PH*, September, 1983.
"Maritime College Day": "M.C. Salutes M.C." *PH*, September, 1983.
1989 Budget Cuts and Tuition Hikes: "SUNY Board Passes Damaging Budget," *PH*, December, 1988.
Cut back on campus services: "From Captain DeSimone . . ." *PH*, December, 1988.
Cutting of sports programs: Floyd Miller, *Letter to Parents*, November 1, 1988. SBLLA.
Edward Regan's recommendations: "Draft Study: SUNY Costs Too High," *Newsday*, April 2, 1991.
Academic Program cuts: College Catalogs. SBLLA.
Private Sector Survey on Cost Control: President's Private Sector Survey on Cost Control
"Three to four times . . ."; "false economy": *1986 Monthly Reports and Memoranda*. SBLLA.
Lobbyist; Miller's efforts in Albany: Interview with James DeSimone.
Resistance to ship-sharing scheme: Floyd Miller, *Letter to Parents*, November 17, 1986. SBLLA.
"It would mean the loss of this ship . . .": "Reagan Cuts Could Sink College," *Newsday*, February 7, 1986. Interview with Hartley Spatt.
Critical mass: Interview with Conrad Youngren.

Joseph Hazelwood hired by Miller: "Exxon Valdez Skipper Hired to Instruct Maritime Students," *Washington Post*, May 8, 1992. "Captain of Exxon Valdez to Take Cadets on Cruise," *NYT*, May 10, 1992.

"I'm doing three jobs now . . .": "On The Water Salt's Life Took Unexpected Tack" *Newsday*, June 20, 1993.

Decline in SAT Scores: *Undergraduate Academic Assessment: The Report of the SUNY Maritime College Faculty Coordinating Committee on Assessment*, January, 1991, 23-24. SBLLA.

"We accepted the same amount . . .": Interview with Hartley Spatt.

"for courses in which I now teach six books . . .": "Bob Sennish Comes Clean," *PH*, February, 1989.

"given up his life for this school": Interview with James DeSimone

"Miller was slow to realize . . .": Interview with Hartley Spatt

"I find it quite distressing . . .": *PH*, October 4, 1985.

"Every maritime school's got the same problem . . .": "Interview: F.H. Miller," *PH*, October 4, 1985.

"chili policy": Interview with Jose Femenia.

"Why settle for just a degree?": College Catalogs, 1985. SBLLA.

"that the general public has working . . .": *Draft of Report of the Faculty/Student Ad Hoc Committee on Recruitment and Retention*, February 11, 1986, 3. SBLLA.

Suggested name change to Maritime Academy: *PH*, February, 1989. *PH*, April, 1989.

Dual degree programs: Interview with Hartley Spatt.

Associate degree program: "DOMER Progress," *PH*, November, 1983.

Suggestion for the intern option: Correspondence with Conrad Youngren, April 10, 2012.

"Some people will resist . . .": "Mission Impossible?" *PH*, February, 1986.

1995–2,900 jobs: Interview with Conrad Youngren. Interview with Jose Femenia. For the study Miller cited, see *Statement of Vice Admiral T.J. Hughes, Jr. (USN) Before the Merchant Marine Committee of the House Merchant Marine and Fisheries Committee on Maritime Bills*, May 1, 1986.

"License Officers Manpower Curve": Correspondence with Conrad Youngren, April 10, 2012.

"correct and sacrosanct": *Middle States Report*, 1992. SBLLA.

"Is the status . . . ?"; Chancellor's visit: Interview with Conrad Youngren; Interview with Jose Femenia.

"no studying of where the institution . . .": *Middle States Report*, 1992. SBLLA.

CHAPTER 19: IN STEP WITH THE FUTURE

"Are we here to train . . .": Interview with Donald Brennan.

Budget Deficits: *Decennial Self-Study Report: Institutional Change and Renewal*, January 28, 2002, 11-12. SBLLA.

"preemptive bankruptcy . . .": Interview with Donald Brennan.

Biographical Information on David Brown: "Where did he come from?" *PH*, December, 1995.; Interview with David Brown.

"much kinder, gentler administration."; on Sheila McCurdy: Interview with Karen Markoe.

Brown's administrative style: *Decennial Self-Study Report: Institutional Change and Renewal*, January 28, 2002, 1-4. SBLLA.

"apologized for leaving me . . .": Correspondence and Interview with David Brown.

Brennan joining the College Council: Interviews with David Brown and Donald Brennan.

Biographical Information on Donald Brennan: Correspondence with Donald Brennan.

"It was dark and damp . . .": Interview with Donald Brennan.

Rethinking SUNY: Interview with Conrad Youngren.

"A letter to Santa . . .": Letter from Youngren to Brown, December 26, 1997. SBLLA.

"more focused presidential . . .": Correspondence with David Brown. SBLLA.

"Structured Community"; long term planning: *Decennial Self-Study Report: Institutional Change and Renewal*, January 28, 2002 Chapter 1, Mission Review. College Catalog, 2000, 9. SBLLA.

Members of the presidential advisory committee and biographical information: Interviews and correspondence with Donald Brennan, David Brown, Thomas Fox, John Ingram, and Thomas Keenan.

"four very accomplished . . .": Correspondence with John Ingram, March 20, 2014.

Nickname of the "Gang of Four": Interviews with Conrad Youngren and Joseph Hoffman.

"Kitchen cabinet": Interview with Donald Brennan.

"Many options were considered . . .": Correspondence with David Brown.

"believe me . . .": Brown, Homecoming Remarks, 1999. SBLLA.

SUNY's options over what to do with the college: Interviews with Donald Brennan and Thomas Keenan.

Transition funds and plans: 2000 Memorandum of Understanding, 3-5.; lobbying and credit to O'Connor: Interviews with Thomas Keenan, David Brown, and Donald Brennan.

Investigating alternatives to the training ship: Interview with David Brown.

Vote of No Confidence against Cline: Interview with Hartley Spatt; Minutes of the College Faculty. SBLLA.

"methods were not cruel . . .": Interview with Hartley Spatt.

"In Step with the Future": *Decennial Self-Study Report: Institutional Change and Renewal*, Janurary 28, 2002 I-1-4. SBLLA; Interview with Conrad Youngren; "In Step with the Future." Briefing by Admiral David Brown. Correspondence with Conrad Youngren, November 1, 2011. Interview with Donald Brennan.

"the ship might be gone . . .": Interview with Donald Brennan.

"turned out to be a galvanizing . . .": Interview with Conrad Youngren

"Don't Give Up the Ship!": *Newsday*, September 26, 1999.

"Does anyone here doubt . . .": Brown, Homecoming Remarks, 1999. SBLLA.

"We could only reach . . .": Correspondence with David Brown.
"no plans at present . . .": Brown, Homecoming Remarks, 1999. SBLLA.
"hard over and locked in": Interview with Thomas Keenan.
Thomas Fox memorandum: "Message to the Alumni Association," September 14, 1999.
Resignation of Fox: Interview with Thomas Fox. "SUNY Ahoy," *Newsday*, May 13, 2000.
"has no following . . ."; "The president has essentially . . .": "Maritime College Rocked by Transistion," *Newsday*, May 21, 2000.
Vote of no confidence in Brown: *Faculty Minutes*, April 18, 2000. SBLLA.
"In all of academic wimpdom . . .": Interview with Conrad Youngren.
"just create another obstacle . . .": Interview with Thomas Keenan.
Gorbachev comment: Interview with Conrad Youngren
"inflection point"; "I felt I had taken . . .": Interview with Donald Brennan.
"Change is never easy": "Maritime College Rocked by Transistion," *Newsday*, May 21, 2000.

CHAPTER 20: THE SHIP SAILS ON

John Ryan's Navy career: "Navy Chooses Admiral from Pa. to head academy," *Baltimore Sun*, February 13, 1998.
Uniform race story: Earl Kelley, "Arnold Duo Set to Follow Path of Famous Twin Cousins," *Capital Gazette*. May 21, 2006. http://www.capitalgazette.com/news/arnold-duo-set-to-follow-path-of-famous-twin-cousins/article_eb5e8533-5e50-5d8e-a555-b093ceb925db.html
Ryan's selection as superintendent of the USNA: "Navy Picks Veteran to Lead Academy," *Pittsburgh-Post Gazette*, February 13, 1998.
USNA resolution: SUNY Office of Communication, "SUNY President Ryan named Interim President of University at Albany," February 24, 2004. http://www.suny.edu/SUNYNews/News.cfm?filname=2004-02-24BOTNamesRyan.htm
"a gentleman"; Craine's Navy career: "Remarks of the CNO Adm Vern Clark Change of Command Ceremony for Chief of Naval Education & Training," May 30, 2001. http://www.navy.mil/navydata/cno/speeches/clark-cnetcc.txt
2002 Middle States Review: *Middle States Report*, 2002. SBLLA. Interviews with Conrad Youngren and Joseph Hoffman.
"What we are talking about . . .": "Admirals Ready to Take Helm at SUNY Maritime," *Newsday*, October 23, 2001.
Ryan's implementation of the transition plan: Interview with Joseph Hoffman.
"Whatever Ryan's magic was . . .": Interview with Conrad Youngren.
Resurgence of the regiment; unification of Commandant and Master: Interview with Richard Smith..
Enrollment and hiring data: AR, 2005-2006, 5.
"You grow the population . . .": Interview with Conrad Youngren.

Alumni Association Separation: Various documents maintained electronically by the Fort Schuyler Alumni Association. http://www.fsmaa.org/independent/BackgroundInfo.cfm. Specific documents noted below, but for the scale of the entire issue, a full reading of all supporting documents is necessary.

Guidelines from SUNY concerning Alumni Association: May 16, 2003 memorandum from Brian T. Stenson. AND Memorandum to the Board of Trustees from Robert L. King, April 29, 2003. SBLLA. https://files.nyu.edu/jmm257/public/fortschuyler/guidelines-2003.pdf

"SUNY tried to convert . . .": Alumni Association, Maritime College, "Contract Issues and Options." October 23, 2003. Maintained electronically by the Fort Schuyler Alumni Association: http://www.fsmaa.org/independent/BackgroundInfo.cfm

Order off campus: Interview with Jose Femenia.

Ryan's comments on Alumni Association: Interview with Karen Markoe.

"really done a great job . . .": Interview with Richard Burke.

"created a sense . . .": Interview with Hartley Spatt.

James Cordara's Story: *NFFS*, September 28, 2001—Volume 5, No. 26; Interview and Correspondences with James Cordara.

Future strengths and weaknesses of the college: Interviews with Richard Burke, Ernest Fink, Kathy Olszewski; Richard Smith, Hartley Spatt.

Wendi Carpenter's Navy Career: "Rear Admiral Wendi B. Carpenter: First Woman to Serve as SUNY Maritime College President," *gCaptain*. July 6, 2011. http://gcaptain.com/rear-admiral-wendi-carpenter?27554

"it's not a cruise . . .": "Doctor Foody," *PH*, March 11, 1971.

"when he comes in as a freshman . . .": Mitch Pitkof, "Professor of the Month," *PH*, March, 1979, 5.

Recollections and commentaries on cruises: Burke.

Illustration Credits

Stephen Bleecker Luce (1827-1917). Library of Congress Prints and Photographs Division.

Students of the New York Nautical School training in boats. Stephen B. Luce Library Archives, SUNY Maritime College.

The sloop of war *St. Mary's* had a storied Naval career. Stephen B. Luce Library Archives, SUNY Maritime College.

The students of the *St. Mary's* wore traditional sailor uniforms. Stephen B. Luce Library Archives, SUNY Maritime College.

Ross Gilmore Marvin (1880-1908). Courtesy of the Peary-MacMillan Arctic Museum, Bowdoin College.

The caustic Boatswain William M. Dreilick. Stephen B. Luce Library Archives, SUNY Maritime College.

Wells Field addressing the boys and public. Stephen B. Luce Library Archives, SUNY Maritime College.

Students of the New York Nautical School being inspected by Executive Officer Christopher Marsden. Stephen B. Luce Library Archives, SUNY Maritime College.

The *St. Mary's* beached. Stephen B. Luce Library Archives, SUNY Maritime College.

Students running up the rigging. Stephen B. Luce Library Archives, SUNY Maritime College.

A student being taught how to use a sextant aboard the *St. Mary's*. Stephen B. Luce Library Archives, SUNY Maritime College.

The students of the *St. Mary's* used the gun deck. Stephen B. Luce Library Archives, SUNY Maritime College.

The *Newport* was the New York Nautical School's second training ship. Stephen B. Luce Library Archives, SUNY Maritime College.

Captain Lay Everhart (right) showing Richard Aldcroftt, Jr., the Chairman of the Nautical School Executive Committee, the *Newport*. Stephen B. Luce Library Archives, SUNY Maritime College.

Frederick S. McMurray and his officers. Stephen B. Luce Library Archives, SUNY Maritime College.

In 1916, Louis Weickum drew this political cartoon. Stephen B. Luce Library Archives, SUNY Maritime College.

Felix Riesenberg. Stephen B. Luce Library Archives, SUNY Maritime College.

John Baylis. Stephen B. Luce Library Archives, SUNY Maritime College.

James H. Tomb. Stephen B. Luce Library Archives, SUNY Maritime College.

The *Empire State I* at Fort Schuyler's pier with the *Annex*. Stephen B. Luce Library Archives, SUNY Maritime College.

Fort Schuyler was built. M. Righton Swicegood, delineator. "Key Plan." Drawing, sheet 2 of 12, June 19, 1924. Fort Schuyler, Throgg's Neck, Bronx, New York. Historic American Buildings Survey, Library of Congress, HABS NY,3-BRONX,3-. http://hdl.loc.gov/loc.pnp/hhh.ny0096/sheet.00002a.

Fort Schuyler was rebuilt for the school through New Deal agencies. Stephen B. Luce Library Archives, SUNY Maritime College.

Fort Schuyler was dedicated for the school's use on May 21, 1938. Stephen B. Luce Library Archives, SUNY Maritime College.

Admiral T.T. Craven. Stephen B. Luce Library Archives, SUNY Maritime College.

Oath of Acceptance. Stephen B. Luce Library Archives, SUNY Maritime College.

Arthur M. Tode (standing) and Lewis Wilson. Stephen B. Luce Library Archives, SUNY Maritime College.

Admiral Leary with Governor Thomas Dewey. Stephen B. Luce Library Archives, SUNY Maritime College.

The *Empire State II* was the former *Hydrus*. Stephen B. Luce Library Archives, SUNY Maritime College.

John J. Foody. Stephen B. Luce Library Archives, SUNY Maritime College.

Meier Degani. Stephen B. Luce Library Archives, SUNY Maritime College.

Alfred F. Olivet. Stephen B. Luce Library Archives, SUNY Maritime College.

Admiral Durgin (center) with Captain Olivet (right). Stephen B. Luce Library Archives, SUNY Maritime College.

This 1952 cartoon published in the student newspaper. Stephen B. Luce Library Archives, SUNY Maritime College.

The *Empire State III*. Stephen B. Luce Library Archives, SUNY Maritime College.

The *Empire State IV*. Stephen B. Luce Library Archives, SUNY Maritime College.

Illustration Credits

Filomena Magavero. Stephen B. Luce Library Archives, SUNY Maritime College.

When Marjorie Murtagh graduated. Stephen B. Luce Library Archives, SUNY Maritime College.

The *Empire State V*. Stephen B. Luce Library Archives, SUNY Maritime College.

The *Empire State VI*. Stephen B. Luce Library Archives, SUNY Maritime College.

James Cordara. Courtesy of James Cordara.

Students in the licensing program. SUNY Maritime College.

Fort Schuyler with cadets in formation. SUNY Maritime College.

Incoming students entering the licensing program. SUNY Maritime College.

Cadets going through training drill on how to plug leaks. Stephen B. Luce Library Archives, SUNY Maritime College.

Cadets mustering during summer sea term. SUNY Maritime College.

Rear Admiral Wendi B. Carpenter became the first female president of Maritime College. SUNY Maritime College.

Cadets on deck during the 2012 Summer Sea Term. SUNY Maritime College.

SUNY Maritime College Campus in 2011. SUNY Maritime College.

Vice Admiral Herbert Fairfax Leary (1885–1957). Superintendent, 1946–1949; President, 1949–1951. Stephen B. Luce Library Archives, SUNY Maritime.

Vice Admiral Calvin T. Durgin (1893–1965). President, 1951–1959. Stephen B. Luce Library Archives, SUNY Maritime.

Vice Admiral Harold Moore, Class of 1924 (1901–1981). President, 1959–1967. Stephen B. Luce Library Archives, SUNY Maritime.

Rear Admiral Edward O'Donnell (1907–1991). President, 1967–1972. Stephen B. Luce Library Archives, SUNY Maritime.

Rear Admiral Sheldon H. Kinney (1918–2005). President, 1972–1982. Stephen B. Luce Library Archives, SUNY Maritime.

Rear Admiral Floyd H. Miller. President, 1982–1995. Stephen B. Luce Library Archives, SUNY Maritime.

Rear Admiral David C. Brown. SUNY Maritime College.

Vice Admiral John Ryan. President, 2002–2005. SUNY Maritime College.

Vice Admiral John Craine. President, 2001–2002 (interim); 2005–2011. SUNY Maritime College.

Rear Admiral Wendi B. Carpenter. President, 2011– . SUNY Maritime College.

Index

A.J. Fuller (ship), 99
Accreditation, see "Maritime College, accreditation"
Adams, Charles Francis, 123
African Americans at the college, 181-182, 255-256
Alabama (ship), 255
Alchiba, 160-1
Aldcroftt, Richard jr., 38, 41, 71, 75, 77-79, 81
Ali, Mohammed, 185
Alleghany (ship), 149, 321-2
Alumni Association, 38-41, 79, 85, 100, 118, 189, 272-273, 275-277, 282-284, 316-317
American Pilot (ship), 145, 318(n); 320-1
Anderson, Henry C., 114
Annex (ship), 123, 138 (n); 326
Apprentice System, U.S. Navy, 5-6, 12
Astoria (ship), 160

Baker, David, 182
Baker, R.J., 136
Balancia, Charles, 277
Balfour (ship), 174, 326
Barr, Robert, 156-157
Barrett, see "Empire State V"
Baruch, Herman, 185, 197
Bassett, Claude, 168
Baylis, John S., 109-113, 117-119
Bedloe's Island, 110, 121, 123
Bells of St. Mary's (alma mater), ix, 41(n), 109
Belson, Joel, 266
Bentley, Helen, 220
Berner, Robert, 242-243

Bett, James, 167
Biaggi, Mario, 255, 261, 261(n)
Bissikummer, Charles, 85
Blackstone, Henry, 168-169
Blauvelt, George A., 82
Blood, Jeremy, 180
Board of Governors, 82-84, 87, 92-94, 100, 102-104, 110-112, 114-120, 170, 260
Board of Visitors, 119-120, 122, 126, 144, 147, 150, 169, 171-172, 195-196
Bombe, A.A., 115
Bradley, John, 284
Branford, Walter Womack, 181
Braude, Beatrice, 220-221
Brennan, Donald, 269-271, 273-276, 278
British and Foreign Sailors' Society, 37
Brocco, Salvatore, 108
Brokaw, Thomas, 154
Bronstein, 235-236
Brown, David, 270-278
Buffalo (ship), 85
Bullock, William G., 181
Burke, Richard, 204(n), 214, 224, 228, 246, 277, 284, 290, 292-294
Burnett, Carl F., 181

Calhoun, Dennis, 248
California Maritime Academy, 91, 168-169, 170, 223
Callas, Maria, 185, 199
Camerata, James, 190
Cantor, Jacob, 34
Cape Cod Canal, 79, 87
Carnegie (ship), 89

Caro, Robert, 126
Carpenter, Wendi, 228, 284, 291
Carter, Edward "Nick", 43, 122
Carter, Jimmy, 238, 271
Celler, Emmanuel, 173
Cernik, Steve, 202
Cerny, Thomas, 238, 252, 258
Chartwells, 249
Christian Radich (ship), 244
Churchill, Thomas, 82
Clark, Thomas, 211
Clark, Vern, 280
Clarke, Charles H., 117–119
Claytor, Graham, 239
Cline, Kimberly, 274–275
Clinton, Bill, 192, 281
Clio (ship), 4
CNET, *see* "Naval Education and Training Command"
Coast Guard, United States, 99, 109, 112, 118–120, 143–144, 150–151, 153
Cochrane, E.L., 188
Coffin, Isaac, 4
Coffin, Tristram, 4
College Council, 189, 195–196, 207, 228, 266, 271–273, 275–277
Collins, David, 126
Conant, Samuel M., 86–87
Conway (ship), 12
Cordara, James, 285–289
cozy mug (nickname), 156
Craine, John, 279, 284, 291
Craven, Thomas T., 146–154, 165, 172–173, 172 (n)
Crossing the Line Ceremony, 294
Crowninshield, Arent, 25, 32–33, 35
Cruises, notable, 1896, 36
Cruises, notable, 1900, 37
Cruises, notable, 1901, 37
Cruises, notable, 1908, 71–74
Cruises, notable, 1914, 84–87
Cruises, notable, 1915, 90–92
Cruises, notable, 1916, 95
Cruises, notable, 1919, 104
Cruises, notable, 1920, 109
Cruises, notable, 1923, 114–116

Cruises, notable, 1933, 132
Cruises, notable, 1946, 174–175
Cruises, notable, 1969, 202
Cruises, notable, 1983, 260
Cruises, notable, 1987, 257
Cruises, notable, 2009, 293–294
Cuccio, Frank, 229–235
Cuomo, Mario, 260

Dalzell, Frederick, 20–21, 83, 93
D'Amato, Alphonse, 255
Dana, Richard Henry, 1–5, 44
De Long, George W., 18, 23
Degani, Meir, 198, 198(n), 224, 292
Dern, George Henry, 136
Desborough, Marilyn, 245
Desertion, 32, 61, 72–74
DeSimone, Guy, 158, 176, 212, 256
DeSimone, James, 212–213, 215, 256–257, 263
Dewey (dry dock), 89
Dewey, George, 39
Dewey, Thomas, 174–175, 181, 189, 196
Dickerson, Mahlon, 124
Dilloway, Phylipp, 148, 149, 154–158
Dombaugh, Harry, 78–79
Dome (nickname), 199, 202
Dorey, Albert, 74
draft deferment, 153, 158
Dreilick, William, 29–30, 49–50, 52, 99
Driggs, James, 84–88
Dugan, Joseph, 288
Dunnigan, John, 134–136
Dunphy, Pat, 211, 219, 219(n)
Durgin, Calvin T., 183–189, 191, 194, 196–199

Edsall (ship), 235
Educational Practices Act, *see* "Legislation, Educational Practices Act"
Eight Bells (yearbook), 109, 153
Eilman, Paul J., 102–103
Eisenhower, Dwight David, 189
Emmet, William, 11

Index 379

Empire State (ship), 123, 129, 132–134, 137, 138 (n), 144–145, 149, 171, 320–1
Empire State II (ship), 174–175, 197, 322
Empire State III (ship), 195, 197
Empire State IV (ship), 197, 202, 213, 240, 247
Empire State V (ship), 240, 255, 260
Empire State VI (ship), 255, 290
English, Frank, 214, 244
Erben, Henry, 29–30, 71, 78
Ernest Renan (ship), 87
Evening Star (ship), 9
Everhart, Lay, 71–78
Exxon Valdez (ship), 262

Farragut, David, 39
Farragut, Loyall, 39
Fay, Reginald, 80–82, 93, 116, 122–123
Females, admission of, 221–228
Females, faculty, 217–218, 220–221
Femenia, Eileen, 283
Femenia, Jose, 180 (n), 203–204, 239, 257, 264, 266, 283
Field, Wells, 35–36
Fine, Judy, 258
Fink, Ernest, 290
Firpo, Luis Angel, 102
Flower, Roswell, 34, 36
Food and meals of the institution, 32, 50–51, 60, 101, 104, 205, 245–249, 258
Foody, John J., 180, 212, 292
Forbes, Robert B., 8–9
Foreign Student Exchange Program, 185, 236–238, 275–276
Fort Schuyler Foundation, 239
Fort Schuyler, 1930s reconstruction of, 137–141
Fort Schuyler, acquisition of by NYSMMA, 124–137
Fort Schuyler, decay of, 125–126
Fort Schuyler, first construction, 125
Fort Schuyler, history under the U.S. Army, 124–126
Fort Schuyler, initial purchase of property by federal government, 117 (n), 124–125
Fort Schuyler, McDougall General Hospital, 125
Fort Schuyler, movies filmed at, 126
Fort Schuyler, New York State obtaining deed of, 172–173
Fox, Thomas, 272, 275–276
Frederica of Greece, 185
Frothington, John C., 153

Gansevoort, Guert, 6–7
Gaulin, Alphonse, 86
Gaynor, William Jay, 79
GI Bill, 172
Gilroy, Thomas, 33–34, 36
Goethals, George Washington, 91
Goin, Thomas, 4–5, 9
Gooden, Richard, 256
Goodman, Oscar, 209, 212
Grace Commission, 261
Grace, William R., 31
Green, John, 157–158
Green, Lucien B., 132–134, 137
Gregory, George M., 176
Grening, Paul, 106–109, 289
Guilford D. Pendleton, see "Annex"
Gumersindo (ship), 132–4

Halsey, William "Bull", 174
Hammond, Charles H., 125
Hanus, Gustavus Charles, 17, 19–21, 29, 37–40, 75, 77, 85, 89
Hard, Douglas, 256
Harold, Charles, 28
Hartford (ship), 39, 85
Hartley, Thomas, 248–249
Hasselbach, Jerry, 245
Hatzel, John, 38, 80, 80(n), 83, 96
Hayes, Jack, 255
Hazelwood, Joseph, 262
Hazing, 43–44, 53, 55–58, 64, 67–70, 79, 155–156, 177, 178, 204–205, 293
Henderson, George Francis Robert, 185
Henry Gibbins, see "*Empire State IV*"

Hess, Fred, 157, 174, 176, 184(n), 203, 223–224
Hesse, Walter, 161–165
Hoffman, Joseph, 224, 272
Hollenbeck, W.A., 73–74
Holloway Plan, 187
Holm, Clarence, 160–161
Hoverter, Terrence, 176, 217
Hughes, George W.R., 137–138, 147
Hughes, T.J., 266
Hurley, Patrick J., 131
Hussar (ship), 255
Hydrus, see "Empire State II"

Ignazio Florio (ship), 105–9
Indoctrination, 155–157, 175, 179, 204, 204 (n), 224–225
Ingram, John, 273, 275
Irving, A. Emelius, 17

Jack's (diner), 158–159
Jacob, Edwin, 36
Jeannette (ship), 23
Jobson, Gary, 208, 246–247
Johnson, Erik, 253

Kedge Anchor, 11–12
Keen, Edward V.W., 119–120
Keenan, Thomas, 273, 275, 276–277
Kelly, James, 104
Kelly, Scott, 28
Kennedy, John F., 220
Keystone State (ship), 148–9
Kingston, William H.G., 88
Kinney, Sheldon, 223, 226, 235–244, 241(n), 247, 249–250, 252, 258
Kirby, Julie, 230–231, 233–234
Kirby, Sean, 229–236
Knight, Telfair, 146–149, 151, 168–169
Kobalenko, Jerry, 27–28
Kohle, George, 106
Kramer, Aaron, 221
Kriv, Laurence, 225, 225(n)

Larr, Timothea, 228
Leary, Herbert Fairfax, 173–180, 182–184, 199, 203

Leavitt, Ralph, 146, 151, 188
Leboffe, Luigi, 105, 108
Legislation, 1911 update to the 1874 Federal Act, 78
Legislation, 1936 Merchant Marine Act, 144–145
Legislation, 1958 Maritime Academy Act, 189, 239
Legislation, creation of the New York Nautical School, 14–15
Legislation, Educational Practices Act, 181
Legislation, Permission to operate ashore, 134–136
Legislation, Transfer to the State Education Department, 110–111
Legislation, Transfer to the State of New York, 79–82
Legislation, Transferring ownership of Fort Schuyler to New York State, 140, 172–173
Lehman, Herbert, 131–132, 134–137, 139–140
Leviathan (ship), 106, 138–9
Liberty Island, *see* "Bedloe's Island"
Littlefield, Charles E., 75, 81, 90, 90 (n), 103
Liverhant, Salomon, 198
Loree, Leonor F., 126
Luce, Stephen B., 5–8, 10–15, 18, 37, 75, 143, 259
Lynch, Daniel, 193–195

Macedonian (ship), 12
Mackenzie, Slidell, 6–7
Magavero, Philomena, xiii, 217–218, 220, 221, 222
Magliocca, Karen, 224
Maine Maritime Academy, 146, 149, 151, 188, 223, 240, 275
Malay, Linda A., 228
Maloney, James, 275
Mand, George F., 127–129
MARAD, *see* "Maritime Administration"
Maria (ship), 133
Marine Journal, 71, 76, 78, 81, 83, 84, 91, 93

Index

Marine Society of the City of New York, 3–4, 75–76, 80
Mariners, mortality rates, 3
Maritime Administration, 186, 188, 214, 220, 223, 240, 261, 269, 290
Maritime College, accreditation, 182, 199, 213–214, 226, 280–281
Maritime College, adoption of name, 180
Maritime College, establishment of college curriculum, 170–173, 175–180, 182
Maritime Commission, 145–151, 168–169, 174, 186
Maritime Industry Museum, 255
Markoe, Karen, 221, 226, 236, 260, 269
Marsden, Christopher, 72, 74–75, 75 (n), 81
Marsden, Roland, 75, 75(n)
Marvin, Ross G., 23, 25–28, 289
Massachusetts Maritime Academy, 31, 149, 168, 240, 261
Massachusetts, see "Reformatories, schoolship"
Matthews, Edward W., 73
Matthews, William E., 173
McCaney, William, 294
McCormack, Emmett J., 129, 131
McCurdy, Sheila, 270
McDonald, Anthony, 229–235
McGowan, John, 33, 35, 88–89
McKee, Joseph, 131, 134
McKee, Ralph, 82
McMurray, Charlotte, 88–89
McMurray, Frederick S., 22, 29, 37–38, 43, 87–96, 98, 102–103, 115
McNiece, Walter V., 171
Megie, Benjamin, 34
Mercury, see "Reformatories, schoolship"
Mercy, see "*Empire State III*"
Merkel, Howard, 208
Miller, Floyd H., 250–269, 271
Miller, J. Hillis, 178–179
Miller, Jacob W., 79–80, 82–85, 87, 94–96, 120, 170
Miller, Nathan, 110–111, 111(n)
Monroe, Jeffrey, 255

Moore, Harold, 198, 198(n), 203, 205–206, 244
Mormacdove, see "*Alchiba*"
Mormacrey (ship), 161–5
Mormactide, see "*Empire State VI*"
Moses, Robert, 126–128, 130, 132, 136, 140–141, 197, 198
Muir, William, 174–175
Muniz, Martin, 254, 259
Munsch, Charles, 203, 276
Murray, Arthur, 157–158
Murray, Robert B., 188
Murtagh, Marjorie, 221–223
Mus, Abdul, 98–99
Museum, see Maritime Industry Museum
Mussolini, Benito, 109

National Marine, 102
Naval Academy, see "U.S. Naval Academy at Annapolis"
Naval Education and Training Command, 239
Naval Indoctrination Center, 147, 149
Naval Militia, New York, 36, 79, 111
Naval Reserve Officer Training Corps, see "NROTC"
New Jersey (ship), 106
New York Chamber of Commerce, 14, 18, 31–32, 34–37, 79, 83, 93, 126
New York Civil Liberties Union, 221–222
Newport (ship), 39–40, 70–79, 82, 84–87, 90–95, 97, 100–105, 109–118, 121, 123, 171, 319–20
Newspapers, student, 148, 205, 211
Nolan, Gerald, 213, 243–244
Nordhoff, Charles, 88
North Carolina (ship), 6
Norton, George, 76–78, 80–81, 83, 84, 91, 93
NROTC, 187, 187 (n), 239

Oaksmith, David, 190–191
O'Brien, Keran, 19–20, 73–77
O'Connor, John J., 274
O'Donnell, Edward J., 203–204, 208–210, 212, 215, 222, 235, 236, 241, 243, 250

Office of Management and Budget, 261–262
O'Hagan, Sean, 230–232, 234
Olivet, Alfred, 175, 177, 193–195, 197, 242–244
Olszewski, Kathy, 290–291
Ontario (ship), 9

Page, Ralph E., 176
Palmiotti, Anthony, 259
Panama Canal, 81–82, 90–92, 122, 174
Panama-Pacific Exhibition, 90–91
Pappas Group, 272–273
Parents Association, 187, 276
Parnham, Harold, 174
Patricia's (restaurant), 249
Patterson, Howard, 36–37
Paulding (ship), 118
Payton, John, 257
Peary, Robert, 25–28
Pennsylvania Maritime Academy, 31, 147, 148
Pershing Rifles, 178, 208
Peters, William, 134
Pfleging, Edward, 256–257
Phillips, Robert, 243
Phythian, Robert Lees, 18–19, 22–23, 29
Pilecki, Billy, 248
Pittman, Milan L., 144
Pomeranz, Janet, 220
Port Royal, battle of, 11
Porter, Albert Ogden, 176
Porter, William, 237, 239, 266
Powers, Jimmy, 191
President Harding (ship), 105–109
Previll, George C., 245, 256
Prinz Eitel Friedrich, 100
Private Sector Survey on Cost Control, *see* "Grace Commission"
Procyon, see "Empire State"
Protests, 208–212, 248
Putnam, Harrington, 93

Quinn, Peter, 173
Quinn-Oliffe Law, *see* "Legislation, Educational Practices Act"

Randall, Robert Richard, 3
Reagan, Ronald, 259, 261
Rebound, 229–235
Reeder, William, 32, 35–37
Reformatories, schoolships, 8–11
Regan, Edward, 260
Reinhart, Roger, 176, 191
Reugge, Carl, 104
Rey, Charley, 245–246, 248
Ridder, Victor, 138–139
Riesenberg, Emily Schorb, 98
Riesenberg, Felix, xii, 29, 43, 96–103, 105, 112–119, 130, 196
Riesenberg, Felix, jr., 115
Riesenberg, Maud Conroy, 100
Riesenberg, William, 115
Riis, Jacob, 32
Riis, John, 32
Riser, George, 156–157, 157(n)
Rockall, 10
Rockefeller, Nelson, 197–198, 260
Rondo, 106
Roosevelt, 26–27
Roosevelt, Eleanor, 220
Roosevelt, Franklin Delano, 123, 126, 128, 131–132, 134, 136–137, 139–140, 144, 151
Roosevelt, Theodore, 39
Roscoe, Theodore, 235–236
Rothschild, Louis, 188
Ruffin, Albert, 19–21
Ryan, John, 279–284

S-4 (submarine), 118–119
Saga/Mariott, 249
Sailors' Snug Harbor of Staten Island, 3
Sallyport Saying, 185–186, 191
Scharpf, Margaret, 160
Scharpf, Theodore, 160
Schneider, William, 115
Schutz, Charles Daniel, 147–148
Schuyler, Philip, 125
Seamanship (textbook), 11–12, 52
Sedco/Phillips, 229
Seel, Richard, 182
Sennish, Robert, 206–207, 209, 211 (n), 263

Index

Servomation, 245–249
Shack, Barbara, 222
Sheridan, Thomas W., 102–105, 109–110, 120, 130
Sikorsky, Igor, 183, 185
Smith, Alfred E., 82, 110–111, 111(n), 117–118
Smith, Craig, 177
Smith, Richard, 281–282, 290–291
Sodexo, 249
Somers Mutiny, 6–7
Spatt, Hartley, 237, 258, 263, 275, 281, 291
Spencer, Philip, 6–7
St. David (ship), 89
St. Mary's (ship), xii, 15, 17–22, 25, 28–41, 43–71, 76, 84, 88–89, 98–99, 101–102, 105–106, 109, 114–115, 117, 119, 147, 155, 291, 295, 319
Starbecker, Eugene N., 160, 179, 179(n)
State University of New York, 180–181, 195–198, 207, 245, 260–261, 266, 270–273, 275, 282–284, 290–291
Stedman, Giles C., 108–109
Stepping Stone Lighthouse, 202
Straus, Nathan, jr., 127–129, 131, 136
Strommer, Charles, 154–155
Student Government, 177, 211, 214, 254
Sturtevant (ship), 235
Subsidies to the college and students, federal, 78–79, 94, 144, 146, 150–151, 168, 186–189, 214, 239
Sullivan, Michael J., 79–82
Sultana (ship), 9
Sulzer, William, 82–83, 85
Sunbeam (ship), 88
SUNY, see "State University of New York"
Sutter, Len, 193
Sweeny, Michael, 169

Temporary Emergency Relief Agency, 137–138
TERA, see "Temporary Emergency Relief Agency"
Thomas, Albert Richard, 187
Thompson, Robert P., 244

Throgs Neck Bridge, xi, 197, 197(n), 243, 253
Tiedmann, Hollie J., 188
Tighe, Franklin, 71–74
Tillman, Edwin, 79–80, 84
Todd, W. Dwight, 221
Tode, Arthur M., 110, 112, 114–115, 117–119, 147, 169–171, 196
Tomb, James Harvey, 120–124, 126–132, 134–141, 143–144, 146–147, 155, 170
Toran, William, 221, 223
Totten, Joseph, 124–125
Tracey, Marcus, 102, 104, 109, 111
Trimble, Richard W., 244–245
Truman, Harry S., 181
Turi, John, 190–191
Tuthill, William, 244
Twomey, Matthew, 178, 192

U.S. Maritime Service, 145, 269
U.S. Naval Academy at Annapolis, 7–8, 11–12, 14, 18, 37, 39, 75, 82–84, 122, 131, 143–144, 147, 170, 184, 202, 207, 235–236, 241, 269, 279–280
Union, 20–21
United Interstate, 249
United States Merchant Marine Academy, see "USMMA"
Upshur (ship), 240
USMMA, 145–147, 169–171, 178, 186, 187–190, 223, 261, 290

vandalism, 190, 206, 244, 247, 250, 254
Vander Clute, Carl, 196
Vaterland (ship), 106
Vecchione, Felix S., 171
Vicksburg (ship), 39
Vietnam War era demonstrations at the college, 208–212
Villella, Edward, 191–192
Vogel, Robert, 246

Wadhams, Albion, 37
Wadsworth, Alexander, 17
Waesche, Russell, 150

War Shipping Administration, see "WSA"
Wauchope, George, 146
Weaver, Charles, 28
Weber, Lewis M., 101-102
Weickum, Louis, 43, 93
Weiss, Leonard, 155
Weiss, William, 190-191
Wellman, Walter, 99-100
Wessel, Roger, 190-191
Wetmore, David, 15, 18
White, Donald, 174-175
Whitman, Charles, 92-94
Wile, Ira, 79-80
Williamson, Charles, 18
Wilson, Lewis A., 135, 135(n), 140-141, 146, 148, 150, 169-172, 172(n)
Wood, William M., 28-29
Worcester (ship), 12
Worden, John, 14
Works Progress Administration, see "WPA"

World War I, 85-87, 93, 95, 97, 106, 119, 123, 161
World War II, 118, 141, 145-146, 148-165
World War II, convoys, 160-165, 235
World War II, merchant marine casualties, 154
WPA , 138-139, 149, 169
WSA, 151-152
WSA, see "War Shipping Administration"

Yanni, Richard, 159
Yearbook, *Eight Bells*, 109, 178
Yorktown (ship) , 39
Young Seaman's Manual, 18, 67
Youngren, Conrad, 229, 246, 252, 266, 271-272, 277

Zimmerman, Alisa B., 228
Zumwalt, Elmo, 241(n)

About the Author

A native New Yorker, **Joseph A. Williams** is a librarian and archivist at SUNY Maritime College's Stephen B. Luce Library. He holds a bachelor degree in History and Political Science from SUNY Geneseo College and master degrees in History and Library Science from Queens College. Mr. Williams has also led graduate and undergraduate courses at Queens College and Briarcliffe College. His work in librarianship and history has been published in several professional journals such as *Seabreezes* and the *Bronx County Historical Society Journal*. Currently, he resides in the Bronx with his wife, Michelle, and daughter, Jamie. This is his first book.